MESSAGES

from

VALLARTA

-The Traveler Series-

DAN CHAPMAN

Messages from Vallarta by Dan Chapman

This book is written to provide information and motivation to readers. Its purpose is not to render any type of psychological, legal, or professional advice of any kind. The content is the sole opinion and expression of the author.

ISBN: 978-1-950101-00-9 (Paperback)
ISBN: 978-1-950101-02-3 (Hardback)
ISBN: 978-1-950101-01-6 (Digital)

Printed in the United States of America.

Foreword

I would fairly say that the following *messages* are an impulsive tale. They began as a collection of minor, candid observations during a vacation. Then, as visits progressed and allowed, they became a compilation of anecdotes from several trips made to ***Puerto Vallarta, Mexico*** spanning five years. Later, when opportunities allowed, my notes were revised and organized into this volume. The visits included all four seasons, eleven of twelve months for various reasons and Angelina, my wife, was my companion with exception of a few months. Most of the following remarks were spontaneous reflections during our stays.

However, the core and gist of this *writing* originated primarily from an excursion planned and fostered as an extended-vacation in 2013. Chronicling that initial, four different months' adventure was an idea forged from ***PV's*** summer heat. Once engaged within our getaway, so many new and adventurous activities prompted substantial and entertaining anecdotes for this personal log. That was when I began notations on people, places and experiences which we encountered. Follow-up visits provided additional, material-impressions for this collection.

Sometime along-the-way, I began using original, personal poetry to expand on descriptions of new impressions, feelings and attitudes. Poetry has always been a personally favorite medium to help sort out some emotionally charged details. It allows me to offer more complete and concise expressions of some story-telling happenings. Each new and varied visit encouraged additional material for the prose and this subsequent volume. The manuscript grew as I chronicled five visits beginning in 2010. Those stays included two, brief-visits, plus three, short-term residencies of three, three and five-month durations from 2013-2015 while living within ***Puerto Vallarta's*** municipality of ***Zonas de Mismaloya-Boca***.

It really was an entertaining process "chronicling" those "happenings" and then adding poetry to emphasize some experiences. Overall, the journey evolved through a total of eleven, seasonally-detached months. This was planned to offer unique, seasonal visits in order to better learn and understand and appreciated the climate changes on human psyche. Visiting the fun, vibrant and beautiful city of ***Puerto Vallarta*** is always a joy. Travelers must just find ways of dealing with the climate changes to better suit themselves. I planned on finding these ways. It was different and challenging, yet we believed it was even more relaxing living in our selected ***Mismaloya*** area near the community of ***Boca de Tomatlan***.

Our arranged residence was only a thirty-minute bus-ride from the city's hub, and that gave us a completely different perspective for our visit. Instead of city-lights and noises, we had jungle background and a constant metronome of surf lapping or pounding on a rocky beach below. Ocean-views filled us with exotic, spiritual and relaxing days. Our experiences offered ample *food* for thought.

Reflecting on impressions of people we met as subjects for this prose was personally entertaining. Some visits were amusing, others thought-provoking, but all were interesting. Poetic verse and their topics made experiences that much more personal. Early on during our vacation(s), I soon recognized that peace and quiet and relaxation were beneficial to thoughtfulness and creative-writing. I quickly understood a healthy and useful aspect for what I was attempting:

Opportunities for quiet, meditative-contemplation and self-reflection are always worthwhile endeavors and good for a soul anytime.

Dedication

I am: ***The Traveler***. Most assuredly, my parents and a special Aunt all helped instill a travel-bug in me from an early age. They all cultivated and encouraged a motivation, curiosity and craving inside me to see new places, meet new people and experience new sights and circumstances. I am beholden to them for my desire to travel. Each of them pursued travel too. Often they traveled together, and many other times they traveled alone or with others. After each retired, they continued to chase their own, "bucket-list" experiences with new places to see, people to meet and things to do. Their influences became trademark impressions left upon me. My hobby, interests, goals, and lifestyle now seem to have evolved into world, travel-site acquisitions thanks to them.

As evidence of their influence, to this day my mother still cracks a broad smile at an opportunity to travel anywhere, anytime and with almost anybody. I know this to be true because she and I have journeyed over much of the world as "travel-buddies." And, I have always enjoyed her easy-going manner, enthusiasm and willingness to go-the-distance anywhere to see anything, anytime. Mom is approaching eighty-nine now, but she is still the Timex watch of traveling: "(She) keeps-on-ticking" and traveling… or, the Energizer bunny: "Going-and-going."... We have shared many planes, balloons, trains, automobiles and taxis, ships, hotels, youth-hostels, tour-excursions, and countless sidewalk and trail meanderings together. I shall never forget any of our shared *experiences and memories.*

That is why with pride and appreciation, I dedicate this volume to my "travel-buddy," family-members: My parents, Guy and Pat, and my aunt Jean. Although Mom is the only one still around and willingly receptive to almost any travel plans, I clearly recognize and sense the influence of them all on my own travel-aspirations. Dad and Jean have already made the biggest journey of all, if not most significant, by venturing into their afterlives. Perhaps, that is why I feel that one day in some cosmic, existential-consciousness, which they have already achieved, we shall all be together again in pleasing, sharing and spiritual travel.

Preface

I have been fortunate enough in life to have spent a considerable amount of time traveling throughout various states and cities within the USA and countries around much of the world. Since childhood, new places, faces and experiences always interested me. As a child growing-up with my siblings, our parents moved around a great deal due to employment needs. I became easily accustomed to new change. To a certain point, I almost looked-forward to it, let alone expect it.

A new location meant new things to see and do and new people to meet and learn about. In accepting my family's quasi-nomadic lifestyle, I developed a kinship at an early age with taking residential changes for granted. Often, I was already mentally prepared on Friday nights when Dad returned home from his job somewhere and announced that we were moving across country to a new, job-opportunity. Probably, the concept of "traveling-light" was figuratively, but permanently, embedded into my psychic during that period of my youth. I need, therefore, to give thanks and appreciation to my parents, Guy and Pat Dork.

Another important influence of my travel appreciations was my mother's oldest sister, Jean, who often subsidized my early travels. Jean brought me along on her camping excursions and other adventures throughout the Western United States. Along with her life-long mate, Phyllis, they encouraged and invited me to travel with them often. Trips to ***Baja California***, north to Oregon on pigeon-release exercises, camping trips, and summer-getaways were examples of shared experiences and influences upon me. In 1962, as an eighth-grade graduation reward, they even brought me along with them to the Seattle World's Fair.

Of course, Jean's major contributions to my restless and curious travel-nature were her encouragement and support for a summer's hitch-hiking adventure throughout Europe after my high-school graduation. That trip would never have happened without Jean's emotional and financial support. She provided the round-trip tickets from San Francisco and Paris as a graduation gift. My "world-travel" experiences obviously would have been much more limited, or at least delayed or curtailed, without her voiced encouragement and fiscal backing. She had a very experienced and adventurous soul and wished the same for me, I imagined.

My parents, on-the-other-hand, instilled in me a more pragmatic desire for travel from an early age. I believe that seeking and finding pleasure from traveling became a quality of my character during childhood. I learned to accept change with anticipation thanks duly to so many residential moves made throughout my youth. My father was a Field-Construction Boilermaker Welder by trade and career. He was exceptional at his craft and seldom had problems ever finding work. The problem was getting to the "work" and keeping our family together.

Our family issue was that Dad's *new work* was always far from wherever we were living at the time. He had to grab a job quickly before it was unavailable. We had to move quickly, too, if we wanted to continue eating regularly. Some people referred to our way-of-life as "feast or famine." We moved, however, in order to be together near his new job... and for his paycheck and food.

There was a term for our lifestyle. We were called "Boomers" like in the old, historically-noted gold and silver discovery periods and oil-drilling days. Dad chased the "booming" areas for work. Sometimes, contacts in distant-places called upon him personally for his skills to help them complete a job. Mom supported his endeavors by readying our family to go along for the ride and the experiences. I fondly remember eagerly anticipating Friday night discussions with Dad. Ever-so-often, he would show-up home late from his present job-site and announce that over-the-weekend we'd be moving to a new location for a new job in such-and-such state and such-and-such city for his new work opportunity.

I cannot fairly speak for my siblings, but, typically, I had already been packed, at least emotionally. I was enthusiastically ready and willing to go to our new destination. It was not that I was discouraged, tired or upset with where we had presently been living. On-the-contrary, I had made the most of where I was, but I was eager to see more. New faces, new places, new things to do.

Granted, schooling got a bit more difficult to manage as years went by, but I managed. I accepted the circumstances and learned to make the most of what was available. I believe those "moves" we made for whatever circumstances may have developed my kinship or understanding and appreciation of other folks' trials and tribulations and dealings. I know it helped develop within me an empathy for others' struggles and identity issues. I became keenly aware of the "new-kid-on-the-block" syndrome. Perhaps, it encouraged me to be a little more outgoing and friendlier for survival's sake. I enjoyed making friends with a school's new arrivals. I identified with their anxiety and tried easing their adjustment by welcoming them. Plus, I was genuinely interested in learning from where they came.

Later, after high-school graduation, I was given an opportunity to travel all around Europe for the entire summer. I was not supposed to travel alone, but my two best-buddy, would-be traveling companions canceled. Disappointment arose, but I just determinedly decided to go it alone. Aunt Jean was the motivator and part-financier to make it happen. It took serious assurances to convince my parents to agree. Actually, I think in some subconscious way, Jean figured she'd live a Huckleberry Finn-type, vicarious existence through me helping finance my hitchhiking stunt around a foreign continent alone at the youthful age of eighteen.

Of course, another option would have been to allow Uncle Sam to train and send me overseas. At the time, my draft-lottery number came up in the first round. By beginning college in the Fall, I was granted my first, temporary, college-deferment. However, the military was a constant, pressing and actually depressing alternative. It would have been quite an experience, though, to have gone then, and it's highly likely that I would have been murdered for their pathetic, futile and worthless cause supporting egos, psychoses, neuroses, and fiscal interests of our political and financial demagogues in Washington, D.C. and on Wall Street.

Four years later, after dropping-out of college during my final semester before graduation to protest, and in-stress, I would get "drafted." As an immediate option to joining the U.S. Army, and likely going straightaway to death in Vietnam, I was given a choice to enlist in the USMCR to fulfill my six-year, military-obligation. It was a difficult but maturing and gratifying experience. My limited travels with the *Corps* included San Diego Recruitment Depot and Camp Pendleton for Boot Camp and Military Occupational-Service training. After that, I bounced back and forth between San Francisco and Sacramento for monthly weekends and various *Camps* for summer-trainings. Modest travel was afforded my "MOS" as a "Remington-Raider," meaning I did my job with a typewriter.

For that Summer of 1966, however, I traveled around Europe mostly all alone and on-my-own from Denmark in the North to Southern Italy and every country in-between. I experienced the spectacular splendor, history, grace, charm, and vitality of Europe's incredibly varying cultures. Granted, there were a few mishaps along-the-way, but happily and successfully I learned to appreciate independence and diversity. Most importantly, and the feeling has remained with me ever since, I developed a kinship-love for travel.

Traveling for any extended period of time, especially alone, can be challenging. Successful voyages, however, can also bring excitement, fascination, revelation, instruction, learning, growing, and development as a person and human-being. Ideally, long-term travel also promotes a sense of independent-living and self-reliance. And yet, if a traveler is on-the-road, more-or-less, there is less possibility to truly grasp lifestyles and communal energy from any single, tentative and temporary location.

That is why it was always a goal of mine to create an opportunity where I might choose various places in the world and make them temporary homes away from home. Living in a foreign destination could promote conditions whereby I might really get in touch with its environment, community and inhabitants. Having this cognitive desire to see and experience the world encouraged a more humanistic quality within me and an inquisitive nature.

And yet, the experiential, growth-and-learning I presumed from traveling to and living in ***Puerto Vallarta*** was both complemented and surpassed by yet other personal elements. There was also my internal, emotional-maturation and an understanding and appreciation of the *Big W's: Who I was; What I was; and Where I was headed.*

Let the tale begin...

Introduction

We all need to stop once-in-a-while and consider a few things: Who we are; what we want; and where we are going. The three, "Big-W's:" Who, What and Where? *What (who) type of person are we?*-What (who) type of person do we want to be? Also, w*hat do we want from life?*-What is it which makes us feel fulfilled? And, finally, w*here are we going with our lives?*-Do we have a dream or plan or design to accept and follow? Are we finding comfort in our lives? In our lives, are we seeking meaning and purpose?

Everybody wants peace-of-mind. If we don't have it, we try to figure out how to get it. I realize that in my past, I did not had much of it. Now, however, I feel focused and clearly working toward maintaining and improving my mind's peace. Naturally, I still have some personal issues requiring continuing efforts, and I have a ways to go yet resolving other aspects of my life; among them include health issues. However, I feel very positive about my direction.

I did not have "it," (peace-of-mind) before and, therefore, initially coming down to Puerto Vallarta was little more than an adventurous escape from stress and an unclear-direction I was headed-in. Fact is, I was radically mistaken as to *who* I thought I was and *where* I might be headed. I suppose that all I really understood was '*what 'seemed important to me or* what I *wanted.* That was *Travel.* I wanted to see the world or at least see as much as I could afford or was practical.

Going anywhere had to be on a right-track for me. I'm a fairly easy-going, mild-mannered, good-natured fellow with extreme intensity, (Ha! Ha!)... and a new adventure in a strange place would almost always satisfy me. It wasn't until serious and pensive reflection in my new *home-away-from-home* in ***la Zona de Mismaloya, Puerto Vallarta*** that I also discovered true, essential purposes of *traveling* for me: *Travel produces desired learning, wanted excitement and needed relaxation. Travel* also yields graceful comprehension of important blessings intended for our minds, bodies and spirits. I shall have a little more to say on that later...

The challenge and quest of coming down to ***Puerto Vallarta*** for an adventurous experience to study, observe and note others' lives helped me. Additionally, it allowed me to appraise and assess vital aspects of myself. By observing and considering others' language and lifestyles and appreciating new places with new experiences in ***Puerto Vallarta***, I was able to reflect upon my own state-of-being. I was able to *come-to-grips*, so-to-speak, and understand some things about myself. Importantly, I learned to really appreciate where I was going.

Unfortunately, there were times when I was alone. However, during my solo "short-term" residences in ***Mismaloya***, I regularly reminded myself that Angelina was back home also "alone." Circumstances made our situations more bearable, usually. Sometimes, Angelina remained at home for personal and family issues. She usually joined me when matters finally allowed or awarded her opportunity. Since writing poetry consumes as much time as any reflections, though, I appreciated periods of solitude when I was allowed the luxury of quiet, undisturbed and pensive thought.

In fact, much of the writing and poetry developed while sitting at my computer feeling moodily alone but lost-in-thought. However, it should be noted that most experiences written about were shared with my wife and/or friends. When alone, however, time often provided and promoted quiet and thoughtful, meditative-opportunities for reflection. Typically, most important were reflections upon *my life* and my world around me. We are all fairly easily self-absorbed when it comes to considering our own life's philosophy. This book is simply reflections of some of those experiences and impressions as they pertain to my own being.

The volume grew as I attempted to chronicle in detail multiple-visits made to Puerto Vallarta, Mexico while visiting, vacationing and/or living for short stints in 2010, 2013, 2014, 2014, and 2015. Each visit was a different experience. Each trip provided its own unique and interesting memories: A one-day cruise stop-over, a three-month visit, a two-week resort-vacation, another three-month stay. And then another five-month lease in 2015 comprised this volume's collaborative effort. Each voyage dealt with different seasons of the year chosen deliberately to presumably experience different perspectives.

Initially, I was unaware of what circumstances and/or conditions might develop and influence this travel-log/reflective-diary. It was the unknown aspect which made the endeavor that much more curious and intriguing. Not knowing whom or what might be encountered made the creative-aspect entertaining. Now, I freely and happily admit and confess that the undertaking was a genuinely worthwhile learning experience for me. For explanation, and for my own amusement, in the beginning of the writing, I discuss the development and planning for our getaway. It was no overnight preparation, and there actually was a lot of fun making the journey happen in the first place.

I offer the substance of those times in this volume. It is designed as a sincere tribute to all those friends, acquaintances and people encountered while we experienced *Puerto Vallarta* visiting and living there. Good, bad or indifferent, I am grateful for their sharing and my learning. It is my wish that appreciation will be obviously noted within...

However, it should be noted that this story, or *collaboration of poetry and prose* is actually a second effort in my: *The Traveler Series.* My first attempt was primarily a book of precise, concise, intricate, yet often laughable poetry for which I am still awaiting reviews. Apparently, sales have been sluggish. In fact, I can't find anybody who *got it*, let alone read it, or for God's sake, *bought* a copy!

That issue, as-a-matter-of-fact, has actually caused one of my premier and personal, *pet-peeves*: "Computer-Hackers" and other *users* who "take" *costly things* from the Internet for free. Just how many "hacker" readers have already discovered my book on some obscure, web-site, craftily downloaded it at no cost to themselves and then sneakily and greedily read my life's-effort? After all, it was my *blood* from swollen and bled, key-boarded, finger-tips; it was my *sweat* from exhausting efforts trying to think of words which rhymed with *bulb;* and it was *tears*-of-laughter hemorrhaged from my own, humorous anecdotes and comic, novel poetry! And those *hackers* got it for free? So, what can I do? Where is the satisfaction? God only knows! The answer is... "Out there... in cyber-space!"

I can't begin to tell you how many *Electronically-retrieved* (pirated)-films, shows, TV movies, sports programs, and games that I have been forced to endure. I have seen with my own, spoiled-eyes downloaded films on others' computers which had not even been released to the theaters yet. Amazing! Of course, most of the downloads had squiggly, green-lines running across the screen, confined viewing frames of about six to seven inches, and constant, extremely annoying, pop-ups of banner-size, red-letter warnings of penalties for fraudulent usage...

Nevertheless, there they were... for *free!* Some of the *worst* ones, I may have accidentally saved in private, computer-folders for any future, seriously boring, down-time. However, I am maybe pretty sure, though, that perhaps, they were probably *pirated* by one of my so-called friends or family in some fashion.

Of course, it is unlikely that I have watched any of those programs on my own TV! But, I suspect who does: They live(d) in Angleton,

TX and/or Hesperia CA. Personally, I use understanding and acceptance of others' unwillingness to *buy* their own copies. However, it is not my human-nature to accuse others who haven't bought my book or may have simply missed it; anything is possible. *In fact,* I am impressed! According to all the people who say that they have read it (well, some of it, a poem or two, maybe), apparently, only one-book has seemingly passed through so many hands. It's amazing! It's astounding! It's impossible!

Anyway, accepting any accidents, mishaps, oversights, or *my-dog-ate-it excuses* (I actually had a dog once who ate my college-homework assignment... Of course, I had already brought the graded-assignment home after receiving it from a smug professor... Anyway,... the dog died from red-ink poisoning... It was ugly, but actually, I had received a B-; it wasn't quite up to "*Goodie-two-shoes, 'B'*" standards, but my GPA wasn't harmed... too much!)...

... Anyway, I am up for *forgiveness*! I have *looked-over* many mistakes in my life; in fact, simultaneously I *looked-over* a lot of people too. I am tall for my age! Anyway, like I always say: *Bye-goners are bye-goners.*

Contents

Prologue

Are you a "Traveler," too (***un Viajero***)? Have you ever lived-abroad or envisioned either in your life? How about for retirement? Do you ever dream of visiting or living in *those faraway places with strange sounding names*? That was always a favorite line of mine from a favorite song (*Faraway Places*) by the incredible John Gary. He sang about unique sights, and people and experiences? I've been humming, or whistling or singing that tune my whole, adult-life.

I believe "traveling" reinforces our learned and trained minds with concrete evidence that the world is NOT flat. Of course, by "not-flat" I don't mean just subscribing to classroom explanations of a glorious, watery and geophysical, wondrous and globular earth. I mean also "seeing" for ourselves that Earth is a stunning design of geography inhabited by amazing arrays of plant, animal and human-life. And, for my own particular curiosities, I have become profoundly fascinated with its human phenomena.

From early childhood, we were provided visual maps of our world transcribed onto flat-surfaces offering two-dimensional explanations of various characteristics of Earth. These included many types for multiple purposes: Physical maps most commonly used to grasp land and water masses, places and regional references; maps for topographic studies to better understand elevation aspects; maps for political analysis to relate to regions and borders and cities and capitals; and climate maps to appreciate weather patterns.

Naturally, we also studied a variety of resource maps and thematic maps to have other unique aspects illustrated for us. These explained variances and differences between many subject topics such as population and economic and production features to name a few. Of course, we cannot forget our use of good old road maps to help us find our way too. All of those specific maps offer unique and specialized visions of our world.

Additionally, we were offered globes to understand the dynamics of spherical longitude and latitude. With those we were able to visualize how we all might reach each other physically and emotionally. Globes helped us appreciate the connectedness of us all. They explained variations and differences of land masses in relation to each other. Yet, more importantly, they provided clearer understandings and appreciation of our unique, human placement on Earth.

Both forms, maps and globes, are excellent teaching-tools. They are common and used often having the best intentions in mind. However, they do not express with clarity or personality the truly incredible diversity and uniqueness of the earth's surface. In the same manner, flat surfaces, diagrams or globes simply cannot clearly and visibly demonstrate the earth's vast differences. Neither can they exhibit the unique humanness of all us different people living in innumerably distinctive environments inhabiting our earth.

Our world is an absolutely amazing orb. Upon it live the most diverse, astonishing and interesting species imaginable. Yet, if we just concentrate on ourselves, human beings, it's a mind-boggling exploration of fascination's making and a study of endless learning. We are an incredibly varied and remarkable species. It would truly make many fulfilled lives traveling and searching to grasp, learn and appreciate the breadth and subtleties of our human sorts

National Geographic magazine and its television affiliates do wondrous jobs bringing "diversity" into our living-rooms. Disney and many other producers do fabulous work illustrating, explaining and promoting the incredible and varying qualities of our earth and its human, and otherwise, species which occupy it. There are so many wonderful, visual-diversions entertaining and educating us regarding the vast multiplicities of Earth. Thanks to networks, we need travel no farther than our television sets to encounter them all. Yet, we can only experience those people, places and things accepting them in somewhat impersonal ways.

Fortunately, however, many of us are able to "see-outside-the 'box.'" We are allowed truly personal reviews by experiencing some of these places and people in person for ourselves. *Travelers* get to familiarize themselves first-hand. They do it by visiting and experiencing on-the-spot these dichotomies and harmonies of Earth's regions, climates and weather, and animal, and other species' kingdoms. Some even get out-of-this-world with space-exploration. Point is, *travelers* accomplish this by *going* there! They do it by getting right into the mix of things. We all can explore and learn from reading material, television and movie shows; however, getting it *straight from the horse's mouth* provides true, "reality-checks." There are appreciable differences between the terms *book-wise* and *street-wise.*

Television programs and theater movies are fun and interesting means to learn. They are both experienced similarly, though, like paper maps and globes, as two-dimensional views. Thus, they deny viewers any substantial or personal and real understanding. The old adage, "If you want something done right, do it yourself," seems to hold equally true for learning and understanding about new places, their inhabitants and new experiences. Surely, if we "rightly" want to see and understand something, we have to go there and see for ourselves.

If you want to watch a soccer game, *be the ball!* Well, maybe we don't need such extreme measures, but the fact remains that we need to look *at* ourselves and *see* for ourselves! Humans are amazing! We are fun. We are fascinating. We are exhilarating, and so are all our incredibly different and unique lifestyles, architecture, talents, achievements, and variable personal and local histories. We only need "travel" to appreciate these points on personal levels.

Over the past few years, my several visits to ***Puerto Vallarta*** have given me opportunities to experience this vibrant community and its inhabitants on a personal level. This volume humbly intends to explore a small part of that region's uniqueness and charm. Hopefully, my observations, recollections and records will provide a varying array of impressions on the region for my readers.

My objective is not a map or chart-study. It is not a colorful description of sights and sounds and foods and clothing. I want to offer something here a little different. I want to explore the heart, mind and soul of ***Puerto Vallarta, MX***. I wish to do this by examining impressions from my own experiences.

I have attempted this with storytelling and poetry. With each I tried to probe my feelings regarding various phenomena experienced, people and friends with whom I observed and/or connected and places I ventured. Everything sent messages to my psychic. This volume, then, is a sort of collection of those varied "messages" received and recorded. Humbly, I offer you: Messages from Vallarta.

In the Beginning...

I do not give up easily. I am no quitter! I had been persistent. There was no mistaking from my comments and behavior that I wished to make a very special extended-vacation somewhere in ***Mexico*** for the two of us. I used a plausible excuse that I needed and wanted to continue my writing and learn Spanish. Soon retired and being of Mexican descent, my wife, Angelina, could reasonably accept my premises. With little truly holding us back, the possibility became a reality. Saving and planning was done, and then we were gone.

Once underway, I began jotting down notes on each new "observation-point." I also took lots of pictures for reminders and references to help jar the memory and offer new ideas. That's the fun thing about going somewhere new. Everything is an adventure! If you've never been there before, or never done something before, then keep watching! Something unique and fun may likely occur. By the way, cameras are so much fun. They instantly grab a slice of our lives and hold it forever for our review. I have always enjoyed being the "picture-guy" like my dad, *Guy*.

And adding poetic verse to the storytelling later came easily. However, poetry came in spurts and runs for me. Much of the time, I was alone at our residence in ***Puerto Vallarta*** because Angelina needed to be back at our California home for personal and family issues. She joined me whenever her circumstances finally allowed or awarded the opportunity. Those periods of solitude, though, allowed me the luxury of quiet, undisturbed and pensive thought. Often, when I conceived an idea or verse, I sat down for marathon writing sessions.

I did much of the writing while sitting at my computer alone and lonely. However, it should be noted that many of the experiences spoken and written about were shared with my wife and/or friends. When alone, though, time often provided and promoted quiet and thoughtful opportunities to reflect on life and the world around. This book, therefore, simply became a reflection of some of those experiences and impressions.

We had, in fact, traveled there during varying visits in 2010, 2013, 2014, and 2015. Each was quite different from the previous stays, and each vacation provided its own unique and interesting experience to chronicler and discuss. One day, two weeks, three months, four months, and more during different seasons of the year offered substantially diverse perspectives.

When "travelers" take notes, or at least reflect upon experiences, it becomes easier to develop from a diary or journal, ultimately, the premise of a book. I have humbly attempted this collection of stories and prose as a collaboration of mind, body and spirit. My mind provided impressionable reflections. My body furnished physical and visual observations for examination. My spirit delivered sincere but often imagined, slanted and sometimes tasteless or twisted parodies.

I am fortunate that, finally, my trusted, traveling-companion is my wife, Angelina. It was slow-and-steady encouragement coaxing her into previous travels visiting family, friends or new sights. Lately, though, she has become more accustomed to my "travel" needs and is more accepting and cooperative. It should be noted, however, that Angelina is not unaccustomed to travel. Being of Mexican heritage, she experienced coming to the USA as a young immigrant. Later, as an adult she made several trips back to ***Mexico*** for various circumstances.

Also, she had flights home for family-matters. At one time, Angelina even moved her own, young children back to ***Mexico*** for personal reasons. That had been followed soon thereafter by a return-move back to San Francisco, CA. Additionally, she traveled cross-country in the USA on-her-own, and alone with her children by car. Those trips were unfortunate, however, and instilled negative attitudes toward travel. In fact, she preferred traveling little at all. With me along, though, hopefully, all that is changing. These days she's my *travel-buddy.*

Initially, to ease matters and minds, it had been necessary to arrange "baby-trips" such as Hawaii and ***Baha California***. Later, bigger steps came enjoying ***Cancun*** and then Costa Rica. Angelina participated with modest enthusiasm. However, a cruise to ***Mexico's*** Pacific coastal cities did the proverbial "trick." Our ship stopped for a day in the beautiful, romantic, accommodating, and inexpensive port-city of ***Puerto Vallarta***. We both fell-in-love that day with the entire ***PV*** community promising each other to try and return soon for a longer stay. In my mind began a quest to fulfill that promise, and I even imagined writing about it.

Originally, this book was meant simply to tell a story of ***Puerto Vallarta***. I was determined to share my observations, feelings and impressions of living in the that region and sharing my experiences existing with its people. ***Puerto Vallarta*** is a luscious, historically relevant and beautiful place to study, think, talk, and write about. This writing, however, casually developed and evolved from serious contemplation and idle-thought during our first three-month visit.

As additional visits and experiences were expedited and progressed, so did self-impressions and self-considerations. I wondered, questioned and analyzed my own being within personal perspectives: *Who was I*? *Where was I* (in relationship with my life)? *What was I doing* (with my life)? And, finally, *Where might I be going afterward* (including death)? I was traveling and learning about ***Mexico*** and ***Puerto Vallarta***, yet I was about to learn a great deal about myself too. It was an interesting and valuable experience for me in all regards.

I offer it now to you for your pleasure or curiosity and my satisfaction...

THE TRAVELER

Tales of submissions' images,
Coerced inside our thoughts,
Send messages of discovery's
Missed feelings, once thought lost.

Exploits, friendships and emotions,
Cornucopia's mixed-appeal,
Yield food for starved devotions
With satisfaction's zeal.

Acquiescence of truth's yearning
For sights merely dreamed of
Sometimes requires coaxing
Begin with humbled shoves.

But, once our course-of-action
Determines paths we seek,
Fulfillment's blessed reaction
Is contemplation's seed.

And memories' flourished musings
Which govern our ideals
Let travels' righteous reasoning
Examine how we feel.

Then, venturing beyond our dreams
Is sought in faith's reunion.
Humanity's passion redeems
Inspired, worldly-communion.

"The Traveler" dwells within us
Seeking some peace from strife.
We need only submit to trust
His journey in our life.

A Well-Laid Plan

When a thought, or idea or impression of something strikes me curiously, occasionally I enjoy devising some reason with rhyme and meter to match the story-telling. Just like anybody else when I do things, or go places or meet people, I am typically affected by those moments. Sometimes, "impressions" left on my mind are amusing or perturbing, but most of them are usually thought-provoking. A few of those "imprints" I even enjoy reflecting upon through use of poetry.

As I was mentally and emotionally preparing for our trip to ***Puerto Vallarta***, I considered the meaning and purpose of such a "poetic" journey. I reflected upon the unique intrigue of travel and its potential consequences. Why does anyone bother? What value is there in travel? What's the *big deal*? I thought about it often and concluded that "travel," and writing stories and poetry about those places visited was a lot like a hobby for others.

Some people relish collecting trains; others delight in recording a ride on the *Marrakesh Express*. Some prefer amassing objects of particular themes; others fancy accumulating vacation memorabilia. Both are valid, entertaining and interesting. Both are extremely subjective and meaningful to the "collector." It is all within the scope of personal pleasure. My own "objective" interests are fulfilled by photo-albums filled with personalized, snap-shot memories of distant visages and often accompanied with related poetry. To each their own.

Although pleasure from travel is personal, having a compatible traveling companion is beneficial to any embarkation. Travelers usually feel more secure when they know someone is "watching-their-back." Usually, it's more fun to share an exciting experience with a friend. Each feeds off the others enthusiasm. Travel-mates need not always prioritize interests the same way, but each agrees to join in on their partner's excursions to assist making a journey more successful, interesting and fulfilling to them both. In return, each is comforted that the "partner" will reciprocate with support and participation in the others chosen expeditions, jaunts or curious adventures. After all, "It takes two to Tango."

A HOBBY FOR LIFE

A hobby for life is obsessive collecting
Memories of innumerable kinds.
We organize, then categorize
And distribute them within our minds.

When experiences are taken-for-granted,
They can become excluded or denied;
Meaningful notions of important occasions
May be thoughtlessly cast-aside.

Everywhere we go,
Everyone we meet
And everything we do
Form impressionable views.

Views become the stories
In chapters of our books.
Focusing on impressions
Makes others take closer looks.

Feelings reflected on memory's pages
Offer anecdotes' purposes we seek.
Places, people and activities pursued
Provide insightful company.

When we open-our-minds to discovery's joys,
Let acquaintances become new-found friends,
Our actions will encourage novel pursuits,
And "Records-of-Our-Lives" begin.

Everywhere we go,
Everyone we meet
And everything we do
Form impressionable views.

Views become the stories
In chapters of our books.
Focusing on impressions
Makes others take closer looks.

KINDRED SOULS

There's no such thing as "soul mates,"
Two minds melding as one.
Although the thought romances us,
Love's work is never done.

Kindred souls seldom think alike;
They agree to disagree, as they say.
They needn't enjoy the same places;
They visit each others playgrounds.

They don't have to enjoy the same activities;
New adventure is boldness for spirits.
They won't always savor the same foods;
Variety is spice-of-life.

And they seldom look or dress alike;
Individuality is their mantra.
They rarely share similar, personal goals;
Each acquires their own, unique achievements.

They appreciate and enjoy each others' successes
And provide comfort and support for losses.
They accept each others' contributions
And share in everything they have.

That's what makes them *kindred souls;*
They are "kind" to each other.
They enjoy "being" together
Embellishing each others' soulful experiences.

It is not easy and requires much
Effort, diligence and vigilance.
But, as they say, "It is worth it!"
Because that's what makes *kindred-souls* mates.

“Mismaloya Blues”

(Author’s Note):

The following reflections are really little more than sketchy travel-logs commenting about traveling to and living in the community of ***Puerto Vallarta, Mexico***. Throughout the narrative, I have hopefully intertwined some original, appropriately-placed verse as sort of "poetic" judgments and observations regarding various aspects of ***Puerto Vallarta*** and its surrounding communities. Ideally, those poetic inclusions will demonstrate examples of the varied emotions, feelings and insight I experienced and gathered from my visits there and travels about the region.

The main portion of the story covers the trip itself, ***Puerto Vallarta*** and especially the area in which we lived, ***Mismaloya***. Naturally, I shall discuss the amazing and beautiful, surrounding communities and areas. So, too, shall I offer conjecture regarding the widely varied and colorful inhabitants of the various regions. Furthermore, the tale promotes commentary regarding the wonderful variety of lifestyles and fun, interesting and unique, local-landmarks of curious interest. Finally, I opted for some personal observations and comments detailing the spectacular raw and natural beauty of the unique terrain with its ***maravillosa*** (marvelous) land, sea, and sky scape images.

Additionally, and in conclusion, I have utilized literary license to embrace a somewhat personal and unique method of Spanish-language learning by inserting various words, terms, and phrases

en espanol with their English translations following in parentheses. Occasionally, I reversed the order for variety, and still in other parts, I let ***el espanol*** speak for itself. My purpose is to demonstrate the commonality of our two languages and to show readers how colorful and easy Spanish is to read, comprehend and appreciate. ***Si este metodo*** (If this method) is entertaining and beneficial (***es entretenido y beneficio)***, then I am humbled and pleased. ***Si no, lo siento.***

"Mismaloya Blues"

Part 1

Mexico Cruisin'...

The time came (Llego el momento) to make our move. Angelina and I had planned and rehearsed and even practiced twice before with varying effects, but the results were the same. It was time (ya era hora) for us to move to ***Puerto Vallarta, Mexico***. We would lease the same condo from a year before, but this time arrange for a long-term stay of ideally up to a year.

However, first, let's back up a couple years to get an understanding of the events which led to our desire for a long-term stay... ***Originalmente, mi esposa, Angelina, y yo*** (originally, my wife, Angelina, and I) had visited the wonderful community of Puerto Vallarta while stopping over for a day during a "***Las Vistas y los Sonidos de Mexico***" cruise. I guess the cruise-line planned on *the sights and sounds of* ***Mexico*** experience for us all. That particular vacation was a celebration for my retirement, and it brought us to a variety of exotic, Mexican destinations. ***Puerto Vallarta*** was the final stop-over before returning home, so it was probably true that we were ready for something unique and special.

Arriving in the early morning to the M***arina de la Cuidad de Puerto Vallarta,*** and with the ship safely secured, we ignored instructions from the ship's entertainment-director and ***decidemos ir*** (we decided to go) on our final souvenir, shopping-spree to the main tourist part of Vallarta, ***El Centro. Inmediamente***, and just after stepping-off and turning from the gangplank to face our last port-of-call, we were stunned with surprise, dismayed, disappointed, and finally amused. Laughter erupted from us newest visitors with discovery of a newly constructed ***WalMart*** directly across the main boulevard from the cruise ships' docks.

Against our better judgment we dashed across the busy avenue, wormed our way through the myriad of parked cars in the huge parking lot and entered the typically massive structure. Noting ***similitudes y diferencias*** from other WalMarts visited back home, we still recognized the same merchandising and sales essence: Here, essentially, could be imagined a person's entire, life's needs enclosed in a box, albeit, a big one, but still a box! Yet, we still found a couple of ***elementos*** (items) ***absolutamente necesarios***... not! and made the obligatory purchases and escaped. But, we had our ***primero*** (first) anecdote for home.

Once outside, we hailed a taxi-driver to take us to our desired location. Our driver, apparently, was a NASCAR trainee who took his task very seriously getting us to our destination ***muy pronto.*** Our adventure raced to the downtown, ***El Centro*** and ***Zona Romantica*** areas of small shops and flea-markets to seek our spoils. Wildly weaving and swerving through bumper-to-bumper ***trafico***, our "Jeff Gordon" wannabe finally dropped us off at a likely turn-around, smugly accepted his fee and tip and disappeared in-a-flash. Our hearts still racing and eyes bulging from a hundred, seemingly-near mishaps, we cleared our heads, laughed with nervous exhilaration and moved into our flea-market destination alongside the ***Rio de Cuale***. A large, white, concrete arch and stairway warmly welcomed us.

La puerta de entrada (The entrance-way) made me imagine we had arrived at some place locals referred to as "Touristville." Or, maybe they just called it "***La zona de los touristos.***" Regardless, we were in for a treat. Wandering down "olde-world," cobblestone-streets lined with brightly colored ***tiendas*** (stores) and markets (***mercados***), the air was filled with delicious aromas of familiar and new cuisine blended to tantalize every nasal sensation.

Our hand-in-hand journey past authentic flows of new ***mexicana*** sights and sounds was thrilling and entertaining. ***Nuestra caminata*** (our walk) was soothing and relaxing, filled with constant "Kodak-moments" and was genuinely romantic. We saw and absorbed so much in such a short time. Everything was experienced while eagerly traipsing about for less than a dozen blocks and a couple hours of delighted curiosity.

Meandering through the ***Rio de Cuale*** flea-markets ***(mercados de pulgas)***, our adventure was filled with colorful sights and friendly vendors selling an array of souvenirs challenging any tourist's imagination. ***Fue aqui y fue entonces*** (It was here and it was then) that we simply fell-in-love with Puerto Vallarta. It was rapturous, and it was ours. ***La Musica*** from brass and string instruments lifted and floated through the community sent from strategic locales by talented musicians playing lively and favorite ***mexicana*** melodies. It seemed from every street corner we heard guitars and brass instruments coloring the air with voices uniting in musical gaiety.

Joining in the spontaneous festival from alongside the riverbank, occasional, lime-green colored, or grungy, gray and orange iguanas crawled overhead on tree branches. ***Los reptiles*** all seemed relaxed and simply enjoying the day's sunshine. They appeared quite unconcerned over any enthusiasm from local children and tourists goggling at them. Perhaps, they were just there enjoying the musical background the same as us; however, I think they were primarily hanging around just to startle and thrill everyone with nervous excitement and contentment.

Our eyes were soothed by nostalgic visages of authentic, hustle-bustle ***de la cultura mexicana*** at work. All the locals were working busily in their shops or stands or watching and waiting for passers-bye to stop and look. ***Muchos restaurantes*** along our way filled our nostrils with amazing and sensual combinations of aromas blended with odors and smells from the ocean and jungle and city around us. ***La gente*** kindly greeted us with warm and friendly sales-offers of food or merchandise. Others, perhaps noticing my wife's Hispanic heritage, were even prompted to light and genial conversation, as was Angelina.

But, no-question-about-it, what was happening to us was the burgeoning of a delightful, love-affair experience, a triage, if you will, between willing and eager partners: my wife, myself and Puerto Vallarta. We sauntered all the way to the beachfront, ***La Playa***, where a fun, noisy and pushy sales, business-area thrived along a concrete, waterfront boardwalk called ***La Malecon***. Restaurants, t***equila*** and liquor stores, souvenir and clothing shops, bars, tour-sales stands, art-galleries, ice-cream parlors, candy shops, and a myriad of food and souvenir, portable-vendors were all pressing each passer-bye for their business.

We only had minutes to soak it all in. Yet, it all made ***una buena impresion*** (a nice impression) and unforgettable experience on the both of us. Eventually (***Eventualmente)*** heading back the way we arrived, we spotted the proverbial *icing-on-the-cake*. It was a quaint, ***mexicana***-style, brightly-colored billboard advertising hotel rooms nearby ***a $16 USD al dia***. That did it! It was a hotel one-block from a delightful beach, smack-in-the-middle of a colorful, vibrant city-life and going for sixteen bucks a day! We could not afford *NOT TO COME BACK!* We sealed the *tryst* with an excited kiss vowing to return one day soon for a longer, more-intimate stay.

Esa tarde (that afternoon), around 5:00 P.M., we sailed away from our new-found lover. The cruise ship slowly exited the pier allowing us opportunity to hang over the viewing-deck railing and gesture haphazardly to whomever motioned from ***el puerto***. Filled with a sort of mellowed melancholy, we waved back dishearteningly. Likely, we each subconsciously wished for the ship's captain to boom menacingly over the loud-speaker system commanding, "Both of you, '***bahar del barco de inmediato***' until further notice!" It would have been to our ecstatic delight. Alas, it never happened, and we weren't ordered "off-the-boat." But, we sailed home "with some wonderful memories" ***(con algunos recuerdos maravillosos)*** and an often recalled "vow-to-return."

In a short amount of time, we had come to realize how beautiful a simple life could be. The people of ***Puerto Vallarta (El pueblo de Puerto Vallarta)*** seem happy without having much money. They seemed content with their places and their beings. Hot, humid weather did not seem to faze them. They understood the grandeur of their surroundings and potential "tranquility" for acceptance.

I understood that what allowed them to sustain themselves in that peaceful, "tranquil" community was something you found only when you finally stopped "looking" for it: *Acceptance and peace.* They "accepted" who they were, what they were and where they were. It gave them "peace." *Peace-of-mind.* It truly was a special treasure for any of them to discover, channel and maintain.

I had much to consider, think about and reflect upon. I couldn't get those genuinely comfortable and apparently relaxed and peaceful people out of my mind. I began contemplating plans for returning to see more of them and to learn and understand more. I wanted to see everything from a new perspective. Like the brilliant, French novelist, Marcel Proust, wrote, ***The only real voyage of discovery consists not in seeking new landscapes but in having new eyes.***

LOST AND FOUND

For anything that's ever lost,
Something else may be found.
But, if you're always looking up,
You'll never see the ground.

Yet, some important things you'd cross
On paths which you are bound
Might be forsaken as corrupt
Because you're looking down

So, never fear your needs be squashed;
Wear them proudly as crowns.
Just take the time to follow-up
And ne'er be tightly wound.

Then, when you calculate the cost
Of everything around,
You'd see your "runneth-over" cup
Gives value pound-for-pound.

Thus, what is gone simply call "tossed."
The advice is really sound.
Your search can end, though seem abrupt,
But ***joys-of-life*** surround.

Returning Thoughts...

The cruise was over. We were home again and forced to return to the same old schedule. Angelina was usually content with her nine-to-five routine. Her career provided personal, fiscal security, a focus on community-service, an amiable working environment, and a social atmosphere with her peers. Perhaps, most importantly, her job gave her self-fulfillment and responsibilities which filled-up her days. When not at work, she visited with family or co-workers or dealt with home-matters such as cooking, cleaning, maintenance, or shopping. Angelina almost always seemed to stay occupied and busy with something.

In fact, I had mentally listed the critical-mass which identified her lifestyle: Work, house, kids, and shopping. Everything, including me, fell into at least one of those categories. Actually, I fit into all of them. I listened to her brag, laugh or rant about her job place; I was the "house" maintenance-engineer which meant I did all the stuff she couldn't or wouldn't do; I visited with the kids, helped them out physically and financially and accepted baby-sitting duties for our grandchildren; and, regularly, I guarded department stores' entrances while casually slumped-over an available berth during interminable periods of Angelina's shopping needs.

Truth-be-known, I realized that I had just identified my own lifestyle's "critical mass." My life seemed to be involved, or rather had evolved, or closer yet, devolved, into a support-structure for my spouse's needs, responsibilities, wishes, wants, desires, and dreams. If that's what husbands are supposed to do, and it's called, "manning-up," then I was a virtual Hercules amongst ***hombres***.

At least, that's how I perceived myself: *Who* I was; *What* I was; *Where* I was; and, *Where* I was going. Oh, yeah, I had other assets too. I was a couch-potato when a good sports game came on TV, and I messed around on my computer for endless hours of business and news reviews. With all that in mind, my life seemed thus summed-up: *It was filled with stuff to do*. But, that was not enough; it wasn't *fulfilling*.

And so, I kept going back into my memory vault for reminders of that wonderful day in ***Puerto Vallarta***. Oh, sure, that coming summer I was taking us to Costa Rica for a couple weeks during Angelina's annual vacation-break, but it wasn't the same. ***PV*** sat in my "vault" like a smoldering ember waiting to ignite a potential firestorm for which it was destined. My personal travel responsibilities were to fill-in edges of empty-time, highlight and delight the exposed weak areas and tie-up all loose-ends that might prohibit travel.

But those were tasks for amateur travelers. I had already visited much of the world, during much of my life, often alone, and I was up to a real challenge. A Summer in Europe, several more vacations to Europe, Russia, Canada, ***Mexico***, Asia, Costa Rica, the Caribbean, and Hawaii were nice. They were colorful and interesting. I always tried to make them so, but they still weren't enough.

I wanted to see the rest of the world from a new perspective, with *new eyes.* I wanted to see a country from the inside. I wanted to go where I could finally really "experience" what it was like to "live" somewhere else. My boyhood, "gypsy" days were festering and sparking, and I wanted to let my present days ignite and roar into an eternal blaze. Or, they could just burn for a little while and then fizzle-out. That was okay too. Just burn-baby, burn!

It was as if each morning I rose and faced the dawn and asked, "Where might I otherwise be, and what would it be like *being there*?" I wanted and truly desired to "be there." Somewhere, anywhere, it really didn't matter, but the thought consumed my fantasies. Each day was like sex in the morning. "Hey, Baby! Hello world! ***Buenos Dias***! What do you feel like doing? What have you got in mind for me today?" I would get so excited, I'd holler in my fantasies, "Bring it on!" I was ready to go, and I really even understood where to go too: ***Puerto Vallarta***! I was just waiting for the opportunity to "arise."

THE ROOSTER CROWS

The rooster crows;
'Tis time to rise and shine.
Part the blinds,
Receive the light
And let fresh feelings grow.

The afterglows,
Following morning's sign,
Removes binds
From stresses' plight
Letting sensations flow.

No need for haste;
Hearts' trust a pulse measured.
Love's treasured
Elation throbs right,
And nothing goes to waste.

Passion's sweet taste
Upon daybreak's pleasure,
Day's leisure,
Already bright,
Compels a pleasing pace.

"Mismaloya Blues"

Part 2

Time to Return...

Months had passed, and every-now-and-then, we'd reflect and comment about ***nuestro dia maravillosa*** (our wonderful day) in ***Puerto Vallarta***; however, we were both still occupied. My wife was busy with her full-time employment in the medical field, and I busied myself goofing-off. But we both kept talking, wondering and imagining the "big break." To fill in the void, we managed a few, break-the-monotony vacations to ***Cancun***, Butchart Gardens and Costa Rica, but memories of the "affair" simply did not go away. When ***mi esposa,*** Angelina, announced her impending retirement to occur simultaneously with her next birthday, (thirty-nine...again!), bells, and whistles and fireworks went off in my brain, and I began formulating "***El Plan!***"

The "plan" was simple enough. My wife would make all the arrangements, and I would buy the tickets. Easy! Well, there was a little more to it than that. I knew she loved ***Puerto Vallarta*** as much as I did, but could we go there for an extended stay, like say, "The rest of our natural lives?" Well, that would be ***un poco mas dificil*** (a little more difficult). I realized it would take time for her to adjust to the notion. We were going to need "baby-steps" I understood, and of course, naturally, I was going to have to *trick* her. I mean, you can't just blurt out straight-on what's on your mind. That's sure to get, "No!" from any woman.

So, my conniving, I mean *planning,* began as I entered the realm-of-play for a game I like to call: Marital-Bliss. That's where one spouse, or mate, wants something and figures how to make the other get it for them and all-the-while think "getting-it" was their idea in the first place! ***Las mujeres*** are great at it; women do it all the time ***con sus hombres***. Consider the diamond, wedding-ring, if you will? Case closed! Oh, alright, I'm just kidding. Nevertheless, for a starter, I was going to have to get Angelina to want and plan a three-month trip to ***Puerto Vallarta*** and think it was all her idea! Isn't this game fun? Ain't marriage a kick?!

Fortunately, I had already played my trump card. You see, my wife just loves to *Google*. *Google* and gamble! You should see how she "googles" her way through Amazon wonderland and slot-machine heaven web-sites... ***por diversion*** and no-profit, just her *Paradise of Fun*! But I digress!... I mean she just gets lost in that incredible, search-engine and finds all kinds of stuff all kinds of ways in all kinds of places. If something's in cyber-space, she'll locate it. She just knows how to ask the right questions.

Me? I can't Google ***un mapa*** to a local pizza-parlor if I'm accidentally parked right in front of one. But, she sure can, and my trump-card paid off handsomely. Previously, I had given her ***el regalo brillantemente considerado*** (the brilliantly considered gift) of a *Samsung Galaxy 4 Tablet* with *Android Power*! Now, with it, she could travel forever anywhere in universal cyber-space!

Of course, I didn't want to travel that long or that far, just ***Puerto Vallarta*** for a few months to begin with. Nevertheless, the "game" was on. I just had to plant a few, seedling-thoughts in her inquisitive mind, add some fertilizer (B-S) and watch an "android-powered" idea sprout and thrive from her creative imagination using her own, and her tablet's, boundless energy.

Now came ***el momento de que la "idea"*** to be sprung or sprouted. My wife's announced retirement and birthday tilled the soil, so-to-speak. I simply offered her a double-whammy birthday/retirement gift, the kind of present that is hard-to-refuse. I teasingly fertilized, "How about a romantic escape to celebrate?"

"***?Eh?***" was her cleverly detached response, and I expected as much, but it was just a lure, a temptation to hear, and dig, and harvest, or taste more.

I softly but emphatically mused, "How about right after your birthday and retirement, say mid-September, we go back to our 'Promised-Land,' ***Puerto Vallarta***, for ***tres meses*** (three months) liked we talked about?" I paused letting the suggestion sink in. Then I excitedly promised, "We'll come back before ***Navidad*** to celebrate Christmas and New Year's holidays with our kids." Okay. Now, I had to wait a moment while thoughts developed within Angelina's curious cognizance. She would quietly consider the point, reflect upon it pensively and when the moment was right, she would inquire further. And so it came… ***"?Como?"*** That's right. "How?" she cautiously but curiously inquired.

"Easy," I baited. "Use your tablet to find a good place at a good price and find the airline tickets for a good deal. Think of someone to watch our ***casa*** while we are gone. She can take care of Smiley, our dog (***nuestro perro***), the birds ***(las aves)***, the indoor plants ***(las plantas de interior)***, and the outside gardens ***(y los jardines exteriores)***." There was silence from her. She was thinking about the idea and a prospect. Silence is often better than "No!" A good sign, indeed.

Then I pointedly offered, "If *she's* live-in, then *she* can do the job for free-rent. Work on it. You can figure it all out." Finally, I casually drifted, "I want to go watch ***mi juego de beisbol en la television***. Call me if you need me or find something." With a sly smirk on my face and my back toward her to hide it, I casually sauntering off to watch my baseball game on TV in the other room.

Now came the moment to set-the-hook. I gently teased-the-line by calling back over my shoulder blurting, "Oh, yeah, by-the-way, I think ***mi hija*** (my daughter), Deborah, needs a place to stay for a few months while she organizes her life and makes some changes. She might appreciate the opportunity."

Angelina considered this point for a thoughtful moment and then quizzed, ***"?En serio?*** (Seriously?) You really think she would? I know she said before that she really needed a change. Maybe if we talk to her... I trust her too... ***Y seria bueno aqui.*** (And she would be good here)." Yes, she would, and "The Plan" was good too. It was working, and I was winning… I knew it all along.

Things were going like clock-work. ***Los peces*** (fish) were nibbling at the bait. That comes from knowing your territory with a little preparation ahead-o'-time. Of course, ***naturalmente***, I had already previously spoken with Deborah about the prospect. She was elated. I actually had to tone her down a little, "Just tell Angelina that you're really interested in the idea, and you'd work very hard to take care of ***la casa*** and everything. Tell her you really adore our ***perro***, Smiley, because he's such a good dog, and say, 'It's an opportunity (you'd) appreciate.'"

Angelina really likes Deborah and is sympathetic to her ordeals. If I let Angelina talk things over and make some kind of plan with Deborah, it would be icing-on-the-fish, or something like that. Anyway, "The Plan" was working.

Pescado para la cena de esta noche! Really, I'm not that fond of fish, but I'd enjoy it for dinner tonight!

Line and hook baited, cast, let drift, feeling nibbles, a strike, set-the-hook, and now was the time to reel in the prize. Offering a tonal tinge of excitement, but in a very straight-forward manner, I declared, "Also, you should know that the whole adventure is going to be paid-for with my special, retirement savings. ***Todo!*** Everything! All you've got to do is figure out all the details." Then came the final nail, or cast, "And if you want, I can call Deborah and check with her. If you like, ***podemos hacer esto***. We can do this! You just have to do the figuring. Hey, Babe, I'll be in the front-room watching baseball." I quietly slipped into the other room to watch the game, and I waited…

I didn't hear from my wife until almost the end of the game. The A's were winning, so I was ***relajado*** (comfortable) and prepared for her visit. If she walked in, or called out, I had to appear nonchalant and fight-off overeager enthusiasm over her successes. I mean, really, I couldn't sound too excited now, could I?

On expected cue, however, Angelina hollered from our bedroom, "Dan, I think I've found out some pretty interesting stuff here on Craig's List. The rent might seem a little high, but the places look beautiful ***con vistas al mar*** and everything." Imagine that! Ocean views! Then, she continued, "They are away from town, though, and I like that. Come and look at these rentals. I don't want to live in-town. It's too noisy and crowded." ***Un momento de silencio*** followed, and then she added loudly with my hoped-for closer, "And the airline tickets aren't too expensive, and there's a lot available when we want to go." It all sounded great so far, but I couldn't show my enthusiasm quite yet. Indifference was still the edge.

The next part was easy. "***Oh, esta bien***," I muttered loud enough for her to catch my quasi-acknowledgment that it was okay, it was good. "Whatever you like," I quipped and then added, "***No problema***. Whatever ***el costo esta muy bien***. I'll be there in a minute right after the game." My mind envisioned Angelina shaking her head with an "Oh, he-doesn't-even-care," attitude. I just grinned, did a double-fisted, air-pump and yelled, "Yeah!" It went undetected because the A's had won the game anyway, so it fit right in.

I was impressed, though! I had tossed her the ball, and she ran for a touchdown. Or, I threw her a pitch, and she hit a home run. Or, my favorite, I gave her a fishing pole, ***y ella cogio*** Moby Dick! No matter. I tossed my imaginary "catch" into my imaginary boat. I gave myself an imaginary pat-on-the-back and victoriously spoke to my inner-self, "Let's go see where we're gonna live in ***Puerto Vallarta***." I smiled to myself again, ***pero esta vez*** (but this time), I once more sauntered into the "Think Tank" of Marital-Bliss. Or, happily I fantasized, "...***Pero esta vez, fue en el 'Centro de Celebracion!'*** "

From that-point-on, it was "blissful" effort as we laid side-by-side on our "work-station," king-sized bed passing her tablet back and forth. We were looking at rental properties Angelina had found and analyzing each. She had found several interesting places, and we were able to narrow them down ***rapidamente'*** to a few possibilities. A couple were in town, which I sort of leaned toward, but others were in an area called ***Mismaloya*** zone or area. I assumed ***que era similar a las ciudades*** with suburbs which generate their own personal names due to local significances but are still within city limits. Like, "Brooklyn" is still NYC.

I recognized this to be ***una estrategia muy importante***, however. The choice could make-or-break our trip. I already knew I would be comfortable in a hammock on a beach anywhere so long as a bar was nearby to visit if it started to rain. But, my Angelina would need a few creature-comforts and doing ***tres meses*** (three-months) of "hard-time" would be unforgivable. I needed her to pick out something that she would feel safe and comfortable with and a place that I would love the view. Safety. Comfort. View. Fair enough to get started looking. Okay, so I just let her "Google." She'll find it.

Things like safety and ***seguridad*** were tops on her list. Angelina, like so many Americans, had been over-hyped by TV and newspaper coverage of horrifying cartel activities, ***el trafico de drogas de Mexico*** and horrendous stories printed and diagnosed. She had typical trepidation derived from reported incidents which had usually occurred ***en las comunidades de la frontera de Mexico y EE. UU*** (its border towns). Reassuring her from my own Google research that ***Puerto Vallarta*** was a safe community with minimal crime did not reduce her anxieties. She needed physical *assurances* to make her ***sentir segura*** (to feel safe) like evidence of locks and gates and access protection to our potential new home...

Las instalaciones de la cocina y el bano (the kitchen and bathroom facilities*)* were her next priorities followed by the living area and bedroom aesthetics. Sure, she wanted a view, but the price of the rental unit was very relevant to her, so ocean-views were a lower factor in her mind. And Angelina did not want to suffer from heat or humidity. Having experienced those conditions during previous times e***n Mexico***, she was well aware of their discomforts.

Yo (I), on-the-other-hand, was all about ***la vista y el acceso a las luces y actividades de la cuidad.*** Give me the views and access to the city lights and activities! I cared less about the cost because I had been saving for a long time for this escapade and was prepared to blow the entire proverbial "wad" on the venture, but I already knew it was going to be very inexpensive. Personally, I had wanted to live right in the middle of ***centro***. I wanted to hear the noises, listen to the voices, see the city lights, and be right next to all the action on ***El Malecon***.

After all, it had been that cheap, hotel-advertisement, $16 USD/ Night, we had seen on our cruise visit that got us all excited about a return trip in the first place. No, I didn't want a disreputable, sleazy ***barrio*** for us, and I did want aesthetics. For me, it was all about: Location! Location! Location! Views! Views! Views! Just give me a comfortable hammock right next to all the action with a drop-dead gorgeous view of the ocean. Nothing much! ***!El sol, el mar, y la cerveza!*** Or, *the burn, the beach, and the beer*! Or, *the sun, the surf, and the suds!* Whatever. ***Lo mismo*** (Same thing). That's all I dreamed about.

Afortunadamente (Fortunately), one of us is the realist. I dreamed of honey-dipped rolls, but I knew who buttered-my-bread. I wanted lights, action and camera to excite my days and nights, but I knew it wouldn't be any fun unless we were both happy. Sacrificing city-life for the outskirts of town was a small offering. If Angelina was secure ***(Si Angelina era seguro)***, then outside-of-town was the only choice from which to pick. I knew if I wanted to be happy with this adventure, she had to be happy. It had to be a place that Angelina chose.

It promoted her to "game-maker" status because ***nuestra seleccion*** (our selection) would have her stamp-of-approval. She would make the choice, and because of her needs ***la seleccion final*** would be hers. And the catch? If the trip turned out to be a disaster, ***una bomba***, it was Angelina's choice so her fault, her blame! If it was great, I'd get credit for "enjoying it!" Surely, a no-lose/win-win for me! Do you get it? (***?Lo entiendes?***) ***?No lo ves?*** (Don't you see?)

There's intricate strategy in this "blissful" game ***que jugamos*** (that we play)!

But, like I said, Angelina was a serious Google-maniac. She always asked ***todos las preguntas correctas*** (all the right questions). She went to all the right sites. She had found ***muchas alquileres realmente interesantes*** (rentals) for variable periods-of-time, and some were ***muy razonable***. Because we wanted to go in mid-September, her research had explained that we were still catching the tail-end of the lower, off-season pricing. She had google-mapped various areas and found the curious "***Mismaloya***" district several miles out-of-town from the main part of ***Puerto Vallarta***.

Many of the ***fotos de alquile (***rental photos) were interesting but left uneasy feelings of uncertainty. Angelina looked for key-words like "safety-gate" or "gated-community" or "very secure and safe." I wasn't as concerned about that issue, and I thought to myself, "Well, heck, I'm not going to bother anybody. Just give me a view!" But I knew when to give in, so we both reviewed the listings for security's purposes and Angelina's wishes. We were still right-on-schedule with "***el plan***." It was time to choose, call and begin arrangements.

Craig's List is a very useful tool. Of course, sellers and buyers need to use common sense and available precautions; however, essentially, people sell and buy just about anything on the web-site. Angelina had asked ***preguntas*** (questions), found categories, narrowed the listings, and identified a source for us to contact regarding potential rentals. She had identified two, available rentals which both suggested safety and security and were reasonably-priced units ***con oceano-vistas*** and/or access.

Both sounded really fun, and we began getting excited. With Angelina's skill and fortitude, Google provided us with maps to look more closely at each site. City rentals we eliminated right away, but there were several others available. They were in an area referred to as ***Mismaloya*** about eight to ten miles out of the main part of ***Puerto Vallarta***. ***Los alquileres*** (the rentals) which interested us were on the cliff-side of the ocean with the ***Bahia de Banderas*** directly below. It looked like we had selected an area pleasing to us both but especially Angelina.

This place called ***Mismaloya*** kept coming up in Angelina's research. It began to have a sense of purpose about it, but it was still several miles, or even more kilometers, away from the main part of town. We are both comfortable with riding local bus-systems when traveling, but we felt uneasy here. We needed to find out more. How far away was it? How easy was it to get there?

The main road which led to our area-of-interest was called ***Puerto Vallarta-Manzanillo/ Hwy 200***. Other than occasional developments or structures, the vast majority of the area across the highway opposite the cliff-side appeared to be pure and simple jungle. It looked fascinating and gave us goose bumps imagining its true, natural beauty and potential danger. Therefore (***por lo tanto***), due to their locations, we were pretty-well settled on these choices, and it was time to go-for-it. With two, interesting listings offering the owner's or manager's name, phone number and email address, it was now up to me ***para el contacto inicial*** (for the initial contact). I would deal with the property-manager who handled the listings.

Me encanta (I love) ***el internet!*** I'm not great at the "searching" stuff, true, but the other stuff I get a kick out of, and what I can do really amuses and amazes me. When I just follow the browser's lead, I go where it suggests ***por mis intereses***, and I see and read what is going on practically anywhere in the world, let alone local news. But it's still the" other stuff" that gives me a real kick.

En unos pocos (a few) ***minutos***, I was about to write an email contacting a person two thousand miles away. Even more impressive, it was over ***tres mil doscientos*** (3,200) ***kilmetros de distancia***, and this person could arrange for our long-term lodging in that distant location. It was ***comunicacion instantanea*** with someone a vast distance away on an appliance other than a telephone. ***Increible!*** My computer is going to make it happen for us.

Sure, I could have even used Angelina's tablet to do the email too, but I've got her checking out more about airline tickets. While

I'm busy doing one thing, she's busy doing something else. It's our thing, if you know what I mean... Fuhgeddaboudit, this "Marital Bliss" thing-of-ours requires teamwork. I call it "***nuestra cosa!***" (our thing) or rather, "***nuestra casa!***" (our house). I mean, I don't want to plagiarize or upset anyone's feelings, especially wonderful ***Sicilianos***! But, we're having fun too. It's nice when two excited mates work together.

Angelina is hooked, too, and I can tell from her laughs ***(y puedo decir de sus risas)*** and "oohs" and "ohs" and "aahs" that she is teeming inside. Usually fairly reserved and conservative, it takes a lot for her to express excitement. However, I've overheard my wife telling ***anecdotas*** of our travel experiences ***a miembros de la familia y los amigos.*** She gets excited sharing her memories with them. ***Conmigo*** (with me), however, Angelina is usually more a model of emotional-containment.

"Yes, Dan, I enjoyed the ocean-swim; ***fue agradable*** (it was nice)." And my wife can't even swim! She was terrified! Sure, she had a life-jacket on, but it was still remarkable. She just gives me pure trust but with "reserved-emotions."

And right now, I just relied on ***recuerdos*** (memories) ***de nuestra primera*** (of our first) ***visita a Puerto Vallarta*** to re-kindle-the-flame and re-thrill her. The photos and map shots and descriptions were sparking some serious interest again. Present details of our planned escapade were on-hand. Our underway-plans allowed her to imagine returning to some ***de los mismos*** (same) ***lugares turisticos romanticos*** (romantic tourist places) which had captivated us and that we had both adored. That, and my genius gift of her supersonic, inter-galactic, all-knowing-and-all-serving, (atomic) powered, *whoop-d-do* tablet were providing mesmerizing interactivity. Together, memories and technology were "doing-the-trick." I just wind her up, let her go, and we're on-our-way!

The e-mail and phone contact were the easiest parts for me. I sent an inquiry to the given e-mail address and quickly received a reply. ***El partido me contacto*** (the party I contacted) was obviously

un administrador de la propriedad responsible (a property-agent responsible) for his clients' rentals. He wrote that timing was important. There were several places available with a variety of amenities. It was a good time to quickly select one we liked and put down a deposit to hold it before it was unavailable. I wrote back requesting ***mas informacion y mas fotos.*** They arrived shortly thereafter, and Angelina and I sorted ***por las selecciones.***

Ahora (now), it was ***hora de una llamada telefonica.*** I made the simple call. The "agent" answered right away and sounded ***muy agradable.*** He seemed knowledgeable and courteous but emphasized the importance of a swift decision due to the pending prime-season for rentals. I learned that the slow-season which ran ***entre mayo a octobre*** was due to heat, humidity and the rainy-period. In ***septiembre***, business began picking up for everything from cruise-lines and airlines and resort vacations to tourist visitors for long and short-term rentals. We were coming during a more desirable period, but our timing was excellent. ***Muchas opciones*** were still available.

After listening to my "wants-list" focusing on safety, security, cleanliness, and views, the agent quickly announced that he had a place which cost a little more but had everything we were requesting. ***Las fotos*** he then sent really got us excited. It was $100 more per month than I had anticipated, but the amenities were more than we had expected. ***Por $800 USD por mes*** (per month), we could get a stunning, 1 B/B condo overlooking the ***Bahia de Banderas*** near the ***Mismaloya*** district with all amenities furnished.

That meant that electricity, gas, water, garbage, cable TV, and Wi-Fi were all included. There would be no ***aire acondicionado,*** AC. However, we were informed there was little, if any, need for AC during the fall, winter and spring seasons. Besides, ceiling fans would likely cool ***las habitaciones*** and make us quite comfortable. We were too excited to question anything about cooling needs any further. After all, we wanted to live in the tropics. What should we expect?... We would learn the truth for ourselves later.

A few more scribbles back-and-forth, and Angelina and I were agreed on our mutual choice. We decided to spend a little more each month and choose the costlier ***condominio*** for the all-around package it offered. Other choices were cheaper but lacked aspects such as electricity-included, size and comfort, or had poor or no direct ***oceano vistas.*** Amenities and views were of primary concern. However, we also desired a place with access to everywhere and everything.

Fortunately, the agent explained, the bus-system we would utilize ran like clockwork with buses passing every ***quince*** (fifteen) ***minutos***. We loved riding buses from past experiences, so that was a minimal factor. True, I did want to live closer to town for the convenience and the action and sights and entertainment, but this choice was a no-brainer. Besides, rentals ***con las mismos comodidades***, with the same amenities, were hundreds of US dollars more per month. Our choice provided security Angelina needed, amenities we both desired and I had my views.

I arranged a ***Cuenta de PayPal*** (account with) ***con el agente***. Then, I transferred the required deposit (one month's rent) to lock up the unit for our planned visit coming ***en septiembre***. We were on our way! Well, almost! We still had plane tickets to purchase, but my "google-geek" wife resolved that matter easily. She had dates, ***16 de septiembre al 15 de diciembre***. We wanted round-trips, non-stops and preferably late-morning departures with early-evening returns.

Have I mentioned ***Angelina es bueno***? She nailed it! It would be a late-morning departure from SFO (San Francisco) non-stop to PVR (Puerto Vallarta) arriving mid-afternoon. ***Dos horas*** (two hours) clock advance for ***diferencias horarias (***time-zone difference) still meant less than a flight ***de cuatro horas.*** Two thousand miles away a new, long-term vacation life-experience awaited, and it would happen in three hours and forty minutes. ***Increible***! Everything went as planned with a few, small glitches to-be-expected. The departure-date arrived, and we had solved or resolved all the issues ***en casa. Mi hija, Deborah,*** had ***la casa*** well under-control because she had joined us a month earlier for personal needs and for training and preparation. After all, a home-residence is no small matter to be frivolous about or taken for granted.

There would be constant, on-going house-keeping and continual up-keep and maintenance. These included, but were not limited to, ***limpieza*** (laundry) and ***cocina y limpieza*** (cleaning) needs. The house-plants needed watering, and there was always plenty to do outside. ***Los jardines*** (gardens) had to be cared for ***y el cesped*** (and the lawns) required mowing and watering.

Of course, we can't forget *Smiley*, our dog. There would be proverbial "piles-of-doggie-do's" spread all across the yards from one end to the other requiring regular pick-ups. Otherwise, the place becomes fly-infested. Smiley, ***nuestro perro***, does not leave "deposits" near or around his eating or sleeping quarters, but it's open-season anywhere else. And although he seldom messes-up our front-yard lawn, our careless, thoughtless ***vecinos*** (neighbors) release ***sus perros*** each morning never keeping-track while their mutts do a "number" (pun intended) on it. But, Smiley, and dogs in general, require care and attention.

My daughter had her own casa-gato (house-cat) with her, and that was a major stretch for my wife's acceptance. Angelina probably considered, "Can't your daughter just keep 'the thing' boxed-up in the garage until we return?" So, if *Smiley*, were to come inside, Angelina should not find out. Deborah would just have to keep him bathed, brushed, clean, and the house free of dog-hairs!... Shhh!

Angelina ***ama*** (loves), ***no, le gusta*** (no, she likes), ***no, tolera*** (tolerates) ***perros. Pero, no hay perros de la casa! Zip-cero-nada!*** Considering times I've been in the "dog-house" for mistakes I've made and for my big-mouth, which, incidentally, coincide remarkably often, I know what she gets upset over. It stinks in there! Smiley, ***te amo***, but ya gotta stop rollin' on ***nuestros vecinos*** (our neighbors') stinkin' lawns.

Anyway, the point is that caring ***de un hogar*** (for a household) ***y especialmente su casa es un gran trabajo*** (big job). Deborah was up to the challenge, I knew, but it would be an experience for her.

Una gran candidad de responsibilidad (a lot of responsibility). Oh, yeah, and there were ***las aves*** (the birds) to care for, ***el correo*** (the mail) to pick-up and sort, ***las llamadas telefonicas*** (phone calls) to filter or serve or take messages. Then straight-faced, I teased her that ***las ventanas*** (windows) only required washing twice-a-week. Noticing a tinge of fear, I just grinned and laughed, "Just kidding! *Never* is good for me!"

My daughter, however, was fine with everything. I knew she could handle all the responsibilities. Besides, Deborah would have support of family-members from both sides of Angelina's and my marriage. Her siblings and step-brothers and step-sister would all help out. Fortunately, they were all pretty much on good terms with each other. It's difficult enough when there are problems between our children and ourselves. At least then, we are aware of whatever an issue may be and can react to it with complete bias. When there are issues between our ***hijos*** (children), often it is more difficult because we are sometimes forced to choose sides. Choosing hurts, often causes more friction and can be complicated.

So, it was good that they were all on speaking-terms on the eve of our departing the country for a few months. Contact amongst them, if not frequent, was at least plausible. So, the night before our leaving, we stored our locked cars in the garage, placed ***todos nuestros articulos especiales y personales en nuestro dormitorio*** (all our special and personal items in our bedroom), I created a humorously designed list of "Do's and Don'ts," and I hung it on the kitchen wall. The packing nearly completed days earlier, we were ready to fly, and my wife's daughter, Cynthia, would take us to the airport.

Flight-day arrived. We were finally on our way. We locked-up ***nuestro dormitorio*** (our bedroom), said our good-byes and drove to the airport as planned. After swift unloading at SFO's departure terminal, required due to traffic congestion and meter-police pressure, we said our final goodbyes to Cynthia and were on our way. ***El aeropuerto internacional de San Francisco*** has stream-lined itself recently. ***Estos dias*** (These days) ***es un proceso muy suave y confort-***

able (it's a smooth and comfortable process) going through ticketing and baggage check-ins. Just show your ID and your passport and turn in your luggage.

The rest of the process was pretty much SOP. These included every travelers' presentation of ticket information, identification and passport checks, carry-on-luggage X-ray checks, and X-rays of persons and their belongings after removal of ***zapatos*** (shoes), ***sombreros*** (hats), ***chalecos*** (jackets), ***gafas*** (eye glasses), ***todos los objetos de metal*** (all metal objects), removal of ***todos articulos*** (all articles) from pockets, minimal liquids and creams acceptance levels, and assault-weapons confiscations such as finger-nail clippers, etc. These are all standard examinations everywhere. You just adapt and go with the flow. Make things difficult for them, and they'll definitely make things more difficult on you.

All-things-considered, we were passing through a relatively high-level ***sistema de seguridad*** serving thousands of persons daily, and we were doing so with minimal disturbance or delays. As tedious and time-consuming the whole process seems, however, I still have a relatively positive attitude about safety they promote and generate for the flying-public. ***"Es mas seguro en el aire que en el terrano*** (It's safer in-the-air-than-on-the-ground)," most say. Yet, it was very evident how times had changed since 9/11. What a difference a day makes! Or, ***"Que diferencia hace un dia!" Gracias, Osama Bin Laden***. You made the world a safer place... not!

Safe, or not... We were on our way. Our new adventure had begun. All the thinking, planning, preparation, and organizing that had been scrupulously and tediously attended to had finally come to fruition. What was in store for us we knew not, but that was part of the thrill. You can only plan and prepare so much, and then you just have to sit back, relax, let the coming events take their course, and go along for the ride to see where it takes you.

One thought-line, however, kept returning which amused me. All the prep work was accomplished to achieve something. What was that? What were we in for? I understood something from prior travel experience, our previous cruise-visit to ***Puerto Vallarta*** and the airport flight. In approximately six hours, our lives would be transformed into a new lifestyle. We would have a different address, different accessibility and transportation means, different neighbors and friends, new sights, sounds and smells, different needs, different accommodations, and potentially exciting, new and different happenings to experience. The thought was amusing to be sure, but it was also exciting, if not thrilling.

To be sure, I was filled with anticipation, curiosity and wonder. Like any "new" adventure, however, moments of angst crossed my mind too: "What had we gotten ourselves into?.. Will we like it?.. What if we hate it?.. Will we have any problems?.. What if something bad happens?.. What if there's an emergency?... What if one of us dies?... What if we both die?... How will we get our bodies home?... We won't... We can't... We'll be dead!... How will our kids get our bodies home?... Will they, or not?... Maybe they'll just leave us to rot there... 'Good-bye and good riddance, you deserting parents!'"...

Oh, stop this nonsense, *Brain*! We are off for *Paradise*! We made it happen. We planned this trip to have a good time. So, we'll make it a good time. If we managed to get us this far, with the excellent support and help of my co-conspirator, we can handle whatever might arise. So, I'm just kicking back. I'm going to relax and enjoy the flight. A *New World* awaits! Everything is going to be just as we had hoped and planned. What could possibly go wrong?...

BEST LAID PLANS

"Be careful what you wish for,"
The clever sage has said, "
If all your wishes were horses,
You'd be ridin' high instead."

And cease wide-eyed 'wishing-upon'
Those fruitless, empty 'stars.'
Dreams are a waste, a fool's disgrace,
Like trying to fly to Mars.

If 'lives are stuff made up from dreams'
And dreams foretell our lives,
Go find that 'needle-in-a-haystack'
And stitch together those lies.

Then, take the cloth from your foolish weaves
Of aimless dreams of straw,
And cover-up whimsical plans,
'A-stitch-in-time's' faux pas.

Adventure is the devil's toast:
"Here's to all follies' quests!"
It's safer to sit and vegetate
And leave your mind at rest.

Your 'Best-Laid-Plans' might come undone
From problems ne'er considered...
So, deny dreams which please your life;
You risk dying embittered.

"Mismaloya Blues"

Part 3

'New' Home Sweet Home...

The flight went off without a hitch, and we soon saw ***nuestro destino*** (our destination) from our window seats. ***Puerto Vallarta*** has a relatively small but comfortable airport. Although there were many ***de los pasajeros*** (passengers) from our flight alone who were going through ***inmigracion*** and customs, it was exciting, interesting, a novel experience, and passed quickly. We dragged our ***nuestro equipaje*** (luggage) through the check-point, answered all the standardized questions, got cleared, and were on-our-way with no problems. It was convenient that Angelina speaks Spanish (***Era conveniente que Angelina habla espanol***). Naturally, my wife's Spanish is homegrown, natural and impeccable, not-to-mention authentic, so she ushered us right-on-through ***las puertas y las puertas*** (gates and doors).

Once inside the terminal's Welcome Center where outsiders and visitors gather, we were greeted by our agent, Trent. As a part of his responsibilities, he was there to greet us and provide ***un servicio de traslador a nuestro nueva casa*** (a shuttle-service to our new home). He appeared like a relaxed, casual ***Gringo*** just as he had seemed ***en el telephono***. I easily recognized his voice from our previous, phone conversations.

He is ***un ex-patriota de Alaska*** (ex-Patriot) who had driven down to ***PV con su esposa***. They had sold everything and closed shop with their Alaska home. All their life's possessions, cold-turkey, so-to-speak, they had brought with them to make a new life down here. They had been in ***Puerto Vallarta*** seven years so far, so something was working, I guessed. That, or they couldn't afford to leave anymore. I figured I'd learn more about them later on. His experience sounded interesting, if not unique, and I was curious.

Once loaded-up into our driver-agent's ***coche de la economia*** (economy car), we dashed off to be taken on some brief but necessary errands. We needed to go shopping, so we were taken to a major, local grocery-market, ***Mega***. There, we picked up some essential items of a personal nature like ***cerveza*** and pretzels, some quick-fix food items and some house-cleaning items typically not included with rentals. Another stop included a USA-friendly bank's ATM service for Mexican ***pesos.*** We had been informed that most proprietors accepted USA cash, but the exchange-rate was never to our advantage. It was better ***tratar en pesos*** (to deal in pesos). Besides, we were going to be living here.

Later, we discovered that in some cases it was ***en realidad*** (actually) ***la ventaja*** (the advantage) ***de un turista a utilizar*** (of a tourist to use) USD cash or even VISA credit cards for exchange-rate benefits; however, it was never as much fun. ***Naturalmente***, I wished to deal with their currency. It's fun to leave your "comfort zone" once-in-a-while and try something new and different. Getting comfortable and used to it would expand horizons. At least, it seemed so to me.

That would be part of the thrill. There would be a chance I might get the wrong change in some purchase because I couldn't count right! ***Ahora*** (now) that would be an embarrassing prospect for a retired, math-teacher. Angelina would just expose the error in a calculation, and she would get ***el cambio correcto*** (the correct change). But me? I'd be walking away, eyes cast downward into my open palm counting pesos with an index-finger and shaking my head in bewilderment. Oh, no, not for me! I enjoy numbers too much not to pay close attention and study their coins and paper-money. It was an early goal to get the money right.

Oh, si, I would become a quick-study of ***Mexico's*** currency-system. Plus, technical and electronic magic would come to the rescue again. ***Cuando sea necesario*** (when necessary), I would use a newly-installed "currency-converter" application on my phone or I-pod to assist me. ***No hay problemas.*** No problems. I loved my gadgets, and I was not afraid or unaccustomed to stop what I was doing and break out the device to convert pesos or translate a word.

The only problem was occasionally not having a Wi-Fi signal to "translate" words or phrases for me. The money-converter was an application on my cell phone and tablet which worked all the time. I asked, "Why not both?" That's the extent of my tech knowledge: I know, but I don't understand (***Lo se, pero yo no lo entiendo***). Sometimes, it worked, and other times it didn't. Make sense? !***Muy bueno porque no lo entiendo*** (Very good because I don't understand)! ***Pero yo no necesitaba traduccion*** (I didn't need translation); ***tuve Angelina*** (I had) my Angel.

Finalmente, we were given the whirl-wind tour through cobblestone streets where we excitedly recognized some landmarks from two years earlier. ***Lugares como el puerto deportivo y Walmart*** (places like the marina and Walmart) were obvious stand-outs, and there were vague recollections of ***iglesias, bazaars y otros lugares*** (churches, bazaars and other sights) from our one-day cruise visit. Our driver skillfully zigzagged through traffic twisting and turning past busy and crowded streets to get us eventually out of the main, central part of town.

Everything was a rush of bright and blurring colors. Rustic buildings, worn-and-weathered ***tiendas*** (shops), thick, untamed jungle, and exotic, modern resorts lined our passage. More jungle, bouncy, cobble-stoned streets, cars, and scatterings of locals mixing with tourists were everywhere. Soon, however, we were being hustled along ***la carretera principal*** (the main highway) ***de Puerto Vallarta a nuestro condominio*** (from Puerto Vallarta to our condominium) ***en la region*** (in the region) ***conocida como Mismaloya*** (known as Mismaloya).

Nuestro nuevo, agente-amigo (our new, agent-friend) gave us more personal history ***en el camino*** (on the way). He spoke briefly of his own exploits traveling to ***Puerto Vallarta.*** According to his sketchy details, seven years earlier, he and his wife had "expatriated" to ***Puerto Vallarta*** from Alaska via a short stint in Colorado. They had made a niche for ***si mismo*** (themselves) using his computer skills to help local, property-owners rent to long-term vacationers like ***nosotros mismo*** (ourselves). ***Vallarta's*** internet-services were weak at best, ***pero los residentes locales*** enjoyed taking advantage of its usefulness as much as anyone. With knowledge of computers and the internet, a person could find work.

Nuestro agente was computer savvy. He knew the web, had used internet promotional-skills in previous employment and was very comfortable with Craig's List as a tool. ***El y su esposa*** (he and his wife) were relatively stable living here. They had lived in various areas but favored rural ***Mismaloya*** and the more remote jungles ***de la region sur*** of ***Puerto Vallarta.*** They were, comfortable with their existence with no desires or plans of returning ***a los Estados Unidos en un futuro proximo*** (to the United States in the near future). We would meet ***muchos otros de mente similar*** (many others of a similar mind) as our vacation progressed.

As we continued on toward our own rental, our agent provided a few tips about shopping values we might wish to consider. ***Ciertos establecimientos locales*** (certain local establishments) were reasonable for certain things, others not. Some "tourist-spots" were musts for all newcomers, ***y otros*** were visitor/buyer-beware targets capitalized by unscrupulous con-artists seeking naive or ignorant short-term vacationers. These "***vendadores de presentacion***" (presentation-salesmen) wanted "short-term" tourists because they knew the vacationers would be leaving soon. We'll scratch-and-bleed these guys ***en major detalle mas adelante*** (in more detail later).

Adding some colorful accounting of past times to our drive, ***nuestro agente*** gave us ***un poco historia e informacion de famosos resorts, residencias y lugares de Hollywood*** (a little history and information of famous resorts, residences and locations of Hollywood) movie-sets as we passed them. ***Varias estaciones locales (Several local resorts) had been, or still were, temporary homes or vacation retreats for Hollywood celebrities.*** Many of us remember the famous Hollywood film from the mid-sixties, Night of the Iguana. ***Esa pelicula*** (that movie), starring Richard Burton and Ava Gardner, was filmed in ***Puerto Vallarta*** in the ***Mismaloya*** district near to where we would be staying.

Por supuestro (of course), it was the tempestuous relationship of the infamously drunken and womanizing Burton and his jealous girlfriend, Elizabeth Taylor, whom he brought along which rocked the community and all of ***Puerto Vallarta***. Almost overnight, ***PV*** became recognized as a "celebratory" location ***en el mapa mundial de los lugares notables*** (on the world map of notable places). During our wanderings, we visited several locations dedicated to memorabilia of Burton and Taylor. There are boutiques, art galleries, statues, private estates, and tours which share their lurid details of those movie stars and their affairs. Fun stuff for all and especially interesting for Hollywood, star-struck tourists.

Cerca de alli (nearby), also, was a side-road to the 1987 main, film-site for Schwarzenegger's famous, jungle-flick, Predator. ***Finalmente***, the wonderful and silly 1970's-80's TV sit-com, The Love Boat, really splashed ***Puerto Vallarta*** on everyone's vacation destination A-list. The cruise ship with its whole "zany-antics" crew made many, weekly-stops ***en esta romantica ciudad*** (in this romantic city). Our guide-agent's point made, we had ***unos pocos mas*** (a few more) "celebrity-style" tourist attractions to visit if it suited us. Our enthusiasm perked with excitement, curiosity and enthusiasm. It was working too! We weren't even to ***la casa*** yet, and I was ready to pitch a hammock and stretch out for life!

Serving many, local property-owners who were his clients, our agent also talked a little about the couple who were renting to us. According to local gossip, ***nuestro propietario*** (our landlord) was an astral-physicist who had personally designed and built his own ultra-modern, multilevel-residence and rental quarters. This couple were involved in extra-terrestrial studies and remained aloof from the community. ***El hombre*** was scientifically reserved, ***y el y su esposa vivieron*** (and he and his wife lived) quite exclusively ***aparte de su barrio*** (apart from their neighborhood).

We were informed, if not instructed, that our hosts were both minimally social. Each would demand and promote mutual privacy. Supposedly, they were both aloof and seldom socialized except with only specific friends. We were not to bother them for miscellaneous needs or issues. Rather, instead, contact the property-manager... This turned out to be ludicrous, if not humorous. Our landlord hosts would become very supportive, friendly and social with us. Our agent-property manager, on-the-other-hand, became little more than useless. For one thing, we seldom, if ever, saw the agent again. He was helpful and useful in the beginning. Afterward, however, he mostly vanished. He did little ever again to assist us with problems or questions.

To our delight, however, we quickly learned that our owner-landlords were gracious, friendly and kind folk. Fortunately, we would get to know ***esta gente*** (these people) ***muy bien***. ***Ciertamente*** (certainly), we would dismiss many of the superstitious and naïve, local-notions about our host-landlords. And yet, others we would encourage for the fun of it. I would eventually consider some neighbors as curious and eccentric.

However, our agent was working now, and it was fun. As "icing-on-the-cake" ***nuestro conductor*** (our driver) stopped a couple times allowing us to absorb the glory and beauty of ***Bahia de Banderas*** and its beaches and surrounding jungle. Our rental agent/shuttle-driver/tour-guide pulled into scenic-view spots to show-off the local highlights. There was ***Los Arcos*** which were ***grandes formaciones de rocas*** (large rock formations) just offshore used in various movie scenes and was a local, snorkeling-favorite site. There was the ***Mismaloya*** community whose side-passages led to the blockbuster film-sites of Predator and Night of the *Iguana*. There was the promise of lots-to-see and lots-to-do and lots-to-learn-about. ***Estabamos emocionados*** (We were excited)!

These, however, were just long-enough Kodak-moments to tease and tantalize while preparing us for an introduction to our new home. We still arrived at our destination during daylight and were met by ***nuestro nuevo proprietario y su esposa*** who would soon become ***en los primeros, buenos amigos*** (our first, good friends). ***El senor y la senora Gomez-Salazar*** met us at the parking spot next to the stairs which led to our condominium two-levels below.

I was impressed with their stately, but casual, elegance and sophistication. From our initial greeting and throughout our meeting, they were very cordial, welcoming, informative, and kind. ***Probablemente***, though, I was likely an embarrassment and distraction due to awed fascination ***con la magnifica vista de la bahia y la costa abajo*** (with the magnificent view of the bay and shore below) and cliff-side vantage point we had. It was a visually stunning beginning.

After cordial and introductory greetings, we followed our host, ***Sr. Architecto Sergio***. He led us down two levels of steep stairs to a concrete, decorative-path winding through native, jungle foliage and a massive, ripened, fruit-bearing ***arbor de aguacate*** (avocado tree). It was immediately noticeable that the walkway and apartment construction had been built upon and anchored within an enormous and massive rock which was part of the mountain side. The rock actually served as part of the structure's walls. Once past a utility and storage area, finally, ***alli y entonces*** (there and then), we entered our new dwelling.

And just like the pictures and previous conversations had suggested, it was a modern, stylish and comfortable one-bedroom/one-bath condominium. I was immediately stunned by its nearly one hundred eighty degree cliff-side view ***de la hermosa Bahia de Banderas*** (of the beautiful "bay"). This was to be our home for the next ***tres meses*** (three months), and nearly the entire bay's view was available to us from our cliff-side patio balcony. This balcony area nearly covered the entire ***occidental, norte y este*** (western, northern and eastern sides) of our rental unit.

The condo-apartment was ***elegante***, nicely furnished and comfortably spacious for two persons. A fold-down ***sofa*** would adapt to any potential over-night ***invitados*** (guests), and the living space was very adequate for us. A well-organized ***bano con ducha*** (bathroom with shower), ***una cocina basica, elegante y funcional*** (a basic, stylish and functional kitchen) and a very reasonable living-area with attached dining space made the unit's design seem ***muy abierto y complaciente*** (very open and accommodating). The master bedroom was large and open and pleasing with modern, urban and ***Mexicana***-themed trappings.

Hanging from every room's walls were fascinating and appealing ***pinturas*** (paintings) done by our esteemed landlord during a "painting" phase of his life. He was gifted, apparently well-known and we would learn much more about that aspect of his life later. His primary career, though, had been architecture. He had designed a very unique, interesting and aesthetically beautiful home for himself and his wife, including an additional, add-on rental for potential renters like us.

The whole building from street-level to below had a stylish, almost futuristic elegance with its design. ***El unico aspecto negativo*** (the only negative aspect) we may have considered was concern over no air-conditioning; ***sin embargo*** (however), we were not troubled ***con eso hasta el momento*** (with that as of yet). ***Nuestro entusiasmo*** (our enthusiasm), the evening's ocean-breezes and awareness of a cooler, mid-September fall season mentally overcame that issue.

Besides, we were all but overwhelmed noticing the extent of glass windows and sliding-glass doors providing and promoting our gracious, outside-views. From every room we could look out and see the expansive ***Bahia de Banderas***. This bay is notable as the 9th largest bay in the world and typically protected from a fervent hurricane season. Plus, an added bonus, we were told that right from our ***vistas de la ventana*** (window views), we would soon see the annual visits of humpback whales ***(ballenas).*** Both bulls and cow mothers would be coming to our door-step vantage-point to spawn, play and teach their young calves survival skills. Mothers would raise them until their departures north the following Spring.

All this would happen and be seen directly by us from our ocean-view backyard. Our vantage-point views furthermore gave us marvelous position to nearly see the entire shoreline from the northern tip of ***Punta de Mita*** to beyond ***Boca de Tomatlan*** and ***Yalapa*** in the south. With somewhat reserved enthusiasm, there was no doubt we were a couple of proverbial "happy-campers."

After the "oohs" and "ahs" subsided, we settled into contractual-matters. We all discussed and resolved our rental-agreement, monthly-payment plan and exchanged required funds. We were informed of other additional-cost amenities available such as ***lavenderia*** (laundry) and maid-service if desired. It was explained to us how we could receive ***por una cuota minima, adicional*** (for a minimal, additional-fee) delivered, bottled, ***agua potable*** (drinking water) to our door-step from the local service company. Delivered, twenty-five liter, bottled-water was everyone's standard. Considering the steep climb to our door from the street and back, ***me gusto la idea*** (I liked the idea) of "delivery" immediately.

Finally, ***Sr. Architecto Sergio*** offered ***instrucciones generales*** regarding our free TV and cable service, free Wi-Fi access and cell-phone information. Pressing high-priority interests, ***solicite informacion a la maravillosa playa de roca debajo de nosotros*** (I requested access information to the wonderful rock beach below us). We were delighted and ready to begin our special-time together. We shook hands and agreed to get together again soon.

Upon parting, our landlords offered to take us into town with them on an upcoming Sunday for additional shopping needs. They volunteered to act as our own personal, tour-guides, shopping-advisers, and lunch-and-entertainment companions. Angelina and I were sure we were ***realmente en unas vacaciones especiales*** (really onto a special vacation). Promising our own reliability with solemn guarantees of cleanliness and quiet, our relationship was off to a good start.

The adventure was on! Alone, at last, Angelina and I hugged and laughed at our good fortune and excitement over her Craig's List find. Immediately, I rushed outside to hang over the metal-bar, protective-railing on the balcony to absorb the evening's ***espectacular puesta de sol*** (spectacular sunset). Angelina joined me to enjoy ***las maravillosas vistas***, and afterward, we both went ***dentro*** (inside) to hunt and search out all the nooks and crannies of our condo unit.

Almost immediately, Angelina made some quick mental and physical organizational rearrangements and had us shifting and switching ***la mesa*** (the dining table) with the living-room ***sofa***. A couple of ***sillas***, or chairs, were moved elsewhere, and a few available but unnecessary items were stored away. Quickly and easily, the place took on a much more open and personalized touch. A couple of family pictures were propped-up on the vanity. Then, my Led Zeppelin posters were taped to the living-room wall... NOT! Okay, I couldn't go there. That's "man-cave" stuff. The great thing, though, was that Angelina was ***feliz*** (happy), excited, involved, and content. That would mean ***muy buenos tiempos para mi***!

Angelina inspected ***la cocina*** layout for its kitchen appliances, unpacked our modest grocery supply and reviewed ***el bano*** facilities with our shower more closely. I checked into the utility and storage aspects such as ***compudora*** hook-ups, cable-orientations, and ***la agua*** supply. Together, we looked over ***el dormitorio*** accommodations for respective, bedside preferences, closet space and passed judgments over whose-was-whose. Actually, Angelina passed all the judgment; I just nodded agreement and acceptance. There would be no disputes tonight. We were here. We unpacked. Life was good. It was ***cerveza*** time!

With the initial unpacking and arranging and rearranging mostly completed, and ***cerveza en mano***, I led Angelina outdoors ***para nuestra primera caminata por vecindario*** (for our first neighborhood walk). Back-tracking on the path leading to our bungalow, we really recognized the severity and steepness of thc tthirty-five or more steps up to the main street entrance. It was going to be a cautious and slow process going ***subir o bajar esta escalera*** (up or down this stairwell). It was somewhat artistically designed, but the tread, or footing area, was narrow with sharp edges; caution was an ally. Coupled with the problem of no handrails, just walls on either side to rest a supporting hand, and we had our first, exercise-workouts laid out for us automatically for all future, outside adventures.

La calle principal (the main road), Hwy. 200, passing our new home, headed either ***norte*** through ***Mismaloya*** and on into ***Puerto Vallarta*** proper and beyond, or it went ***sur*** to ***Boca de Tomatlan*** and all further points south. It was a narrow, two-lane highway with no specific walking lane on either side. We had to be careful about both on-coming and rear traffic which seemed to pass by with zest and urgency. ***Los vehiculos grandes***, trucks and passenger ***autobuses*** would roar by forcing us to scramble for the roadside's far edges into brush or weeds to avoid conflict. This was definitely not a pedestrian-friendly walking area. Another concern was the realization that the highway was a two-way, passing-lane too.

Con la seguridad como nuestro principal objetivo (with safety as our primary focus), we ventured down the road a kilometer, almost 2/3 of a mile, or so. As we carefully strolled along, we noted ***las casas de nuestros nuevos vecinos*** (our new neighbors' abodes). ***Algunos edificios*** (some buildings) and developed areas looked like wherever it had been deemed possible to build something, somebody had constructed some sort of concrete structure as living and/or rental quarters. There were ***grandes edificios blancos*** (large, white-washed), cinder-block buildings with multiple living-units tucked away in various sections and corners. Some buildings suggested that they had originally been built as enormous, fantastic, cliff-side, single-family dwellings for wealthy ***las familias locales mexicanos,*** or as their one-time, vacation retreats.

Perhaps later, as the economy surged or plunged, demand for use or demand for income respectively occurred. ***Al parecer*** (apparently), owners had blocked off sections and had added additional ***bano y cocina*** (bathroom and kitchen facilities). They turned large, mansion-type homes into miniature villas of many, small rental-units. Our closest neighbors were part of one such construction referred to as ***Villa del Capricho*** (Caprice) or 'Caprichoso' meaning Whimsical. Go figure...

We would make ***amigos con muchas*** of this place's inhabitants. We would discover that our neighbors were made up of local owner-landlords, Mexican nationals' renters, short and long-term renters similar to us, and ex-patriots, or foreigners mainly from the USA or Canada but elsewhere too. Each were interesting with their own lives' tales, and some were even ***incluidas en las memorias de este escritor*** (included into this writer's memoirs).

Durante nuestra maravillosa, de tres meses de estancia (during our wonderful, three-month sojourn) ***a Puerto Vallarta***, ***mi esposa y yo*** did ***un buen trabajo*** (a pretty good job) exploring the quaintness and authenticity and touristy aspects of ***Puerto Vallarta***. Angelina and I traveled the width-and-breadth of the entire area covering half-a-dozen city-towns from ***San Blas*** in the north to S***an Sebastian*** in the east to ***Manzanillo*** in the south. We also visited a variety of coastal resorts in the inter-connected states of ***Jalisco*** and ***Nayarit*** as well as each ones' commercial aspects. ***Finalmente***, but just as fun and entertaining, we had taken several boat rides cruising and traversing the entire vastness and beauty of the ***Bahia de Banderas*** too. We visited special, private and gorgeous beaches along the coastline as well as ***las Islas Marietas*** (the Marieta Islands).

And, naturally, we did the typical tourist-stuff such as all the tours: We took the ***Puerto Vallarta*** city and surrounding area tour; we did the deep-jungle tour into the forest to see authentic tequila being manufactured. We joined party-boats to go to "by-boat-only" ***(por barco solo para)*** private and unique beach tours for fun and interest. We rented a car with a driver for a distant, unique city-visit, ***San Sebastian***. Then we traveled to other destinations for horseback riding and more beaches and local communities. We did as much as we could afford on a very modest budget. There were so many inexpensive things to do too.

Angelina signed up for art classes at the ***Centro Cultural Comunitario***, and I enrolled in an ***Universidad de Guadalajara*** extension program ***de clases de espanol. Entre tiempo para el estudio y la practica*** (Between time for studying and practice) and the typical shopping and laundry-needs days, we squeezed in ***paseos*** (promenades) through the city's walkways and park-like areas and bazaar and flea-market zones. We often did our ***caminando en la Malecon***, a three-kilometer walking stretch of attractive, concrete boardwalk to enjoy the ocean breezes and surf and artwork along the way.

While walking, we would stop to chat with local shop-keepers selling everything from authentic, Mexican souvenirs ***hecho en china***, to truly authentic, ***tequila mexicano***. Of course, nearly everyone working along the Malecon tried to sell us something. Storekeepers asked us to buy their souvenirs or hats or clothing items. ***Los propietarios de restaurantes*** offered the finest meals available anywhere regardless what we wished to eat. ***Las tiendas de licores*** (the liquor stores) and tour kiosk salesmen all tried to convince us to attend their hotel, time-share presentations and receive cash and/or great offers for tour deals. It was business and industry working at full-scale to keep the system running. Yet, there was a charm and beauty to it all-the-while understanding and appreciating its need.

Por ultimo (finally), ***estaba el arte*** (there was the art). Puerto Vallarta is well-known for its art themes and galleries and sculpture throughout the city.

Artistas come from around-the-world to live there cheaply and demonstrate their talents by attracting clients and customers. ***Las exposiciones de arte Malecon*** (the Malecon art displays) were ***especial y original*** and very worthwhile. Each was a permanently placed sculpture evenly spaced apart throughout the entire Malecon walk. The art-pieces symbolized and complimented a special theme or practice ***de la cultura mexicana o Puerto Vallarta***. In addition, several means are encouraged to promote the many city-wide galleries.

Tambien (also), along-the-way were ***varios artistas locales*** (several local artists) presenting their own, ***pinturas autenticas*** (authentic paintings) for sale. There were nick-knack shops, ice-cream vendors and ***pharmacias*** (pharmacies) scattered amongst every block. And there was no opportunity to avoid the dozens of street-vendors. These were the 24/7 street-salespeople pushing or carrying their wares while casually weaving through the crowds ***de turistas, lugarenos y nativos*** (of tourists, locales and natives).

Irrespectively, they promoted their portable showcases of ***joyas*** (jewelry), ***ropa*** (clothing), ***piezas de arte*** (art pieces), ***artefactos*** (artifacts), ***comida*** (food), ***dulces*** (candy), ***chicles*** (gum), ***o cualquier otra cosa*** (or whatever else) they might sell to make an honorable living. These vendors came in all shapes, sizes and ages too. Some were elderly ***hombres y mujeres*** (men and women), time-and-experience tested salespeople with hard-sell lines to their prospective buyers, and ***todo el mundo*** (everyone) was a "prospect." ***Otros eran ninos pequenos*** (others were small children), barely into grade school, offering small toys or dolls for sale or even little packets of C*hicklets* gum for a ***peso*** (6 ½ cents) each.

Throughout the entire ***Malecon*** walkabout were convenient areas set up for numerous, incredible and amazingly varied food-stands. Although there were multiple, delicious duplications of some food items ***para la venta*** (for sale), still there were so many wonderful offerings. Everything one might enjoy savoring with a Mexicana flavoring was ***para la venta***. Of course, there were ***tacos, tamales, burritos, enchiladas, y quisadillas*** to devour off a paper plate as you walked, but the sweets and treats were everywhere too from gum and candy to ***helado*** (ice cream) and so many cakes and pastries.

Mexicana candies are pretty good. Many, you might imagine, specialize in coconut flavors. You could have coconut chips, coconut drinks, coconut shakes, coconut bars, and on and on. Also, it's no secret that ***mexicanos*** like their "hot ***tamales***" or '***tamales*** hot,' but it became obvious that they liked their ice-creams too and have *sweet-teeth* to go with it. However, it was other aspects of food and nature that could float-your-(taste-bud) boat, so-to-speak.

The beautiful ***Bahia de Banderas*** was right there in front of us with waves gently splashing on pristine, sandy beaches. It allowed us to thoroughly relax and enjoy the delightful and remarkable experience ***de la mar y la gastronomia*** (of sea and cuisine) with a metronome of surf in the background. ***La bahia suave y relativamente tranquila*** (the smooth and relatively calm bay) was full of ***embarcaciones de mar*** (sea craft) amusing and beautifying our contentment. It was a really lovely ambiance for anyone's taste buds.

With the dynamic sea, surf and sand in the background, ***vendadores de comida*** (food vendors) were busy selling everything from fried-bananas to grilled corn-on-the-cob as munchies items. To tease us, or top-off our meal treats, ***desiertos y refrescos*** (deserts and refreshments) available consisted of widely-assorted ***variedades de*** (varieties of) ***tortas mexicana*** (Mexican cakes), ***pasteles*** (pies), ***galletas*** (cookies), ***dulces*** (candies), ***frosties*** (frosties), ***batidos*** (smoothies), ***y helados frutales*** (and pop sickles). The soothing ***mar*** was a constant, and it seemed that the other constants were unique foods and drinks and treats ***para la venta*** to tantalize anyone's taste buds.

In fact, we did a very memorable visit throughout ***nuestra estancia de tres meses*** (our three-month stay). We remained busy with studies, travel, visiting, sight-seeing, shopping, and dining-out for every meal or occasion. We had favorite establishments for ***desayunos*** where breakfast was their specialty. We had lunch, ***(almuerzo)***, anywhere we chose. ***Hora de la cena*** (dinnertime) was unique because ***cena*** was everyone's favorite, and offerings were endless in cuisine style.

We did not eat-out often, but usually we would stop for the occasional and variable meal for each visit into town. Our home was ***quince kilometros*** (fifteen kilometers) away or thirty minutes by bus. It was just far enough out to make each trip pass through a mealtime period. If we went to town early, we'd find a fun place for breakfast. Our favorite was ***The Pancake House*** where Mexican or traditional American breakfasts would be served. Lunches and dinners would find us exploring and seeking out fun and curious eating establishments. A rule-of- thumb was finding a place which had plenty of customers. If lots of locals ate there, it likely served decent Mexican dishes. Good service keeps you at a restaurant longer, but it's good food that brings you back.

Anyway, eating out became a regular practice because of the journey we went through getting into town. ***El viaje en autobus*** (the bus ride) was always ***agradable*** (enjoyable). There was always something new and different occurring.

However, it did require some planning for chores and needs and meals due to time and distance restraints. Yet, our sojourns ***en el centro*** were always interesting, scenic and useful. ***Para los dos*** (for us both), those trips to town meant another adventure, and we considered them to be treats and always special and fun.

We made ***un monton de amigos*** (a lot of friends) and met some unfortunate characters. That's life, though, everywhere you go, isn't it? Win some; lose some. Make some; break some. It was, overall, a wonderful visit, and we enjoyed ourselves immensely while getting ***un gusto de la comunidad*** (a taste of the community) and the feeling, if not flavoring, of living out of our own country. We became very efficient at using ***su sistema de autobuses en toda la cuidad*** (their city-wide bus-system). Our bus rides to town and all around became an integral part of the overall travel experience.

We even used ***los autobuses*** to travel to ***communidades distantes de Jalisco*** (distant communities out of ***Jalisco***) ***a los estados de Nayarit*** (to the states of ***Nayarit***) ***al norte de Puerto Vallarta*** (to the north of ***Puerto Vallarta***) ***y Colima, al sur*** (and ***Colima*** to the south). ***Al final de nuestra*** (by the end of our) ***estancia de tres meses*** (three-month stay), we were confident traveling anywhere or anytime.

Algunos de nuestros amigos (some of our friends) became long-lasting, and we kept up correspondence with them in planning a return the following year for an even longer visit. We would plan to pick-up where we left off and enjoy ***Puerto Vallarta*** throughout the really beautiful ***temporados de invierno y primavera*** (winter and spring seasons). There were still ***muchas cosas*** (many things) to do and countless ***lugares*** (places) to see for which we had neither time nor budget for this trip. But, that's what planning vacations is all about. It would make for another memorable, long-term vacation ***durante nuestra proxima visita*** (during our next visit).

So, when the vacation's end was on-hand, we repacked, said good-bye ***de los amigos y vecinos*** (to friends and neighbors) and readied for the brief, non-stop flight ***a casa a*** San Francisco. ***Uno de nuestros hijos*** (one of our children) would be there at the airport to pick us up and shuttle us home. Our landlord hosts drove us to ***el aeropuerto de Puerto Vallarta*** expressing sadness ***en nuestra partida*** (in our departure) along with well-wishes and promises to remain in-contact ***para nuestra proxima visita*** (for our return visit).

Angelina and I recognized that we had made ***amigos especiales*** (special friends) ***con este tipo y gente interesante*** (with these kind and interesting people). Because of them our stay had been so much more enjoyable and interesting. They had taken us sight-seeing and had joined us for dinner outings. We went to the local cinema together, and they even joined us attending the local theatre for a visiting Russian State Ballet production of *Don Quixote*. On-top-of-all-that, we went grocery shopping and even special, curio-shopping together.

And, I absolutely must mention that to our shocked surprise and delight, they so generously and kindly organized for us an old-fashioned, turkey-and-all Thanksgiving dinner. They had invited another local couple as guests, and we all joyously ate and drank until nearly bursting, talked and joked, and played an amusing and favorite ***mexicana***, table-game for laughs and entertainment.

And with our hosts introducing that particular game at that particular moment came one of those Letterman "Top-10 List" items entitled: *Personally Unforgettable, Embarrassing Comments*. I actually prayed with thanks to God for those others' ignorance, deafness or rudeness. I had jokingly said something, and I was immediately so grateful that no one understood, was listening or had simply chosen to ignore me. Regardless, it was one of those *guffaws* when you wish you could simply say, "Cut! Back up the tape. Let's re-do that scene!"

Oh! Okay, I suppose I've got to come clean now, huh? Do you understand how embarrassing this may be for our hosts and other guests there that night? Everyone there at the gathering (*Thanksgiving*, for *God's* sake), were socially upstanding, sophisticated, righteous, and influential people, including my wife; especially my wife! She's going to kill me! Oh, alright! If you must know...

It's really just another simple "Open-mouth and insert-foot" routine. I sort of do it all the time, so I'm kind of used to it. Unfortunately, others, especially those with me for a first experience, may not take (it) so well... Anyway, for your whimsical curiosity, devious mind or sick and decadent humor, here it is:

Once after-dinner conversation had ebbed, and table-cleaning had been completed with everyone pitching in, our benevolent and gracious hosts, Sergio and Deyanira, provided a fun and entertaining table-game for our after-dinner amusement. Although apparently fairly common amongst ***la cultura mexicana***, I had never before heard of the game. So, it came (no pun intended) as a surprise to me when the game's title was announced as "Mexican-Train."

Instantly, with mouth racing *faster than a speeding brain*, I jokingly quipped. "Oh, what is this, one of those Mexican, sex-games?"

Do you recognize any of those agonizingly embarrassing moments in your own life when you've said something, and immediately, your face flushes into beet-red retreat and you seek instant-shelter? Unfortunately, I could not recover and leave that quickly. Everyone was right there in front of me. All I could do was pray while rapidly glancing around the room checking closely for each person's personal attentiveness. Fortunately, God had seen my mishap coming, so He deliberately had everyone ignoring me... again. Thank you, God!

Anyway, I had survived another one of my spontaneous *in-bursts*, and the evening ended with special and unforgettable memories. For us two Americans away-from-home-and-family, our hosts and friends, ***los Salazars***, had made a "gracious and unforgettable" evening for us. ***Senor Sergio y senora Deyanira*** were more than host-landlords. They had become friends.

We certainly wished to get to know them better ***en un futuro proximo*** (in the near future). There were fascinating aspects about both of them of which we hoped to learn, understand and appreciate more ***durante otra visita*** (during another visit). We would surely see them again. We would be in touch once more, at least.

Nearly all the people we had met in Puerto Vallarta, and especially near us in Mismaloya, had been kind and gracious friends. Conversations were always warm and congenial. The locals knew how to handle the weather and environment. They remained upbeat and casual about the heated and rainy months yet spoke appreciatively of the approaching, comfortable winter months of daily sunshine and lots of business. It was peace, contentment and acceptance of their lives, and they seemed to enjoy the tranquility of where they lived.

We needed to return to see what we would miss ***durante los proximos*** (during the coming) ***meses de invierno y primavera*** (winter and spring months). We wanted to return ***otra vez*** (another time) and take advantage ***de la amable hospitalidad*** (of the gracious hospitality) ***de nuestros anfitriones*** (of our hosts). We would want and need to enjoy once more a vacation retreat at ***nuestra maravilloso, oceano-vista Mismaloya casa.***

LA GENTE

La gente,
Surviving summer's duration,
Are mellowed
To casual populations.
It must be
Heat and humidity's sensations
Which explains
Negligible apprehensions...

Nearly all
Have stability in their lives
With earnings'
Blessings as business thrives.
Successes
Reflect focus on "the prize"
Most agree
Means: "Having enough to survive."

Membership
Requires support of society
Promoting
Tourism and culture's history.
Of pressure,
An unwelcome guest's company,
Mantras tout,
"Be happy; it's only money!"

Tourists' cash
Demands petty tolerances
From locals
While indulging their own senses.
Will they learn:
"Tranquility means peacefulness"
Accepting
Dreams of *la gente*: "No-more-fences?"

Giving Thanks

Giving special thanks on distinctive days or occasions is not a uniquely American tradition by any means. History reflects celebrations and appreciations occurring throughout the world and throughout time over many generations, centuries and even millenniums. A commonality, however, is a customary and special day or period for "Giving-of-Thanks" to God, or Gods and Spirits for generous harvests and good years with hopes and prayers for new and better ones yet to come. Oktoberfest is one such typical and similarly known occasion. However, in the United States, there is a unique day (fourth Thursday of November) set aside and celebrated specifically for this custom.

***Thanksgiving**, a traditional American celebration since 1621, originated with the Pilgrims' experience of that fall's bountiful harvests and reaping. It coincided with their North American Indian neighbors' annual-celebration of thanks. In both cases, they had much for which to be grateful and "thankful." Having experienced dreadful times previously, the "good year" was definitely worthy of celebration and festivity.*

Pilgrims and Indians, side-by-side, laughed and joked merrily. Together, they prepared and shared food and ate fully and heavily. Teasing and challenging each other, they played their unique games exploiting hunting and sports skills. Furthermore, commemorating their festive-spirit, they all gave solemn, unique and personal thanks to their own God and/or Spirits for support, guidance and salvation. It has been recorded that both thoroughly enjoyed each other's company.

Indian and Pilgrim alike were grateful for the past good year. Both were joyous that crops had come in so abundantly. Their harvests had helped guarantee provisions for a safe and secure winter with promise for a potentially fulfilling planting-season in Springtime. Both were appreciative of each other's support because, likely, neither would have succeeded that year without the other providing helping-hands and encouragement. They were friends, and that is what friends do: Help each other to get past difficult times.

In fact, that is how "friendship" should be defined: "Being there to support and help one another during challenging times thus earns and deserves welcome invitations celebrating each other's successes." Friendship is an alliance or bond between associates. I believe that is what "Thanksgiving" is really all about, and that is what it was really about for the Pilgrims and Indians during that joyous fall of 1621.

Perhaps, Thanksgiving should be less about "thanks" for crops or successes, and, rather, more about giving appreciation for all the support and assistance from those whose love, care or help make our lives more complete. Of course, we may give Creation and Nature their due; however, we also need to express our gratitude to family and friends. We should assist each other during struggles and difficult times and then be welcomed by each other to share in celebrations of accomplishments.

Naturally, support comes from verbal means as well as physical. We all value and appreciate helping voices along with helping-hands. Vocal support provides encouragement and 'heart' for each of us to 'keep trying.' Side-by-side effort is blood-and-muscle teamwork which assists all toward reaching goals. Emotional support and physical support are mutually beneficial. Everyone benefits and is stimulated by encouraging words. Everyone profits and is gratified by added muscle.

In a sense, that is what Angelina's and my uniquely shared "Thanksgiving of 2013" signified. We were celebrating a happy and successful season in a new country. Much like the Pilgrims of 1621, we had similarly "succeeded" because of new found friends who had been so supportive and helpful. Together, we celebrated joys and successes on that special occasion by sharing food, showing appreciation, joining in entertainment, and mutually offering prayers of thanks. We were all appreciative of each others' support, friendship and companionship.

As Angelina and I relaxed and enjoyed those final days before our destined return home, we both came to recognize and appreciate what was really important to us at that time: Our new(Giving Thanks continued...) found friends, who had been there for us throughout new and challenging times, had been essential to our success. Many interesting, unique and valuable experiences for us happened primarily because of our special friendships. Genuine pleasure had been derived and enjoyed from selfless acts of kindness and support extended to us by these friends. We felt honest and grateful appreciation for their thoughtfulness and caring.

Truly, it was a Thanksgiving worthy of "giving thanks."

Dedicated to:

Our friends, Sergio and Deyanira
Mismaloya – Boca de Tomatlan,
Puerto Vallarta, Jalisco, MX
Thanksgiving Day, Nov. 28, 2013

"Mismaloya Blues"

Part 4
Going Back Again...

Like the famous warning, or threat or promise of Arnold Schwarzenegger's character in Terminator, the "I'll be back!" slogan became my calling card and a comical code-line for friends and acquaintances in ***Puerto Vallarta*** and my lovely ***Mismaloya***. I was feeling pretty certain that it was nearly inevitable that we would return the following year. During our trip's initial preparations, we had made vacation plans without true understanding or appreciation of the natural beauty we would desert when departing as previously scheduled. The weather was just starting to turn incredibly beautiful when our farewells were required.

Leaving on December 16th had meant that the best weather was still ahead. The enormous humpback whales had just made their appearances, and all the dolphins were drifting and playing regularly into our sight. It was actually a time to arrive, not leave. But those had been our circumstances, our conditions and our plans, so the timeframe had to be followed. We had returned home as planned. But, a wishful and desired return to ***Mismaloya*** was already in-the-making.

Planning went much easier and more swiftly for the "Return-to-***Vallarta***" campaign. There were a few changes and differences, however. This time, initially, I would be returning alone. Angelina had many family conditions to work out, and she was absolutely not willing to experience our condominium, ***Mismaloya, Puerto Vallarta***, or ***Mexico***, in general, during any summer months.

The previous year in ***Puerto Vallarta*** had given us a rumble with the rainy-season's ending-period. September, and part of October, had still been very wet, very hot, very humid, and the biting-insects were a severe annoyance. My wife, having been raised in Jalisco as a young child and recalling our previous vacation, wanted no part of it. This trip would begin as a solo stay for me.

One of my "bucket-list" adventures had something to do with living in a foreign country for each of the twelve months of a year. We had visited Mexico in previous years, but we had lived there only during September, October, November, and December of the year before. Now, I had a chance to add July, August and the first-half of September to my "bucket-list" before Angelina joined me again for the more reasonable climate of October. So, those were the plans: I would return, set up camp, begin my studies, and start writing again while waiting for Angelina to rejoin me in mid-September or early October at the latest.

Being familiar with the turf, the return was easy. For this trip, I brought a few, specialized items along like a fishing pole and gear, more electronic gadgetry for music and improved internet-connection wiring. I already knew what not to bring: Heavy shoes, long pants, long-sleeved shirts, and anything else not appropriate for hot, steamy weather. It would be tank-tops, cargo shorts and sandals for me 99% of the time. Even the winters were comfortably in the 80's, so there wouldn't be any problems. If I became desperate for something else, I'd buy it. Otherwise, I was travelin' light and livin' lighter! It would be boxers or nothin' for me, well, inside my condo, at least!

Our landlord, ***Sr. Sergio***, met me with enthusiasm, shuttled me around for basic, shopping-needs and sped us rapidly home to our mutual destinations. My favorite line for our host was the familiar, "Remember: '***Mi casa es su casa!***'" Upon arriving at "***la casa***," and even beginning while traveling along the course to our ***Mismaloya*** residences, there had begun a gradual, transformational relaxation which imbued throughout my body. I was really feeling comfortable and happy. I felt like *I was home again*.

It was going to be a time for me to really focus on my Spanish instruction. This time, I would be teaching myself, however, with the aid of some computer applications and Spanish-learning programs. I set a goal to focus on vocabulary this time concentrating on nouns and verbs with some attention toward conjugations of verbs. I wanted to develop conversational skills. Knowing words for things and action words to get points across might make me sound like a fumbling illiterate, but at least I'd be communicating.

I mean, I could point at my mouth or belly and cry out, "***Cerveza, por favor***!" and they'd understand. Anyone would. Plus, so many Puerto Vallartans depend on their own English-skills. They need them to promote business dealings with the tourist population which mostly speaks English. Besides, ***Vallartans*** know the rest of the world likes beer as much as they do. Well, almost as much, but *fuhgeddaboudit* when it comes to ***tequila***!

But, I had a lot of other goals that I planned to work on too. I would strive toward discovering some new snorkeling and dive-spots for fun and entertainment. I would struggle to seek out new beaches to sun-bathe upon and find new trails for exploration through the nearby jungle. Inside ***mi casa***, along with ***mi clases de espanol y estudios***, I would practice daily on my guitar thumpin' 'n' strummin'. I would wail away on my harmonicas until my heart was content or the neighbors complained. It would be alright, though, because I would be alone, so my noise shouldn't hurt anyone. Furthermore, until my wife finally rejoined me, I could play all the rock-and-roll and jazz and classical music I desired.

I was fond of large doses of any and all kinds of musical genres. Angelina, though, could only take a little for a short time. She was a "Golden-Oldies" girl which satisfied me too. Sometimes, though, I needed The Stones, Santana, Brubeck, the Marsalis brothers, or Tchaikovsky to ring my bells and set me free. But now, I was free. Free to do as I pleased and come and go as I saw fit.

And, furthermore, getting "fit" was another goal. Nice segue, huh? I would eat properly, but sparingly, and lose fifteen to twenty unwanted pounds. I was here, and I was ready to get skinny rockin'-and-rollin', swimmin' and sunnin', walkin' and talkin', ***espanol, que es!*** I was formulating my own personal, "liquid-exercise-language" diet. I had it all worked out in my mind's eye...

My plan was to walk to any local pub, three times-a-day and order a beer in Spanish! ***Manana, tarde y noche, quiero caminar, caminar, caminar!*** (Morning, noon and night, I want to walk, walk, walk)... ***"Buenos Dias! (Buenas Tardes!.. Buenas Noches!) Una cerveza, por favor, mi buen amigo: Corona, Pacifico, Dos Equis. No importa*** (It doesn't matter). ***Muchas gracias! Adios!"*** Oh, alright. I said, "...formulating..." I meant "fantasizing!" It's just a "plan," a goal, but it's my fantasy. Okay, fine. I had made promises to Angelina. I would be a good boy, eat right and not drink too much. So much for promises...

FORGOTTEN PROMISES

It's not that I forget;
I just don't always remember
Like somber differences
Between "losing" or "misplacing."
The thing is "gone" or "not-for-long."
I just cannot find it right now,
But I will... when I remember.

However, if it's lost,
Fuhgeddaboudit; I'm to blame.
It's the same thing as if
I just threw all of it away.
It is a big mess, you would guess.
Now, I have to make another
As soon as I clean-up this one.

'Promises' are like that.
We make them with our best intent
Not meant to be broken.
Sometimes, we may get all confused,
Or even drop the ball and fall.
We make them like they are steel.
But sometimes they are just cheap tin.

What must not be forgot':
"We make promises with fresh starts-
Crossed hearts and hope-to-die!"
They are held in highest regard,
But our minds change or rearrange.
And all those heartfelt promises
Are not forgotten, just recalled.

HUNGER PANGS

I get those hunger pangs
When spirits wane,
So, I want to quench my thirst.
I need to go someplace
Where it's no disgrace,
And its liquor makes me burst.

I am a party-boy
Who drinks for joy;
I've got to find some release.
I want a place to go
Where I always know
How my habit needs to feast.

What I am looking for
Cravings explore
How "party-boys" seek pleasure;
It's from bars, I believe.
Hunger is relieved
By the booze that lets me soar.

(Chorus)

No time to be petty;
I gotta get ready.
I'm gonna paint Vallarta red.
'Cause I want to bleed
With drunk company
Where my thirstiness is fed.

There is the Malecon
Where clubs are fun,
And bars serve their booze with lime.
Music will always go
Where the liquor flows,
So, I will have a good-time.

Yeah, it's a party-town
When suns go down,
And its laughter never sleeps;
But, it's the morning's wake
With awful headaches
When my spirit always weeps.

(Chorus: *Once more, with feeling!****)***

No time to be petty;
I gotta get ready.
I'm gonna paint Vallarta red.
'Cause I want to bleed
With drunk company
Where my thirstiness is fed.

"Mismaloya Blues"

Part 5:

Here and Now and Hereafter...

Living in ***Mismaloya*** District is so quiet and lovely. The serenity and tranquility are very evident on this side of the bay. My "south-side" of ***Puerto Vallarta*** stands in unique and pleasing contrast to those frantic, neighboring districts on the (other) east and north sides of ***Vallarta*** in the State of ***Jalisco*** on the ***Bahia de Banderas***. Here, where I live, life is blissfully peaceful and calm.

There, in the distance, within the "other-sides," I can see an evening's hectic, city-sights and blazing lights chronically burning to inflame the rushed and toiling mayhem of downtown ***Puerto Vallarta***. Ceaseless flows of air-traffic arrive and depart hourly in conjunction with seasonal, bi-weekly visits of cruise-liners adding yet more tourists and more frenzy to the commercial and hotel districts located in those areas, or "zones." The city-lights burn all night, and although things do quiet down a bit after late hours, it's still a city that is open all night long.

Within ***"La Romantica," "El Centro"*** and ***"La Marina" zonas***, the hungry hustle-and-bustle of anxious, local hawkers squawk and promote their wares and deceptions to naive and unsuspecting innocents. It is a necessary, yet unfortunate, fact and reality of ***Puerto Vallarta's*** financial stability which plagues the business and beach front areas. The streets and beaches are crammed with booths, shops, vendors, and transient-workers all pushing their products and prodding potential clients. Although souvenir-sales and pitching tequila by offering free-samples, and then encouraging its chronic consumption, are landmark, city-traditions, the worst of the sales-lot are the "resort, time-share promoters."

Every street and corner, it seems, maintains pitchmen promoting "time-share" purchasing concepts for the hotel and resort industry. Their job or "scam" is simply to get short-term tourists to the resorts by offering cute, convenient, useful, grandiose and typically phony promises of "free gifts" just to look at the resorts. No obligation required. Then, once these naive tourists arrive, the resorts' high-powered, persistent, sales-closers take over with charm, finesse, and non-stop jabbering in attempts to overwhelm, bewilder and intimidate clients into buying "time-shares" of the resort(s) vacation-condo availabilities.

Tourist-buyers are temporarily transfixed by the delight of their newly purchased time-share often from the very resort at which they are vacationing. While playing out their one or two-week rendezvous, the "new-owners are treated like royalty. The resort really offers them everything they need or want, if resort-life is all they need or want. Often, it is not.

Unfortunately, the reality-check occurs once they return home. There, they unpack, look at their bank accounts, and reread the small print of their contracts. The overwhelming, financial-burden and vacation limitations now placed upon them becomes obvious. That compounded by the difficulty utilizing membership advantages becomes evident. And it gets worse.

Just consider all of the actual costs involved. Now, when you wish to utilize your incredible, spectacular, resort time-share ownership is when they discover all the fine-print and critical rules hidden somewhere between the lines of their owner's-contract: The whole ordeal can be very expensive when compared to planning their own vacation on their own or through an agency. Plus, they can get all the desired upgrades they want with their own efforts or agents' for any resort in the world at their time-of-booking. So, it's not such a good deal after all.

Furthermore, there is little chance to return or cancel a purchase; Mexican laws prohibit such acts and protect the resort-owning corporations. New owner, purchase-contracts typically involve significant down-payments charged to high interest, credit-cards. Additionally, multiple, incidental-fees, annual-dues and maintenance fees, transfer-plan membership fees and annual dues seem always "due." Finally, significant availability issues with the resorts' make time-share schemes just that: A scheme.

And consider the real deal. To add insult-to-injury, resort shysters simply continue selling and re-selling the resorts' never-ending resources. With new units to sell and old units to resell from upset, frustrated and broken owners, the sales office was always open. One condo unit may be sold for potentially fifty-two (52 time-shares (52 weeks in a year). Or, fifty-one if you want to give the poor folks one week for clean-up. Nevertheless, each resort has potentially hundreds of units. Foreclosures provide on-going returned units too. Time-shares? What a deal...if you own the resort or work for them. Buyers beware!

Unfortunately, but truthfully, the hundreds of smaller, large and enormous resorts are the blood-life of the area. They are what maintain ***Puerto Vallarta's*** thriving economy because they bring in fortunes in tourist-dollars annually. The entire city seems for sale, and scams are daily rituals and common practice. Everybody is selling something to tourists, and the closed-sales maintain the hoax.

Tourism, the root of this evil, invades every edifice with glibly bargained and acquired delights of transient glee and celebrations of frantic zeal. If money-makes-the-world-go-round, ***Puerto Vallarta*** spins deliriously from it. Yet, the vast majority of "***la gente***" work so hard for so little. Typical of everywhere, those selling "nothing" for something make it hard on everyone.

But that was not the lifestyle meant for me and my wife. We freely chose to live in ***Puerto Vallarta***; however, we deliberately preferred to dwell on the distant, southern-outskirts of town away from inner-city chaos and, rather, on the fringes-of-enchantment. One direction takes me backward into the blood-and guts of the beast: anxiety, stress, pressure, and rush-hour traffic. The other takes me forward to the heart, mind and soul of home: relaxation in my comfortable, ***Mismaloya***, cliff-side residence.

Here, in my easy-livin' "comfort zone", everyone and everything in ***Mismaloya*** appears so relaxed. Even the buzzing critters and chirping birds innocently hum and twitter about hunting and nesting throughout the area carefree and prosperous. Little, jungle-creatures and crawling insects of astonishing varieties scamper and move about my condo quarters and surrounding grounds seeking food and shelter with curiosity and purpose.

They are welcome unless they become a nuisance, at least until Angelina arrives. The mere sight of an insect or bug or gecko would nearly paralyze her with stress. I am personally fine with most of them...outside! Buzzers, biters and spiders are nature's wonders and fascinating little delights. If they crawl, they're cool. Oh, yeah, but no snakes. I will definitely help them to go outside!

I mean, I have to face it: It's a jungle out there! Snakes were here first, this is true. I respect that. But they are out! The other critters are relatively safe with me for the time being. They aren't too much of a bother, but we have to draw a line. In fact, one was already made, and it's called "the highway!" Critters can stay on their side, and I'll stay on mine. If I go over there, I deserve to get bit'. If they cross over here, I hope they get hit...by a truck... before I squash them!

Anyway, bugs and spiders and other "crawly" things aside, there are always the gentle and kind voices which greet me from my neighbors' ***casas***. My new-found friends, I believe, have already discovered nirvana. Their meaning-of-life seems to be absolving themselves of sin and guilt and being aware of their surroundings. They seem to lead meaningful lives of caring, sharing and humanism. All-the-while, they speak and act as though they truly appreciate and respect nature and its spiritual energy.

My neighbors personal and unique abodes all provide individualistic color and primitive-art-deco which add character to the surrounding cliff-sides. Private balconies and deck flood-lamps offer-up creative and dramatic luminescence to the evenings' shoreline below. Many have adorable, personal pets, typically puppy-dogs, which greet passers-by with singular emissions advising owners of potential guests. You can see them throughout the days joyfully parading the grounds for daily exercise acting like lords and ladies of the realm. The precious, little canines seem as free and contented as their owners living comfortable lives of simplistic tranquility.

Across the dividing bay, city-life shudders from over-crowded streets. Touring multitudes of travelers aimlessly parade the toiling streets. They visit umpteen shops of pushy vendors and flea-market hawkers all peddling the same cheap, "***Hecho-en-china***" tick-tack in every shop or booth day-after-day. Their explanation is that the city's street-businesses and vendors are designed for "flea-market" mentalities and "here-today-gone-tomorrow" customers. The "same-ol'-shi-!" is not "the same" for new folks.

New faces means the same-old-stuff is new again, and the "same-ol' sales pitches can be rejuvenated over and over, "Hey, ***Amigo***, come take a look. Is no charge to see. Is free to come inside. We only charge when you leave!" It adds a pleasing tone to the amusing and carefree gaiety and ambiance of the entire souvenir-shopping experience. Also, the tourist soon learns the two most useful words in the ***Puerto Vallarta*** shopping atmosphere: ***"No, Gracias!"***

Everything always looks new and shiny to "new" visitors. And the "natural-law" of "barter-economics" still exists and thrives throughout the land: "Whatever the price, offer half." At first, the seller acts insulted, and then you both meet in the middle. Guaranteed 25% discount. Less, you got taken; more, you haggled more and got an even better deal. But not to worry, the vendor still makes a profit! The Chinese make cheap stuff for everyone!

A "one-size-fits-all" philosophy primes the trade-store dynamics. Every vendor has exactly what the curious onlooker seeks: "What you looking for? I got it here. Come, it's free to look...," and "No! Is no too small; is just right for you!" The bartering, bargaining, and wheeling-and-dealing never ends. To the souvenir-industry's credit, however, usually some curio or clothing item or art-piece is desirable to all seekers.

A variety of studios offer local sculpture, artwork, and photography for a wide-range of tastes and interests. I believe it is thought in ***Puerto Vallarta*** that if you need money and won't do anything else, do art and try to sell it! Zealous sculptors, painters, and photographers create all sorts of modes and methods of art and place them in curio-shops or galleries for potential buyers. Beauty truly is "in-the-eye-of-the-beholder." Sellers even "wrap-it-and-ship-it" to assist buyers who are returning home.

Artists from all over the areas converge on Puerto Vallarta collaborating with local galleries and shops. They display primitive-art styles, neon-deco contraptions, surrealistic and impressionistic art-forms, quaint scenery-settings and portraiture, living and otherwise, in hopes of selling their work to art-collectors or souvenir shoppers. Every artist hopes to line their clients' homes' walls and shelves with their artistic endeavors; similarly, they wish to line their pockets with starving-artist, needed cash.

Museums, historical architecture, and sites-of-interest, though scant, are scattered throughout ***Vallarta's*** domain for enthusiastic visitors. Usually, there is something to see or do for everyone if sights are not set too high. Of course, every resorts' goals were one-stop shopping for their vacationers. They want to provide their visitors with every imaginable entertainment right there, on-the-spot, at the resort...for a small fee, naturally. True, you could spend a whole week doing a resort's bidding and then miss everything.

Fishing boats, sailing boats, party-boats, and various water-rides abound the ***Bahia de Banderas*** providing unique entertainment and exciting sport to all customers. If those don't "float-your-boat," so to speak, then limitless varieties of contrived activities are available. Gambling, sports-betting, exotic dance and show reviews, and tours and activities of all sorts are on-hand and in close proximity to anywhere. The hotels, resorts, hawkers and vendors will make sure you know all about them. Most of those folks all get a piece-of-the-action, or commission, on any sales.

Adventurous souls can go dirt-biking, hiking, horse-back riding, zip-lining, bungee-jumping, para-sailing, and take bus-tours to see all kinds of sights. Tourists can also take tours of city-attractions, zoos, marine-life exhibits, exotic shows on distant beaches, and even go on inner-jungle, tequila-tasting adventures. Although seasonal, even local, bull-fighting is accessible in the city's arena.

Until recently, there was even a large theater for concerts, ballet, opera, and dramatic performances. It closed, however, due to overhead costs, lack-of-funding, public-relations, advertising-rates, or just not enough care. But, I am certain it will reopen again under proper guidance. However, two ***grande*** malls, two WalMarts and Sam's Clubs, Costco, Office-Depot and Home Depot are big attractions as well as the malls' local cinemas which show prime features. Almost anything locals, tourists, transients, or short and long-term visitors need can be found at one of the "outlets." If not, the computer-savvy can find it online and have it shipped to a postal service.

If tourism is the "blood" of ***Puerto Vallarta's*** economic health, then city and district-wide ***autobus*** systems are the veins that carry it. Literally, hundreds of buses are en-route at any given time throughout areas from early mornings until well-past midnight. The coaches are color-coded for serviced areas and clearly identify their destinations on the front, wind-shields. The main, longer-distance boulevards are often paved, but the inner-city streets are typically cobble-stone. Thus, jittery and jolting rides provide unique ambiance or else painful ordeals.

The buses will take you anywhere you need to go within Puerto Vallarta districts' limits. Still other bus-lines will take you beyond. Of course, we cannot forget the taxi-drivers. They are everywhere, readily available for reasonable prices, and they will also take you anywhere you desire. Plus, they love to "chatter-up" pleasant conversation about ***Puerto Vallarta's*** sites and beauty in hopes of encouraging ***muy grande*** tips.

Beware! Bus and taxi rides are somewhat like amusement-park attractions. Every destination seems to involve a race to reach it, and big-city drivers have nothing on these guys. If you can distract yourself while riding along, do so. Read something, stare at the floor, or talk to someone, but don't involve yourself with traffic congestion. If you do, you may suffer from "congestive" heart-failure. Offensive-driving, or take-the-hill attitudes, are "rule-of-thumb," operational-techniques for driver-skill. Driver-training in ***Puerto Vallarta***, regardless of the vehicle, is a basic, ruthless art-form.

Mealtimes find vacationers carousing and stuffing themselves within vast arrays of restaurant-life savoring local cuisine or international flavors. Though tacos reign supreme, taste-buds for every desire are satisfied and hunger is vanquished with varietal, caloric, blissful glee. Every restaurant or ***taqueria*** guarantees the best food in town at the best prices. Tourists' suckling thirsts are easily quenched by the staggering number of liquor stores, bars and upscale saloons, beer halls, and ***tequila***-tasting merchants competing for short-term drinkers and dollars. ***Mexico***, in general, promotes its beers and tequilas, and ***Puerto Vallarta*** is, happily, no exception.

However, I don't deal with that environment inside my friendly Mismaloya. If I want a beer, "***Una cerveza, por favor***," or a mixed-drink, or wine, soda, coffee, tea, or just plain water, I can have it served quietly and efficiently in a mellow atmosphere on a multitude of pristine beaches nearby. Yet, my favorite location to relax and drink-and-think is my own, private balcony. There, I can absorb the sun's radiant shine, inhale the sensual, sea-breezes and ponder the magnificent glory of the ocean's spectacle below. Each morning, I settle in my lounge chair for my first coffee. Later, I take a relaxation session to read or study or just take in the view. Another couple of times during the day, I stretch out again to enjoy a beer or a drink and just sit and think and relax and enjoy the serenity and beauty of it all.

It is my own, personal "zone-of-contentment." I relax there, consider the outside-world, or not, and meditate on the purpose-of-life, my own life, to be more specific. I sit and think, or sit and drink, or think and drink, or just do neither. I have resolved so many issues for myself in that manner. And, just as often, I have actually become intoxicated by the revelations I've discovered. Well, probably the liquor may have had an influence too, on the "intoxicated" part, I suppose.

Throughout each day, however, I am mellowed by the soothing and continual play of the ocean's mirthful laughter while it softly laps upon the surf-and-sun-bleached rocks below. It is supported by a constant and vast source of clear-blue ocean promoting its own special pleasures to water-lovers everywhere. In the winter months, the bay is home to dozens of porpoises and humpback whales which return each year to spawn and raise their young for spring's departures heading back north.

These wonderful creatures add to the sea's spontaneous color, intrigue, excitement and entertainment for boat-viewers and cliff-side watchers alike. The sightings are so close from my home in ***Mismaloya***, I'm tempted to reach out to touch them. They are part of what makes the location so incredible and special. Other spectacular and amazing sea-life abound here too. Schools of fish dance in abundant pools to the ocean's movement and tides. Large groups of manta rays leap, flip and flop on top of unsuspecting victims to feed upon. The reefs directly below are home to multitudes of aquarium-like, multicolored fish species. And "home" is the objective. This is where I call "home."

While each day the bay is a continual parade ground for visitors of all sorts, fascinating samples of watercraft and vessels take fishermen, sportsters, players and diners, sailors, cruise ships, and passenger boats of all sizes and shapes to various destinations. People go out to party and carouse, drink and dine, fish and snorkel, catch the "mother-of-all" big-game fish, feel the wind and sea mist in their faces, visit unique attractions only available by boat, and/or just enjoy nature's wondrous sea-life.

Evenings bring heavenly, brilliant, sun-setting experiences. Clouds and fog on the far horizon, with Father Sun dipping below, cascade spectacular sprays of vivid reds and pinks and oranges across the fading skyline. Keen observers can identify the wide berth of the sun's settings depending on the time-of-year. Seasons spread the sunsets' shows from far northern views seemingly touching the ***Islas de Marietas*** off the coast of Nayarit to the far south well behind the coastal mountains. The key point is that no matter when or where, sunsets are always dynamic and inexplicably beautiful.

During the rainy-season on many nights, in remote distances over the ocean or hills, the sky's magnificent displays of nature's own baseball-drama unfold with brilliant, lightning strikes and thunderous ovations unleashing electrifying experiences of dynamic power, beauty and entertainment. Yet, the crashing waves from the storms' violence are metronomes of reverent sound and pulsating seduction. Never ceasing to provide visions and sounds of timeless strength, determination and sheer will-power, they force viewers and listeners alike to acknowledge their omnipotence and submit to their dominance and control.

What wonderful companions are these natural beauties with whom to share a delightful meal and a drink. On any-given-day, I carry food and beverage in hand, settle into a relaxing, lounge-chair on my balcony, and engage myself with all these majestic sights and sounds. I absorb the dynamics of the ocean's beauty and its surf below. I am content and relaxed as I realize the slow and steady changes taking place around me and beyond.

I become fascinated by the incredible skyline and endless and continually changing cloud formations. I watch and sense how the powerful storms begins developing and dark, gray and ominous cloud cover blankets the overhead skies. Lightning rods crack in the distance, sometimes bringing near daylight to an otherwise black seascape. Thunderous booms follow to add excitement and thrill to the rapid weather change.

I share them equitably with all my senses including those of the spirit. I relax, observe His glory and give thanks for God's magnanimous offerings. I study and learn to appreciate what is really important in my life. And my life is in the here-and-now, and it's not available to me downtown in the "moan zone" but only here... in Mismaloya...just inside heaven's gate.

Earlier, I had been reflecting on "best laid plans" to appreciate how quickly things could change... Since my last writing, I have already returned home again briefly for an emergency trip to be with my children while their mother passes through the final-stage of her terminal illness. Although I've been divorced from her for many years, it seemed appropriate to be home and available for my kids needs while they struggle with remorse and grief. All I can really offer is my shoulder and a promise to be there to comfort them.

Child-births and funerals seem to be crystallizing moments. During both occasions, family members and friends become significantly aware of how grateful they are for each other and how tentative and special this life-experience truly is. New life emerges and family and friends gather to share in its splendid importance. Everyone is in awe of the incredible occurrence of this new child and its potential. With months of prior, emotional preparation, giving-birth still always brings cheerful and hopeful well-wishing. It ushers in a welcoming spirit.

In a similar way, deaths often reunite family and friends but rather to share in tribute, consolation and appreciation. These are times when we contemplate the hereafter and the wonder and meaning of life's existence. It is then when we acknowledge life's tentative briefness. We wonder why it ends so soon, and we often challenge it. We question the purpose of our brief and curious existence. We ask ourselves, "Where do we go from here?" And, it is during this grievous period, regardless of circumstances, that family and friends join together and offer condolences and support. Once again, well-wishing is prompted by hopeful spirits. Mourners wish all to carry-on with newly-modified lives.

I hurt for my children's sake. I know that their grieving is important, yet I also understand that we all have personal and epochal tasks in this existence to make the most of life-and-death. We are all together in them both.

FOR GOD'S SAKE

Before we can understand ourselves, we must first understand our meaning and purpose. Before we can understand our meaning and purpose in this life and on Earth, we must first appreciate the glory of our universe. Before we can appreciate our universe, we must first accept God. Before we can do that, we simply must accept a basic premise: Our Universe is God.

God is the Universe. Everything within us, about us, around us, surrounding us, and away from us is part of our Universe. Everything is part of God. We are all part of our Universe, and that makes us all part of God. We are of God. We are God.

Everything is of God's essence. We are all partners together sharing mutual relationships. As we share in our Universe each other's meaning, value and purpose each shares its Universal Truth: "Life is brief."

It is here; we are here. Then, it is gone; we are gone. Life is significant, but its duration is not. A millisecond or a million years are both trivial within the scope of Universal Eternity. We are eternal.

With new life comes a new member, a new partner, a new part of our Universe. Once anything becomes part of our Universe, it is forever linked with it. Everything becomes members of our Chain-of-Communion. Life forms, all created matter, and all energy become thread-links of an everlasting, eternal Fabric-of-Consciousness. We are one.

All new life and creations increase the volume and magnitude of the universe. With their manifestations expansion and development occur within an ever-growing Cosmos. We are expanding.

When life, matter and energy expand, they grow in dimension and number. We grow, develop, propagate, and regenerate. When we contract and/or expire, we still remain physical or energized parts of all existence. We continue forever as abstract fragments of our Universe and God's ubiquitous power. We are all-powerful.

Once conceived, born or created all things become manifestations of our physical and energized God. New life enlarges our universe; God becomes greater. Once expired, all things change their unique, physical interpretations yet remain concrete or abstract forms of our universal and eternal Existence. We are everlasting.

Humans share unique placement within the everlasting fabric of our Universal God: Bodies *supply concrete growth for our material Universe;* thoughtful-minds *advance considerate understanding of our Being;* souls *provide abstract energy to the entire Cosmos. Each expands and develops and embellishes God. We adorn God.*

Nothing ever ceases to exist. Once created, it grows, and then may perish yet transcends into omnipresent and omnipotent Energy. All Energy defines our Universe, and our Universe defines Energy. Energy is God; God is Energy. Our Universe is expanding. God is growing. We are growing.

Alive or departed, everything is part of energy, our Universe and God. You are always part of God. God is always with you. You are with God in your life with your body, your mind and your soul. Loved-ones may be gone, but they are in our Universe and with God forever. They were created to make God greater. You were created to make God greater. You are with God, and God is in you. I know this because We Are GOD.

For my grieving children mourning
the passing of their beloved mother: *Kathleen*
October 16, 1951 – August 6, 2014
DT Chapman-Puerto Vallarta,
Jalisco, MXAugust 2014 –

DON'T ASK WHY

What purpose is there for anyone's
Existence?
What value shall we find in our deaths?
After spending a lifetime seeking bliss
As a calling,
What cost is our final-breath's resistance?

What are the meanings of these lives
We are leading?
Is there purpose or reason behind them?
Are we here for some dutiful creed
We should follow
Or merely to perpetuate breeding?

Is life a game played for winners
And losers?
Are there rules that both sides should follow?
Will "winners" collect the "Good News"
When it's over
And others be forsaken abusers?

Are our lives examined like science
Experiments
Where hypotheses and theories abound?
Are laws-of-nature covenants
For human-truths,
Or are laws-of-man here to convince?

Are we simply reserved as amusing
Diversions
Meaning little more than some tryst
To be toyed with like dollies' devotions
As companions,
Then cast-aside with waning elation?

Curiosity has no boundaries,
Ends or rules
If taunted just to see what happens.
When "fire-and-brimstone's" threatening fuels
Ignite uproar,
Are we enlightened or burned in conversion's pools?

One final possibility may be
"Creations"
Occurring to do as we please.
If gullibility, then, offers convenience
For answers,
Don't ask why, just have patience.

"Mismaloya Blues"

Part 6:
I Miss My Bliss...

I've been distracted with family affairs of late. It is time to get refocused. Unfortunately and begrudgingly, however, I must venture into the "stress-zones" occasionally if only to pick up supplies at better-bargained prices. Even in ***Puerto Vallarta's*** market places supply-demand economics rules their price-setting. More availability of product lowers prices compared to the outward areas like my Mismaloya. There are a few exceptions but not to many. We're too far away.

Therefore, with serious reservations, and I don't mean tickets, I climb to the roadside coach stop. Here, I wait to catch the local autobus filled with its myriad of colorful, local passengers and ***mexicana*** charm. I shall enjoy the unique and pleasing ride to the outskirts of "anxiety-theater." We'll get more into that later... It's a bit of an awkward, if not dangerous bus-stop. There is a narrow area to stand and wait and flag down the bus-driver as he approaches. It must be nerve-wracking for passing cars who must hurry and get past the bus before another car comes whizzing up or down the road. However, schedules are fairly accurate; you can almost tell time by their arrivals. Buses pass each way every fifteen minutes.

Anyway, the bus stops for me, and I step-up into a personalized but seriously worn-out coach. I am pleasant to the ***conductor del autobus*** and am typically greeted warmly by him. Depending on the time-of-day, the bus may be near-empty or near-full because of work-shift changes. Regardless, by the time we reach our city-stop destination, our bus will be "standing-room-only" and packed like sardine cans with passengers going home, going to work, or begrudgingly, doing the same as me: Leaving *Shangri-La* for a time in purgatory.

Yet, the ride is pleasant enough due to the local sights and the colorful entourage of riders making the voyage. All shapes and sizes and colors and sexes and ages and nationalities venture forth. Everyone keeps politely quiet and to themselves, seemingly, so as not to upset anyone's harmonious state. All types of people use the bus-system: Short and long-term visitors like me; ex-Patriots from everywhere desiring wondrous and inexpensive lifestyles; locals going to jobs or shopping or home; occasional tourists; and some unique regulars. These are men and a couple women taking advantage of the bus to make their livings.

Each trip usually brings aboard a crusty and rusty old, guitar-playing crooner. These troubadours play and sing authentic, Mexican romantic pieces or local, favorite folk-songs for tips. Each time, after a short-distance and a few strains, they conclude with a warmed-over monologue about how difficult it is to make-a-living and how they need donations. While some players are actually talented suggesting past-glories in the music-industry, others just screech and plunk and agonizingly fake-out a performance. They are more comedic than musical, but their "closing-speeches" are typically longer with more pleading. The better performers seem too proud to beg much. Befittingly, good players garnish better tips. Sadly, it's depressing considering the fates of any of them.

Local, small-time fishermen climb aboard, too, with their daily catches of smelly, sea-life to sell to the town's smaller restaurants and fish-markets. They catch anything and everything themselves, or they partner with others fishing off the shores and rocks or diving and spearfishing from tiny boats. The daily "catches" are transported in recycled, five-gallon (20 liter) plastic, paint-containers. The fishermen are hard-working, weathered, and modest but proud individuals who usually enter the bus bragging about the morning's successes-in their buckets.

Once arrived at the "staging-point," however, the "trip-to-town" entertainment is over. Now, I have finally arrived at "Anxiety Theater." It's starting to sprinkle again, but that will just encourage my focus on finishing quickly and going back home before the serious rains begins The time has come for my bold entrance. I mentally focus preparing myself for the inevitable, up-coming, one-act play, ***Scourge of the City***. I leave the bus area, take a deep breath and... Enter Left.

Scourge of the City...

A One-Act Play: "Scene One:"

I deal with the opening, chronic monologue and constant batter, chatter and noise from offensive crowds and traffic. Avoiding salespeople with little eye-contact I move swiftly around and past them. Occasionally, greetings spring out from open doorways, and I am briefly staggered by some torrid, sales-offer, "Hey, Amigo, come look. Let me help you spend some of your money!" I briskly respond with brief but polite, yet to-the-point retorts, "No quiero nada, gracias!" (I don't want anything, thanks). Continuing my bee-line course to desired, shopping establishments, I am emboldened to seek all my required needs from these sites of necessary but evil mercantilism, purchase them and get out!

"Scene Two:"

Once inside a selected establishment, I swiftly locate and snag wanted produce and product and toss them into my shopping-cart with apparent frenzy. It's like I'm participating in some sort of Reality-TV, shopping-spree contest where the faster I shop, the more I get to keep for free! Racing through the aisles in maniacal style, I am proudly aware that my taxi and bus experiences have rubbed-off on me. I shove my cart like a Tijuana taxi-driver; no, make that a PV driver! Smoothly, efficiently and recklessly I maneuver my cart around and past and through awe-struck, dismayed and, sometimes, fear-struck shoppers who instinctively assist me by leaping out-of-my-way!

The registers become the "finish-line" where I empty my cart, vigilantly observe the cashier ringing up my charges, briefly question any uncertainties, pay the clerk and carefully count my change, tip the bagger, and hastily make for a fast getaway. "I win!" I imagine as I quickly retrieve my initially checked-in backpack from the Customer Service Center. Repacking my purchases into my satchel and backpack, I swiftly weave through the parking lot and maneuver myself into the bus stop where I shall leap aboard a bus that will take me to El Centro and then another bus that will take me home.

"Scene Three:"

"The Finale" is where I again zigzag and dodge my way through snarled traffic and hurried crowds. This time, however, I am burdened by my heavy load. Yet, I am compensated and aided by the tired and crazed look on my unshaven face. My time in Paradise has allowed me the frivolity and freedom of forsaking appearances. The unkempt hair, the growing and graying beard, the worn and wrinkled attire, and the weary eyes are not a disguise. They are my Puerto Vallarta costume for just such dramatic performances.

However, "the look" probably influences peoples' choices. They choose to leave me alone or get-out-of-my-way. The play, and thus my "make-up" countenance, is designed to encourage other actors to finish the scenes as quickly as possible. In any case, I still race full-force and focused to my welcomed bus stop for the catch-my-breath junket back to the Promised Land...

Exit Right!

The End.

"Epilogue"

In this final, closing scene, I respectfully and appreciatively board my bus for home, flopping into a vacant seat on the bus's right section to arrange a cliff-side view. The earlier, ever-building tension and climactic anxiety-attack steadily releases its stress as we near my beloved home. It is raining hard again and probably will continue all night. But soon, I shall be dry, safe and secure again.

It had been a nearly overwhelming experience of emotional discomfort and physical and mental effort to survive, but I had made it. The day's adventure marked success from the day's toil and performance, "And the Tony Award for 'Best Performance Under Unbearable Stress' goes to..." You get it! I got it, and my "award" is simple, basic and perfect: Once more, the hero in our little drama, a *star* in his own mind, finds peace and comfort in the tranquil beauty of his cherished and precious nirvana-promoting ***casa*** within his lovely Mismaloyan surroundings.

BEARD TODAY/GONE TOMORROW

Beard today/ gone tomorrow?
What is the fuss?
Do nothing.
Whiskers grow on you.

If you have to shave them off,
Razors, and soap
And lost time,
And they just come back.

If you try to trim your fuzz,
Keep on trimming
Victim of
Chronic OCD.

Dyes and designs are not free.
Altering beards
Is costly
And repetitive.

Shaving, trims and adorning
Are wastes of time,
Mental state's
On-going expense.

Better to leave it alone;
It will not hurt.
Let it grow.
Beards can change your life.

Hairy-faced originals-
Each is unique,
Artistic.
Try one on for size.

When you stop shaving to see
What quality
Is in you,
Let-it-all-hang-out!

HAIKU BEARDS

Whiskers are faces.
Beards are natural to us.
Why is there conflict?

Avoid stress; keep them.
Hiding man's appearances
Will just bring both out.

If we trim our fuzz,
We shall continue clipping,
OCD victims.

Shaving wastes money
As do trims' and adornments'
Chronic expenses.

Beards are not costly;
They need no dyes or designs-
Anxiety's waste.

Better left alone,
Beards arrive to change our lives.
They will not hurt us.

Artistic, unique,
Hairy-faced originals,
Try one on for size.

Men have qualities
Unseen until they have beards;
Let-them-all-hang-out!

SKY'S THE LIMIT

Today, I saw Godzilla
In a raging battle with Rodan.
While each fiercely attacked the other,
Godzilla gobbled-up Rodan's upper-arm.
His shoulder ripped-off and swallowed whole,
Rodan was forced into casual retreat
As its upper-torso hung vaguely
From Godzilla's bleeding, disfiguring mouth.

Slowly, with Rodan morphing into an enormous snail
Shifting carelessly and crawling steadily away,
Godzilla nonchalantly transformed
Into a gargantuan, spike-horned alligator.
This day was obviously Godzilla's,
But who will play or fight tomorrow,
And how many shapes can they take?
I guess the sky's the limit.

Tonight, there is nothing but darkness;
No afternoon's militant monsters
Joining together as whimsical creatures
Merging steadily and methodically.
Now, a foreboding and seamless blanket
Covers imagination's blotted vision
With brooding and spontaneous outbursts
Growling from occasional flashes of violent anger.

Taunting, striking, crooked spears-of-fire
Are cast at an agitated and frothing sea below.
Moments pass as each flash narrows
Its gap between an enemy's furious retorts.
Outraged roars bellow incensed upheaval
As weather's warriors fiercely rage again.
How long will they keep this up?
I guess the sky's the limit.

"Mismaloya Blues"

Part 7:
Getting Bugged...

I am still really enjoying this little escape of mine. I pretty much remain indoors most of the time and focus on ***mis clases de espanol*** and my writing because that's why I'm here. I still go into town only when necessary, and I try to reduce those visits in number and duration. Besides, the weather doesn't promote much outdoor activity. It's so hot and humid, and the rain is always here or on-its-way. During the all-too-few exceptional weather days, I have been kept mostly inside due to two circumstances: Business or loneliness.

I'm busy for many reasons. Two of them of course are spending as much time as I can practicing my Spanish lessons and also focusing a lot on my writings for this publication. Both demand a majority of my creative day's juices. The remainder of my time, however, is also pleasing. I venture out to visit friends and neighbors and typically have daily interaction writing to family and friends. I stay in touch with everyone via email, *SKYPE*, and *MagicJack* telephone-service

These family and friend contacts are my connection to my other life, the "outside-world." I depend on them for updates and current information on matters of "relative" importance, pun intended. It's usually the standard greeting stuff, "Hi. Love you and miss you. Hope all is well. See you soon enough when my stay here in Paradise is over, and I must return home to hell again." I know they all understand this. That's probably why most of the contact is performed by me.

Another productive time for me down here is serious and of a relevant nature. I figure out various ways and means to keep insects away or dead. The hot, humid weather and the incessant rain keep me indoors where I am mildly cooler and dry, but it also constantly brings the insects to my doorstep too. Their task, their goal, their motive, and their desire is to breach the enclosure I have developed for myself. Those insects and little crawling creatures don't just gather at my doors and windows for whimsies' sakes. They are attacking. They are on the offensive. They mean to do me harm. I am in harm's way. If I don't fight back with frenzied fervor, I'm... food,... finished... fertilizer... Phooey!

Insects and bugs and critters don't want to live with me; they want to live in me! And I, for one, cannot stand it. If I did, I would fall, and they would eat me. It's that simple. No rocket science here. It's man versus nature. It's me or them, that's all. So, I am obsessing with ways and means and methods to discover them, chase them away and preferably kill them and dump their remains in trash cans or even over the cliff.

My life has become another triage, another "affair-to-remember:" Me, my work, and bugs. And,we are all alone together here inside this cubicle fighting for our individual freedom and trilateral survival. But, in reality, I am the only lonely one. I am alone reading and studying, I am alone writing and emailing, and I am alone repelling and killing insects. Mine is a solitary existence. It is a lonely job, but I've got to do it. I must create. I must let the outside world know that I exist. And I must kill! I will not go-down-quietly-in-the-night without a fight! I refuse submission and acceptance of defeat. I'll play no role as "feast-for-the-victors," mere fodder for those disgusting, degenerative, lowest of all life-forms, bugs!

GECKO GUEST

A gecko guest has come to stay.
It showed up unexpectedly.
It was not invited;
I am not excited.
I'd be thrilled if it just went away.

It never gives me a warning-
Late at night or early morning.
When I want it to leave,
Then it tries to deceive
And make me believe it's sleeping.

Sometimes, I spot it in the bath.
I get startled and may even laugh.
But, anywhere-anytime,
It's considered a crime
Inviting noxious tones of wrath.

It simply won't listen to reason.
It acts like I'm committing treason.
If I chase it away,
It comes back the next day
Behaving as though in delusion.

I've tried everything I know.
It's making my spirits swing low.
So, a new strategy
For "my" gecko and me:
A pet's name is the key, "ALONZO!"

Dedicated to my step-son, Alonzo

"Mismaloya Blues"

Part 8:

A Call for Help...

I miss my wife, Angelina. I really want her here with me. It's just getting harder to keep carrying-on with this routine all the time by myself. I need an ally, another combatant, someone to share in my struggles and end this solitary conflict. Of course, I want her nurturing and her touch and love. However, there are also other important things she can do. She can help me cook and clean. She can go to town shopping with me, or she can even go all by herself without me having to come along. She can scratch my back and other parts I can't reach. And yes, she can help me kill bugs! There's so many and plenty to share in this agonizing war. Angelina hates them worse than me. She'll fight! Then again, maybe she'd just pack up and run. I couldn't blame her.

But hallelujah, she could even go with me to the beach and relax in the sun once in a great while. That is providing mother-nature isn't having another bad day like yesterday, and the day before that, and the day before...and, and, and always. But, I know that Angelina would never accept the heat and humidity issues for this summer season. In truth, I've been told there are really only six months of decent weather down here and only four months of those where tourism really makes business profitable. Those are December through March with November and April acceptable. However, May through October is pretty miserable here in this humidified-heat and rain-soaked torture chamber without air-conditioning.

Point-in-fact, we had returned here for a brief, but fun, two-week visit last July. The difference? We had "five-star-conditions," that's all! We came to visit friends by taking advantage of a resort-package special we had earned last year. We had received an incredible discount to stay at one of the swankiest resorts in all ***Puerto Vallarta*** and region, thereof. The Grand Mayan was the genie inside a lamp. Make a wish and it could be granted. Whatever pleasures were desired the accommodations and staff offered them. Everything we wanted or needed was there for us for the asking. Yet, a desired and essential ingredient was nice weather, and summer just doesn't give it to you. It was bad when I enjoyed visiting a Walmart just because of its vast oasis of air-conditioned coolness. That ain't "cool!"

Like we anticipated, it was hot as hell and stick humid outside, but it was actually bearable because we had an igloo to return to each day at our resort. The air-conditioning unit in our room was wonderfully chilling, especially in the "Hi" mode, and we maintained that setting constantly. AC and humidity! There's kind of a ring to that rhyme. I would stagger at the utility bill of those resorts. Ninety-nine per cent of their overhead is probably keeping people like us comfortable.

And yet, there are many folks living here without air-conditioning ever, let alone the summer months. I know this because I have seen them. They are the poor souls who look so burned-out, wrinkled and exhausted staggering every-where. Some tell me that one "gets used to it." After a while, the insects won't bother you either. I wondered if it was because they have developed a new type skin which will not let ultraviolet sun rays penetrate their course, thick hides, and thus, the same factor regulates the insects' behavior.

But, there's no AC in our Mismaloya condo either, and that factor coupled with the heat of July? It would never fly, and neither would my Angelina...to here. So, yes, I'm on my own until she arrives, but it's tough fighting this war on my own. I need reinforcements. And what am I going to do if she arrives, and the little suckers are still here in force? She'll spot them first thing upon entering, scream, pack-up, and leave me stranded until a better day another month away!

Yet, I understand. Angelina hates bugs, all of them, but especially the ones that crawl or jump or fly. And they're everywhere, and they are in constant, state-of-emergency starvation phases, it seems, to feed...on me! There seems to be no time that they wish to be anywhere else except inside this condo keeping me company or taking a meal with me. Sure, I understand that it's heat and humidity which let the little critters thrive, but why do they need to thrive ***en mi casa***?

They never seem to rest or sleep even though they are always in bed with me. They're always eating and drinking in bed too, and it's driving me crazy! I feel a sting and leap up and out-of-bed in the middle-of-the-night screaming, "Get off me! Get out! I'll kill you, you little *so-and-sos*!" Scrambling for my nearest can of Raid to gas them, I begin a relentless counter-attack. But to what end? They just keep coming back for more, and they're such inexorable guzzlers causing me such restless nights. I continually awaken imagining or dreaming that I'm being bitten, and often-as-not, I am. First, it's the bite, then it's the fight, and it goes on and on… Sleep… Then, the sting. The slap. The chase. The spray. The drowning. The kill. The bed. Sleep. And then it begins again. Over and over…

And don't forget about itching! I feel like my life has been condensed, no condemned, into two prospects: Itching and scratching! Well, three aspects then, and *killing*! I get bit, then I itch and I scratch, and then I go on a killing rampage. I need to get on the internet, contact my broker and buy some stock in Raid insect-repellant. I think I'd get rich from dividends just based on my own purchases.

Anyway, the insects keep *coming*, and I keep *killing*. Yet, some of these little suckers manage to avoid and escape their *destinies with toxic-death* by holding-their-breaths and breaking through my poisonous barricades. Then, those tiny, parasitic, zombie-like, vampire-suckers still succeed in seeking out their tantalizing target and feasting on (my) flesh. I don't understand. I'm not nice to them, but I sure must be good for them. I swear, I need a vacation. Oh, yeah, I'm on one. I almost forgot... Must be the blood loss! I'm not thinking clearly anymore.

I used to think it was my beard which may have frightened people and forced them to keep their distance. Now, when I stretch out my legs and arms, or twist around in the bathroom to get mirrored-reflection of my back, I see the possible real truth. I look infected! I look like I've got "the pox" or leprosy, or The Plague. My body has been ravaged by those little suckers,...and I mean that literally! Not only do they buzz around and torment me, but eventually they find a landing spot. Once they do, they're pretty much home free to "suck" away on me. That is, the ones that I don't smash or chase down and drown with sprays of Raid!

Unfortunately, some make it safely onto my body and quickly go to work. Insert and suck. Zip! In goes their stinger or teeth or fangs, or whatever-in-hell they use, and sluuurp! Out goes my blood. Sure, I let out a yelp and frantically swat at the pests, often squashing them, but not until the damage is done. Occasionally, I spot them attacking in swarms it seems. It's a group campaign!

They are comrades-in-arms, and I am their enemy. They're like little, friggin', self-sacrificing, Kamikazes swooping in, crashing and dying for their glorious cause: To *cause* me pain and suffering!

It's working for them too. I look like I'm a seriously damaged survivor from multiple bombing-raids victimized by miniature shrapnel injuries. That, and I may be suffering from internal-poisoning from all the Raid fumes I've been forced to inhale. Plus, there are sprays I've needed to spread all over my body for protection.

Of course, ointments and sprays are needed for relief from itching too. After I take multiple, daily showers to keep fresh and clean allowing less body-odor emissions to attract insects to me, I use recommended creams and salves and ointments suggested by friends and local pharmacies to ease the itching discomfort. I've even attempted the highly-recommended technique: "Leave-it-alone." I'm advised,

"Don't scratch, and the itch, pain, discomfort, and agony will pass in time. Just don't touch it!"

Yeah, sure. "Oh! There's a monstrous mosquito sitting on my eyeball! Why, I'll just calmly sit still here for twenty or thirty minutes and relax after it has pissed on my pupil, stabbed me in the eye, guzzled its blood-thirsty fill, and then buzzed away! ***No problema***! And I won't "touch" it either!" Yeah, right!

Lime juice is a little trick that seems to help, though. No, I don't drink it. Well, yes I do, as a matter-of-fact, but that's a "trick" I use to flavor my ***cerveza***. The "trick" with the bugs is a different kind of strategy. I rub a lime's acidic fruit all over my body, and, hopefully, bugs don't like it. I'm not too certain it works, though, but I'll bet I taste pretty good,... like I'm marinated.

Naturally, I must spray and cover all the chairs and bedding and floors and walls and doors and windows for defense too. Also, I have resorted to counting my kills. This act is relevant because each morning I begin calculating daily, dead insects. I'm either seeking an increase in their deaths caused by my defense system or a decrease caused by the weather's cooling trend as Fall approaches.

This preparation is critical and imperative for those moments when I try to rest or lie down. Typically, it's due to finally collapsing in bed or on the couch or chairs from sheer exhaustion. The killing-frenzy is wearing me out! Sometimes, I am imagining things. I can hear them or see shadows of them flicking about my room. I'm seeing things. The miserable creatures are driving me mad!

But, there is method-to-my-madness. I have insect-repellent candles that I place on the dining table and night stands. I burn them whenever I am sitting or lying nearby. Also, there are electric, wall-outlet insect-repellents that I strategically place around the condo to kill and ward off the evil-doers. Those are supposed to work round-the-clock, but who isn't? Bugs sure are, and I sure am!

I love my cans of Raid, of course. A can for every room and two for the bedroom, one on each side of me. I spray until a gaseous, insulating cloud hovers above my bed, and the room glows with a shiny, outline from poured and virtual liquid sealing all my window and door openings. There is no way for insects to get in without making contact with the fatal toxin. But, if they do, they'll NEVER get out ALIVE!... *Aaaahhh!.... Ha! Ha! Ha!* The toxic substance won't just get attached to their bodies and poison them, they'll be forced to drink it and die that way too! *Ha! Ha! Ha! Ha! Ha! Ha! Ha!...*

APPARITIONS

Apparitions appear, then fade.
Supernatural emissions
Let our imaginings invade
For instructions to be obeyed.

Illusions, mostly mysteries,
Affect with moody visions
Allowing us to largely see
What minds envisage them to be.

Some ghostly and mystical scenes
Approach on silent missions
Engaging within subtle means
Recognizing their haunted beings.

Yet, other mysterious views
Configured with conceptions
Instill fear or perhaps amuse,
Nevertheless, leave us confused.

But spooks aside, my fantasies'
Heavenly apparitions
Are observed when desire to please
Partakes upon a moment seized.

ONE TOO MANY

Alonzo, the gecko, has a mate.
It's his sweetheart, or a little pal.
They chase each other
Over ceilings and walls
'Til one-or-the-other
Makes a slip and falls,
And I retire to consider my fate.

What shall I do after midnight?
Their sneakiness gives me the creeps.
Will they climb on my bed
While I'm fast asleep?
Will they crawl on my head
As I wake with a leap?
I'll just lie there and ponder my plight.

What can I do about mayhem?
My fatigue is becoming complete.
If I spray them with Raid
And force their retreat, Is my karma betrayed
Before their defeat?
Does peace mean accepting their freedom?

I was getting used to *Alonzo*.
Even though he startles my brain.
But geckos bring crowds
If you don't block their lanes,
And their silence is loud
If their presence is pain.
So, tomorrow, those critters will go!

"Mismaloya Blues"

Part 9:

Another Week of Burnout...

And the sun, when I can see it, burns like hell. Usually, it just hides behind the clouds, but it is there, and it is radiating like crazy. The heat is painful too. A few minutes outside without protection and I am toast. Cloudy days do not make a difference. They will fool you, though, and you'll think, "Oh, good, cloud-cover. No worries!" But, you'd better worry. Those U-Vs will get you, and it can be bad. Fried flesh… Yummy for insects!

Yet, even with the heat, it's the humidity that is exhausting. It's so bad, I'm sweating-in-the-shower! By the time I dry off and shave, I've got to dry-off again. Humidity is caused from all the moisture in the air. Okay, I understand climatic phenomena, but where does all the moisture come from? Where? Where? I'll tell you "where!" From all the rain! And it won't stop, and I'm drowning!

It's been raining almost every day, and there's no clockwork or reason to it. Except, it rains every night, and I'm never sure when it might rain each day, just that it will. It must rain because that's what makes all the moisture which causes all the humidity which joins with the heat to suffocate me and bring all those nasty, torturous creatures buzzing and flying and biting and sucking and swelling me with itches and infectious sores! And I scratch and kill! It's a violent and vicious circle.

I am a survivor, though. I have made it through the worst times. Well, actually, I've heard that May and June are pretty bad for rain and heat and humidity and insects, too. In fact, I've also heard of the wild, crazy and enormous migrations of little frogs and crabs sliding down the mountainous jungle behind us seeking the waterfront. Apparently, it seems, they traipse over everything to get where they've got to go to spawn, or something. Now, if their destinations were any of the of local, OXXO liquor-store markets that are so abundantly placed on every street-corner around town, then they'd sound like some friends of mine on late Saturday nights. But, I digress. Truth tends to do that a lot.

Anyway, the worst has passed for me, at least, for the time being. I can feel a change in the air and see a difference on the ground. The "dead-zones" are less-stacked with little bodies. My clean-up time has been virtually reduced to mere seconds of daily, swift swipes with paper towels. No more push brooms! Oh, sure, I'm still getting "vamped" once in a while, but the frequency has diminished significantly.

I mean, those filthy, little, disgusting transfusions were really starting to get to me. I felt like my screams were becoming howling(s)-at-the-moon. Now, however, my new name is: Sir Vivor, Loyal Visage of the Realm of ***Mismaloya***! Finally, there is peace-in-the-valley for me. Well, at least here, once-again, in the sublime and serene tranquility of my lovely ***Mismaloya***.

And my Angelina, ***mi esposa***, my better-half, my comrade-in-arms will be joining me soon. Although, the worst part of this horrid, rainy-season has passed, there are still plenty of rain-showers and insect-wars to share. Her company will be both appreciated but deserved, however. After all, I have held down this fort from all the invasions for so long on my own. My strength is waning. Her fortitude and imagination will be joyfully accepted. Also, she should recall last year's ordeals, so it won't be that bad, I hope. Angelina's tolerance is less than mine, though. We'll probably be applying affecting new strategies, no doubt.

But life here, so far, had been an adventure. True, I have been under attack so much while conditions permit. Sometimes, I let my guard down, but it's getting better. I have had so much opportunity to relax, and study, and read, and write that I cannot complain. When circumstances allowed, I have mostly been immersed in the glory and beauty and tranquility of ***Mismaloya*** and the ***Puerto Vallarta*** visage. I sit by my bay-windows enjoying the spectacular, million-dollar views ever-mindful that I am observing and enjoying some of the earth's finest scenery for a very modest expense. It really has been what many refer to as: A poor man's paradise. Whatever. It's worth it. I'll take it anytime.

THE DAYS WE ARE BORN

The days we are born
Mark journeys begun.
Our ways through life's maze
Will test us 'til done.

Paths that we follow
Determine our fates.
Uphills and downhills
Test character's traits.

Lessons we acquire
May challenge our truths.
To bleed while we lead-
Veracity's proof.

If meaning in lives
Is "*give,*" not to "*take,*"
We learn not to yearn
For others' mistakes.

A traveler's course
Confused in the black
Let lights in the night
Become beacons' tracks.

Sharing from our hearts
And caring with soul
Will pay freedom's fees
Worth more than our toil.

When judged for value
By deeds that we do,
Confessed will impress
Divine points-of-view.

Lives are like gambling
On pathways we choose.
Choices are voices,
"What is there to lose?"

SECRETS OF HAPPINESS

Up long before the rising sun,
Fishermen have already begun.
Todos sus barcos se preparen
Not for glamor and not for fun
But love of work which must be done.
A prayer within, not uncommon-
"May this day's catch bring good fortune
With blessings shared among our friends."

Morning's light means starting chores.
Merchants and shop-keepers ready their stores.
Sus trabajo es sus amor
Arranging merchandise and sweeping floors.
Watchful eyes seek out the tours
With hopes that should it rains, it pours
Bringing customers through their doors,
For when cash flows, the spirit soars.

Restaurants open at break-of-dawn,
Good food and service served-up with fun.
El desayuno es una comida importante,
But people must eat all day long.
"Our food is the best!" may sound like a con,
But proprietors make clients feel at home.
Duty and purpose in places belonged,
Owners please tourists before they are gone.

Daybreak brings charted boats on the bay
For fishing, sight-seeing and tourists at play.
La Bahia de Banderas es un mar de placer
Offering food, drink and revelry throughout the day.
Exotic vessels originate ways
Seeking adventure for tourists who may.
Each vessel wants passionate sailors to stay,
But enjoying their work is why they don't stray.

Finding *secrets-of-happiness* isn't so hard
If we open our eyes and let down our guards.
El amor no es deficil de encontrar
When we love what we do in our own backyards.

A POEM OF GOD

'I Am God'

The Universe is God.
God is the Universe.
Everything is part of the Universe.
Everything is part of God.
We are all part of the Universe.
We are of God.
We are God.
I am part of the Universe.
I am of God.
I AM GOD.

Everything is of God's essence.
As we share in our Universe,
Each shares its Universal Truth:
"Life is brief."
It is here,
Then it is gone.
A millisecond or million years
Are insignificant
Within the scope of
Our Universal Eternity.

Once anything becomes
Part of the Universe,
It is forever linked with it.
Everything becomes members
Of our Chain-of-Communion.
Life forms, all created matter,
And all energy become thread-links
Of an everlasting, eternal Fabric-of-Consciousness.
All creations increase and manifest themselves
Within an ever-growing Cosmos.

When life, matter and energy expand,
They grow in dimension and magnitude.
When they contract and/or expire,
They still remain physical
Or energized parts
Of all existence.
They continue forever
As abstract fragments
Of our Universe
And God's ubiquitous power.
Once born or created,
All things become
Manifestations of

Our physical and energized God.
Once expired,
All things change
Their unique, physical interpretations
Yet remain concrete or abstract forms
Of our universal
And eternal Existence.

Humans share unique placement
Within the everlasting fabric
Of our universal God:
Each Body supplies concrete growth
For our material Universe;
Thoughtful Minds advance
Considerate understanding of our "Beings;"
All Souls provide abstract energy
To the entire Cosmos.
Each expands, develops and embellishes God.

Nothing ever ceases to exist.
Once created,
It grows and then will perish
Yet transcends into
Omnipresent and omnipotent Energy.
All Energy defines the Universe.
The Universe is Energy.
Energy is God;
God is Energy.
The Universe is expanding.
God is growing.

Alive or departed,
Everything is part of God.
You are always part of God.
God is always with you.
You are with God in your lives
With body, mind, and soul.
Loved-ones may be gone,
But they are with God forever.
You are with God,
And God is in you...

I know this because
I AM GOD.

UNA POEMA DE DIOS

'Yo Soy Dios'

El Universo es Dios.
Dios es el Universo.
Todo es parte del Universo.
Todo es parte de Dios.
Somos parte del Universo.
Nosotros somas de Dios;
Nosotros somos Dios.
Yo soy parte del Universo.
Yo soy de Dios.
Yo soy Dios.

Todo es de la esencia de Dios.
Como compartimos en nuestro Universo,
Cada uno comparte su Verdad Universal:
"La vida es breve."
Es aqui,
A continuacion, que se ha ido.
Un milisegundo o un millon de anos
Son insignificantes

Dentro del ambito
De nuestra Eternidad Universal.

Una vez que todo se convierte
En parte del Universo,
Esta siempare ligado con el.
Todo se convierte en miembros
De una energia de la cadena de.
Formas de vida, toda la materia creada
Y toda la energia convertido en hilo enlaces
De un tejido eterna, eterna de la conciencia.
Todas las creaciones aumentan y se manifiestan
Dentro de un Cosmos en constante crecimiento.

Cuando la vida y la materia
Y la energia se exanda,
Que creen en dimension y magnitud.
Cuando se contraen y/o caducan,
Siguen siendo partes fisicas
O energizadas de toda la existencia.
Siguen siempro como fragmentos abstratos
De nuestra Universo
Y el poder omnipresente de Dios.

Una vez que nace o se crea,
Todas las cosas se convierten
En manifestaciones
De nuestro fisico y energizados Dios.
Una vez caducado,
Todos las cosas cambian
Sus interpretaciones fisicas unicas
Aun permanencen formas concretas o abstractas
De nuestra Existencia
Universal y eterna.

Los seres humanos comparten
La colocacion unica entro de la trama eterna
De nuestro Dios universal:
Cada organismo suministra hormigon crecimento
De nuestro Universal material;
Pensativo mentes avance
Comprension considerado con nuestro "Ser;"
Todas las almas proporcionan energia abstracta
A todo el Cosmos.
Cada expande, desarrolla y embellece Dios.

Nada nunca deja de existir.
Una vez creado
Crece y luego puede perecer
Sin embargo trasciende en

Energia omnipresente y omipotente.
Todo La Energia define El Universo.
El Universo es La Energia.
La Energia es Dios;
Dios es Energia.
El Universo se esta expandendo.
Dios esta creciendo.

Vivo o muerto,
Todo es parte de Dios.
Ustedes estan siempre parte de Dios.
Dios esta siempre con ustedes.
Ustedes estan con Dios en sus vidas
Con cuerpos, mentes y almas.
Seres queridos puedan haber desaparacido,
Pero que estan con Dios para siempre.
Ustedes estan con Dios,
Y Dios esta en vosotros...

Lo se porque
YO SOY DIOS.

"Mismaloya Blues"

Part 10: Bully Pulpits...

It seems like I spend a lot of time down here thinking about God... and the Universe too. It must be the weather, or vistas, or solitude, or all-of-the-above which bring on these meditative moods. I know I've reflected and thought and considered things through many times before, and yet I always conclude with the same finding: We Are One. Still, I cannot help reconsidering just what part I play in the whole scheme-of-things... in my present state of being... right now.

Alright, then, "scheme-of-things" may be a bit crass. How about "thread-in-the-infinite-fabric" of Almighty-time? Okay, I'll buy that. Then, how long a portion in the entire design is it (am I) included? How long is my "thread?" How thick is it? What's it made of? What color? Am I part of a theme or just the background? Am I on the edge and growing out or just hanging on the inside? No, I've got to be "on-the-edge" because I'm not dead yet! ***Que pasa? Que esta pasando? Hacia donde voy con esta la vida?*** What's up? What's going on? Where am I going with this life?... Where am I going with this rambling?...

It's thinking... thoughts... reflections... self-reflections... I believe when it comes to ourselves and eternity, we really get all hung-up on *ourselves*. It's the "me, myself and I" moments which surely start us postulating. There's no-better-time to become self-absorbed, it seems, than when we think and talk about God. Most everyone's got an answer. Some even declare, "I have 'the truth!'" Give us a break!

Nobody knows for certain, not even those who talk to God. Not even those who hear from God! I've got mine. You've got yours. Let's agree to disagree.

I wish others would refrain from telling us "their way," showing us "their light," or giving us "their truth!" Most of those characters, and many are professionals, prey on others, pretending to pray, while seeking converts or followers from amongst the weak, fragile, unsure, and indolent multitudes. Often, they seek quarry from other potential bullies like themselves whom they believe to be manageable and controllable with imposed, rigid hierarchies. It's a power trip for ego-maniacs, and for some, it's just a job, a means to earn a living.

This "prey-preaching" gives these "self-anointed" zealots a sense of purpose and a power-base which they cannot find, earn or deserve elsewhere. It's as though these "soul-suckers" believe each convert earns them brownie-points or reward-points redeemable from the Almighty Redeemer, Himself, when they personally face the Pearly Gates with its Judgment Book determining entrance or rejection. "Look at my list of 'converts!' I get special privileges now, right?" For many, however, it's just a personal, power-trip which they can perform requiring little skill or knowledge but rather just a trumped-up charisma and a guidebook.

Many of these people claim to have conversed with the Almighty already. Perhaps, so. That, in itself, is no big deal. Just start talking, and you can claim the same experience. Probably, most of us already have. Regardless of our method, it's comforting, in some way redeeming, and maybe even transcending. With honest-to-God believers, I have no problem. It is just when their "beliefs" are forced on me that I take offense. If someone "believes" in their heart and mind, then good for them. But, one's beliefs are not necessarily "good" for others.

We all have very different lives filled with unique experiences from varying backgrounds, families, education, and socialization-processing. No two people can possibly share similar visions. In more recent history, that visionary, belief-system difference can easily be demonstrated with Hitler and his Nazi Party creeds. He had answers, visions and "truth" so many that even Christians considered and even accepted. In time, most realized their mistakes-in-judgment. All demagogues gather followers from false *preachings* only to eventually fall.

More-to-the-point recently, no two religions agree on creed or purpose. Within each religion, themselves, are multiple faiths or sects with enormous variances in belief-structure. For examples, look within Christianity for differences between Catholics and Protestants. Dig deeper and you will easily find variances within each of those churches. Notice the extremism on either end of each spectrum of teachings and doctrine from Fundamentalism to Universalism.

Observe the present crises developing among Islam countries. Sunnis make up the vast majority of Muslims (85-90%). Shi'ite Muslims make up between ten and fifteen percent (10-15%). Several other very minor sects also exist with extreme differences in belief-structure. The Sunnis and Shiites continually struggle for domination in different areas and countries and resort to horrific violence within some extremist branches. Supposedly, they all follow the same edicts from the Qur'an but have serious issues interpreting its instructions or teachings, themselves.

Notice any historical similarities here within Christianity's development? Around three-fourths of Shia live within four countries: Iran, Pakistan, India, and Iraq. Shiite's have a vast majority of governmental control within Iran, but among others, they share equal footing. Sunnis make up nearly ninety percent (90%) of the Muslim world and have strong power-bases all around the world on many continents including Asia and Africa and, of course, the Middle East.

Now, review Christian communities. Catholics have strong religious and governmental influence of so many countries. Look at Southern Europe, Mexico, Latin America, and South America. Protestants have their own power-bases amongst powerful nations. Look at England and Northern Europe. Other Western countries share power-bases between both sects, Catholic and Protestant. Look at the USA and Canada. Both these camps attempt world influence and domination.

Everywhere historically there have been power-struggles for domination between one sect or another. Today, Jews and Christians are aligned, if not united, but it has not always been that way, has it? Today, the Muslim world is in turmoil, if not crisis. It's a terrible struggle involving horrific violence and power-struggles. Who knows how, where and when it may ever end. Will there ever be world-wide peace-and-order amongst all religious organizations? History suggests otherwise.

The point is that religiously partisan groups and organizations and churches and faiths have our globe fairly well covered, sectioned, split-up, and controlled by each other. Continents, countries and governments are heavily influenced by religious groups. Religion is big-business. Regardless of peace or war, good sides or bad or righteous or heathen, religions are ever-present because that is what makes for good business. They are ever there, steady-at-hand, busy at their pulpits voicing for calm or violence, choosing sides regardless of right or wrong, good or bad. Who cares? War is religion's business and business is good. Taking sides is good for business, and business is good for religion.

And what about goings-on within major religions, themselves? Presently, there is relative peace among the Judea-Christian communities, but that has not always been the case. The early Christians had a few hundred years of difficulties. How about within their own group? Remember the Inquisition? Reformation? Nor has there been peace among Judaism-Christianity and Islam.

Remember the Crusades? Today, there are cries of Holy Wars among extremists on all sides. Religion is a messy business, and there are always religious zealots who are willing to fight and die, and let others die too, for what they feel is right regardless of consequences. They have a voice, and they will be heard. They have a following, and they will lead. They have a struggle, and they might win. Victory means significance which equals power.

And then again, others even claim to have heard from God. Given the right circumstances, no doubt so. Even I had a moment, one time, when I heard a voice. I was physically and emotionally drained at the time. Actually, the "voice" had come after a near-death experience, and I had awakened from a one-week coma. I was exhausted from pain's awareness, survival's tears-of-joy, and prayer. I cried out in appreciation for life and giving thanks, and I heard a *voice*. And it was good. I was stunned, and I cried. Thank God it was in English, and not Hebrew or Greek, or I'd have really been confused! Maybe now is not a time for me to be joking... At least the experience was profound and has lasted my lifetime since.

Over-the-years, I have attempted similar communication, but it's been too difficult to duplicate. I guess I wasn't prepared mentally, emotionally or physically to face dying again just to attempt divine-communication. I failed, or else cosmic prayers are mostly just meant as one-sided conversations. We give thanks, and we make promises. Sometimes, people ask for things, if that is their way. Maybe I just haven't heard, or listened. Maybe that makes me weak, or frightened, or confused, or lazy. Maybe I should listen more often to those guys with their "direct-lines" to God as they prey, I mean pray, from their "bully-pulpits."

For some, it's too difficult to believe what might be discovered from our own efforts. Have you ever tried reading the Bible, the Qur'an, Buddha's writings, or any other dogma of teachings? Even Atheists have a strict doctrine. Do you follow a belief that there is only "one-way, one-truth, one-path?" Have you ever listened to others reading or preaching and interpreting those books' messages?

Try these on for size: "We are all 'born-in-sin!'" Or, "Heathens (non-believers) must die!" Or, "When you point at the sky, do not focus on the cloud formations, or you will miss the cuticle on your finger which needs trimming!" Okay. I'm exaggerating, over-simplifying a little and even jesting, but you get my point. Whether it's the Torah and Old Testament, or the Bible's Gospel and New Testament, or Al Qur'an of Muhammad, or Buddha's teachings, they are all up for interpretation. Who's right? Who's wrong? Who says? Who cares?

To me, it's all a bunch of mambo-jumbo, babble, crap, and bull. But, it's so difficult to read, study, decipher, and explain for ourselves that we cordially accept a co-opted menagerie of teachings and philosophies and preaching from others thoughts: Why re-invent the wheel? "Seek, and ye shall find (what I give you)." Or, just accept what someone else says because it sounds "cool." Yeah, that's easier. It's weak, though. Sorry, I have a brain, and I learned how *to think*.

Believe or burn! Some religions, and especially right-wing, extremist factions, really know how to play upon fears of simple folk. They speak of an ever-lasting and eternal after-life, but they warn that it will be either splendid or agonizing. Follow their truth (God's supposed *truth),* or burn in Hell's fires forever! Dear *God*, what kind of babble is that? Even the more soft-spoken, middle-of-the-road sitters have devastating finality to their tones, "Oh, no, you won't 'burn-in-hell.' You just won't go to 'Heaven!' You'll spend eternity in Purgatory until He returns. Then, you'll be given another chance to redeem yourself. His "Acceptance" is the only ticket through those Pearly-Gates. Fear not; just follow. Do what I say. I mean, what 'He says', and you'll be alright."

I'd choose the other direction seven-days-from-Sunday if it meant having to tolerate eternity with a bunch of self-righteous, zealots like that! Can you imagine? They, and their God, want to scare me into submission and into following them. "Heil Hitler!"-A promise of *security* for doing what we're told.

"Follow me, (sinner), and I shall lead the way to the Promised Land, and I shall be a 'favored-son' and help rule (over you) in Heaven!" A person has to be a very timid-soul and afraid of shadows, and death and its aftermath to believe in that line-of-crap: A *frightened-follower...* It's difficult for me to deal with such ignorance. Even if I did "believe" in that nonsense, I'd rather not spend one minute in a Heaven with people of that sort. Let me out! I'll find my own way just fine, thanks.

What's that silly quip? "Ignorance is the devil's playground!" So, we contemplate our navels. Many claim to have a standardized belief-structure which works for them. If it does help them sort out their lives, I often sense that it is just a cop-out for too many. They use their *structure* to satisfy issues which they do not want to consider or for which to find honest, realistic answers. When pressed, most do not even want to consider let alone discuss alternative meanings. Perhaps, it is a way for them to accept otherwise *unacceptable* things about themselves.

And, of course, there are always *wishy-washers*. They gravitate to whatever or whomever strikes their fancy at the time. That, in itself, is not so bad because at least they are searching for meaning and truth in their lives, and they are open to various possibilities. It is when any of them get so enamored and inflexible with their choice, any discussion and reasoning with them is impossible.

But, I like questions. I like to ask them and consider them. Mental exercise leads to mental breakthroughs. When you ask questions, you are thinking. When you are thinking, you will entertain new ideas. New ideas lead to new and deeper and higher-level contemplation. However, mental breakdowns occur to those unwavering group members who never allow any different light to shed its brilliance on their imagined paradigms. Those people are ones who seem so self-possessed, they cannot afford any wavering, let alone acknowledging and accepting reasonable debate: That every single person virtually lives by their own developed paradigm formulated over years of trial, error and experience and study, learning and socialization. None of us are the same. Thank God we are all different too. It makes life more interesting and challenging.

And then there are always those who keep asking the same questions over and over and...

OMG!

"Oh, my God!
I just don't know.
What should I think?
Where will I go?
Am I good or bad?
Should I be happy or sad... or afraid?
The anxiety drives me mad!

"Am I going to Heaven?
Is there really a Hell?
Is there any after-life at all?
Will I finally be with family,
Or better yet, with friends?
When they go in the end... (to somewhere else)
Will I ever see them again?

"Must I sit on a cloud
Playing a harp
Dressed in a shroud
In some cosmic time-warps... forever?
I don't like harps... They're too whiny...

"Will there be a second-coming?
"An 'apocalypse' in time?
If Heaven's not for sinners?
Is there something less sublime... somewhere?
For 'little-sinner types' that aren't too bad...

"What's gonna happen?
Is there really fire in Hell
With pain and anguish and suffering
For whom the bell tolls?
And who's tolling that damned bell?' Anyone I know?

"Or, is it all just bull-shit,
There's nothing afterward?
You mean, we die, and there's no more, that's it?
That's jerking too hard
On all our umbilical cords, and it hurts!

"For Heaven's sake,
I feel so used!
If nothing's left
After life's abuse.
No wonder I'm so confused...

"Earth to earth...
Ashes to ashes...
Buried so near birth...
With no free-passes...
For the ignorant masses.'

"Mismaloya Blues"

Part II:
Ignorant Masses...

How about those "ignorant masses?" Befuddled targets are some of the juiciest prey for "*pulpit*eers." Just season-up those poor saps with something spicy and reasonable to hear. Make it easy for them to read and follow the recipe, and they'll willingly dip themselves into religious stew-pots of condescending atonement. They want truth. They seek truth. If told, they'll gratefully pick-up the Good Book now, or some other similarly relentless entertainment and believe what they are told. It becomes a life's force source from which they can feed and fill the void in their easily managed and crap-sustained brains.

"See-no-evil. Hear-no-evil. Speak-no-evil." Ignorance thrives on kindred company. The simpler the "bait" is to swallow, the smaller "hook" can be used. When leading by taunting who follows, bigger fish can be fried. Ignorance is the cesspool of religion, and preachers never stop fishing there. On-the-other-hand, without ignorance or religion, preachers would have very little to talk about, would they? OMG! Educate thyself! Go fish in your own mind. It's more fun. Entertain your own brain. Do it on your own conditions.

Of course, there is always the lazy-man's way, the easy-way-out. Let someone else or something else be the guide and light-giver. If you don't have to think very hard, just regurgitate back what you read, hear and swallow. That's the slothful approach to a simpler existence. But, it is simple and convenient and non-compromising: "The answers are right here. Look for yourself. Read it. See? The truth will set you free!" Yeah, sure... Truth is I need a break from this...

No discussion, no debate, the subject is not up for review. It's like a catalog or a commercial: "It's got to be good because it says so right here in this advertisement. Look for yourself. Read it. See? I told you so!"... Just read, memorize and reproduce. Salvation is imminent... Yawn!

Some earn an advantage over others because they enjoy reading and thinking and mental exercise. They do not seek simple answers to complex questions from single sources or one book of thought. They test and challenge. True, solutions may be so basic they are difficult to recognize and accept. Nevertheless, the challenge, the ordeal and the task are so critical, and viable, they deserve attention to detail. It's not destinations which matter but rather the discourse which follows.

Read and listen and study everything possible about life and death. What we work hard to earn or learn is more meaningful than anything given to us... freely. Ask questions. Challenge what others say! Naturally, there are those who would willingly give their "truth" for free, but it isn't the same thing as earning it ourselves. Even simple minds can appreciate oppositional points-of-view and make decisions for themselves which seem practical and self-serving. After all, isn't that what we all look for in the first place? An answer that "serves us well." We should do it the hard way: Earn it! It will mean more to us.

The last group probably bothers me more than the others. It's because they think of themselves as "anointed-ones." Their purpose and mission in life is to provide salvation to the unfortunate and sinful multitudes. For them, that includes just about everyone else. Many even question the vindication of their peers. Appropriately, I suggest that they have contracted a common illness I refer to as: PSRS, or "Professional Self-Righteous Syndrome." We are led to believe that only these professionals "know-the-way," and only they can "show-the-way." Many affected, or infected, with PSRS preach and speak in emasculating garnishments suggesting, at least to themselves, esteemed eminence with God and proprietary knowledge of His word.

Some revered personalities have learned to do well within the confines of their chosen religion and sect. When they stay humbled, yet focused and ambitious, they may steadily work their way up the ecclesiastical ladder of popularity, eminence and influence. They have jobs to do, orders to follow and rules to obey. If their congregations grow, or their church's financial accounts increase, then career-opportunities will improve respectively. After all, religions are very much a business in every sense of "The Word," aren't they? Last time I looked, the Pope was the largest religious property owner in the world.

Religions offer a commodity for sale at a reasonable price: "Your saved-soul for your obedience." They have Boards-of-Directors and hierarchies of leadership which guide their decisions and movements promoting successes. Religions are distribution-centers for the weak of mind and spirit and needy. They are unique, "soulful," investment-opportunities for laymen. They are career paths for ambitious, pulpit-masters. They are gold-mines for their hierarchies.

Religions are tax-havens for the rich. They are crime-fighters and socialization instruments for societies. They are safeguards and diversions for governments and rulers. They are very powerful and influential and attempt to govern all aspects of our lives when given opportunities. Often, they are asked to do so. Often, they take control and do it on their own. Just read history books and learn for yourself.

Other crustier, grass-root philosophers prefer ranting and raving and using threatening methodology to admonish, harangue and terrorize others into obeying their will and their message-of-truth: "Our God is an angry God, and He will destroy and burn you in hell forever unless you follow His word. Fortunately, for all you sinners here listening to me today, I have "The Word" for you, and I will grant it to you freely... Just come on down!...

"All you need do is provide me "freely" a modest token of your appreciation which will allow me humble provisions and opportunities to reach-out and save others. Dig down deep in your pockets, Friends, and pay for your souls' deliverance. The more you pay, the more I'll pray for your salvation! And lucky-for-you, I've got God's ear! We're on speakin' terms, and I'll talk to Him about you! You can bet your bottom-dollar on it! In fact, put 'er there! Right there in the basket, Friend. Amen. Hallelujah! Lord be praised and pass the basket!"

To be fair, organized religions have done some good. Decent, kind, well-meaning followers supposedly adhere to strict codes-of-behavior. Sometimes, it's that "behavior" that worries me, though. But, church leaders and parishioners provide many benefits to the needy. They offer faith, hope and charity to those who might not otherwise survive. Baptisms, marriages and burials keep checks on their flocks within tangible, governing realms-of-influence from birth-to-death.

For tithing and donations, preachers teach and offer believers eternal, desirable and colorful afterlives far more appealing than the difficult and painful existences some of their parish's "flock" in this life. They counsel, direct and administer to the needs of their congregations keeping everyone in compliance and supportive of the church and its leadership. Cleric attempt to give meaning, purpose and order to a chaotic world.

To me: *The mind is such a terrible thing to waste* on one form of *believing.* I study historical growth and spread of organized religions in the world including Judaism, Christianity, Islam, Hinduism, Zen, Confucianism, and a multitude of others. I also study viewpoints of agnostics and atheists. It is evident that all these groups have played significant roles in world history. They have spear-headed the world's amazing growth and development, and they have ushered-in destruction and utter damage of societies and governments and nations throughout history.

If they share glory, they must share shame. I enjoy comparing and contrasting them all. I seek to examine, review and determine each religion's overall contribution to the betterment of the world, its regions, nations, and people they are supposed to serve. Naturally, given circumstances of our present, chronically similar world-conditions, this "search" remains a "work-in-progress."

At least, it is a solution or examination that serves me. At first glance, I am pretty hard on organized religions. I'm another couch-potato philosopher who quips, "I am faithful; I'm just not religious." Fact is, I'm very much both. I simply have problems and issues with "organized-faith." I recognize its good deeds and value, but I wonder if we might not have prospered even more as a species without it. There was a time, perhaps, when religions were relevant and useful organizing and educating, tending to poor and sharing its magnificence. Sadly, too often religions shared ignorance and superstitions instead while craving gold and power.

I am reminded of a story of certain impoverished, African nations... The citizenry share their dismal history with this lament: "Once, our mighty nation's people were proud and industrious. They were overjoyed with gold and prosperity. Then, the foreigners came with their religions. Now, we have their religions, and they have our gold."

Africa is no exception. That story is a metaphorical example of world-wide, historically similar case-studies. ***Mexicanos*** can relate. Once, magnificent civilizations such as the Aztec and Mayan existed and ruled empires here for hundreds of years. The Mayans lived and ruled over thousands of years and are still surviving within Mexican culture. The incredible Incas Empire lived further south but still dominated their Andean region for over a hundred years. Yet, they all caved-in to religious invaders. Furthermore, let's not forget how Native American Indians were "civilized."

The point is that the world was connected by outreach-programs sponsored by various governments for economic and power gains. It was then converted by the same "outreach-programs" who were sponsored, instead, by religions for economic and power gains. *Rule their souls and you rule their pockets.* Talk about teamwork... government sponsored religions.

Then, *holibejeebees!* I wonder how things might have been had we left everything to politicians, God forbid! Pun intended! Unfortunately, preachers and politicians seem to be comfortably in bed with each other... in manipulations, er, well, in matters, not sexual... except... no, I digress. One depends on the other, yet both hold themselves in higher regard. Both believe they are serving the highest-calling, God and Public-Service. Sadly, both typically seem to focus mostly on "serving" themselves. Apparently, it's a nice view from the top especially when one is not caught in the muck below.

I believe, however, that humanity is slowly transcending to higher-levels of consciousness, understanding and communion among nations. It will not long require potent, religious bases to encourage peace, growth and stability. Nor will humanity tolerate for much longer the promotion and spread of hatred, bigotry, prejudice, nationalism, war, killing, and death. However, organized religions and resourceful leaders continue to carve out niches for themselves remaining active, viable and comfortable. They still maintain enormous power, riches and influence and will continue to do so for as long as they can get away with it.

In the meantime, I shall continue to carve out my own philosophical niche which keeps me active, viable and comfortable. Hopefully, I'll continue to do so for a long time too. To-each-their-own, I guess. Just don't try to tread on my beliefs, though. My grass just seems a little greener to me, that's all.

PREACHERS ALLEGE

Preachers allege they talk to *God*
Who tells them how to pray.
But, I deny with snubbing nods;
Sermons won't show the way.
For, I have always felt it odd
Fresh ideas are kept at bay
When preachers teach us to applaud,
Yet lead our minds astray.

Church shouldn't tithe for Godly sense.
We talk to ***Him*** for free.
Exemplify what ***Jesus*** did;
Interpret without fees.
Souls are not sold once we confess;
Preaching will never *let-us-be*.
His ***Word*** comes within to caress,
And seeking truth is key.

God's light is ***love*** we all receive;
It's here for free taking,
And it only requires beliefs
Which cease our forsaking.
Light's love comes from what is conceived
In bodies', minds' and spirits' makings.
Be not confused; others deceive.
It is *awakening.*

Seek answers from your impressions.
Lives are here on-purpose.
Finding our ways is tradition
Not meant to make us nervous.
God's ***universal*** creations,
Love is everywhere in surplus.
Giving is our simple mission,
And ***God's light*** will surface.

“Mismaloya Blues”

Part 12:
Together Again...

When you strategize, politicize and exercise together, chances are you'll plan as far as both you might go together. We finally reconnected on our third, no, fourth encounter with this exotic location. Angelina was finally rejoining me at the end of September. She had taken care of all the required family details and business details, locked the car in the garage, set the house-alarm and was driven to the airport for her exotic getaway to her awaiting husband in Puerto Vallarta.

She wasn't returning a minute too soon either. Under normal circumstances, no couple should be separated like we were for nearly two-months. It wasn't right that she remain at home dealing with continuing struggles of family-support, and I was carrying-on a quasi-bachelor existence in La-La Land! The obvious solution, naturally, was for me to go back home, focus and concentrate on family-issues, and once everything was resolved, then make plans to return to La-La Land, if possible...if convenient...if appropriate... NOT! I wasn't going anywhere!

So, I went to the airport to await my escape-artist wife who was finally on-her-way here! Of course, a small influence on Angelina's current decision to finally join me may have been all the phone-calls and e-mails I placed. Daily whining and pleading could have eventually broken her resistance. I convinced her that she was really needed here to keep me company. All this surf-and-sun was too much for one to handle alone. It worked! She would be with me for the final month of this three-month stay in lovely Mismaloya.

This time, we are planning to return home together in time to break out Ol' Mr. Bones for my almost-annual Halloween Festival. "Bones" is our six-foot, Tuxedo and top-hat dressed skeleton who haunts our front porch during late October through Halloween night to spice-up the occasion. He has an attached motion-detector, so he starts flopping around and haunting every passer-by with prerecorded, silly and humorous, scary messages every time someone moves. Each year, and this year in particular because we were in PV for the last one, old, "Mr. Bones" amuses us at first; however, after the twentieth go-around of generic, wise-cracks, we are ready to put him back in the storage-box for another year of agreeable exile.

But, I 'm getting ahead of myself... We have a full-month ahead yet to share as husband-and-wife again in Paradise. Adam and Eve! And Eden is just down the road, around the bend and up the hill. Oooohhh boy! Where's that apple tree? I'm hungry! During a two-month sojourn apart, each of us was forced to re-connect with our private, solo-existences and reflect on the disadvantages of living alone, or at least without each other's "significant-other." Truth-be-known, no doubt, we would both concur that there's distinct advantages for us both, but fortunately, there are disadvantages!

For instance, our marriage-of-commitment does not allow for too much frivolous and scandalous fantasizing. At some point, one-or-the-other partners steps into the psychic, babble-drama and puts an end to all the whimsical, nonsensical and mental video-taping of extra-marital fantasies. It was time for us both to focus on real-life and present-day reality. We have a good marriage and a lifelong commitment on which to focus. Good thing, too, because I was just starting to have some fun! She probably was too, so let's reset that camera. This is supposed to be a story about two love-birds in Paradise. Let's see what happens... Lights!.. Action!.. Camera!.. "Hey, Babe, what's for dessert?"

THE DRINKIN' SONG

Thank god the bars are open
'Cause I need a place to think,
And while I'm figurin'
These messes I'm in,
I'll just have me a little drink.

The banks keep callin' for money;
No food's in the kitchen to eat;
My kids' got clothes
With holes everywhere.
I need that bar just down this street.

The landlord is gettin' nervous
'Bout me missin' another month's rent,
But I ain't been workin'
Since I can remember,
So thinkin' and drinkin's a vent!

Clothes can be fixed with stitchin'.
Landlords 'n' lenders 'll have to wait.
I'll borrow some beans
From next-door-neighbors,...
Yeah, this drinkin' is easin' my fate.

So, Barkeep, pour me another;
Make 'er a double for where I'm bound.
If this lottery ticket
Comes up a winner,
I'll be back for another round.

Thank God the bars are open
'Cause I need a place to think,
And while I'm figurin'
These messes I'm in,
I'll just have me another drink.

"Mismaloya Blues"

Part 13: Fun in the Sun...

October is still part of the rainy-season down here. The rain really begins in June and continues right on up to November. October is still warm too. The days can be steamy with modest humidity, and its enough invitation to maintain a substantial existence for some insects. Oh, they have tapered-off tremendously compared to August and September, but rest assured, some are still around.

Angelina and I have our hands full keeping the critters in-check. She just does not realize, or remember from last year, the significant differences. No huger, flying bugs the size of canaries smashing into the glass or screened-windows and doors. No more, or vastly fewer, tiny, little, blood-sucking, black flying-insects easily crawling through the screens and lying-in-wait on the bed-coverings and anywhere else they chose, like my body. Vigilant cleaning and spraying warded them off, but before Angelina's arrival, they got their fill from me. Now, they're mostly gone. There're still some mosquitoes hanging around, but it's drying up for them, and the air is changing. Thank goodness! Angelina doesn't have to struggle like I did. We can concentrate on relaxing and not repelling bugs.

We had participated in almost all the typical, tourist-attractions in the area last year ***(ano pasado)***. We had wanted to see as much we could during our first, three-month escapade. So, we planned visiting everything possible from ***San Blas*** in the north to ***Manzanillo*** in the south to ***San Sebastian*** in the east and westward into the bay with several ***Bahia de Banderas*** boat-excursions. In every direction were interesting, entertaining and varied sights and sounds and activities to please our curious, tourist natures.

Boca de Tomatlan, a quaint and small village for fishing, tourism and water-taxi port and just a few kilometers from our residence, served as a getaway base for many excursions. We had taken the small, taxi-boats to several distant, lovely and private beach communities of ***Playas las Animas***, ***Quimixto*** and ***Yelapa***. Each was uniquely different in lifestyle and community offerings, yet similarly promoted their own charm and personal qualities of solitude and service.

Playas Yelapa was probably the most well-to-do, private community. It attracted major tourism with long-term rentals and home-owners from around-the-world probably due to its inviting economy and distant seclusion and beauty. Each beach destination was accessible only by water-taxi, so the communities were serene, quiet, peaceful, and pleasurable. The boat-rides, however, were just as bouncy and bone-jarring as the town bus-rides, it seemed, but you could choose a particular destination based on distance and time or personal, sight-seeing desires. From all locales you could find beach-and-surf relaxation, Mexican and seafood cuisine, jungle-hikes, horseback-riding, or just pleasant meanderings through authentic, ramshackle, beach-front communities. Lovely trips, each of them.

One of the biggest deals of PV and another near-bye, beautifully private beach offered a world-famous, evening extravaganza and exclusive event, Rhythms of the Night. Only available for transport from the city's marina harbor, tickets were practically available everywhere from the literally dozens of tourist-attraction vendors. On our assigned reservation day, we took that evening's scenic cruise across Banderas Bay to the isolated cove of ***Las Caletas***. It was a stunning and exclusive beach and a colorful backdrop for our evening's entertainment.

Once shuttled from the cruise boat to shore by smaller craft, we were escorted to the dining area. There, everyone was treated to a wonderful, buffet of steak, chicken or fish complimented with fresh vegetables, salads, tortillas, and an open-bar. Once mealtime was finished, we were all ushered to a jungle-setting, semi-amphitheater for an exhilarating and hypnotically entertaining show. Often comical, always fascinating, an excellent and talented dance-troupe performed a magical spectacle interweaving history with innovative and contemporary music and dance. Finally, the romantic, moonlit cruise-ride home capped-off one of Puerto Vallarta's highlight destinations and amazingly beautiful and unique experiences. Anyone in Puerto Vallarta can tell you about it and give directions.

Alright, enough of that... There is so much to see and do in Puerto Vallarta, but I'm not turning my story into an exotic-destinations, travel-brochure. I'll touch on some of the specific sights and sounds that we encountered and visited along-the-way, but I'm going to skip most of the rabid and touristy, mambo-jumbo of destination-fever. There's so many inner-feelings regarding my new, tentative life in Puerto Vallarta which I must first challenge myself to explore.

Quickly, I want to return to the main focus of this tour-d-force, romantic saga. I need to describe the personal, emotional and soulful transformations which took place for Angelina and me. I must tell our epic journey's tale of two, forlorn lovers. Beginning as lonely, pathetic, shallow, and transparent vacationers, they become lost within the deepest, darkest and evil jungles of the Amazon. But, fate evolves within as they become righteous and clairvoyant, travel-brochure writers.

Oh, wait! No! Just a minute... That's not this story. That's a highlighted excerpt from my next science-fiction novel. Like I said earlier, it's so tranquil around here, I get carried away and lost in my thoughts and fantasies. Whew! I'd better knock that off and get back to reality. Angelina's here! I've got to stop worshiping my imagination and start worshiping her. And that's the "truth!" But, first, some messages from our sponsors...

If you want to have a little fun-in-the-wild around PV, you can rent a car and drive up to ***San Blas***. It's a couple hours north on the coast, but it's an interesting and scenic drive. Several fun stops are available on-the-way for exploration including Alligator Isle. Once arrived, you can catch a jungle-boat ride and motor deep inside the sloughs of tepid, fresh and ocean-water to watch live alligators sunning themselves while eerily watching you watching them. There's lots of other wild-life with gorgeous foliage too. It's a fun day-trip. ***San Blas*** is another quaint, coastal town with expansive, spectacular beaches and many beachfront restaurants for inexpensive meals or fine dining.

Still north from PV, but accessible by local, PV buses is the slightly more exclusive community of ***Sayulita.*** Attractive town, great beaches and lots of tan bodies lying everywhere. It's got all the typical ocean activities you could desire, or you can rent and ride horses until your bu--blisters. It's a little pricier than PV probably because of the "exclusivity" and elusiveness. It's a well-kept village and very clean. However, it's a bit too shiny for my tastes. It has a sort of cookie-house, tacky and unauthentic look to it. Very *tourist* oriented. However, its a little different and fun, though. I'm told Europeans really favor this coastal community.

Within the same general area, and also available directly by buses from the PV ***Zona de Marina*** near the Walmart/Sam's Club complex, is ***Punta Mita***. It's also an upper-end resort community with golf courses and gala tourist stuff, but it has a special highlight. From there, you can catch a fun, group-boat ride to the distant ***Islas Marietas***, a small group of islands once used for Naval weapons target practice but now a tourist-attraction, swimming site. With required life-jackets on, everyone jumps overboard and swims to the islands for frolicking and fun. There're caves to explore and a beautiful, hidden beach for relaxing. Lots of Kodak moments arise, and they even provide secure shuttles for anyone's camera equipment to be brought in to the main-attraction island for tourists..

Once again, however, I must use my breezy and delightful, touring-entries as a clever segue to digress for a moment...

My loving wife, Angelina, along with her sister, Teresa, who had joined us for a week's visit and this day-trip, both jumped into the ocean and swam to shore with me and the others. Yeah? What's so special about that? Neither of them can swim! Both are relatively terrified of water depths anywhere near their waistlines. But, with enthusiasm as their propulsion and sheer trust as their guides, they swam to the islands, or dog-paddled, and did so against a moderately abrasive current.

I was so astonished and proud of them that I could spit. Actually, I did. I was so shocked and amused and laughing, my mouth was agape, and I swallowed plenty sea-water. But they made it there and back again, and they both had a fun time on the island between rather nervous ventures from and to the boat. Trust and courage: Both are wonderful, amazing and very complementary qualities. I was so proud I bought them both dinners. Oh, alright. So, what if I was the only one with any money that day! My treat! Happy to reward and toast them!

Okay. Where were we? Let's return again to the topic of "tourist-traps." Or, rather I mean, "...valuable, worthy and entertaining 'attractions' in the beautiful, serene and tourist-friendly Puerto Vallarta area."

Honestly, there are so many more inexpensive and noteworthy places which we visited that I certainly feel compelled mentioning a few others. Although any specific day can be designed with a variety of activities and tourist-sites to visit, price-ranges can vary significantly. However, lots of activities will complement any budget, and there are a few which we heard about, ventured to and truly enjoyed. They were worth every peso spent, and they all really helped make our short-term, vacation rendezvous a special memory.

Like anything, though, there are some occasional risks involved. Try to be aware of what you are doing and what you expect. Angelina and I have plenty of stories of others having taken advantage of us. However, it's useful to remember that tourists need to be careful. Like any barter-system economy, even if Mexico is a "modified" one, prices for many open-ended activities can vary dramatically. It often depends on who from and where you get your tickets.

Most attraction-tickets are sold on a commission-basis. Even though there is a base price, any vendor may try to get top-dollar for his sale. It means, "Mo money!" Just refuse at first, attempt bartering, and if you have time, check elsewhere. But, salespeople will not let you leave easily and will attempt to get your business. Just "... make-'em-an-offer-they-can't-refuse."

Ah, ah, ah! No guns, no bloodshed! Mexico is pretty mellow, but their laws are very severe. I hear you do not want to get arrested or go to jail even in tranquil Puerto Vallarta. ***Morditas*** (little bites), or rather illegal, police pay-offs, can be an occasional, cultural reality to avoid some issues, I have been told. However, any violations, regardless of circumstances, are obviously best avoided. Back to the fun, though...

Like credited to ***Sayulita*** and the boat-taxi, beach and resort communities of ***Yelapa*** and ***Quimixto***, horse-back riding is popular, plentiful and available at numerous locations throughout Puerto Vallarta and its surrounding neighborhoods. Even in my beautiful ***Mismaloya***, which is normally a sleepy and relaxing resort community, there are horses for rent. Although it's a larger, outlying zone of ***Puerto Vallarta***, ***Mismaloya*** has plenty going on. Its resorts and beach workers offer a variety of fishing and ocean activities. One vendor in particular, however, owns a stable and rents horses to anyone for riding. You can follow a guide up the canyon and venture all the way to another popular, tourist-attraction. Remember my mentioning Schwarzenegger's Predator film site? There you have it! It's "Yippee ki-yay!" Sadly, though, their ponies do look a little worse for wear.

The largest touring and activity provider in Puerto Vallarta is Vallarta Adventures. Whatever you may wish to entertain yourself with, within reason and legality, they can get you there and on your way. Vallarta Adventure's open-sided, tourist trucks and buses are seen regularly carrying passengers to all sorts of exciting destinations and activities. Certainly, they can hook-you-up with many of the horse-back stables all around PV and beyond.

And they can take you on seemingly endless adventures. Go hiking, biking, motorcycling, ATVing, zip-lining, bungee-jumping, cruising, fishing, jet-skiing, para-sailing, tequila-tasting, touring, and even sea-shell hunting, if that's what floats-your-boat. You want some unique, special activity? They can probably arrange for you to get it. Entertaining adventure-lovers is their job, and they're pretty good at it.

City-bus tours may be a bit of a con, though. They bus you around on a scenic and informative, getaway city-tour and conveniently stop at multiple tourist-trap locations to sell you silver, souvenirs, tequila, and unique dining. There's got to be kick-backs involved, but that's not unusual, and it certainly livens up the escapade. It's "Buyer-beware," though! The silver might turn green if it gets wet; "souvenirs" might come from China; tequila is usually satisfactory but is likely way over-priced; and a cuisine experience may be costly for a restaurant's tourist zone location. Nobody is forced to buy anything, though, so it's always up to the individual. For me, I now possess a collection of *verde de plata* (green silver) jewelry to match my naivete, official sombreros straight from Beijing, empty tequila bottles to remind me of undesired brands, and an empty stomach.

But now it's back on the tour-circuit plan again, and there are countless roads and highways to take you to all sorts of interesting places. San Francisco, the locals call it San Pancho, is a fitting destination because it's a quiet, authentic and really fun, oceanfront town. Plus, it's fitting because my son-in-law is named Francisco, and we all call him "Pancho." However, he is not "quiet" but definitely authentic!

Heading inland toward Guadalajara, also in the State of Jalisco, just like Puerto Vallarta is the wonderful, out-of-the-way, and remote village of San Sebastian. Fairly small as villages go, this town is like stepping into-the-past. Everything looks like it looked a hundred fifty years ago. An old town square, a beautiful church, and a single-cell jail all offered appealing authenticity. Nice.

If you are willing to rent a car and brave the crazy drivers in town, then you will open-up a universe of new opportunities and places and activities.

There are numerous rental agencies in town to accommodate your needs, but just use precaution. It is always highly recommended to rent a car with the maximum insurance available. True, it can get pricey, but it is insurance against the worstcase scenarios. No issues, you are only out some money. If you have an accident with minimal insurance, or none, you may be in for a nasty showdown. That could be a time when the "mordita" factor plays into matters to avoid it altogether,and get adequate insurance.

Anyway, with your new (insured) rental all you need is a map, curiosity, Google, if you've got it, and you are set for a treat. Fact is, if you're anything like me, it wouldn't matter which way you drove. It's all new, different, exciting, and you can't get lost because you just keep driving until you get somewhere. Learn this phrase right now: "?Donde esta...?" or "Donde hay...?" (Where is...?) It works for so many things: Donde esta Puerto Vallarta? ?Donde esta la bahia? ?Donde esta el bano? (Where is the bathroom?) ?Donde hay un buen restaurante mexicana? Or, my favorite: ?Donde estoy? (Where am I?) However, "Donde esta el bano?" is my most commonly used phrase. Of course, I always preface the question with, "Por favor, mi amigo(a)" and then "Muchas gracias!" They're the two best phrases in any language...or three!

It will be exciting to see how far you can go with your new car, and it will be rewarding to see how far you can get with your Spanish. The Vallartans, and Mexican people in general, are very kind, helpful and courteous as seems to be a natural part of their cultural behavior.

Kindness to them, or anyone for that matter, usually always generates kindness in return. I cannot speak for other "travelers" when away from home, but I love my country, and I am proud of the USA. Therefore, when I am visiting a foreign country, I want to leave a positive-impression. I feel like I'm sort of an honorary "Ambassador-at-Large," so-to-speak. I appreciate native locals' hospitality, their beautiful country and wonderful climate. I am a guest, though, and I always act accordingly.

Let's leave "rental-car businesses," for a moment, though. Rental cars can sure expand your horizons, but they are hardly necessary. Here, in Puerto Vallarta, the city's incredible bus-system takes you almost anywhere you want or need to go. Just learn routes, ask people at bus stops, read destinations on bus's front-windows, and you are good-to-go.

I mentioned earlier that I enjoy taking buses and just riding along to see where it goes. I know if I stay on it long enough, it will return me to my initial starting point, so I have no fear of getting lost. I also know that no matter where I get off the bus, another will be coming along shortly which can allow me to continue explorations. We have discovered some really interesting and beautiful locations that way and also some pretty delicious, authentic, cocina mexicana.

Earlier in the story, I also mentioned about all the souvenir shops and galleries and storefronts which can fill any day's adventure needs. The buses can get you to a new location anytime you wish. Furthermore, the further away from the central area you travel, the more likely it is that you will be dealing with only resident-locals, and the language-barrier will likely become a factor. But, it is a real treat to learn and attempt communicating with these kind and hard-working people in their own tongue and in their own backyards.

Oh, sure, sometimes, when I speak, they look at me with as much confusion as I feel trying to say something, but it's all done with well-meaning. If the little communication session ends up successfully, we both part with a smile. I guess we do. Maybe, as I walk away they are shuddering and shaking their heads in bewilderment, and I'm just smiling and walking away. Sometimes, for both of us it's, "No entiendo!" (I don't understand), but we tried. Although I may butcher their beautiful language, I believe they appreciate that I try. They are usually cordial and supportive. Hablo un poco de espanol ahora, but I'll learn more.

Well, that highlights the city's tours and activities on land. I did forget to mention the wild and crazy night-life. From my balcony in Mismaloya, I can see the city lights of Puerto Vallarta as illuminating proof that it's a city that does not sleep. Something is going on somewhere all the time. There are the dance clubs, the exotic bars, and the casinos which are 24x7. Some nightclubs along the Malecon remain open all-night long, too, to accommodate the night-crawlers, I guess. Of course, this is second-hand information, please note. Pure speculation. But, like I said, "I can see the lights!" However, the Chapman household lights are going out earlier than those. After all, I need to get my beauty-sleep, so I can get up early tomorrow and go to the beach and take a nap!

What I should do to conclude this travel-log portion of my story is write a little bit about, probably, the most important aspect of Puerto Vallarta's mystique... La Bahia de Banderas! After all, it was on a cruise-ship which brought Angelina and me to this incredible bay and parked at the "port" right in the marina-zone next to Walmart. For goodness sake, it is "Puerto Vallarta," Port Vallarta! The wonderful and modern marina is actually one of the more recent improvements. Although it's been here and active for a hundred fifty years, it was not until the federal government got involved in the 1980's and 1990's focusing on PV's tourism potential. The government sanctioned developing the international airport and the important cruise-ship welcoming marina.

This beautiful bahia and marina are a port-of-call to Vallarta's number one industry, tourism. Cruise ships from nearly every cruise line visit this fun stop-over for a day's excursion. The Bay of Banderas is a beautiful, protected and smooth ride for those monstrous "floating cities." Each time one arrives, two thousand or more tourists disembark for a day's frivolity. That's money in the city's till, and it's a driving force for the port and the city. The bay got them here, just like it did for us a few years ago...

Now, it may be true that even more people visit Puerto Vallarta by plane. Dozens of aircraft from many airlines from all-over-the-world fly into Puerto Vallarta International Airport (PVR) every day. Where are most of these visitors staying? At the resorts, of course. And where are most of these resorts located? On the beaches! It's the Bahia de Banderas and its countless, pristine beach-front properties that drew the resorts. People love the sandy and even rocky shoreline. They come here to take advantage of everything the water can offer.

It really is a spectacular bay. Cruise ships are coming through three and four times a week and more. Party boats of all shapes and sizes churn along all day long heading for various beach destinations, or for whale-watching. Swimming, snorkeling and scuba, surfing and jet-skiing, kayaking and para-sailing, and motor-boating, yachting and sailing can easily fill-up a day's activities on the bay. Everyone is out there having a good time.

Go Fish!...

Of course, one of the most popular and famous Bahia de Banderas experiences is sport-fishing. The hard-core, avid fishermen or first-time enthusiasts can rent a boat with its captain to take them into deep water and a thrill of a lifetime. Captains typically muse, "The big-ones will not get away today!" From my experience and stories heard, everyone comes back with a catch. These boats and their captains go out to deep water for some serious sport and others for serious fun. Big catches like Tuna, Marlin or Sailfish require longer and further outings. Thus, those excursions will take longer and likely cost more.

However, the main game for half-day excursions (four hours) are Marlin, Sailfish and Dorado (Mahi-Mahi or Dolphin fish). It partly depends on the season, but it's always a good idea to wear a hat and bring along sun-block. Usually up to four or five passengers can go along which proportionately lowers the cost per person. Everyone is responsible for their own lunches, snacks and beverages. The price ranges between $160-$200 for four hours. However, as I mentioned, bigger catches may require longer outings and, therefore, potentially twice as much.

The entire experience includes the boat-ride and trip, all gear, supplies, assistance, and the captain's knowledge and experience. You're not going to catch Moby Dick, but if it's the season December through March, you sure might see some acrobatic, humpback-whales. Often, dolphins are whooping it up for fun and thrills too while chasing boats and whales. Not the type of dolphin fish you want to catch, but it's in the same family species, I guess. Ooops! Your decision.

For an unforgettable and relatively inexpensive experience, the local sport-fishing may be pretty much unequaled. Did I mention, "Whatever you catch you keep!" Throw it back, give it away, eat it, or have it sent home for a souvenir.

The locals are fully aware of the attributes of PV's fishing industry. The fishermen are always prepared to call ahead, if necessary and wanted, and have a local taxidermist available to assist an avid visitor-tourist fisherman and stuff the catch of a lifetime. Additionally, in November each year in Puerto Vallarta comes the world-famous Marlin-Sailfish tournament offering fame and fortune to the fortunate winner. Fishing is a seriously big-deal in Puerto Vallarta!

A Fish Story!...

Now is a good time to convince you that not all fairy tales are "fish stories." Some *fishy tales* are true. Take a read of our own experience... My wife's young son, Adam, came to PV to spend a week visiting us and taking in the sights. He is an avid fisherman and has caught fish just about everywhere he has tried. Deep-sea fishing, however, was one form of fishing that he had only attempted once before as a young child with his father. Coming to Puerto Vallarta was a definite challenge for him, and he was excited and eager to try his skill and luck.

Before his arrival, Angelina and I had researched the various fishing zones for potential boat rentals and captains for our outing. We settled on a friend of ours, Sr. Ricardo Petrocena, who sold excursions for various activities to local tourists. We arranged for a full-day, eight-hour venture to the distant, deep seas to hunt for the big ones. Actually, a key factor was that our friend's arranged boat had an on-board bathroom to accommodate Angelina's needs. After all, eight hours is a good while. Me? I've got no shame out at sea, but my lady? C'mon!

Up, at the crack-of-dawn, a taxi-ride to the Marina Zone and our host met us at dockside to escort us to the boat. We purchased a few, inexpensive items to add to our prepared lunches. Okay, it was cerveza, of course! Then, we headed to the boat. It was named *Kathy*

II, and it was nice. It was a 22' Seafarer launch with a large umbrella cover. Nice for shade. It was plenty big enough for five people.

The boat had twin, 150 CC Evinrude outboard engines to power us nicely across the relatively calm ocean waters. There were two back-seats for fishing chairs and plenty of room up front to lounge away the day... my style. The boat was also geared with seven, heavy-duty, ocean-fishing rods at the ready. Also, on board was a large, built-in tank for live bait. We looked like we were ready for bear. Well, that's just an expression. There're no bears in the ocean,... are there?

Our driver and man-in-charge was *Captain Freddie*. Of course, the local joke is that the Captain is always the Master-Fisherman, and his first-mate is always the Master-Baiter! All our introductions completed, the five of us set sail. Well, actually, there were no sails, but rather it was a big motor boat with a ***bano.***

Our captain steered us smoothly out the harbor and straight toward the ***Islas Marietas*** and beyond. About ninety minutes out from shore, the first-mate prepped the fishing lines and poles, baited the hooks and set the rods for trolling. We were fishing, or rather the boat was, but we were there in attendance with full gear and attitude enjoying the moments!

Barely underway, Angelina and I were already stretched out enjoying the sun and sea. From the get-go, Adam sat frozen in a fishing chair. It was obvious that he was staring intently at the rods and their lines. His gaze never seemed to leave the half-dozen baits skipping along the sea's surface at varying distances behind our boat. Angelina and I were ready for nice naps; Adam was ready for "Thar she blows!" It was my kind of fishing: Let the boat do the work.

Adam admitted later on after the fishing expedition, though, that he did not like giving up the rod to the boat's rod-holder. He really prefers salmon fishing or striped bass or trout where he does everything. He gets to search, hunt, find, tease, taunt and snag the fish, himself. Nevertheless, Adam was deep into the experience, waiting and diligently watching.

After nearly four hours out to sea, we had seen nothing, and we were all getting a little anxious or bored. The all-day fee for the boat and crew and rigging and assistance was around $340, so we hoped to get something for our money, if not our trouble. I had minimally hoped for something to eat that night and maybe something else to give away as gifts to friends or well-wishers.

I mean, nobody in their right mind (most fishermen aren't) wants to spend all day in a boat at sea and not catch anything. However, I had already heard of several other expeditions and outings of several hours where their catches were limited or nothing. Oh, well, I was relaxed, though. Only once did I need to relieve myself while out there. I mentioned as much to the captain, and he had his mate hand me a small bucket. He asked in earnest, "Is this okay? Is it too big?"

I laughed, and retorted, "Hell, no! It's *way* too small!" Then I added with my best gravely, Mexican accent, "Bucket? Bucket? I don' need no stinkin' bucket!" Of course, I immediately scanned my audience to note any scowls due to any potentially offensive behavior. No way. I got the laughs I anticipated.

Then, when I began unzipping my swimming trunks to relieve myself over the side of the boat, the mate cautioned, "Don't go on the motor!"

I laughed, quickly pointed out to sea, looked sternly at the mate and responded seriously, "Don't worry, I'll aim way out there!" Then I quickly let out a shivering, "Brrrr!" added a gushing, "Wow! That ocean is cold... and deep too!"

Again, the desired laugh. It was one of those special *male-bonding* moments. Then, I went back up-front to my special spot. I noticed right away that Angelina wasn't as amused as the others with my *Shrekish* behavior, but what can I say? She has little sense of humor... when it comes to my jokes anyway! Aye, mates! Regardless, everything was swell. I was *relieved,* and I was getting a tan, sippin' on a cerveza, feelin' *tranquil*, and I was fishin'. Life was good...

Suddenly, a shout came from the mate: "There's one! It's going for the bait! Steer into it!" We were all on our feet and watching in awe. A huge, dark, spear-nosed fish leaped high into the air and crashed down into the boat's wake and submerged. Then, it broke the surface again leaping high into the air, twisting and turning and crashing down again in the wake's surf. Honestly, it looked like it was chasing us. It was zigzagging coming right at us.

My mind was racing as I recalled those thrilling, reading-moments of whale-hunting accounts from Herman Melville's *Moby Dick* . I excitedly focused on that greatly feared, albino whale, *Moby Dick,* and the revengeful search to kill it by the obsessed, and likely insane, Captain Ahab. An incredible, heart-pounding segment detailed that legendary, ambiguous, yet fantastic whale charging Ahab's whaling vessel, the *Pequod,* in angry defiance, or subjective intolerance or even sheer evil? The subject is still debated today 160 plus years later in literature classes. It still remains my favorite book of all time... next to Mario Puzo's *Godfather.* Sorry, I'm a sucker for rags-to-riches stories.

Of course, back to my present senses, I realized that our fine, energetic visitor/attacker was black, not white. It had a big, long bill for a nose, not a battering ram like Moby. And it was a fish, not a mammal, sperm whale. But that is what is so much fun about imagination. That's where "fish tales" come from. Everybody who tries or accomplishes catching a fish imagines that they *hooked* onto Moby Dick. Well, at least I do. Or, rather, I did, once, when I caught a monster fish in the Yuba River as a teenager. Oh, alright, it turned out to be a big, fat sucker-fish, and I caught it with my bare hands, but I was thrilled. *Thar she blows!* The bigger, the faster, the badder, the better. When the fish races, let your imagination compete with it. If it gets away, or even if you catch it, let the contest determine its final size. The older the story, or the more retelling, the bigger!

Back to our fishing expedition that incredible day... Swiftly, Captain Freddie reared right cutting in front of the frantic fish. He shouted out loudly to his partner, "It's a big Marlin! It's chasing the bait! Grab the pole!" The mate grabbed a nearby fishing rod, but it was already too late. The Marlin was gone.

That huge, black fish had charged after us, leaped into our mindful vision, dazzled us with its brilliant bravado, and then, with a seemingly similar urgency, left us as swiftly as it had come. It was as though it were warning us to stay out of its territory. We were all thrilled, though, and highly energized and encouraged. Even the captain and his mate were hyped and joyfully chatted about the encounter. They had apparently been going through a long, dry spell with big, sport-fishing, so they had been reluctant, but now were excited, to tell us.

After a little while, things calmed down again. We went back into our previous routines. I was sipping and tanning, Angelina was watching the ocean and Adam was intensely focused on the trolling fish-lines. A couple of casual Tortuga floated by completely unaware or uncaring of our presence as we cruised on. A dolphin skipped alongside us briefly for our pleasure, or his own. Dozens of seagulls and pelicans lay casually around in groups on the open water. I think I saw some of them yawning. They were probably waiting and preying on some ignorant fish to come swimming by as an easy dinner. Or, they were all exhausted from earlier efforts and were just kickin' back relaxing, sunning, and taking in the pleasures of the day. Life was good for them too.

Then, just as abruptly as before, but this time it was Adam, his loud, cheering yell hailed out excitedly, "The line! The line! Fish on! Fish on!" We all jumped up again and raced for the rear of the boat to be near Adam and all the fishing equipment and commotion. We watched as the mate rushed to Adam's side, grabbed the pole from its holder nearest Adam and gave it a swift jerk.

"Here! Quickly, take it!" the mate yelled. Immediately, I stepped back out of the way to let Adam ease back into his chair. This was going to be his fight, his catch and his fish. The mate handed the pole to Adam and swiftly adjusted it between his legs on the seat.

After brief instructions, the mate stepped back to watch as Adam fleetly took over full-control of the fishing rod. Instantly, Adam was thrust into a momentous conflict struggling against an unimaginably powerful force fighting and challenging Adam's mental maintenance and grip. It was a battle between the *energy of escape* versus the *will to hold on for dear life!*

Previously, the first-mate had set all the tension-levels on the various reels while Captain Freddie steered and courted us all out to sea. The mate had then re-checked the reels again when he baited the hooks with live bait or lures and tossed them over and into the boat's white-washed wake. All that time and effort seemed to make little difference for Adam's struggle.

The reel buzzed and whizzed and whirred unfazed as it unstoppably spun from the angry, anguished and desperate fish fighting, pulling and dragging the line from Adam's pole as it attempted to escape and race away. Adam's arms were bulged and tensed with blood vessels nearly exploding. Every muscle strained to an intensely hardened state while he fought and forced himself to maintain his grasp of the deeply arched and cruelly, bending rod. We were all frantically hollering encouraging words, "You've got it Adam! Hang in there! Fight 'em!" Yet, all we could do was stand by in helpless and delirious but emotional requiem just watching. Everyone understood that it was Adam's battle to win... or lose. He was absolutely smack in the middle of a once-in-a-lifetime quest.

After a moment, in spectacular awe, we all caught sight of the monster! It was an enormous Sailfish, and it leaped and struggled and weaved back and forth in our boat's froth. Adam was forced to keep up his intensely quiet but struggling vigil. Steadily and busily he continued his progress pulling and lifting on the pole, spinning the reel's handle frantically but methodically as his experienced thumb guided the line back onto the reel evenly during the draws. Then, expertly he took-up the line's slack smoothly reeling-in between masterful and intermittent tugs. It was obvious to us, though, that Adam was stressed and holding on with all his might. He was being challenged by an obstacle forcing his absolute determination and will.

Instantly, another yell bellowed out! This time it was from our captain: "There's another one in the front! Get him!" The mate, however, was forced to maintain his assistance backing-up Adam... After all, *a fish on the line is better than two in the sea...* Sorry about that. I couldn't resist.

And for Neptune's sake, or for crying-out-loud, ***El Capitan*** could not have been shouting instructions to me! I was as useless as flip-flops in a twisting contest... Or, a trap-door on a lifeboat... Or, a one-legged man in a butt-kickin' contest... Or, traffic lights in *Grand Theft Auto.* Or, or, or *me* just being *me...* I was too busy flopping around rummaging for my camera. I don't have to *be the ball,* I just want to *see the ball!* I'm happy to watch real players catch fish. I just take pictures. I live vicariously through others and occasionally take a *selfie.*

I'm the official "recorder," not the fish-catcher. Angelina was just as excited as I was. We were both busy watching Adam, and we were trying to catch glimpses, if not pictures, of the other big, fat fish jumping in front and to the side of our boat. Captain Freddie, quickly recognizing his dilemma, instead set the boat on auto-pilot, ran to the front of the boat, snatched a close-by rod from its holder, and vainly attempted casting a few, frantic tosses out at the new fish.

I'm not sure, but I think I overheard him anxiously mumbling some stressed and muffled Spanish about ***turistas incompetentes***, but I wasn't miffed. Long ago, I had accepted that status and had actually grown to embellish it. That way, people lowered their expectations of me. If I screwed up or simply did nothing, it was expected, and no ill-feelings were cast. But, if I did something clever or imaginative, then everyone was in awe. I maintained a win-win state-of-mind.

However, "Sorry, Captain Freddie, but you're on your own!" was about all the glorious support I could muster-up. So, after a brief, stressful couple minutes for the captain, the rush was over; the fish was gone. But, fortunately, I had finally managed to dig through my belongings and rummage up my camera from my back-pack. "Where did it go?" I pretended "Oh, darn!" I exaggerated. "Well, c'mon Captain. There's plenty more fish-in-the-sea. And I still want Moby Dick!"

It was thrilling, though, almost magical. Just as quickly as the initial Marlin startled us, this Marlin too had vanished. Maybe, it was the same one as earlier. Maybe it was attempting to lead us away and was just making sure we were leaving. Maybe, it was laughing at us and taunting us for its having escaped... twice! Maybe, it was attacking us for snagging his bill-fish brother, Adam's Sailfish. Maybe, it was hoping one of us would fall overboard from all the excitement, and it would eat us! Maybe, it was Moby Dick's cousin! Maybe!

That brief distraction over, we rushed back to the rear of the boat and reestablished our *oohing* and *wowing* while Adam continued his stoic struggle fighting with his giant Sailfish. All we could do was just watch with continuing awe and occasional, positive-reinforcement, "OMG! It's huge! Oh, wow! Hang on, Adam!" To his credit, Adam did just that. Steadily, he pulled and reeled and pulled and reeled, and eventually, he dragged that fish up close to the boat's side.

Once the Sailfish was up close enough, the first-mate reached over the side and snagged the Sailfish by its gill with a long, hooked pole He struggled with the Sailfish's weight but finally hoisted it up and over the boat's side flopping it onto the deck. It was enormous! Captain Freddie gleefully and proudly began exclaiming, "It's a championship fish! It's a 'once-in-a-lifetime' catch!

Truly, that Sailfish filled up the whole width of the boat's deck. Both the captain and his mate seemed genuinely pleased, if not thrilled. Each eagerly requested having their pictures taken holding up the catch and then having pictures with Adam holding up the Sailfish. In some snapshots each one grabbed the fish's "sail" and spread it out in all its glory. It was a sight to behold. Biggest game fish I've ever been up-close-and-personal with. Especially important to me, though, was that it was the first time and one-and-only fish that I had ever actually bared witness to Adam's catching! I was amazed and proud!

The Sailfish surely was a beauty, though. It measured out to be ninety-five inches and right at 120 pounds. I figured we could stretch the nose, or bill, and bend its tail a little; plus, we could leave the hook and bait inside. That would fairly round the stunning catch out to an even eight feet and fifty-five kilos! WOW! It really was the *catch of a lifetime*. The pride was all Adam's; it was his catch. The thrill belonged to us all, though. A great day of deep-sea fishing.

After a little more trolling around with no luck, winds began to kick up, and Captain Freddie advised that rough waters impeded good fishing. My worn-out jokes of not being satisfied until we captured Moby Dick were beginning to make "Freddie" nervous. We still had over two and one-half hours on the clock for our day, and I kept taunting, "No! No going home until we ALL catch one!"

But we were all exhausted from the excitement. We were genuinely fulfilled from Adam's catch, and we were all getting a bit weathered by the day's heat and sun's reflective powers off the ocean's glare. With too much rocking on the choppy waters too, Angelina was beginning to feel the worst of fishing overindulgence. So, after a little more faked intensity straining my neck to catch a glimpse of good, 'ol Moby, I grinned and teasingly relented. "C'mon, Captain, take us home. Besides, I'm hungry. I want a hamburger!"

The end of this tale actually arrives in a couple months. Adam was so hyped, as were we all, that he chose to hire a local taxidermist. Of course, the captain and his mate eagerly and adamantly advertised stuffing the fish. It would mean a sizable commission for them, no doubt. They kept repeating and emphasizing to us that for a sport fish like that one, "You have to keep it and put it on your wall! It's really *the catch of a lifetime*!" The advertising pictures will do them some good too, I'm sure. Oh, I'm such a skeptic, but they were right!

However, for an additional $1,100, Adam's Sailfish would be mounted in all its splendid and glorious colors and size. The taxidermist would ready it for wall hanging, crate it, and mail it to Adam's chosen address back home. Now, all Adam needed to do was buy a new house to show it off! That fish was going to be amazing on anyone's wall, and Adam had a great story too. It had turned out to be a spectacular day's end, and there was a terrific fish-story to close it with. Imagine: ***20' & 2,000 lbs.***!

"Mismaloya Blues"

Part 14:
Character Flaws...

So, there you have it... We just trudged through a rundown of the city and community and nearby cities and villages of interest. We looked at many of the surrounding, tourist-spots and unique places to see for fun and interest. You've read about my impressions of Puerto Vallarta and its "layout of the land." I've described the marvelous bay and activity-schedules for both. I even took you on a exciting fishing trip on the bay, and I most importantly invited you to my favorite hang-out spot in Mismaloya, my place. My private joy.

If the city and the bay with their tourist-offerings weren't enough, you've read about the spectacular settings of jungles and beaches. I've taken you on a virtual tour from way up north Puerto Vallarta to way south describing places and sights and fun things to do. We visited many of the incredible beaches that Banderas Bay has to offer. We even went out on the bay and learned about the islands to swim around. And, of course, we mentioned the jungle, jungle everywhere around you. It's what sets the place apart so vividly. You're in a city, and wham! You're in the jungle. It's amazing and gorgeous and adventurous!

Finally, the wonderfully inviting weather was offered as a clincher. True, there were a few jokes about the heat and humidity, the rainy-season and the bugs. But, c'mon! What did you think? It's a jungle out there! It's wild with fascinating creatures, natural beauty, serenity, adventure and excitement, and... memories.

Now, it's time to look into a completely different aspect of the area. I'd like to explore the people who live here. I'm not interested in typical tourist visitors. We are all pretty much cut from the same cloth. We've all seen them for ourselves, and most of us have been them, ourselves. No, the one and two-week "guests" are worth their own humorous novel, but they are not right for this one.

Puerto Vallarta, mi zona Mismaloya and pretty much anywhere in this whole-wide, incredible world are filled and complemented, or littered, with all sorts of characters calling certain places their homes. That's the target-group that I wish to elaborate upon in this portion of my story. Sure, the ocean, and the jungle, and the cliffs, and the beaches all display a glorious, visual experience of this wonderful part of the world. Nature is fine; it's beautiful and, well, *natural.* We can't get along without it... However, that's not what I want to share in this segment.

It's always people who make everything possible and interesting. If it weren't for, well, us... nothing would ever get done! Nature makes the world go round, but people are along for the ride. People are the ones who see it, use it, change it, abuse it, destroy it, even create it. Without people, who cares? People make this world and life more interesting. It's not always fun; it's not always pretty, but it's always "human." Just about everything we need, use and cherish has a human-imprint on it. People may be "along for the ride," but they give it some zip to its spin. It's the conversation, behavior and activities which make life newsworthy. It's "people" who keep everyone from being bored.

People I've met down here and friends I've made are all curiously and uniquely different and interesting. Some are permanent, native-residents who have never lived anywhere else. Others have traveled here from distant parts of Mexico to make this particular area their home. Then there are the long and shorter-term ex-patriots who have left their native homelands to find and carve out a niche for themselves here. Additionally, there are long and short-term visitors who return here annually like migratory-creatures, and some of which purchase homes in the area for their return stays. Finally, there are the short-term vacation-visitors, much like me, who have enjoyed returning whenever possible for several months at-a-time.

Therefore, this section is not meant to be any diatribe. I am casting no stones. I shall "...call 'em like I see 'em!" One man's friend is another's "gossip-column." That is not my intent. These are all folks who left impressions on me." They (we) are all here from different places and for different reasons, but we've all got stories to tell. Some are worth repeating. Here's a few that I'd enjoy sharing...

Money Makes the World Go...?

The local working-class is an interesting group. It is comprised of all Vallartans and life-long residents of all the surrounding areas. They have all figured out means-of-survival in this "tourist-driven" economy and serve it well. To their merit, many are bi-lingual, or rather I should say, "They also speak English!" Either through necessity, interest or abundance, these people pick-up enough English to survive amongst a primarily English-speaking tourist crowd. It's hard to sell something if you can't tell customers how much it costs. "Savvy" survive. They learn communication-skills, and they learn how to accept obnoxious behavior for sake-of-a-sale when subjected to it. Besides, even most visiting foreigners also speak English. It seems like a one-way street.

Who knows what is really going-on in their minds, though. My experience suggests that they are pretty much like everyone else everywhere else. They have work and business lives where they adapt as necessary. They also have private lives where they relax and share their feelings with family and friends.

Two elemental themes seem common among the working-class: First, is "acceptance and appreciation." They accept what they have and appreciate where they live. Most of them speak about pleasurable weather and the "tranquility" of the area. Truth is, though, I never was sure whether this was just a "pimping" exercise preceding a sales-line pitch. Everybody working in restaurants and on beaches or street-vendor shops and taxis was so "tranquil," but nearly all of them had something to sell or a hopeful tip to collect. They were friendly and enjoyed joking around, but I usually sensed there were alternative motives to that "friendliness." And yet, everyone had jobs, although they likely earned very little.

Thus, the second element suggests "meaning and purpose." Foreigners are potential customers. The goal is not to let them get away without selling them something." Always smiling, the "customer-is-always-right" philosophy prevails and reigns supreme. Do not dispute; negotiate. Leave 'em smiling. One happy customer may mean another one. Ten "Noes" for every "Yes." Since nearly all businesses in Puerto Vallarta are directly, or indirectly, related to tourism, nearly everyone is a salesman. And every passing tourist is a potential client or sale.

I must admit that it got tedious after a while. I was never certain of the true intentions of any acquaintance. I learned to smile back and retreat with humor at the remotest sounds of a "pitch" coming my way. I'd laugh and move on. I had learned this fact the hard way because all too often I had remained with the "friendly-salesmen" and subjected myself to their indirect-approach. Thus, I became victimized by their sales-technique. To be fair, by far most were straight-up honest. There may be something they wanted to sell, but they accepted "No" for an answer. They might push their moments-of-opportunity, but they let you go.

Nevertheless, however, the vast majority of "Vallartans" are industrious, hard-working, honest, and kind. Unfortunately, that old "ten-percent rule" plays into their business environment. There always seems to be a percentage of nearly every group, who make things harder, more difficult, embarrassing, and bad for the diligent majority. Down here was no exception. Some resort to lies, bullshit and deception to make a deal and always do it smiling. These were the "con-artists" whom larceny typically served well. Seemingly happy, good-natured, and glad to see you at their doorsteps, they handed out fake and phony promises like they were passing out goodies to Halloween trick-or-treaters. "Yum! Free candy!"

Consider yourself hereby advised, "Never take an offer for a purchase or deal where the sales-person promises to 'pay-you-the-balance' or 'complete-a-deal' at a later time." You will likely never see the person again nor your "balance-due." These "cons" go to great extent to avoid paying-up or with ever having to see you again. If they do see you again, they will have countless excuses and time-honored explanations of misconceptions and misunderstandings. It's often the old adage, "Buyer-beware" where you don't always get what you bargained for. You simply need to use a little caution when dealing with strangers. It's the same anywhere.

Actually, there is an "anti-unscrupulous-vendor," government-agency available for tourists to file complaints. However, reports are sincerely taken, but losses are seldom accounted for nor refunded. Really bad vendors simply change companies, move to different locations, or vanish. When they did disappear, I fantasized that maybe "Dexter" from the Showtime series had actually heard of these nasty characters and sought his revenge or act-of-public-consciousness. Oh, but it was my naivete, my ignorance, my trust-worthiness, and my fault to enter into business dealings without acceptable warranties. They may be the "bad guys", but I was the "fool." Just be careful with whom you do business regardless of the transaction or the location. This is good advise for Puerto Vallarta or ...New York City. C'mon! Common-sense is a good tool to carry and use anywhere/anytime.

Examples might come from rental-car agreements and the notorious "Time-share-Presentation" vendors. Beware of car-rental services. If you stray from reputable car-rental dealers and go to some "activity-vendor" for your ride (because they made you a seemingly cheap-offer), you may get just that: Something cheap! Some are not even licensed to "rent cars" to the public. Regardless, what you get may not be what you expected. Ignorance ain't always blissful, and buyers usually need to beware and watch out for their pennies or others' ill-tidings. It's your money. Give it away freely without remorse, or count-your-change. There are those out there who will take all-they-can-get and "slight" you without remorse.

Another would-be, con-artist salesperson worth avoiding can be "Time-share Presentation" vendors. Many of these "unscrupulous" salespeople will use any sales-line available to get a customer. They prey upon and warm-up to potential clients who are typically short-term vacation-visitors leaving in a week. These tourists have activity needs, and these dealers make extravagant and grandiose offers to lure them into visiting one of the local, magnificent resorts.

The agents tell the tourists about the special gifts offered by the luxury-resorts just to come and take-a-look. Naturally, these salesmen are looking specifically for happy, naive and gullible tourists. Gifts like beautiful, scenic, evening-cruises on-the-bay may be offered, or even cash, or... even "rental-cars." The tourists are informed that they simply join the resort staff in an amenable, forty-five minute, short-visit and presentation of the facility.

These "street-agent" sales-pitches always begin amiably and with lies. At first they ask if you're having a good time and if there is any entertainment that you might be interested in. Often, they immediately reach for some colorful brochures which they make available for your review emphasizing, "No! Take them. They are free to you." Then they carefully segue back to their proposition which may go something like this: "NO PURCHASE NECESSARY! Just be nice and smile. Tell them (the resort people) that you like what you see, but it's not for (you). They'll understand, and you'll get a wonderful gift, the one you want just for visiting. No questions asked. It's fast, man, and it's easy, and a good deal! C'mon, ***amigo,*** take their gift...I promise you won't be sorry..."

Well, you can't be "too easy," so you counter, "You mean there's no-pressure? And it won't take too long, and we'll get a free

"Midnight-Cruise-for-Two" without any problems?... Just for showing up? Honest? Are you serious?"

"Sure, ***Amigo***!" they assure you, "It's easy! Just make sure you both show-up, give them a fake name of some hotel where you are (supposedly) staying, tell them you are leaving in two-days, and show them a good VISA or MasterCard. You've got one, right? Maybe it's a Platinum, ***si***? Go for an hour, and then go home." Sounds TGTBT!? It is...

From our own, personal and embarrassing experience with these slime ball, "time-share, presentation-vendors" and their associated resorts, we learned the truth. Initially, I'd become immediately suspicious due to a couple of those early conditions, "Give them a 'fake name' of some hotel where (we) were staying, and tell them (we) were leaving soon." I understood for potential purchases that both spouses needed to be present, and a reliable VISA seemed acceptable. However, we were renting a single, condominium for three-months from a private-ownership party, not a hotel.

Something was amiss, but the resort-agents informed us that hotel-guest policies insured privacy; the resorts could never confirm anything. Plus, these good ol' amigos were so friendly and supportive and sincere... We agreed to this dubious activity, however, and accepted our non-committal and conniving role. Our requested gift was a rental-car and a city-tour. We were told what hotel's name to provide our hosts and given our phony, pending, departure-date (supposedly three days later). That was where the "easy" part ended.

In the early morning of our agreed-upon-visit, we arrived by taxi to our destination. After reviewing our prompted credit-card for background and eligibility purposes, they quizzed us about our (suspicious and fake) hotel information. However, they were completely satisfied, just as we had been advised, and we were led off for a nice, complimentary breakfast. I already assumed and got a sense that this courtesy was to soothe and relax and soften us up... for the kill. "Wine 'em. Dine 'em. Sell 'em!"

Then, with a full-stomach and an empty-head, the hard-part began, and an agonizing series-of-events took place. Over breakfast the sales-staff began ganging-up on us. "Where do you come from? What do you like to do for fun? How often and how long do you vacation each year? How much money do you earn? What if (we) can show you how to "own" for less than you spend now? But wait! Don't decide anything yet. Let's go look at this marvelous resort and see what you've been missing!" OMG! We were nervous and exhausted from the initial cross-examination, and we hadn't even seen the place yet. But it got even worse.

After hiking and touring the vast premises of their honestly and truly remarkable and beautiful mega-resort, we were led to view potential "time-share-ownership" condos of all shapes and sizes. They were models of those available for purchase. Once the required, "Oohs," and "Aahs" were completed, we were ushered to the sales room. Now, the hard-core "closers" stepped-in and began their onslaught of arguments outlining, high-lighting, emphasizing, and strongly urging purchase of something right then. It was "an-offer-of-a-lifetime!"

Some of the salesmen and women were like children. I've never experienced grown-ups behaving so childishly when forced to take "No" for an answer. It was an exasperating arm-wrestling challenge to determine who broke first. They wined-and-dined us, then whined-and-primed us to take special-advantage of their offer then and-here. They just refused to take, "Thank you, but No!" for an answer.

Our anxiety was ignored, and our requests to leave were postponed until all of their staff had a shot at us. Each new salesman was higher-up the "closer" ranks. Each lowered the sales-price or sweetened the deal. Some "higher-ups" even attempted intimidation and leaned toward antagonism. That was a pathetic sales-tactic for me to easily brush aside. Nevertheless, it was an awful experience.

Even Angelina had to fake nausea, or did she, to get away from the pressure.

Begrudgingly, and many hours later, they finally relented and released us to return home via their taxi. Our redeemable "city-tour" tickets were given to us by a stoic, smile-less, businesslike secretary/clerk. Exhausted, we accepted our partial-gift and then inquired regarding instructions for receiving our "rental-car" coupon. "What agency do we go to see? What would be available? When should we make arrangements?" Uh, oh! We were informed that we needed to talk to the vendors who had sent us to the resort in the first place. The "resort" never resorted to that type of accommodation. Oh? Well, that wasn't explained to us in-the very beginning. Of course, it wasn't... None of those people are stupid, just conniving.

However, had we purchased a "time-share" from the resort, we likely would have received full-fare coupons for a Rolls-Royce of our choosing. For the cost to us for one of those dicey condos, they could have afforded to provide a chauffeur, too, free-of-charge, to guide us anywhere we chose for our remaining stay. But,it didn't work that way. We had to locate "Slick-Willy" and his partner, "Slim-Pickings" to get our just rewards. And, honestly, that's what we deserved and got.

The "rental-agencies" which did business with our "vendor" accomplices, unfortunately, were all out-of-stock. There was just no way that they could accommodate us unless we paid extra for a different agency's car. One of the vendors had actually become a close friend of ours during our stay. He had even joined us for multiple activities in the area including celebrating his own birthday. So, we accepted his participation and company. Besides, he could act as a tour-guide and get us to places easier.

I'll conclude this tale of shortcoming-characters with the following description of our rental car: Old, broken-down import, dirty, greasy, unclean inside-and out, and empty...out-of gas! Additionally, our vendor-friend-driver was broke. We needed to pay his way throughout our weekend, touring-adventures. When our car-rental was half-finished, our "friend" needed additional funds to get the car returned to its owner. It turned out that the car had actually belonged to the resort's "vendor-sales" affiliate. The car had been missing for two days.

I was delighted to tell them where it had been, though, "All-to-hell-over-the place! Hill-and-dale! Canyons and creeks! Mountains and valleys! Beaches and jungles!" We had gone everywhere we could. It had gotten stuck in mud in the mountains, stuck in traffic in cities, and stuck in sand on some distant beach. And all those Kodak moment tidbits advised the rental-vendor "where their car had been." I happily forwarded the car's "whereabouts" with emphasis to its owners.

I would have been delighted to "tell them where they could put it!" But, I didn't want to seem bitter. After all, this is "tranquility country!" Find your Zen...

We had experienced a brutal, unforgiving sales-experience with those time-share people, but we did get our "city tour" and our "rental car," although not exactly as promised. Eventually, it made for a laugh and a story. A real concern, however, is the resorts' dependance on those deceiving, vendor-agents. Also, they should beware of "professional" tourists who play-along, lie, say, "No," and take resorts' gifts for a living. Among "time-share" vendors they are called, "Strokers!"

Resort to the Worst..

The Grand Mayan Resort and its affiliate "Mayans" through expansion are the biggest, grandest and most aggressive mega-resorts in the whole dominion of Puerto Vallarta, Jalisco, MX and Nuevo Vallarta, Nayarit, MX. These two connecting states of Mexico house a multitude of high-end resorts providing vacation resources and potential time-share ownership to the entire Puerto Vallarta tourist crowd. The Mayan's goal, and every other "time-share" offering resort in the area is to sell fifty-one weeks' worth of time-shares for every, single unit in their complex. The fifty-second week is used for maintenance purposes required by law.

All resorts, but particularly the mega-resorts, offer incredible and extravagant accommodations, amazing aesthetics, beautiful grounds and amenities, and provide typical views-to-die-for. All this gorgeous experience has a price, however. A visitor/owner is provided a king's court with all the anointed surroundings and appropriate attributes. Unfortunately, the deal comes for an initial price-offering of a "king's ransom!"

Granted, savvy-buyers may haggle with the resorts' agent-sellers, twist-their-arms and negotiate more favorable sales prices, but the same, final results always exist: First, the resort, sales-staff closes another sale from a "cold-case" client opportunity provided by a local "time-share" presentation-vendor; second, the new buyer-couple had better make plans to return to that resort or its trade for one-week-a-year...forever...to even remotely gain a possibility of earning back a reasonable percentage of their investment.

Now, it's true that "time-share" resorts offer some special advantages to owners not available to the general public. First-of-all, the resorts are almost always extremely enticing to first-time potential buyers. The ultimate, negotiated-offer typically reduces the user-cost significantly for a newcomer and possible customer. To come and stay as a renter for a week's vacation at any glorious resort would likely be expensive and prohibitive to most of the average vacationing crowd. If buyers returned to the same resort year-after-year, they might save.

The point is emphasized during negotiations, however, that few do this. The resort continuously offers enticing deals to "potential" clients through various media-exchanges providing cut-rate discounts to visitors . They offer vacation cheaply simply by agreeing to attend one of their "presentations." A resort's ultimate goal is to sell-out all the time-share ownerships to newcomers.

When one resort is effective with successful sales, then it may expand and adds on new-units. Or, the parent company builds yet another mega-resort nearby and begins again. Plus, the resorts always have re-sales to offer from disgruntled client/owners wishing to sell and void their ownerships. This, of course, comes for a price to the owner which can only be deemed advantageous for the resort.

Regardless of which upper-end resort or hotel where any vacationing couple resides within the entire region of Puerto Vallarta, every time-share selling resort seeks-out potential, new clients. To keep the industry flowing, they need new prospects, fresh meat, new blood, and more cash. Although resorts' sales-agents use vacation enticement strategies to bring their own, first-time vacationers to a time-share, sales-pitch, they are also extremely receptive to clients brought in from any of the other hotels and resorts as potential purchasers. So, they formulate aggressive techniques through use of "time-share vendors" to send these tourist couples to one of their affiliated resort's "presentations." Once in a resort staff's grasp, so to speak, these naïve, but curious and excited, first-time visitors are figuratively thrown-to-the dogs of hard-core, closer, sales-negotiators.

These sales-persons' purpose is to eat their new prospects alive including their bank accounts. Their goal is simply to "close-a-deal." Regardless of the final price, the ultimate objective is just to get another sale. Their job is to close the deal of another time-share sale for one of their unique, and ***muy caros*** (very expensive) ***pero negociables,*** resorts. Good luck! However, with all the continued growth and development and expansion of "time-share" concept resorts, I can only imagine who are the real winners. I am furthermore continually amused at resorts' sales-strategy techniques such as modifying the somewhat tarnished "time-share" conceptual name to "...a new, unique and special-type of purchase..." called: "fractional-ownership..." Yeah, right! "A rose by any other name...," huh? No, I don't think so. It's more like: "You can call it manure, but it's still bullshits!"

BULLSHITS!

I've got experience with talking and writing
And even pimping a little prose.
A career of terse verbosity
Embellished with permeable pen
Often defined my art-of-persuasion,
Turning a thorn into a rose.

A career as a high-school teacher
Facilitating knowledge from A to Z,
My daily exercise and performance
Hinged upon aggrandizing
My academic acronyms:
BS, MS, and PhD.

Finessing and shoveling on students
Such dialog steeped in academia's mound
Of cryptic *bullshits, more shit*
And *piled-higher-and-deeper*
Made heaps of steer-manure
Appear like a child's playground.

I made cattle-muck seem pleasant
And even shaped it with cunning and wit.
Ostensibly, it posed as a rose,
But, only God makes precious flowers
That smell and feel like a garden's blush.
And so, in-the-end, mine was just "bullshit!"

So, hawkers, or squawkers or "*bull-shitters*" alike,
Keep your salesman's crap to yourself.
I've been there, done that,
Spoken and written all about it before,
And laid it on thicker than you ever could,
And I'm still trying to validate myself.

A STROKE OF GENIUS...

It just so happens that a significant number of returning and permanent visitors to Puerto Vallarta learn of this resort sales' technique. It has become a game for them to outsmart the resorts and take advantage of them. The tourists, or visitors, would pretend to be interested in looking at the resorts' "time-share" opportunities. After an appropriate measure of time, they back-out of the discussions and refuse any further dealings. Once excused, they collect their prearranged, free gifts. The experienced and really brazen ones go for mega-resort offers with hefty cash gifts as incentives. Others comfortably agree to visit the resorts for "tourist-package" incentives such as tours, attractions and dining.

The most successful "fakers" (visitors) are referred to as "Strokers" by the vendor-agents. These scammers join forces against the resorts in order to swindle resorts for the highest returns in cash and other gifts. The vendors set up all the appointments for their stroker partners at the ritziest, super-resorts offering the largest cash incentives and nicest tourist-package gifts. The vendors receive their valuable commissions regardless of sales-or-fails just for getting the "potential-buyers" to the resorts. It behooves vendors to have "strokers" working with them in these "scams" in order to continue receiving excellent commissions.

"Strokers" schedule visitation-bookings as often as possible with their vendor accomplices for as many different resorts as possible.

Some even arrange for morning and afternoon visits if time and scheduling allow. They do these multiple-visits, obviously, to increase their prize earnings. Some of these experienced connivers come down for a two-week vacation to Puerto Vallarta and spend the first week "working" the resorts for scammed gifts. Strokers take the cash prizes to pay all their vacation expenses. Other gifts received are used to relax, enjoy themselves and see the sights during their free time.

For some of these stroker shy locks, it's even a living. Actually, there are many, permanent and long-term ex-patriots who play the "stroker" game. They develop close ties with various vendor-agents of the resorts. When the mood or need strikes them, there are always vendors ready to line them up for new resort visits for their mutual benefit. There's really no end or limit to their shenanigans.

Enormous, mega-resorts with hundreds and hundreds of available units ready for usage and sale need these time-share sales. Remember, each unit can sell fifty-one times or more because of the "time-share" concept: "Attention, WalMart Shoppers! How would you like to buy and 'own' your very own piece of this incredible, extravaganza resort? Why rent from us and pay outrageous costs, when you can become a partner and own your very own 'week' of this amazing resort?!" It is an enormous, revenue-earning industry for Puerto Vallarta.

It is a key source of revenue for resort owners too. In fact, foreign money pumped into these resorts by short-term, vacationing tourists is staggering. "Time-share" concept visitors become overwhelmed by sales tactics and regularly accept and buy into the enterprise. These "buyers" were screened, so resort-staff know if they have sufficient credit-card funding and available cash for down-payments. The resort people want good, highly-qualified guests to visit and view their extravagant offerings. Of course, sales-staff closers are confident that they can "twist-the-arm" of any guest into buying. However, apparently, resorts do not keep records or analyze their methodologies to help determine reasonable and potential buyers from the "strokers."

Of course, you get-the-drift of the "stroker" term. These folks know how to play-along with the resort personnel. They "stroke" their hosts with feigned interest over subtle, sales intentions. They display just enough phony curiosity to get through the ordeal. At an appropriate juncture, strokers then bow-out with mocked denials and refuse any time-share purchases. Smoothly and swiftly, they request their contractually agreed-upon cash and gifts. There is little worry because client-resort "agreements" are governed and controlled by agencies within the city. Once gifts are received, strokers make a quick getaway.

Also, resorts move their sales staff around too. It's usually due to relocation needs and staffs' acquired stress. Sales-agents come and go. The resorts are breeding grounds for potential "killer-shark" closers. They also dump sales slackers (or anyone with a conscience). Also, successful sales personnel are typically a transient breed themselves. They travel from one country's destination to another picking out preferred locations, resorts, lifestyles, or potential incomes. When one area has been gleaned successfully, they move on to greener pastures. Really successful ones move up the resort hierarchy or transfer as desired.

Furthermore, after reasonable periods have lapsed, resorts actually don't even mind returnees. They want another chance for a sale. Top-notch, qualified visitors are valuable to the resorts. Resort sales-agents view qualified visitor-tourists as veritable cash cows. Buyers are valuable to them. That is why resorts pay out significant commissions to vendors and cash and gifts for guests whom their affiliated vendors send. The highest echelon resorts pay-out to qualified guests up to one-thousand dollars and gifts. It's a huge business to take seriously.

Apparent issues abound: Resort sales-personnel do not care who comes through their doors as long as they are qualified. Closers will take care of business. Some time-share, presentation vendors, and it's far-reaching, will send anyone to the resorts claiming "qualified-status." Often, they even assist their tourist-customers with appropriate responses including lies and deceits during resort-staff questioning. This grave situation promotes corrupt vendors and "strokers" to play along and take advantage of hotels' sales-strategy flaws.

Resort, time-share, sales-staff don't care about their potential clients. Their jobs are to get the sales. They want clients' money to keep the enterprise afloat. It's a huge business with enormous profit potential. They could not care less about the ultimate shock, agonized reality, stress, or financial-ruin of their victimized, time-share buying clients. It just means money-in-the bank and nothing personal; it's strictly business.

Unscrupulous, time-share vendors connive with con-artist tourists to beat out resorts for their prizes and commissions. They don't care either about potential pain or loss to tourists. Some scheme with professional "Strokers" to cheat and beat the resorts at their own game. There seems to be little loyalty when it comes to money.

Occasionally, some *strokers* are recognized, disqualified and sent away. "Pros" just move on and look for their next vendor and resort-target. If a vendor is challenged by a resort for sending them a "sand-bagger" (slacker), commissions will be denied. The vendors, however, with faked innocent and false naivety earn academy-award worthy performances when they simply claim ignorance to the resorts' inquisitions, "Those tourists lied to me, Boss!"

SATAN CLAWS IS COMIN'

You'd better watch your back.
You'd better not be found.
You'd better back-track,
'Cause you'll never hear the sound.

Satan Claws is comin' for lost souls...

He's made a long list;
He can hardly wait to play.
His evil can't resist
Finding ways to make you pay.

Satan Claws is comin' for lost souls...

He's glad when you are cheatin'.
He's laughing when you're bad.
He sharpens his claws for misguided fools,
So, get ready to feel sad.

Oh, you'd better confess;
You'd better do well.
You'd better seek forgiveness,
Or he'll drag you straight to hell.

Satan Claws is comin' for lost souls...

He knows if you are cheatin'.
He's laughing when you are bad.
He sharpens his claws when you're slippin' up,
So, get ready to feel sad.

Satan Claws is coming for lost souls...

He's plannin' to see you at Christmas,
But his bag ain't full of gifts...
It's oozing with bloody and filthy souls...
To fill up his abyss.

Satan Claws is comin' for lost souls...

Will he find yours?

Scary.....Christmas!

"Mismaloya Blues"

Part 15:
The End is Near...

How I just managed to just go from "Bullshit" to "Satan" was actually a pretty clever segue. My three-month vacation was coming to an end. Angelina had been with me for the final month, and I'd had plenty of time to reflect on all the sales gimmicks used against tourists including us. In fact, I had reflected considerably on those times when we had been a target. In a twisted way, money was lost, but that was worth any experience. To me, though, what was unfortunate was losing those supposed friends, locals with whom we'd connected through our transactions. Those "cons" moved on; they were gone. Likely, they had already even forgotten about us. Now, at least, their personages may live on within this whimsical tirade.

Also, I transitioned to an evil version of "Santa Clause Is Coming to Town" because of our "up-coming" return home to California for the holidays. This year, we shall arrive back in-time for Halloween, Thanksgiving and Christmas. First, I'll break out ol' Mr. Bones for our front porch Halloween display to add a touch of demonic aire to the festival. The next month, we shall celebrate all that we are "thankful for" again. Finally, Christmas plans and gift purchases have to be made. It is pretty easy connecting all the dots from dubious and unfortunate experiences with unscrupulous hotel, sales-agents and vendors in Puerto Vallarta to reflections upon their own potentially uncertain holidays, especially Christmas.

Additionally, before departing for home, it was time for my promised hair-cut. I'd considered my options and fantasized about remaining unshaven and keeping my hair longer. I believed I could return home without shaving or cutting my hair and have a glorious surprise for all our grand kids. I explained sincerely to Angelina that I would be a good candidate for a family "Santa Clause" this year.

Her snippy retort was ingratiating and uncompromising. She quickly but snidely remarked, "Oh, *yeah*? You'll look more like *Satan* than *Santa*!" Had I been half-ass, quick-witted, I'd have retorted, "Oh, *yeah*? Well, *you* better watch out! *You'd* better not...."

We had enjoyed ourselves the past month together. October is an important conversion month for Puerto Vallartans and definitely for folks in Mismaloya. A desired cooling trend starts moving in slowly. We recalled that the previous year's October had been more pleasing than September. This year, we were experienced returnees of last year's spectacular November and December . We could easily and comfortably use them as comparisons. Nevertheless, I could tell the difference. It was getting nice... really nice. And just in time for us to leave.

Humidity begrudgingly was drying-up. No longer were we demoralized by those chronic frustrations over continual, under-arm-sweats and shirt-backs stained from perspiration. I'd even gotten comfortable with occasional short-sleeved shirts instead of insistent, tank-top apparel. Even the local, dress-code made subtle changes too, it seemed, accommodating new changes in weather and temperature. More long pants were being worn and even long-sleeved shirts.

Autumn and winter tend to do that regardless where one is, I guess. Unless you're on the bottom-half of the globe. I've heard that countries in the southern hemisphere have a reverse, or opposite, cycle to their seasons as do nations in the northern hemisphere. Don't know for sure, though. Never been there. I can only surmise. Maybe I studied or read about it in a book or saw it in a picture show or something. That, or it was a *National Geographic* special. You see,

I've never seen it. Got to go there some day, though. I need to see it for myself...

Also, finally, insects were beginning their decent into hell, I imagined. Or, at least we were grateful they were dying or departing from our domain. Their presence definitely brought on anxieties to otherwise delightful times. Oh, bugs do make for candid conversation. Jungle folks, those of us out here in the wild, Mismaloya and Boca zones definitely know about insects and critters. It's much less a problem in town because of their concrete jungle, though. Bugs and lizards enjoy creeks and streams and dirt and mud. You don't find that as much in the city.

Here, however, in my blessed, Mismaloyan sanctuary of wooded forest and cliff-side, jungle vegetation thrived ample, open-water sources contributing to infestation melees. Those of us without air-conditioning were blatant, neon-sign invitations. Little creatures sought out our tempting habitats in which to thrive in appetent heat and humidified coziness. If those little monsters were totally gone tomorrow, it would be one more day too late. We had been having several days in a row recently without rain or even threats. It had allowed for comfortable visits outside anytime without fear of sudden downpour soaking us. Finally, the "dry-spells" were seemingly drying-up insect populations and none-too-soon.

I think that a hurricane which had passed through last month on its destructive path of mayhem to Cabo San Lucas and Baha California had left in its wake follow-up changes in weather patterns. Rain, though lessened, still lingered with us as if waiting for its master, *Hurricane Odile*, to return with reinforcements. In fact, it had been a combination of heavy rainfall and surges from storms associated with *Odile* that left a swath of minor, coastal damage.

Regrettably, it had even indirectly caused the deaths of two, naïve and foolish, tourist observers. Rains poured during *Odile's* close proximity. Heavy winds churned up the bay and coastline with enormous, pounding and dangerous waves. It was no time to be teasing, taunting and toying with an enraged sky and provoked ocean. It was a time better left remaining secure indoors. It was safer and wiser for me to simply venture onto our deck and watch in humbled awe as nature took its course.

There were times when I surmised with certainty that next-door neighbors had inexplicably fired-off shotgun blasts *baaam!* only to realize that it was thunder cracking and booming across the bay from distant, lightning-flashes. Other times, my heart ceased beating from a startling yet mistaken *crruushh!* when deafening crashes were simply doors in our neighborhood housing complexes left ajar and smashed themselves shut due to wind forces. Occasionally, *craack!* and *boom!* were nearly simultaneous revealing that lightning had struck extremely close-by. All of it was thrilling and exciting and awesome. Yet, it was also extremely unnerving and left many of us pitiful, anxious observers feeling a sense of helpless subordination.

The two, local deaths indirectly caused by *Hurricane Odile* were both unfortunate tourists visiting the area on short, vacation-breaks. One of the casualties occurred when a middle-aged male ventured down to the shoreline of a nearby beach to watch up-close and personally as huge waves broke, crashed and rolled onto shore. Unexpectedly, a singularly powerful wave of enormous, thirty-foot amplitude crested and broke close to shore sweeping up the man, dragging him back out to sea and swallowing him. Although agonizingly tragic, yet it was a meaningful warning to others not to dare, challenge or tempt Mother Nature. She could "call-your-bluff" anytime she chose and most decidedly would always win.

The other unfortunate but similar loss was a younger tourist in town who ignored "danger-zone" signs deliberately and specifically placed on the city-pier's entrance. Instead, he chose attempting a close-up experience of the dangerous surf and foolishly edged his way to the pier's end. Suddenly, with little warning, a series of gigantic waves burst over the pier sweeping him off the platform. He disappeared in an instant. Mercilessly, he had been engulfed, condemned and entombed within an eternal, watery grave. Lessons learned from others' mistakes...

Due to the storm's violent conditions, we never heard further details about either case nor whether search parties had ever recovered and returned the victim's bodies to their agonized families. They were gone. Both cases were considered and accepted as pathetic, unfortunate accidents. Yet, both were inexcusable and unnecessary. Sad errors of judgment by some are often internalized lessons learned by others. Indirectly, some teach by mistakes they make; others learn from admonitions. We all determine our own truths.

BEWARE THE SEA

Beware the sea.
It has no friends.
It tolerates
But for a fee.

We take its worth
And play upon,
But rest-assured,
It feels no mirth.

The greatest men
Who sailed true
Are anchored in
Davey Jones's den.

Do not go near
If you're afraid.
The price you'll pay
Is constant fear.

Captains en route
And those in ports,
Trained to prepare,
Still have their doubts.

They know the depths
Of the sea's force
That in a storm
Can drown their breaths.

So, play along
The sandy edge.
Swim if you dare, But hum this song:

"Row, row, row your boat
Gently back to land.
'A safer place,' all sailors warn, '
Is not to swim but stand!'"

"Mismaloya Blues"

Part 16: Gotta Get Going...

Those unfortunate, hurricane-related drowning accidents were exceptions, however. They should not be considered the rule. Not everything we do which can be deemed risky should never be condoned. True, some risks we take which end-up mistakes might have been better left alone. But, some choices in life which might cause strife aren't always best unknown. There are things we can do just because they seem true from dreams we believe we are shown. So, with attitudes that dare, let the devil beware. Take the bull by the horn's... danger-zone.

Oh, okay, I'm not ready to jump into some bull-ring with cape-in-hand shielding a sword and shouting, "Ole!" Especially if there is a monstrous, previously-injured and totally-pissed-off creature charging straight for my groin area. In fact, no longer am I prepared, willing or desirous to race off to Pamplona and "run with the bulls" for that matter. It wasn't too long ago, though, that I yearned for such stunts. Fact is, I fantasized about both those crazy exploits.

There have been a few eventually famous matadors who began their illustrious careers by simply taking a highly "risky" initiative. As foolish and impetuous youth, a few leaped over a protective barrier in some ***plaza de toros*** to challenge a crazed-bull before an astonished crowd and upset and frustrated picadors, bandoliers and/or matadors who expected to receive all the attention and glory. If the imposter actually performs admirably, he may have a chance at a new profession. If he is injured, or looks ridiculous, he may have a chance at jail!

Regardless, I have no interest anymore in being chased by bulls, injured, looking ridiculous, or ending up in jail... or the hospital. What I'm trying to express is choosing "risks" with appropriate caution. One man's "risk" may be another man's death... Yet, a stone left unturned gathers moss, and I'm not ready to settle down for a bunch of nasty, clingy plants growing all over me. I still want to do some stuff, but within reason. Like Clint Eastwood's famous character, Harry Callahan from *Magnum Force*, "A man's got to know his limitations!"

Okay. So, we all just figure out what are our limitations. We all can do that. We simply need to qualify what "risks" are foolish and which ones are feasible and could become unimaginably entertaining and fulfilling. We need to choose something that suits us best. But, we need to choose. Start small and go bigger. But go! We all need to get out of our comfort-zones and try some "what-if" zones. If we've got any spontaneity inside us, then go for it! But, whatever is holding us back, we've just got to let go of it. Let go and go!

TAKING RISKS

The only risks never to take
Are never taking risks.
Betting our fates to: "Make-or-break!"
Steps into the abyss.

Sensations felt when we survive
Will measure us by deeds,
And "actions-over-words" revive
Our satisfactions' needs.

But, opportunities-of-chance
With promises so vane
Are "acts" derived within a trance
And seldom *gain-from-pain.*

Yet, dreams are stuff lives are made of
And worthy of our toil.
Fulfillment is redemptive love
Remaining ever-vigil.

We may not always reap rewards
From seeds sown for success,
And pleasures gained may ne'er afford
Their cost, we might confess.

Yet, lives survived taking no risks
Chance emptiness inside.
But, satisfying dreams insists
Consciences be our guides.

Some of us labor; others dream.
There is no shame in choice.
We each devise our ways-and-means,
And effort is our voice.

A family's needs or Mt. Everest
Both demand fervent quests.
Let every worthy soul insist
What challenge serves them best.

"Mismaloya Blues"

Part 17:
I'll Be Back!...

Nevertheless, it was time for us to "get-going" home again before we suffered the "risk" of wrath from family members and bill collectors. We would be back home for the holidays, but there was no question that my heart was in another place. There is something to be said of lifestyles where the most difficult issue faced was finding a decent phone or internet connection. Yet, whenever I used my computer for newsworthy updates, I became regularly frustrated from current affairs in the States and the world. Typically, it was bad news, and I was seldom inspired to read details...

For instances: In news headlines, Congress, politicians and nations were fighting with each other as usual; in sports were hi-lights of the most recent, heroic winners and resentful losers; in entertainment, Hollywood continued its narcissistic love-affairs; with lifestyles, everyone focused on rich and famous or scoffed at wannabes; in finance, stock-markets loomed to new heights while doomsday-prophets warned of imminent collapse; and in weather-patterns, there still was some everywhere. The commonality between news and weather is always consistency: good and bad.

Incidentally, "Attention, Walmart Shoppers: The above-mentioned (generic and figurative) forecasts were brought to you by none other than your *AOL Homepage*-providing confounded distributors of refined tidings and undefined merit'..." Got to give them credit, though, even for their miserable, boring and stressful menagerie of news coverages.

Our weather here was fine, though. I could read about rain and cold and the snow storms and blizzards back home, but I just couldn't relate to it. How could I when I still needed sun-block whenever I ventured outdoors. And regarding news? I survived just fine with second-hand headlines. World-news controversies went on fine without me. I appreciated experiencing life without them. It is absolutely invigorating and exciting when I am heading for an airport to *get outa Dodge!* True, my expectations are high, but my blood-pressure lowers.

We gotta get out of this place
If it's the last thing we ever do
We gotta get out of this place
'Cause, Girl, there's a better life for me and you

The Animals – 1965

Anyway, living here or anywhere else away from pressures back home offers distinct benefits. We travelers can remove ourselves from all the pains, anxieties and frustrations caused by unnecessary stress. For a while, at least, we can forget about those innate emotions of families, communities, nations, and everywhere else. We can take well-earned and well-deserved hiatuses from all the deafening noises. It can be honestly refreshing and relaxing and rewarding. Let's stop making excuses and start making plans. Let's cut those binds holding us back. Let's *let go and go*!

When we are no longer players living "in the belly of the beast," it's actually energizing. Once removed from daily onslaughts and barrages of all those gripping influences hanging onto us, we may be given opportunities to review our lives from new vantage points. Those "views" can be more objective and unique perspectives... or not. It depends on who "let's go" of most and longest.

However, our business is finished here, this time, at least. It has been another interesting chapter or episode in our visits and travels to Puerto Vallarta and our second home here in Mismaloya. Quite a bit happened over the unusual stretch of vacation this time around: An early-on, emergency departure and relatively swift return for me; an amusing struggle (in hindsight) with me and nature; and Angelina's return and our adventures continuing together dealing with nature and its elements. I loved it all. It's so much more amusing fighting bugs than fighting traffic.

We have made some new, solid friends because of our conditioned-response, visitation-behavior. We mutually look forward to future visits. We are no longer considered *one-time rookies* with conditions. We are relevant. A first-name basis encourages expectations of annual visits. We'll make plans to return and then follow-through. Maybe not exactly "snowbirds" yet, but we're working on it.

In fact, an obscure objective may yet unfold. I still want to live in this area through Winter into Spring. It's a "bucket-list" thing for me, important stuff. New seasons-same reasons. I want to experience Puerto Vallarta throughout most of a year, anyway. I'd like to say, "I *lived* there," and believe it myself. There are still places to see, people to meet, things to do, and stories to write about.

The driving force is still the same: I want to get away and have a new day... Try change just for-the-sake-of-it... Who knows? Maybe when this "gig" becomes too comfortable, it will be time to find something else for kicks. Maybe we'll be ready for that Amazon adventure. For now, I just want to think about Mismaloya. I want to think more about God and the Universe and my place in it. I want to learn more from other friends and acquaintances about their own *cosmic* experiences and opinions.

So many neighbors and contacts, including locals, ex-patriots and visitors like us, seem to have curious, if not profound, viewpoints on all sorts of topics. Just *drop a nickel in the slot machine*, and watch 'em spin! A good topic and a better question will set most of them off on irreversible tangents. And they are all eager to share opinions regarding anyone's place within the cosmos.

Religious stratum's range, from extremely devout to atheism, all share a commonality of understanding and appreciation regarding each's own, fortunate circumstances living here. All share a willingness to purport positions on anything including: *Life-and-afterlife*, *extra-terrestrial life*, *alien life-forms*, and even *permanent, alien-visitors...* from outer space! Which ones ? I can't wait to hear all about... "abductions!" For now, though, we've got to go, but, *I'll be back!*

INCLINATIONS

Inclinations to talk when we should listen
Disgruntle another's delay.
Expounding upon every self-actualization
Tends keeping an audience away.

Everyone desires focused attention
While emotions are scattered astray,
But possibilities for shared communication
Encourage other voices to stay.

Mysteries-of-life are games of contention
When tossing words into the fray.
Fairness demands everyone's participation
Where all are required to play.

Even solitary lives' repentant confessions
Pleading for mercy, pray
For soul-searching, humbling, divine-intervention
From another listener who may.

Life encourages everyone to speak of devotions
With rapture, often kept at bay.
Yet, voices are silenced by the strongest opinion
When death leaves us no more to say.

"Mismaloya Blues"

Part 18:
I'm Back!...

How did you like that segue? To go from quoting two, dynamic screen-personalities, Arnold and Jack, from two, thrilling motion-pictures, *Terminator* and *The Shining*, really required foresight. And then, I connected them both with my driven-ambition to return to lovely Puerto Vallarta. Well, I just astonished myself! Of course, all "true-believer," movie-trivia geeks would challenge my *I'm Back* quotation from *The Shining* because it was actually used as a sales-gimmick rather than a true quote from the film. If "geeks" really want to get down-and-dirty, they could remind us that, in fact, it was Arnold (and a dozen others) who said, "I'm back." Arnold's turn was in Kindergarten *Cop.*

But, so what? Everyone remembers both obsessed characters from those films, and they'll also "remember" those attributed lines, if only supposed. In the same fashion, all *my* readers will remember my "obsession" to return to my second-city, love-affair with Mismaloya... Oh, there's another clever segue again. But, "It's gooood!" Uh, oh! There's another famous, film-quote, and this time its from Jim Carrey and Morgan Freeman in *Bruce Almighty.* Eat your hearts out, Geeks! *Now, cut that out!* Ooops! That was Jack Benny. Alright, enough! Back to the segue... Back to "The Plan."

The Plan...

Right. I guess I'd better explain how I (we) got "back" to Mismaloya... There had been a continual stream of activity transpiring during an interminable period of time after returning home. It had been a relatively uneventful flight home with no customs/immigration intervention. This time, we chose to rely on our own initiative and rent a car from the airport to take us home. Doing so brought zero harm and disturbance to our conflicted children further proving our own self-reliance, and more importantly, non-reliance on family-assistance or support. It worked alright, except that it cost us over $100 to get home. Hey, never question family-costs: "Family" costs you going and coming.

But, we were home again... Home in California... Back to where we started. Don't get me wrong. After any period away, its usually nice to reacquaint myself with my "natural" surroundings... There was the house. Yep, it still looked the same. There were the lawns and plants and flowers and trees. Yep, still needed cutting and pruning. Wow! They really needed cutting and pruning! There sits all the furniture just like we left it. Got to re-hook-up all my electronics, though, that I brought back from Mexico. No matter, I have got to be *plugged-in*.

Now, isn't that a pathetic, *social-commentary*?" First-thing-in-the-morning, when I awaken and grab my cell-phone to check for messages, I've received health-notice warnings advising me, "Avoid developing neurotic, OCDs where first-thing-in-the-morning, upon awakening, (you) reach for (your) phone to check for messages." Damn! It's too late! It's got me already. Why don't they just stop "texting" me? Then, I'd be fine! Guess I'd better go "Google" and see what's going to happen to me. Or, better yet, I'll take a *risk* and *fuhgeddaboudit*! I'll find out sooner or later, anyway. My kids can worry about it after I'm gone.

Alright, but looking over the home-zone, things aren't too out-of-shape I can deal with most confusions and intrusions. What is that beautiful, Zen-like motto? "Do unto others before they do it to you, but have the strength to run away afterward," No, no, that wasn't it. It was, "Grant me serenity to accept what I can't and change what I can, but recognize both." Yeah, that was it! The *AA* and

NA club prayer. It's good advise especially coming from a bunch of alcoholics and drug-addicts. However, it's a peaceful and meaningful *mantra* for anyone. Its abidance could help keep all our proverbial boats *sailing on smooth seas.* I guess it means a little more, though, if you *fell overboard* while drinking or doing drugs.

There's a slow but steady stream of visitors to our house over a few days. Family, friends and neighbors haphazardly appear through the woodwork and network glibly joking, "Hello, Strangers! Are you just back from somewhere? Well, welcome home. We've missed you. Where did you say you were?"

My initial response was puking, but I contained myself. Instead, I'd quip apologetically but sarcastically, "It *will be Mexico.* Actually, Puerto Vallarta. But, we haven't left yet. We've been inside packing. Getting ready to leave in a few weeks!" I chuckled at my quick-mindedness but then recognized the *big-picture.*

Immediately, I scanned my crowd for amusement, confusion or curiosity. There was a distinct strategy to my cynically humorous retort. First, of course, was letting everyone know that the neighborhood, comedian-wannabe was, in fact, back. Second, and most important to me, was the affective advisory to friends and family, especially my spouse, that I was calculating yet another absence.

Amidst laughter and hugs, or handshakes, my loving Angelina was forced to consider "the plan's" intended notice: "Huh? What in hell is he talking about again?" Truth hurts, but this time it was with a considerate but calculated warning. That's a type of "compromise" sort of, kind of, well, hopefully...isn't it?

Successful relationships are all about compromise. Angelina's and mine possess the same elements, sort of, kind of, well, hopefully. Regarding most matters, we have agreements: We *agree* to do whatever we want; she does what she wants, and I do what I want. The only potential conflict is when something "wanted" by one of us affects, conflicts or interferes with what the other wants. Those are circumstances initiating "real-compromise:" 1a) a settlement of differences by *arbitration* or by consent reached by mutual concessions or, b) something *intermediate* between or blending qualities of two different things; 2) a *concession* to something derogatory or prejudicial <a *compromise* of principles>.

Right! If I don't get to go back, and soon, it will compromise *my* principles! It was still early, though. We had just arrived home... again. There would have to be "compromises" in the near-future regarding departure times, but let's leave *sleeping bears* alone for the time-being. Who might we use to *arbitrate* any differences would be a forthcoming issue. What was an *intermediary-blending* of our wishes? Finally, who was going to *concede* what? Whew! Heavy stuff. Where's my suitcase? Didn't I pack a bottle of Tequila in there somewhere?

Alright! Back up! I'm not being completely honest and forthright. "The Plan" had already been in the making. We had already loosely, predetermined that we would be returning. There would be at least one, final return-trip to fulfill our (my) "bucket-list" objective. Two years earlier, we had begun our sojourns. Over four years ago, we had briefly dropped-by and promised ourselves to absorb everything we could someday(s) about the wonderful area of Puerto Vallarta. So far, we had completed two-legs of that goal, that dream, but it still wasn't enough.

Oh, and I forgot mentioning that I sort of cheated. We (I) left nearly all our belongings back at our home in Mismaloya. That was sort of my preconceived guarantee of a return-trip: "Babe, we gotta go back and get our stuff!" I had arranged to leave almost everything behind with our benevolent landlords. They were agreeable and more-than-happy obliging us because, partly, it meant basic certainties of continued months' rentals. However, I preferred to believe that they stored our belongings because they really welcomed another return visit from us.

Additionally, it was to be the last opportunity to complete my book's writings ***si no mis clases de espanol.*** Furthermore, Angelina had to return to her "art-throb" maestro for help and instruction to progress with her painting endeavors too. It was obvious. I mean, we had to come back. Seriously, we had made a new home for ourselves in ***Zona Mismaloya de Puerto Vallarta***. Yes, it was only a rental, but it was *our* rental. We had established a new, secondary life for ourselves. It was real and relatively comfortable and meaningful.

We had a unique and particularly special-arrangement with our landlords, Sergio and Deya, to return anytime we wished with due-notice. We would be the first, if not only, considerations for any future rentals regardless of the season or month. Considering the excellent rental-fee, which included all additional expenses, it seemed inexcusable not to return. The currency, exchange-rate make it very feasible for living expenses. Plus, it was in a beautiful and scenic part of Puerto Vallarta next to good friends, neighbors and company. It was very comfortable living there. The difficulty was always when leaving.

It's normally awkward saying, "Goodbye." There are usual and typical misgivings and uncertainties of any return from us partly because we rent and because we are still green. Many "ripe," old-regulars are comprised of native-locals, ex-patriots, owners and renters who live here permanently. Some owners return during specific periods each year like "swallows" to Capistrano. Thus, of course, comes the term s*nowbirds* because those are the annual returnees always coming back when cold, winter-weather hits home in the USA or Canada.

But, oh, yes, I knew we would return at least once more. It was too much to consider anything permanent yet, and my own beliefs challenged any likely candidacy as an "ex-patriot." I'm still a fervent "flag-waver." We had a while yet to deal with those distant parameters. First, we had to get past these "holidays."

We were home, and we would take care of business. In the meantime, I would wait and strategize for an appropriate "get-away." We would go back *asap* to where "I" needed and wanted to be. Hopefully, Angelina would be along, but a looming possibility, if not probability, was rising that another "solo" venture would occur. Initially, I might have to go alone and wait for an appropriate time for Angelina to join me.

We still had Halloween, Thanksgiving and Christmas, at least, to get past. Attempting to get myself, I mean *us,* back after Christmas, but before New Year's Eve celebrations, would need some serious and effective plotting, I mean *planning*. Convincing Angelina to return sooner-than-later wasn't going to be an easy-trick. This was "family-season," and there would be many family gatherings.

I would need to be careful about springing any holiday surprises like, "Merry Christmas! Adios, Amigos!" Or, another of my honest, soul-felt offerings, "Hey, Everybody! Guess what I got Angelina and myself for Christmas? *Return ticket to Puerto Vallarta*!" No, I had to be methodical, choose my words carefully and prepare for potential debate. For the time-being, and my, I mean *our*, best interests, I chose to use the most clever strategy of all: Shut-up and wait!

SILENCE

Sometimes, the best thing we can say
Is simply saying nothing.
When words seem to get in the way,
Silence hears its call.

When pictures cannot illustrate,
Quiet can be impressing.
If science will not demonstrate,
Noisy research stalls.

When math just does not calculate,
Silence helps reasoning.
If socializing instigates,
Language hits a wall.

When music cannot resonate,
Quietness makes hearts sing.
If dancing will not stimulate,
Talking makes us fall.

If caution advises to wait,
Let silence be pleasing.
We must learn to appreciate:
"Meditation is 'all.'"

So, save your breath with notions bent
On talking where silence is meant.
It clears the air like ceiling vents
When silence ***says it all.***

Letting Go...

Angelina and I were still relatively new with only a couple returnings under our belts, but our *Snowbird* title still remained ambiguous. We had yet to "prove" ourselves. Another visit would encourage our hosts of our commitment. It would assure friends and neighbors in Puerto Vallarta that we were serious about annual return-visits. Furthermore, and just as relevant, it would advise family, friends and neighbors back home that we were becoming regular, annual-absentees.

In Mismaloya, we could only verbalize another return. They were reluctant to accept annual but non-committal renters. Their lives went on regardless with or without us. However, with our families, I needed to be a little more sensitive and reassuring, "We are not *deserting* you at all. We are taking our retirement seriously, that's all, and trying to enjoy ourselves. Of course, we *enjoy* our grand kids, but "bucket-lists" demand attention too."

Now, there's another great film worth mentioning, *The Bucket List*. Written by Justin Zackham and directed by Rob Reiner, guess who *returned* to star in this movie? Right! Good ol' Jack and Morgan again. That film did more good to help retired-folks, like us, make excuses to get away than nearly any other reasons I can come up with. "Kids, it's a *bucket-list* thing! Climbing Mt. Everest requires significant time-away and attention to detail. Gotta go! See you from the top!" Of course, you can relate later that you only made it as far as

Las Vegas! They'll understand. Tell them that you went there first to help *finance* the trip, but things *got out of hand,* and you lost all your money, instead. They'll understand!

Our *bucket list* item was still another return, and I needed to vociferate my conditions. Some people, parents in particular, and especially mothers, have a difficult time "letting-go." In most extended-families, and ours was no exception, there were always continual streams of news. Some could tie you down. Some could drag you down. Typically, it usually regarded any latest ups-and-downs, here-say and they-say, and dramatic, pathetic or general and incidental events.

Much of family member contact was by telephone or cell phone and cell-messaging services anyway. Granted, there were physical contacts too, but for the most part, I observed that mutual calls made from fifty miles away were common, efficient and sufficient. Grasping that, I rationalized that calls made from two-thousand miles away could achieve similar results. Don't get me wrong, visitation times spent with children and grand-children are special and precious to be sure. I don't mean to discount or deny any value from them; however, I think there is something to be said about the old standard, "quality-over-quantity."

I developed a tangential belief too, or maybe it was a "flip-side" of the quality/quantity thing: "Absence impresses presence." It's sort of similar to "Absence makes the heart grow fonder." True, Grand kids are *impressed* with *presents*, but the concept still works. Daily, typical run-of-the-mill stuff can be handled from long-distances. "Newsworthy" propaganda can be handled in more depth and detail over a "Welcome-Back" party and a cup of coffee.

It's like watching and listening for politics and world events on TV: I sit on my couch at home in California, watch CNN or Fox and become incensed at what I see or hear of what is going on. I yell with or at any company and complain and/or feign abject outrage or indignation. Regardless, naturally, I can't or won't do anything about it. Two-thousand miles away in Puerto Vallarta I can choose to watch news, or not, and do exactly the same thing. I'll deny or refuse any involvement, but I can still complain or agonize over matters. One subtle difference is that *being away* influences my tendency to remain relatively ignorant of home-base, local, state, national, and world-events. Life goes on. Ignorance really is *bliss.*

Using similar, self-persuasion, family may be dealt with in the same fashion.

Phone contact, and now we can add e-mails to connectivity, keep just about all standard, general news abreast. Serious news causes a little more hardship, but absence does two things: First, it requires clarity and brevity; parties need to get to the gist of situations and determine what actions to take, or they can provide reasonable verbal and moral support. Second, absence tends to focus contact on items of more serious nature and avoid much of the incidental stuff; it prepares both sides for more meaningful gossip when physically reunited.

Another issue, but not insignificant, is the aspect of *independence.* That is mutual-independence. Children need to learn to resolve issues without parental support, input or solutions. Once parents are deceased, kids are on their own anyway. Being *absent* on extended getaways, long-term vacations, or even *getting-to-hell-out-of-Dodge* are practice-sessions for family during absences.

I believe in offering *heads-up*, encouraging *head-starts* and getting used to *head-ons.* Advice may be valuable, but it can be transmitted over phone-lines. I can serve as an idea-wall, objective-listener or family-supporter very well from long-distance via phone or e-waves. Finally, I appreciate becoming an outsider too. *Relative* decisions regarding personal, family-issues should be handled on their end, on their own and without our guidance.

There are so many family-conditions in which we need not be involved. By removing ourselves from back-and-forth drama-circles, we break the cycle. They become self-sufficient, self-reliant and independent. We, in turn, finally gain opportunities in this *twilight-of-our lives* period to again become responsible only for ourselves.

We compromise, sort of, by giving-up some pleasant, interaction with family. Granted, this is difficult, but in exchange, we receive an opportunity to distance ourselves from stress, anxieties and pressures caused by family-issues. In the long-run, it is healthier for all sakes. I know that I like the idea. I feel better just thinking about it...

Sometimes, I just want to get away to some place where I don't have to think about too much at all. I just want to sit down, relax and think about nothing. I'm actually pretty good for simply staring... Even Angelina doesn't appreciate that about me. While I'm concentrating on writing, she thinks I'm just sitting on my ass doing *nothing*.

Well, okay. Sometimes, she's probably right. My mind tends to wander a little. Occasionally, I can't remember what I started thinking about originally. Angelina believes it's the onset of Alzheimer's disease. I simply just deny it and advise that it's not a problem for me, only for her. I explain that I've had the same problem since I was one or two... that I can remember. That makes her mad or frustrated, but she ignores me, and I go back to my writing or *staring*.

But I think it's a *guy thing*. That's all. Men have the rare capacity and unique capability of doing absolutely nothing at all. I mean, meditation was invented just for me as long as we don't have to focus on any mantras or stuff. And it's not that we're brain-dead. We can be almost flat-lined yet still thinking, just not about much. I believe it takes extreme concentration. Maybe it's an inherent "Zen" thing: "Little-Grasshopper, you must focus on 'nothing.' Think about your sex-life."

By focusing on *nothing*, we men can recharge our mental-batteries, so-to-speak, so we can deal with everything else later. It's an *art,* I'll tell you.! I call it, "Meditation on the *Essence-of-Nothing*." Men bond with it and share it easily with each another. Women, on the other hand, will never understand it... or appreciate it.

MALE-BONDING
(OR)
"THE ESSENCE OF NOTHING"

Eh!
Sup?
Nudin'.
Oh....
Whatryadoin?
Nuthin'.
Oh....
Whadryadoin?
Nudin'.
Uhhu.
Wan' compny?
I 'oncare.
Cool!
Uhhu...

Eh, Dude.
Eh. Eh.
Sup?

Nuthin'. Nuddin'.
Nuthin', huh?
Uhu. Uhu.
Cool.
Uhhu. Uhhu.
Wansommocomny?
Don' care. Don' care.
A'ri'!
Uhhu. Uhhu...
Amigos!
Hey! Hey! Hola!
?Que' pasa?
Nada. Nada. Lo mismo.
?Nada, huh?
No nada. No nada. Lo mismo.
?Ustedes quieren hablar?
(You guys wanna talk?)
Si. Si. Claro.
Esta bien.
Si. Si. Uhuh.
Todo es bueno.
Si. Si. Uhuh...

?Ustedes quieren hacer algo?
(You guys wanna do something?)
No. No. Nada.
Esta bien.
Uhuh. Uhuh. Si.
Es bueno que no servimos para nada.
(It's good that we are good for nothing.)
Si. Si. Uhuh...

Only men can say so little,
Yet come to terms so well.
Women will never grasp their riddle,
And men can never tell.

Breakaway...

We never really know what's behind the next bend, let alone the next day or week or... None of us have crystal balls. We can only plan, prepare and hope for the best. Unfortunately, it doesn't always turn out *best.* Remember Forest Gump's T-shirts: *Sh-t happens!* (Happy Face) *Stuff* can instantly change plans if not destinies. What was that prayer again?.. G*rant me the serenity to accept...* Alright then, we'll just shift gears, drive around this obstacle and switch to Plan B. There was always *Plan A:* We successfully and happily scurried aboard an expectant and welcomed plane and flew-off together, hand-in-hand to our lovely, awaiting Neverland. *Plan B* was similar, but it had some less warranted modifications.

I realized during our return, home-stay that some unexpected circumstances were likely going to require and deserve Angelina's attention and support. Further, those activities would be time-constraining and likely not allow her to return to PV with me. She probably wouldn't get away until the end of January. Naturally, I was frustrated and disappointed, but I worked on *accepting what I could not change...* Instead, it was a time for "compromise" to rear its ugly face again.

With a little wind lost in my sails, I knew I would not want to bring in New Year's Eve without Angelina especially under present circumstances. So, I just explained to her that after the holidays, all of them, her responsibilities no longer necessitated my presence.

Like last year, I could return to Vallarta and set up household again returning to my Spanish lessons and writing. As soon as she felt comfortable, she could rejoin me in Paradise Lost (Mismaloya). *Paradise* wasn't *lost* yet, but it was getting difficult to relocate. A final, up-my-sleeve card-trick offering and yet another *compromising*-initiative was my promise to pay for her round-trip tickets for this next adventure.

Angelina agreed. Furthermore, she understood. It would not be pleasant for me hanging around needlessly while she raced all over the place with family members resolving necessary matters. Furthermore, it would waste a prepaid month's rent. Finally, she knew where my heart was, and she wanted me to be content. I wanted the same for her, but I recognized that it wasn't with me at that time. We had done this act before; it had been successful. We would do it again.

Return to Never Land...

Our compromise resolved, agreed upon and put-into-action, I departed once again alone but back to Mismaloya for my third major visit. A childish part of me imagined I was off again for *Never Land*, and I'd start carousing once again with my ex-patriot, *lost boys*. Unfortunately, *Wendy* wasn't with me. It was January 2nd and still (sort of) the beginning of the New Year. I had agreed to remain home for all the holidays to be with Angelina and our families. She, on-the-other-hand, had agreed for me to return to Puerto Vallarta solo again. That's compromise, I suppose. At least, I knew that she would be okay for awhile to handle her required responsibilities with family. Afterward, Angelina would rejoin me when an opportunity allowed. For the time being, though, I was on my way.

Another flight from San Francisco to Puerto Vallarta made me satisfyingly aware that we were both getting comfortably experienced with the routine. Taxis, although not that expensive considering the distance from the airport to our rental, were not even required. We knew our ways around town pretty well by now. The local, bus-systems were just about our answer to all our transportation needs. We'd already had bus-rides throughout Puerto Vallarta for variety of reasons including shopping, entertainment, visits, touring, and sight-seeing. We had even taken several, long-distance trips well beyond the city; a few of those were even hours away and included overnights. We were pretty savvy bus riders by then.

Besides, I was traveling light this trip. I'd left just about everything in Vallarta from last time except for my electronics. A basic, carry-on piece of luggage allowed me to easily grab a local bus to or from the airport. In town, we'd take the bouncy and racy, milk-run, sight-seeing trips to any destination but always end up at ***El Centro*** bus stop. From there, like clockwork on any quarter-hour except late-at-night, we'd take the last-leg home on a ***Mismaloya-Boca*** bus.

This time, however, I'd made arrangements for friends to pick me up. I was met at the airport as scheduled, and after two, brief-stops ***para el dinero, comida, tequila y cerveza***, they whisked me conveniently back to my lovely ***Mismaloya*** home. ***"Muchas gracias! Adios! Nos vemos mas tarde!"*** I was finally back again. Piece-of-cake!... It wasn't *Never Land*, but I'd thought I'd *never* get here.

HOME IS A PLACE

To kiss such faithless shores from home
Absently waiting hope's return
Leaves hearts aware tracks left to yearn
Were covered by an ocean's foam.

Remorseful love's examined fate,
When minds reject lessons to learn,
Lets absence substitute concern
With vague promises cast to wait.

Faint memories' abandoned wombs,
Intended for passion's sweet burn,
Are blighted by incessant turns
Anticipating love to roam.

But, reaching inside Heaven's Gate,
Resurrected flesh may rise reborn
Exposing idle-threats concern-
Indifference from a doubting mate.

Then swept away by Clair-de-lune
With seascapes stirring hearts to churn,
Skeptics partake when they discern
(Vallarta's) *Moonlight* is doubt's catacomb...

Denials are all mental-states
Which simply need to be adjourned.
Commitment's love can be reborn;
Home is a place that hearts create.

"Mismaloya Blues"

Part 19:
Un Poco Historia...

Everybody's got a story... Most of them deserve to be told. The better ones are repeated, and the best ones get told over-and-over again. What is sometimes so entertaining is the re-telling. Do you remember playing *Post-office* as a child with friends or classmates? The object was to whisper a brief-story or statement to one person, and then they would whisper it to the next, and so-on until the last person had heard the "whispered" story. That *last* person would then repeat the story aloud typically to hysterical laughter from other participants who recognized the evident and absurd distortions and inaccuracies. The initial, story-teller would then restate the actual and true, first-version to unabated laughter once again emitted by all players. When *truth* is told, most of us are surprised and shocked at its *reality* compared to what is *supposed.* Fact *is* stranger than fiction...

Post-office is an innocent, fun and inviting game for anyone to join. I used it often throughout years as a high school teacher for two reasons: First, it was a connectivity-thing encouraging all class members to participate in social-activities with others (classmates); second, the game served as a lesson as to how *gossip* and, particularly, *history* can be perverted and disguised, if not completely changed, over multiple telling and time. Some students actually enjoyed embellishing their "whispered" versions to add spice to the story. I would tell them that doing so was very natural and typical. People enjoy and prefer colorful accounts of events over brevity. If you want to sell a book or a newspaper, make it interesting.

History is like that; so is gossip, but we'll refrain from any personal vendettas at least for the time-being. A little later forward I can have some fun with a few neighborly remarks. However, history can be mind-boggling especially if you want to get it right. Recall this lesson: *History is written by victors.* Who knows what losers thought? They were probably killed if not culturally destroyed.

The point is that we need always to look at topics and recognize biases.

Who wrote the article or story? What was its focus and purpose? To what audience was it intended? For example, heroes of the (US) American Westward Movement are likely not considered so heroic or glorious according to Native American Indian tribal accounting.

How about our (US) American *Manifest Destiny* or our *Monroe Doctrine*? I'll bet there were a few, Indian tribal-hearings and Spanish and Mexican or other European legislative-sessions which were provoked into a little outrage and indignation over those decrees. It even caused a couple of provocations to go to war. And yet, examples came from wars which followed which gave evidence: "To victors go the spoils." That, however, doesn't necessarily include explanations of why or how "spoils" were attained. *Who did what* depends on *who wrote what.* And even after that, who kept track of what inside the libraries?

Research accounting's of the Crusades Era from the Persian's point-of-view suggest a significantly different outlook. From their writings, you will discover a very contrary perspective on plot, storyline and results. *World History 1A* taught in Asian schools varies significantly from European and Western education. Try this on. Look at my own California history for variances of historical accuracy.

California became the 31st State of the United States of America in 1850. That conveniently followed gold being discovered there. Before that, Indians had lived unrestrained for perhaps thousands of years or more. Of course, prior to gold discoveries, these Indians had been subdued, subordinated and subjected to subtle powers of passive Christianity or conquered by Spanish influences from priests, explorers and soldiers. Later, the whole countryside was usurped by Mexico. Finally still, Mexico was defeated by... you got it, the USA whose *destiny had been manifested!* Today, California is certainly a unique state with a history qualified by several varying but reasonable claims to historical accuracy.

The next portion of this "*fable*lous" story is devoted to a little discussion of Puerto Vallarta's history. The region which is now Vallarta missed some major, epochal milestones which had affected its Eastern and Southern neighbors. Apparently, according to historical records, Vallarta avoided imperialistic restraints or spectacular growth its neighboring Aztec and Mayan Civilizations. Similarly, however, the Spanish ultimately stepped-in to develop the quiet, beautiful and pristine areas of the presently called region, ***Bahia de Banderas***, for their benefit.

The story of Puerto Vallarta is long-time coming. Vallarta began as an ageless and unadulterated, sleepy and practically abandoned coastal area. Then, in relatively recent times, it developed into a modern and international, fast-track, tourist-attraction. Going from a quiet, sleepy, little village to a wide-awake, bustling municipality took a bit of slow-and-steady, nestling encouragement.

Vallarta's history may be more easily digested or understood with a simple and silly simile like the following: Vallarta was like having a nice pot of richly flavored coffee freshly-brewed on a stove in the early morning. Gently the aromas whif past taunting your nostrils to begin flaring. Dragging yourself into the kitchen, you pour that first cup. *Aaaahhh!* Then, with hot and savory, java-juices flowing down your welcoming throat, your brain gets a kick-start. You begin perking up, gaining some energy and becoming partially aware of your surroundings. Another cup o' Joe to say, "Hello!" and you're ready-to go. Finally, with briefcase in hand, you step casually outside your front door to instantly discover *a tornado heading right for your front porch!* Now, you're awake! Life has got your attention!

Vallarta was like that! It was asleep for several millenniums, or more. Now it's awake and moving forward in a turbulent frenzy. At the same time, it struggles to maintain its calming, mesmerizing and tranquilizing effects. More and bigger crowds visit its shores every year. Hustle-and-bustle and growth are evident everywhere. Yet, every vendor or tourist-attraction invites its guests to sit down, relax, have a cerveza or tequila or a taco, and enjoy the beauty and harmony of jungle meeting ocean on this sensually gorgeous, and emotionally, seductive bay.

Its relatively recent growth-cycle, when compared to the hundreds, if not thousand(s), of Aztec and Mayan years' influences is reasonably significant. If we just consider its modern history, like say the past 100 years, Vallarta has painted a vibrant and colorful story of itself. It's a tale worth repeating. Let's take a look...

Once Upon A Time...

In the beginning, dinosaurs roamed Earth we are taught. A few even wandered down the Pacific coastline to ***la Bahia de Banderas*** we're told. Other non-scientific theorists of somewhat different persuasions even believe with a slightly contrary twist that ***Mismaloya***, a valuable and important ***Zona de Puerto Vallarta,*** may probably even be where *Eden* was located. Adam and Eve lived there happily, for awhile anyway, under an apple tree. Right. Sure. I'm not going to debate the issue, though. It's actually kind of cute. In fact, I even got a chance to visit ***Eden*** in a tour of ***Mismaloya*** and its vicinity. ***Eden*** is located way-up a nearby canyon, and I even saw a sign: *Welcome to Eden*. It is very beautiful, no question about it, seemingly a *Paradise.*

Adding to debate, with some confusion, is the fact that much later on, a film was made right there in the exact, same-location. That's right! Arnold Schwarzenegger and Carl Weathers starred in *Predator* where they fought against violent, but sportsmanlike, alien-visitors from another world. Go figure! Three, conflicting-theories on the *origins-of-humanity* in one spot: *Evolution* with Charles, *Creation* with Adam and Eve and *alien-invaders* with Arnold! That just goes to show how you can mix provable, significant and sensible pieces of data with non-sense and trivia...

For instance, I know Arnold was here because I saw the movie! Case closed. But, can you believe all the rest? I mean, it's just a little bit much to grasp. To think that dinosaurs actually tramped all-the-way down here to Puerto Vallarta of all places? Wow! Really? Of course, there are lots of alligators all over the place, and that sort of defends ol' Charles's theory, but there's no "Dino-tracks." Also, please understand that local museums don't offer much reference, if any, to dinosaur theories. Nor, for that matter, do they even discuss Adam and Eve much except maybe during Sunday School lessons at ***Our Lady of Guadalupe Church*** in ***El Centro***; however, there are dozens of references about Arnold and Carl fighting alien-invaders in and around Eden. Got it? Right! It sells tours!

I mean, like I tell you, I was there! I even saw a supposed helicopter that crash-landed in the jungle. Took my picture in it for proof. Ask me, and I'll send you a friggin' copy. So, what are we supposed to believe? In a thousand years or more, who's going to be talking about dinosaurs and Adam and Eve? But, you can bet your last computer-chip, however, they'll be *Googling* or watching *You Tube* videos of Schwarzenegger and Weathers battling an arch-enemy from another Galaxy. History is like that: The exciting stuff sounds good and sells...

History often advises and teaches us about what seems *entertaining* to believe not necessarily the actual truth. *Truth* always leaves a little room for speculation and "literary license." That is what sells books, even history books, and in this case, movies. For goodness sake, everyone loves an embellished story. From baby-hood to old-folks' homes, we enjoy hearing a clever tale. Sometimes, the most outrageous *history* comes from actual, recorded, human-conditions; other times, it may come from historians turned wannabe, Sci-Fi writers. Even already accomplished, successful authors often get to re-write history with personal slants.

In our youth, we start off with Princesses and Prince Charmings and their dealings with terrible ogres and evil kingdoms. Eventually, we end up fighting monsters in outer-space. One single author alone, Jules Verne, did it all. From his authorship, our fantasies and imaginations blended fact mixed with fiction offering us vicarious experiences through his charismatic characters. They (Jules) took us inside

Earth, under Earth's oceans, around Earth, and *From the Earth to the Moon.*

Just think about all the sci-fi fantasies mixed with non-fiction sold to us with popular cover-stories: *Dinosaur BBQ: Yummi!; Alien-Trash: Litter They Left Behind; Abductions: Who Took My Cheese and My Wife?;* and *Alien Bounty Hunters: Out-of-This-World Rewards!* Or, do you remember any of these: *Journey(s) to the Center of the Earth, 10,000 Years BC, 20,000 Leagues Under the Sea? Mars Attacks! 2001: A Space Odyssey,* (and we passed that date already). Need I go on... "To infinity and beyond?" And what about Network TV, Cable TV, DVDs, or *Netflix?* Why, we're just getting started!

And the *Bible* is full-of-it! I mean, *OMG!*, it is filled with enticing, unique and relevant fantasy and fiction, er, I mean *historical drama.* How about: *Daniel in the Lion's Den*?.. Without a chair and a whip? C'mon! Exciting, though, huh? And I should really have gone for that one in a "roaring" frenzy (pun intended) because Daniel was my *namesake.* Well, he and Daniel Boone were. Anyway, I always enjoyed imagining *a lion-stand-off*... Yeah! Just me, hungry, violent and angry lions, and my trusty, Remington 1200, 12-Gauge, semi-automatic, slide-action shotgun: Good ol' "Lick-Ticker." It's the kind of stuff *B-movies* and history are made of.

Anyway, my version might have been a little more realistic, though, but not as colorful. Bullshit walks, but *faith* talks and sells books! Yet, I wonder what the critics might have written if only Daniel had put his head in a lion's mouth for special-effects? Wow! And the audience roared, *"Ooooohhh!"* and they bought souvenirs... and *books.* Dens and cages filled with 'em!

And how about Jonah in a whale's belly? Compelling, right? But, have you ever seen the size of a whale's esophagus? Well, neither have I, but I *Googled* it once, and *it's* very small,... smaller than Jonah, for heaven's sake! The poor creature was probably choking-to-death and spit Jonah out for self-survival. Of course, maybe Jonah was very small; a dwarf, perhaps? That would have changed the scale of the story, (pun intended) somewhat, but it might have made the fable a little more *believable,* although not as impressive. The Bible doesn't mention Jonah's height, though, does it? Of course not!

That's the point. It's a *big deal*; a big story! The plot has got to be captivating and relevant. It helps a lot when the characters are *bigger-than-life*. That's what Hollywood celebrities used to say about Charlton Heston when he played characters like Moses and Ben Hur for the big-screen cameras: "He was like *GOD* stepping onto the stage!" Big people equals big characters equals big gigs equals big bucks!

Like, for instance, that *showboat* story? How about Noah and his arc? Modern science tells us that there are over seven million (7,000,000) species of animals alive on planet Earth. Even if Noah did try stuffing pairs of them all into his boat, it would have reached capacity by the time he finished loading just the alphabetized "A's." There wouldn't have even been enough room to load up the *baboons,* for God's sake! I mean, for heaven's sake. And *forty days and nights in a stinking-storm?* And how about all the crap to clean-up? And can you imagine how much air-freshener they needed to bring aboard too? And feeding-time-at-the zoo? Gee, I'll bet that was a picnic! Gimme a break! But, it sounds cool! It makes great movies. It's interesting, if not intriguing, and we all know it sold a *lot* of books! I mean, *ship*-loads of books… all printed in China!

Alright, now we're on-a-roll… Let's bring back *Moses* again, and, of course, Charlton. Moses was an enigmatic-character played on screen (and off) by a modern, cinematic-god, Charlton Heston. As an infant slave, Moses avoided death by being rescued and adopted by a barren, Egyptian Princess who raised him as her son, a Prince. When Moses discovered in adulthood that he was, in reality (sure), born of slaves, he rebelled and set his people free by parting the sea and drowning all the enemy.

Of course, by that time, he had already determined that he was also one of the "chosen people" and deserved to live. All the poor-sap, working-stiff, Egyptian soldiers who drowned in the Red Sea didn't count. On that fateful day, thanks to Moses's evil, adopted-brother, the Pharaoh, orders were commanded to all his soldiers: "Catch the runaway-slaves!" Little did anyone know, understand or appreciated of God's plan to deal with those meaningless, Egyptian, scum-sucking, scavenger-type, disposable beings who did not deserve survival while following Pharaoh's orders.

"Hey, Yasser, Jr., whatever happened to your dad, Pvt. Arafat when he was in the army?

"Oh, apparently, Allah drowned him while he was running after Moses trying to catch him for the Pharaoh. Allah be praised!"

Gee whiz, that makes me second-guess our American forefathers. Maybe our *Constitution* should have had us electing *Pharaohs* of the United States, not *Presidents.* Weren't a lot of those guys and Congressmen running around chasing slaves everywhere too. George and Tom must have flipped-out when they heard about a few attempts "Movin' on up to the East side!" I think my hero, Barack, would have absolutely floored them... But I digress.

Besides, Moses was looking for the *Promised Land.* In forty years, why didn't anybody mention ***Puerto Vallarta*** to him? The answer is simply because that would have been the end-of-the-story, that's why! ***Mismaloya*** with ***Eden*** square in the middle of it meant *tranquility* for all. Perfection! There were still tribulations and Commandments yet to come.

Peace did not have a chance. And as far as I can tell, Israel is still looking for some today, from outside and inside. I don't know about "Chosen People," either. Chosen for what? Superiority in Heaven? Is that some kind of a private club sporting a fancy, Yiddish, entrance sign: *No Heathens Allowed*? Or, were they simply chosen for the rest of the world's ridicule? If that's the case, then God must really have a *bent* sense-of humor. Funny, though!

Okay. Enough of that *Old News*. How about n*ew news*, the "Good News*?*" For nearly two-thousand years now, a large chunk of humanity has been deciphering, interpreting, preaching, and politicking supposed teachings from one of the greatest minds of all time. And yet, anything recorded of Jesus' *teachings* did not occur until at least forty years after his death. Some re-telling came even much, much later than that. Forty years! Wow! I forget what I promised last night. And, just look at some of the stories which are told:

Jesus saved a *prostitute* from certain death when he commanded, "Ye, who have not sinned, cast the first stone." Well, for cryin'-out-loud, most of those spectators had been putting-up pretenses for years. Why wouldn't any amongst the group rain a volley of boulders down on the sinful woman's head just to keep up their "act?" In today's societies, the list of self-righteous volunteers would be staggering. The whore would not have just been bludgeoned by stones, she'd have been buried alive under a rainstorm of pebbles.

I've seen plenty of "rock-throwers" on TV. Every Sunday morning, they scream, rant-and-rave, fake-heal, promise salvation, and beg constantly for money. Heck, those *sinless-pretenders* would have used heavy-duty sling-shots to do their *self-righteous,* dirty-work. A few of them probably would have even known the woman intimately too. Their shame. Some of the biggest mouths or the loudest ones also seem to have the biggest churches. I think they probably sell the most books too. It figures.

Now, don't get me wrong. I'm not questioning... I'm just sort of challenging what *real facts* exist. I've got faith. Why, when it comes to *faith, I'm full of it!* I mean, I believe! I just don't believe in others ramming their mission down my throat, or ears... I don't appreciate one hand on my shoulder while the other reaches for my wallet. Yes, I challenge what others say because I often think they have selfish purposes in mind. I don't deny them their God-given, er, well, *constitutional-rights* to speak, or even preach or believe whatever they wish. I just object to what they determinedly attempt to belay or portray on me.

However, on the contrary, though, let's get this clear for argument's sake. I *am* a believer. I believe in Jesus. I know He existed. I am certain that He achieved a *higher-plane* (plain?) that I can't even spell let alone comprehend. Yet, I accept Him as a voice, a leader, a guide, and as a mentor. Jesus is an example of someone I really look up to (no *pun* intended).

I even conversed with Him once. Well, I mean that one-time during my early thirties, after a near-fatal, car-accident, I awakened from a one-week coma. There, alone in my hospital bed lying in a full-body cast and suspended in the air to avoid all movement, I was overcome with the realization and nearness of my potential demise. I clearly understood with my stifled and near-frozen vision on the hospital wall before me that I had almost died.

I still didn't even know why or what had happened, but I was sobbing and overcome with gratefulness for surviving. I cried. I sobbed uncontrollably, and I thanked God for His mercy and begged for forgiveness and for Jesus to be in my life. And He answered me. It was so simple yet so pure and understandable,. His words were so gratifying, reassuring and blessed.

Oh, sure, I was hysterical at the time, but it was *my hysteria* and *my reality*. It was very private and very personal. At least, I believe He answered me. *And it was good...* You see, that's what I'm talking about. It doesn't matter what history books report, or what others say, sometimes. It only matters what we "believe" for ourselves and how we believe in ourselves. Ultimately, it is always our own interpretations which guide us toward all things.

We all need to find things, solutions and answers to our needs or prayers which we can comfortably put our *faith* into. *Don't confuse me with facts; my mind's made up!"* It's all about what works for any of us. What floats our boats? What gives us meaning, purpose, significance, and hope? If it seems right to us, then we should believe in it. Go with it! Feel it! Live it! Just don't hurt anybody! However, if we break laws in the process whether social, civil, federal, or international, and we end up going to trial and even to jail, then our shame and crime go with us. That we can believe! And then, we deserve everyone's snubbing, too. "Fool! You hurt someone, and you got caught! Shame!" Now you really must live with it.

But, who am I to challenge what happened to Jesus's prostitute? *Mary, Mary, quite contrary!* Oh, I know it's a different Mary, but it's still not my place! How dare I question whether dinosaurs romped around Puerto Vallarta or not. You see, that's not the point... Tell a story. Make it *fabulous*! The fatter the fish, the funnier the fable. But don't tell your family; they'll just think you're nuts! You've got to tell perfect strangers; they'll believe anything!

Remember this: When President Barack Obama gives the annual SOTU address, people are glued to their TVs and focused on every word. However, when our president goes home to Chicago each year for his Annual Obama Family Reunion, he's just good ol' Big Ears to the aunts and uncles and cousins. They all just want to know if he will be on their team for horseshoes or sack-races and if he can fix a traffic-ticket for them, or something.

So make up a fantastic story, like one of Barack's SOTUs, or something! If you want to do some serious misleading, then remember that creative, old adage: If you can't blind 'em with brilliance, then baffle 'em with bullshit! I call it, *Pulling-a-Presidential-on-the-People.* And just tell strangers! They want to believe. If it's exciting enough, people will remember it and repeat it. That's the object! Get your story repeated. Get your version out there! Get it all on-record. Take plenty of pictures, too, if you can. Get it all into history books.

Then, all the little, school-ground kiddies will be reciting memorized verse from legends of your exploits! You, and the likes of you, will make hysteria, I mean *history*! Even if it's not a nice story, it will be entertaining, and you'll sell books, piles of 'em for the annual Censorship Book-Burning Events. Your words will *light-a-fire,* and then they may *be on fire!*

And now, you understand why I love to write poetry. My stuff is going to be *burning* off the pages in all the history books that include it someday! If I can't be famous, then I'll be infamous! Children everywhere will be repeating and performing my poetry during recess-time (and then get disciplined, maybe)... Professors will challenge their classes' intellects to decipher *what-in-hell* (I) meant... Martial-Arts

Masters (sifu) will require to-dai (students) to repeat favorite stanzas before entering dojos or training-halls... I'll be revered by some and damned by others... But it's attention, and talk is good,... cheap, but good!

I'll be a legend-in-my-own-mind. First, however, I've got to sell some books, a bunch of 'em, maybe even a million... If you're reading this, though, then my fifteen-minutes-of-fame ain't up yet, unless you're a speed-reader. So, slow down and savor my minutes! "***Muchas gracias***!" I'm on my way. Read on...

PAST TENSE...

Speaking of,... it's time to deal with a few true *legends* of Puerto Vallarta. Excusing dinosaurs and Adam and Eve, and excluding Arnold and Carl, still leaves a multitude of historically accurate and important characters who helped shape and transform ***Puerto Vallarta*** into what it has become today. Many recognized this area early-on for its beauty and incredible potential. They may have had varying opinions, however, regarding that *potential* and how the area might have best served themselves, Spain, or today's ***Mexico***, and even the world.

They all agreed, though, that the beautiful, safe and beneficial ***Bahia de Banderas*** (Bay of Flags) offered a destined-place among favorite, exotic-locations. Some of them had already been to Hawaii and Bali or had heard of them. They all understood Vallarta's comparable potential and dreamed of sharing its vitality and tranquility. Yet, some of them had never even been to ***Mismaloya***!

Many of us have seen Mel Gibson's film, *Apocalypto*. Absolutely brilliant! From it, we might sympathetically imagine a few, remote Indians having lived quietly, peacefully and serenely amongst the abundant beauty and prosperity of deserted beaches now known as the Municipality of ***Puerto Vallarta***. That would have been here long before the bay, its beaches and all the incredible potential were discovered by Spanish explorers in the mid-1500's. Likely, any potential Indians were chased away, Christianized, enslaved, killed, or otherwise expelled by conquering, sea-captains or Conquistadors seeking wealth and prosperity for Mother-Nation, ***Espania***.

I mention this only because there seems to be little mention of any "Close Encounters of the Third Kind" by local, tribes-people. Today, there are multitudes of locals and non-native visitors who love to share their incredible "encounters" with alien sightings especially doing so over complimentary shots of tequila. Also, there appears to be few recollections of native-contact from former sea-explorers entering the area. I think like Mel does that there were sparse sets of independent-minded, anti-government, westward-ho, type-Indians living along the shorelines.

These people, in my imagination, had all broken away from their ***Aztec*** or ***Mayan*** ruling-civilizations. They sought, "*Freedom*!" Oh, wait! That was another Mel Gibson movie, *Braveheart,* but you get the point. It was a quiet, peaceful life of sleeping, eating and no taxes.

The natives had discovered and chosen, instead, private, personal and non-governed lives for themselves and their families offering them *true* freedom! Hunting for food, fishing, playing, chasing wildlife, getting chased by wildlife, sleeping... other stuff too, made the *real* "American Dream" real. What a life! Maybe that will be my next book, after the Amazon gig. I've got to talk to Mel about a potential *spin-off.* He'd love it!

Can you imagine, though, for a minute, the stunned and shocked disbelief of those horrified and terrified Indians when first laying eyes upon those enormous and fantastic, white-bellowed, god-like vessels floating into their once calm and gentle, front-yards? Those poor, peace-loving, anarchistic, Native-Indians were likely then to have believed "alien-gods" had sailed into their bay and set foot upon otherwise virgin shoreline. What these pathetically disturbed and frightened Indians may have done to their undershorts, in light of anxious fear of reprisals from their would-be Aztec rulers (in theory), gave evidence to some of history's first examples of ***Montezuma's*** *Revenge*!

Take heart, co-sympathizers. Records reflect that after a few, initial Spanish beach fronts, the area was forsaken, forgotten and left alone for another 300 years. The Natives must have jumped out of their trees rejoicing! How would you like a three hundred-year reprieve from *invasion of your privacy*? Heck, I'd put some of it up-for-sale at those prices! Another theory I suggest is that the early explorers had simply arrived and visited during the summer months. Without air-conditioning and no insect-repellant, they probably just couldn't stand the place for very long and begged their Captain to sail away for an ocean's breeze. I mean, how long and how far will mosquitoes chase you over the ocean?

But, let's give credit where credit belongs. I would not even be sitting here right now giving this accounting of ***Puerto Vallarta*** had it not been for those amazing, brave, adventurous, and visionary explorers and developers who came here first. Well, second, if you count my anti-***Aztec*** rebels. Anyway, remember my "book-seller "theory? It's not just *winners* who write history. They also have to be educated. At least one among the horde of sword-swinging conquerors must have been able to jot down a few notes of accomplishment like dates and stuff.

Maybe that is why we know so little about *Vikings* and their expeditions westward. Today, for history's sake, television offers us a great show, *Vikings*, on cable TV. It's sort of a spin-off of *Dallas,* but it takes place during the Middle-Ages, and is not as violent, emotionally at least. Vikings were supposed to be the first discoverers exploring the *New World.* Well, let's revise that to *second,* right? Remember the Indians and dinosaurs and Adam and aliens?

Of course, that simply complicates the issue because neither of them, Indians or Vikings, could write. How do we know what either of them did? We have to rely on television programs to tell us. Who knows now what *really* happened? In the future, history will teach whatever their current historians research and determine from cable-television programs' library-research. Some of them may even have their own, private DVD collections.

The point is that Vikings left no written-records behind of their potential exploits and few mementos detailing their achievements except for a few hacked-up human carcasses. Most of those were probably Indians too. So, who cared? And the local Indians? Most of their communication probably went up in smoke. It's hard to record gestures and even more difficult to recognize them unless you're there. Little is now known of either except for the vivid imaginations and creative impulses of Hollywood, script-writers. *That's it*! Hollywood determines history!

The Spanish, on-the-other-hand, could write, *and* they won. History was theirs to record. What now comprises the ***Puerto Vallarta*** region, according to recorded Spanish history, was that the bay's magnificent beaches were first discovered by ***Don Pedro de Alvarado*** in 1541. It was named ***Bahia de Banderas***, *Bay of Flags,* due to a significant battle between ***Hernan Cortez***, conqueror of ***Montezuma*** and the ***Aztec*** Empire. The battle comprised upwards of 20,000 ethically-challenged Indians protesting the encroachment. The name ***Banderas*** was offered as a tribute by ***Cortez***, himself, after receiving reports of his army's rather subdued victory. It came from his admiration of all the colorful banners indignant Indians used during their losing protest. Red was his favorite, blood red.

Alvarado and other future, explorer-adventurers believed the bay promised multiple use, port-potential for ships seeking supplies or safe-harbors for trips to the Philippines. ***El Capitan Pedro de Unamuno*** is credited for first proposing a settlement on ***Bahia de Banderas***. Other famous navigators like ***Sebastian Vizcaino***, ***Lopez de Vicuna*** and ***Gonzalo de Francia*** all dropped by more than once and encouraged Spanish colonies. However, an unresponsive ***Madrid*** left the incredible potential of ***Bahia de Banderas*** to almost nil attention with its unwillingness to devote finances to ***Vallarta's*** development. ***Alvarado*** and the others finally simply sailed away never to return. Desertion and being near-forgotten overcame the area for over three-centuries until the mid-1900s.

Actually, there were a few left-over, ardent-believers in the area's tranquil prosperity who hung onto their dreams of its potential. Other than them, however, ***Vallarta*** went virtually unrecognized.

Serious attempts to develop ship-building enterprises in probably what is now ***Mismaloya*** failed during the mid-1600's due to lack of government support. Slowly and steadily, however, the area grew and developed particularly because of the nearby silver and gold-mining industry. ***Vallartan*** population swayed to the wavering of those mountain enterprises.

Finally, in 1851 because of thriving businesses aligned with all the silver and gold mines in the mountain communities, big changes began to occur. An industrious and far-sighted businessman and developer, ***Don Guadalupe Sanchez Torres***, brought his family to the area now referred to as ***Las Penas de Santa Maria de Guadalupe***. He, and several others, truly saw the vast, apparent opportunities available from the area. Under ***Guadalupe's*** enthusiastic leadership, everyone focused on developing agriculture and cattle-raising.

With silver failures, the population actually retreated, adjusted but then grew and thrived due to farming. Agriculture became a major enterprise because of the incredibly rich and fertile soil. Many families migrated there from mountain communities such as ***Cuale*** and ***San Sebastian*** to establish farms. The port was opened to national, maritime-traffic following its official naming of ***Las Penas*** in 1885. By 1887, the community, now a significant town with a growing population of over 1,500 inhabitants, was given political and judicial authority by the ***State of Jalisco*** legislature in the governing capitol of ***Guadalajara.*** For many years following, with thanks and appreciation to ***Don Guadalupe's*** leadership and vision, ***Las Penas*** thrived. Today, in the city's square thrives a church with his name called: ***Nuestra Senora de Guadalupe*** (Our lady of Guadalupe). Some say, the parish is a honorary tribute to its namesake Cathedral in Mexico City. Is it just coincidence? Perhaps, but personally, I like to think maybe good ol' ***Don Guadalupe*** had something to do with it all. The people got two tributes for the price of one. Two birds with one stone. Pretty clever.

In 1918, the city had been prospering so much that by congressional decree, ***Las Penas*** was finally granted the title of Municipality.

Furthermore, in memory and honor of a beloved lawyer and Governor of ***Jalisco***, ***Don Ignacio L. Vallarta***, a new name was given to the port, and it officially became ***Puerto Vallarta.*** The reach of its municipality ranges all the way from the north where the coastal state of ***Nayarit*** borders ***Jalisco*** with their powerful ***Rio Ameca*** borderline to the sleepy, quaint, little fishing and tourist village, ***Boca de Tomatlan,*** in the south.

Vallarta continued steady progress with development in farming, agriculture and cattle-raising industries. Major setbacks occurred, though, when the government discouraged outside investors with legislation supporting Mexican farmers but not outsiders. During the later 1920's, those congressional decrees affected foreign-investors in the farming industry. As a direct result, ***Vallarta*** faltered and stagnated for several years.

Then in 1931, during the earliest years of the Great Depression, the Mexican government took dramatic and positive action to help solidify and encourage growth in the ***Puerto Vallarta*** region. By decree, the government advanced and supported native, Mexican people to participate and share in future growth and development of the ***Vallarta*** region. It enacted dynamic legislation referred to as ***del Ejido*** which provided large parcels of land to be shared among the locals who lived in areas of ***Mismaloya*** and ***Boca de Tomatlan*** and many other areas too.

New, local-users' responsibilities were to live on the land, develop it for future growth and pay appropriate, property-taxes accordingly. A key factor for ***Ejido*** was that land-occupiers could use the land, but they could not *own it.* Land "title(s)" remained with ***Ejido*** districts. Would success come from feudal-style, *non-ownership*, or could this simply blow-up literally in the faces of everyone? Who knew? Stay tuned, Readers...

However, for a short-period during war years of the 1940s, ***Banderas Bay*** did become well-known as a source of wealth for its sharks. In famous, New York Chinese restaurants, shark fins turned-up on tables feeding glamorous, wealthy, gourmet-gulping elite clientele. Also, shark liver oil became a nutritional supplement for USA WWII soldiers. And further, when clever entrepreneurs changed unpopular shark steaks to *white fish*, they created a hugely popular food source from ***Vallarta.***

Present Tension...

Finally, I was born, and that delightful fact brings us to more recent stages for ***La Bahia de Banderas*** transcendence into a place of welcoming tranquility and harmony. It's a good thing, too, because by the next century, I was going to need a place to go and get away! That must have been the godsend inspiration for ***Puerto Vallarta*** to really take-off and begin prospering: "Prepare Thyself, Oh, Bountiful Presence. Your long-awaited, loving-son (me) shall pass this way soon. Be ready to welcome him. In other words, 'Get your act together!'"

Throughout the Depression Era and WWII, tourism had actually steadily climbed as more and more visitors came each year to relax in the vivid sunshine, pure beachfront, and spectacular weather. Of course, it stagnated somewhat from time-to-time, but a few who could afford it steadily trickled down this way due to word-of-mouth from others who had basked in the area's delights. It is still obvious today that once anyone comes here to enjoy and appreciate the calming effects and *tranquility* of the area, they will likely talk and even brag about their experiences and encourage others to share in its nirvana-like sensations.

Over time, roads to ***Puerto Vallarta*** slowly improved. Trains developed and increased their runs to the area from contributing cities and the State of ***Jalisco's*** capitol, ***Guadalahara***. Even airlines jumped, or flew, onto the bandwagon by engineering new and better airfields for long-distance visitors. It was the beginning of a new future for ***Puerto Vallarta***. Suddenly, ***Vallarta*** and its nearby vicinities, including my beloved ***Mismaloya,*** would be put on the map. Curious discovery occurred from the unique friendship of two expressive and influential visitors: A brilliant, Mexico City engineer, ***Guillermos Wulff***, and a Hollywood giant, ***John Huston,*** who wrote about his experiences when first visiting the area:

> *When I first came here, almost thirty years ago, Vallarta was a fishing village of some 2,000 souls. There was one road to the outside world– and it was impassable during the rainy season. I arrived in a small plane, and we had to buzz the cattle off a field outside town before settling down.*
>
> (Huston, 1980. An Open Book)

These two visionaries bonded and brought about amazing and incredible popularity and growth to ***Puerto Vallarta's*** next phase of development. As a designer, ***Guillermo*** introduced the incredibly popular, Spanish-influenced ***cupola*** as an architectural element to the area. Visitors can still see everywhere the dome-like toppings on so many of the casas and buildings which exist today. Its unique and evident architecture can be seen all the way between ***Gringo Gulch*** area in ***Zona El Centro*** to the outlying ***Zona de Mismaloya*** giving ***Puerto Vallarta*** his, and its, unique influence. Some ***cupolas*** are presently used for water storage facilities while others are added for sheer, popular-design. Many are stoic, white domes; others are beautifully ornate with visually stunning colors. Regardless, they all make a special statement about their architectural presence.

By perhaps sheer coincidence, ***Wulff*** and ***Huston*** met in Los Angeles where ***Guillermo*** encouraged John to consider a beautiful area (***Mismaloya***) that he was familiar with for Huston's new jungle-setting film, *Night of the Iguana.* Huston had these penciled-in words to commemorate the event in his later autobiography:

> *In Los Angeles, I met a* Puerto Vallarta *architect and entrepreneur named Guillermo Wulff... I was thinking about locations for* Iguana, *and Guillermo urged me to go to* Mismaloya... *and although* Mismaloya *was Indian land, Wulff said he had a lease on it and could build anything he wanted there.*
>
> (Huston,1980. An Open Book).

Needless to say, this agreement and collaboration was the beginning of putting ***Puerto Vallarta*** on the world stage. The filming of *Night of the Iguana* was only the backdrop to much paparazzi-flooded attention that all the communities received. Hugely famous, Hollywood celebrities adorned the streets and shops and restaurants and taverns. Led by the ***Puerto Vallarta*** charmed Elizabeth Taylor and her lover/husband, Richard Burton, the once quiet, primeval beauty of ***Mismaloya*** and ***Puerto Vallarta*** was forever splashed across international tabloids. Gossip and outright Burton-Taylor lover's-warfare brought priceless attention to the area. ***Puerto Vallarta*** was a tourist spot to be reckoned with.

John ***Huston*** built a private villa in a nearby cove and lived there until shortly before his death in 1987. His impact on ***Puerto Vallarta*** was enormous.

He is still revered as a wonderful, gringo influence. Today, you can casually saunter through ***El Centro Cultural*** grounds next to ***el Rio Cuale*** and see a statue of John Huston honoring his contributions. And close by, you are able to climb up to ***Gringo Gulch*** and find the villa palaces owned and remodeled by Burton and Taylor which provided stationary and concrete evidence of their tumultuous and fanatically popular relationship.

With ***Puerto Vallarta*** now on the world stage, government funding and celebrity-level architects and developers converged on the area to begin serious development of ***Puerto Vallarta's*** long misunderstood potential. ***President Ascencio's*** government signed decrees declaring "residential and tourist development on all the lands surrounding ***Banderas Bay***." In 1970, a few years after the filming of *Iguana*, President Nixon from the USA and President Ordaz of Mexico met to sign and commemorate treaty negotiations between the two countries and publicize the international airport built in the area.

To encourage growth and tourism, the government in 1973 had already authorized the founding of the ***Puerto Vallarta Trust.*** This act opened up vast lands in the area and paved the way for new and significant investments instrumental in promoting development in ***Puerto Vallarta***. After that, development boomed, and construction increased while tourism expanded exponentially with new energy. By 1980, the earliest, mega-hotel/resorts, started springing up with the onset of the S***heraton Buganvillas***. To aid with this amazing growth period, the Mexican peso was devalued, actually cut in half, so builders had twice as much money to use for growth. Exotic hotels and resorts were built in a seeming frenzy.

Hollywood jumped back into the fray with a lovable sit-com, *Love Boat,* which showcased Puerto Vallarta as a preferred, tourist-destination. With humpback-whales and dolphins frolicking in the bay-waters, a sport-fishing industry drawing international participants, jungles, wetlands, lagoons, and incredible beaches, ***La Bahia de Banderas*** was accepted into the prestigious *Club des Baies plus Belles de Monde* (The World's Most Beautiful Bays Club).

Puerto Vallarta was now on the inside-lane and charging full-throttle into its future as a serious world contender for attention. The population proceeded to double every several years . Its new vision brought with it millions of pesos in new revenue each year for ***Vallarta's*** growth. Prosperity was well on-hand.

The ***Puerto Vallarta*** Tourism Fund was created in the mid-nineties, and funded by a 2% tax on hotel occupancy, 100% of the fund was used to promote ***Puerto Vallarta*** as a national and international vacation destination. The airport expanded with greater size and more contributing airlines from more cities. The astonishing, beautiful and enormously popular ***Marina*** was also developed which brought a wealthy class of vacationers seeking extremely reasonable rates for their yachts and glory on the gorgeous bay. Hotels boomed, new restaurants opened everywhere and along with highly satisfying tourism, ***Puerto Vallarta*** prospered and earned a solid position among world-class beach destinations. ***Acapulco*** and ***Mazatlan*** both had identities; ***Vallarta*** began giving them a run for their money.

Tourism thrived and increased. Foreigners came to ***Puerto Vallarta*** to make it their new home. These *ex-patriots* encouraged others to follow. That steady-wave promoted even more permanent homes to be built. Developing into an inexpensive and spectacular, though seasonally prohibitive, place-in-the-world to visit or live, ***Puerto Vallarta's*** popularity has persisted and magnified. With an advantageous exchange-rate between the US dollar and Mexican peso, ***Puerto Vallarta*** and Mexico in unison have encouraged tourism's monies to return.

In fact, to remind readers of our own, personal case again, Angelina and I dropped-by on a cruise, ourselves, in 2010. We were literally overwhelmed by Vallarta's beauty, character, charm, and inexpensiveness. With mutual promises to return and learn more about ***Puerto Vallartan*** grace, we set our goals. We researched, studied, learned, and made plans to return for our first, extended-visit.

Now, we have visited several times, including three, long-term stays, and accomplished multiple escapades. We may even be considered part of that special group who make return visits as often as possible, if not annually. Like many others who happen to find their niche in certain locations, we were fortunate to find ***Mismaloya***. We can now look forward and plan for annual, pleasing retreats.

Our goals are similar to many other foreign-visitors who enjoy partaking in the entertaining and tranquil glory of ***La Bahia de Banderas, Puerto Vallarta,*** and their surrounding-communities. Naturally, for us this includes coming back year-after-year, if we are able, to see our second-city love, our friends and our preferred home-away-from-home in ***Mismaloya-Boca***. If you enjoy living next to the sea, absorbing its grandiose vistas and along with that, basking in its soft and soothing metronome of surf-on-the-rocks or ***playas***, our location will soothe your bones.

If you prefer lights, action and camera and all the hullabaloo-activity generated from any city-hub, then you need only find your fulfillment in or nearby town. You can find park-settings, jungle-settings, river-settings, mountain-settings, harbor-settings, or concrete and steel-settings, and all with authentic, cobblestone streets to fill your needs. It's beautiful, it's good, it's fun, and it's all here waiting for visitors to share in its pleasing serenity and positive vibrations.

Also, the internet offers a vast array of information about nearly any aspect regarding ***Vallarta***. One need only *Google* and ask the right questions to find out more. Or, just ask my wife... Like the printing says on the funny T-shirts in ***Vallarta***, "I don't need Google. My wife knows everything!" That's because my wife *is* the *Supreme Googlist*! Anyway, resorts, hotels, villas, casas, apartments, condominiums, flats, and ***palapas*** are almost all available to review online. Photos and descriptions are offered of many of them on websites. Rental agencies, also found online, offer their services, and many can be found on *www.craigslist.com*.

Anyone can find an ideal place somewhere in or around ***Puerto Vallarta*** if they search well enough. Angelina and I feel fortunate to have found our niche so quickly, smoothly and easily. Now, we are always making mental-plans for potential, return-visits. There are conditions, though: Supportive relationships between our two, nations' governments must endure; there are no catastrophic developments in world economies (so Angelina and I can maintain our humble pensions); continued, universal-harmony for me...continues; and, God willing, "*the creeks (*and oceans*) don't ris*e!

If those stipulations persist, then Angelina and I might just pull-off our *never-ending-story* of *bucket-list*, check-off items by trekking on down to ***Vallarta*** *'till-we-cain't-trek-no-mo'!* Returning, however, requires one rule, "Not during the Summer!" We love our ***Mismaloya*** casa, and we really do enjoy being here,... but we're not crazy! We've just got to have air-conditioning and no bugs!

Future Tenacity...

Do you recall earlier historical information referencing highlights of the 1930's Mexican legislation providing home-building opportunities to the local gentry? It was called, ***del Ejido:*** Opportunities for poorer, working-class people to receive rights-to-build and live on some government-agency ***(Ejido)*** proffered *land* which would thereby encouraging family-attachments. The catch, however, was that the people would not own the properties provided. Later, in time, they might be given an opportunity to purchase the land outright, and throughout many parts of Mexico, ***Ejidos*** offered land-use to its constituents for building homes. Yet, free and clear *titles* were not, initially, part of the equation.

Like so many laws most of us have experienced in our lifetimes, ***del Ejido*** sounded *great-on-paper.* Words to live-by! Words to celebrate! Once enacted, and celebrations subsided, though, and that can be a long-time in Mexico because of its festive-nurtured mentality, typical behaviors were germinated. Several different attitudes sprung forth. There were those postures of benevolent "givers;" attitudes of thankless "receivers" or *takers*; and finally, there were actions by chronic and constantly "greedy."

Initially, an important factor to reckon with is the Mexican-culture, itself, and its in-cohesive *attitude* toward land-ownership versus land-possession: "*Titles*? We don' need no stinkin' *Titles*! We live here, and we work here. That's all we need. *Fugheddaboudit*!" Oh, wait, sorry! I'm mixing cultures again... The point is that the people got something from the government that they expected. Possession was ownership in their eyes. A mutually distrustful relationship with government led people to essentially feel, "I'll take it, but I won't worry about paying-for-it."

Another issue was perhaps an old, paraphrased adage, "What is given to you is less important than that which you earn." Mexican families are large, extended social-units. Mexicans do not look at land in similar viewpoints as their northern neighbors. We, in the USA look upon land more as a *commodity.* There are few, family-homesteads anymore. American homeowners buy homes and then sell them on the average of five to seven years. Does the expression, "Movin'-on-up!" ring a bell? We all see ourselves sort of like the *Jeffersons.* Land and its dwellings are investment opportunities. Land does not have the same, emotional mystique in the States like in Mexico. For us, to own is good, but why keep it? Land is a commodity. Instead, we profit from it!

In Mexico, however, land and one's home are almost as sacred as being free. Their great and beloved revolutionary hero, ***Emiliano Zapata***, made that philosophy his war-cry: *Land and liberty!* The people enthusiastically and joyously responded with, "***Viva Zapata***!" Land is a sanctuary for all the family. It would be maintained, developed and passed-on down through a family's descending generations.

Of course, that meant more and more domiciles needed to be built in order to accommodate generations of growing families. Some of those abodes were poorly constructed. Some became virtual eye-sores. Furthermore, land was useful, so it could serve more than just a place to "hang-your-sombrero." It had potential. Land could be used for building businesses, rental units, little stores for the local community, even some special portions could be donated to local professors to build a school upon. The children could stay nearby and then work on the property when they were released from classes. Religious enthusiasts could even offer some portions of the land to build a church.

Anyway, you can see where this is going... The land was not being utilized in the manner for which it had initially been promoted by ***Ejido***. Those who followed and received free-rides were hardly concerned with payments or taxes or fees and property maintenance. When government officials approached with questions, concerns or investigations, the people responded by hiding or avoiding such agents. Original ***Ejido*** families sold out their ownerships. Issues arose and developed several times over the years with new user-locals now redefined as *squatters*. Sometimes, they they were thrown off property by the new, legal, deeds-of-trust owner who had been paying all along the taxes for the properties.

Thus, a third and unfortunately grave-factor with our ***Mismaloya*** case arose. We all have heard the long-time, well-documented and understood social-law, "Greed is a magnet for money, wealth and power." Perhaps, we should investigate all three above-mentioned issues especially because they involve my lovely ***Mismaloya*** situation. Let's try to understand these curious and relevant groups.

How do people react when all-of-a-sudden, a government steps in, or *up*, and gives them something like the 1931 "***Ejido***" decree? How about, "Hurray! Let's party!" Seems logical. Mexico is no different than anywhere else when someone wins a "lotto." It's celebration time! The small but significant difference with this Mismaloya situation was that many residents had been quietly living in their respective locations for many years already, if not generations.

Originally, in the ***Zona de Mismaloya*** a total of ten families were given ***Ejido*** rights to all the land in question today. The members would live on and develop the properties and pay their required taxes to the ***Ejido's*** local jurisdiction. Withing forty-five years, however, all those initial land-recipients had sold out. They either forfeited for profit or sold their rights to any ownership to the land. Furthermore, a local and prosperous land-owner-developer bought everything.

The first problem resulting with today's fiasco began after those early-on sales and purchases. Some families from the ***Ejido*** land sellers remained on the land as *squatters*. In fact, even more families moved onto the parcels. They were all advised and warned that their presence on the land was tentative and temporary. *Selling* families counseled new arrivals that they could not remain there forever.

However, the remaining family members and new families making their own homes on the borrowed land began building dwellings. Most of them were poorly constructed and all without required permits or permission. Furthermore, these continued land-users, or *squatters*, and newcomers and generations of descendants down through the years thus encouraged, built and opened-up businesses on the land to make money from visiting tourists. The land became their homes and their livelihoods. They loosely joined forces and even built a school for the local children. To make matters even worse, presently, with stick-in-the-eye attitudes, the semi-anarchistic community provided land for a church to be built right off the main highway.

The community, itself, became a ramshackle development of mislaid structures and meager abodes crudely fashioned and, most importantly, illegal.

Furthermore, without permission for anyone to be there on any continuing basis in the first place, there were no rents paid to the land owner. Nor, especially, were required taxes paid to the legal owner or government. In fact, because many years earlier, the previously held ***Ejido*** lands had been sold out to complete ownership by one man and his family, ***Mismaloya del Ejido*** was dissolved due to no need.

Needless to say, scornful attitudes toward a *government* ignoring the situation and a land-owner who did little or nothing to get people to leave, a status quo standard developed. When pressed or routed by the land-owner, due to decades of exemplified and chronic distrust, it became obvious that people were not willing to simply uproot and leave. Force might be necessary.

Old, if not ancient, family-legacies in Mexican culture do not always mean or require *legal, title-documentation*. This is especially true among poor, indigent, uneducated, and naive populations. For them, "land" is something which is passed-down through generations; it is inherited by newborns. No *piece-of-paper* is necessary to recognize a family's heritage. "Let government be damned!" became innate in attitudes. Today, however, the future is catching up with the past.

The next issue focuses on that old warning, "Something easily-gained is something less-appreciated." A *thing* simply given to you is basically just taken-for-granted. In ***Mismaloya's del Ejido*** property-possession issue, "some *things* taken-for-granted" were, perhaps, the "grants" themselves benefiting the original involved families. Either because of required, steep and annual property taxes, purchase offers for their parcels that *could not be refused*, or typical and standard "take-the-money-and-run" attitudes, the original, ten ***Ejido*** families chose to sell out to one local owner with his own vision for personal gain and ***Mismaloya's*** development.

To emphasize again, part of the present issue was negligence in follow-up to the rightful owner's newly-purchased acquisitions. The new owner just allowed families of the sellers to remain, grow, develop, and thrive on his property.

Furthermore, when buy-able and corrupt, government-agents pressured or squeezed too hard, ***morditas***, or acceptable "pay-offs" to complacent and unscrupulous officials, became the norm. This aspect continued for years with indignation's occasional outbursts, but always with the same results: Status quo.

Because the entire culture and government structure was developing a laissez-faire or "pay-off" mentality, corruption became prevalent in all walks-of-life. The government seemed to ignore the issues and the situation until it developed into crises. When, occasionally, *squatters* were pressured at various times over the years, they assembled into organized fellowship voicing outraged indignation and collective protestations. They raised angry banners for passers-bye to read, and exclaimed of the doleful *injustices* being done to them. That is what is happening once again in Mismaloya.

As previously mentioned, a successful *routing* of local *squatters* in 1983 forced the land-users to flee for their lives. The move has the legal support and backing of the local officials and the government. The people ran. The area was bull-dozed and burned and developed. Today, it is the grounds for large and magnificent resorts modeling Mismaloya's upbeat, current and progressive look. However, additional lands purchased in the same huge ***Ejido*** deal lay on the opposite side of the river splitting Mismaloya into equal halves. That property was simply ignored by the owner. No immediate plans were issued for its development after its purchase. People were advised to leave, and their families' choices to remain were largely unheeded by the new owner.

Today, the son of the wealthy land-owner and developer has decided it is his turn to do something. The courts have already given him sanction to proceed. Therein lies the social and, most recently, political crises which has developed. Does the family heir have the formidable power to uproot the *squatters*? Will the local and federal government face potential blood-shed from the naive and mostly ignorant youth from the *squatters'* families? Their basic, bottom-line claim is that they have been living there for many generations without disturbance. Now, the land is rightfully theirs. It is called: *Squatter's rights*. However, the land-owner says that they are *squatters' wrongs*, they are criminal trespassers with no rights and that they must leave immediately.

Finally, there is the last grievous issue, and it may be the most heinous, if not significant of the lot. "Greed" causes people to do extremely inhumane things to other people. Money, and power for that matter, tend to blind some people from actual day-to-day pressures, struggles and dealings of otherwise honorable, working-class folks. "The *end-result* defines the *means*" is a sort of twisted, Machiavellian practice employed by much of the world's wealthy and power-hungry. For *greedy* people, however, it seems to be the *rule* not the *practice*.

If one person possesses something that another desires, then "the-rule" defines *doing whatever is necessary to get the desired result* as "the-means." If a greedy landowner wants all adjoining lands to his own, then the "practice" allows him to do whatever is necessary to get it all for himself. "Whatever-is-necessary" is defined by "whatever-it-takes." With ***Mismaloya's*** historical, yet misunderstood and sadly misplaced circumventions, pay-offs, greased-palms, ***morditas***, and potential investment-opportunities are types of leverage which "greed" can use to buy and change history.

Apparently, that is what is occurring today in ***Mismaloya***. On one side of the river, the village is safe and legal and secure. Violent, government-sanctioned actions over thirty-years earlier had resolved legal ownership at that time. Local inhabitants had been forced to move out. Homes and grounds were bulldozed and burned. Legal, property-ownerships were later established and developed. Hotel Resorts and new homes were built.

On the other side of the ***Rio Mismaloya,*** which sectioned the community into two halves, is where the present crisis grows. Over 650 ***habitaciones*** (rooms), 300 families' homes, a new, under-construction church, a many generation elementary school serving children from all over the region, a half-dozen successful and flourishing restaurants, multiple, souvenir-shops, small ***tandias*** for grocery-items, small, independent proprietor-ships such as spas and souvenir stands, and finally, many anchored-boats for fishing and tourism industries are all in serious jeopardy of being completely displaced or dismantled.

Recent court-orders have given a local landowner supposed complete ownership rights and authority to modify, upgrade, develop, or sell an enormous section of the community which happens to include everything mentioned above. According to the owner's position or argument which was upheld in court recently, the land-users have persisted over the years as "squatters." According to the owner-complainant in the case, ***Ejido*** claims lapsed years ago. The land-dwellers forfeited, sold, gave-up, or otherwise forsook their possession of the land. The only thing they did not do was leave and abandon it.

The supposed legal and rightful landowner, according to testimony, attempted several times over the years to remove the illegal inhabitants but without success. In the past, land-users have risen up in arms protesting any potential displacement. The entire half of the ***Mismaloya*** village in question is angry with the supposed owner and are seemingly ready to *go-up-in-arms* if necessary. Their protest posters scattered all along the highway for viewers passing through Mismaloya ask for sensibility and sympathy, for the most part, and few warn of or suggest violent actions... so far.

Wealthy, potential investor-developers have been mentioned in much of the gossip and real-estate discussions. Local home-makers, if not homeowners, are in aggravated dispute over recent court-rulings. Opposition and appeals are in-play. The federal government has entered into the fracas. Hearings are to be held. Demonstrations and vocal denouncements are under-way.

Altercations and violence have been prompted and have occurred in the past over similar upheaval attempts at inhabitant-displacement. Locals have always survived but not necessarily victoriously. Their case has always been founded on the principle: "Possession is nine-tenths of the law." Some, if not many of the land-dwellers are, in fact, legacy-descendants from the 1931 ***Ejido*** court rulings.

Furthermore, in ***Mismaloya***, itself, the community is split in attitudes. Residents on the highly-developed side of the river which splits the town complain that their own residences are rightful and legal property to them. "We have titles. We pay our mortgages and rents and taxes," they exclaim. "It is not so for them (the other half across the river)," the disgruntled and jealous legal, landowners argue. "(Those villagers over there) are users and abusers and should not be allowed to receive a free-ride with no rent, no taxes and many all-the-while operating businesses for free without fees," seems to be a general consensus. Mismaloyan townspeople are truly split on feelings bordering. This case, however, involves state court-rulings against land-dwellers and land-users. More court-activity is required to resolve this matter and satisfy all affected parties. A significant possibility of violence remains a potential option on both sides of the issue. Legal and, therefore, police-action may result in home-dwellers being forcefully removed from their homes. This case also has historical precedent from 1983 circumstances when the other portion of ***Mismaloya*** was burned and bull-dozed down by authorities supporting land developers against the home-dwellers. The property was thereafter developed into profitable resorts.

Yet, this case may also be no different than past attempts to circumvent existing circumstances. Who can tell? Who shall prevail? Will civil-law, social-law or Machiavellian-law prevail? Stay-tuned, Readers! Same-time, same-place, same-channel... Return tomorrow for another exciting episode of "As the World Burns!" Or, "As the Stomach Turns!" Or, "Squatters Rights or Wrongs?"

It's the kind of relevant, emotional, storm-gathering tempest which may ignite into full-fledged fire if something unusual sparks the situation. For my memories, it's reminiscent of the 1960's and 1970's. I don't understand this matter as well as I did marching against the Vietnam War and for Civil-Rights, but it does spark curiosity. Also, I can't fight or run, if needed, like in the old days, but I can still observe, take some good pictures and reliable notes hopefully.

However, it's obvious that the *natives are getting restless.* A big protest is planned for ***manana*** at the town-square in Puerto Vallarta. I shall attend as a Gringo observer and pretend to know what all the shouting is about. Hopefully, I will be able to learn more about both sides' arguments. That will be interesting too, because I must travel through ***Mismaloya***, the center of all the disturbance, in order to get home. Let's see what happens. ***!Viva cambio*** (change)***! or !Viva Zapata!***

So far, I have also been allowed in-depth interviews with representatives of the court-ordered, legal land-owner. From them, I have received a significant version of their history and present review of the case. Naturally, I was understandably imbued with somewhat prejudicial comments too. After all, they do represent the land-owner and want-to-be developer.

Furthermore, I have spoken with many outside observers familiar with the ongoing conflict present in ***Mismaloya***. I sought their combined input, insight and opinions in order to develop a fair and objective coverage of the situation. As might be accepted, those opinions were split with about half going for, or against, either side of the issue. Some favored leaving the tranquility of Mismaloya alone.

They appreciated its old, worn-down and authentic look of third-world Mexico. Others, of course, were all in favor of cleaning ***Mismaloya*** up and allowing for future growth and development. They resented "free-rides" and wanted to beautify the area by recognizing the rightful dreams and claims of the legal owner.

Additionally, I have talked and questioned several and with several older and younger inhabitants of Mismaloya who offered grave concerns for the future. Several of those people I interviewed spoke hauntingly of remembrances living through previous attacks by the developer attempting possession rights and control of his Mismaloyan properties. Some say that they lost before, but not again. In loose references to the old ***Ejido*** rules, they claim that they have been living-on the land for several generations and working the land, so it is theirs. Of course, that does not include paying taxes, but that's another issue to them.

I am concerned. The situation has all the ear-markings and potential of an outright rebellion. How far will an aggressive-takeover go? Who may show-up to assist the long-time dwellers of Mismaloya? How far in defense might some local ***Mismaloyans*** go supporting either side? One young leader, after directing a 200person protest march through the main streets of ***Puerto Vallarta*** boldly warned, "This afternoon, we shall all return to our (***Mismaloya***) village and prepare ourselves for a (potential) catastrophe tonight... with machetes!

Stick around, Folks. I'll try to keep you posted on updates. Unfortunately, in Mexico, *updates* occur on slightly different schedules than many of the rest of us are used to seeing. For now, something might happen, or nothing might happen. Should I fall under unfortunate time-restraints with this publication and am unable to offer anything more to report on the current topic, then just "Google" it!

Type into the search bar: *Mismaloya Land Grab,* or *Mismaloyan Waste Makes Haste,*or *Mismaloya Usurper Slips,* or *Mismaloya: Eviction of the Squatters.* All the search-engines will find and provide lots of historical and recent information on the potential crisis.

Like I have mentioned, ***Vallartans*** and ***Mismaloyans*** promote the region as tranquility centers for relaxation. Dependent on tourism with its constant state of hustle, locals are still just like most of the rest of us in many ways. They have pride in their neighborhoods. They have homes and want safety. They have children in school and want a good life for them. They have responsibilities and jobs and desire security. They pay taxes, and they look for ways to avoid it. Finally, just like us it seems, they too have governments or banks or creditors or always somebody breathing down their necks wanting something from them.

You want "tranquility?" Plenty of Mexicans laugh about *tequila and cerveza* to find theirs. Actually, it ain't too bad! Works for me! However, if you want inner-peace, go join a Buddhist Temple in Tibet somewhere. Anywhere else, you've got to work, pay dues, save your dough if you can, and if you're lucky, you can retire and spend some blissful-time in the serenity of lovely ***Mismaloya***...

Uh, oh... Ooops! Well, like I was saying, "Let's just hope for the best." It is bothersome, though, to observe these diabolical conflicts-of-interest taking place. On one-side, owners and resort developers want to profit by improving and building-up ***Mismaloya's*** and ***Puerto Vallarta's*** economy and their own bank accounts. From their process, supposed improvements to the community's image would come. Their vision is more in-line with modern, tourist-promotions.

Resorts would centralize and govern local, labor-forces and employment options and possibilities. Resorts would create many new jobs. All the same services provided to visiting tourists now would still be provided except then services would become elegant and come through the resort's teams. Everyone could work for resort-management. Restaurant owners and workers could still operate restaurants, but then services would be upgraded and offered by the resort. Previous restaurant owners could become resort restaurant-managers; restaurant workers could become resort restaurant-staff. Sure...

Furthermore, they defend that modern development would beautify the entire region. A new, mega-resort would remove unsightly construction and ramshackle abodes from their shabby and shoddy locations. Instead, it would add a polished and shiny, distinctive, renovated face-lift to the area. Then, foreign visitors and their investment-money would generate increased prosperity for all. Pleasures and tranquility of Mismaloya would be exponentially increased and shared by more. Mismaloya would blossom. Everyone would win.

The predicament would be clearly defined as *People versus Big-business.*

On the other-side-of-the-fence are all the residents and small-time individuals (Mismaloyans) seeking status-qua in order to continue scraping out their modest but independent incomes. Mismaloya is their home. Many have lived and survived there for multiple generations. Where are they to go and do what? Must their lives be defined by what wealthy conglomerates determine? What happened to Zapata's teachings?

Their case can be argued with historical reference: Forefathers were given ***Ejido*** rights to the land to live on and develop. The law clearly stated that the "land-user" must live on the land, improve it and abide by it forever. Furthermore, the edict stipulates that a land-user and land-owner must live on the property and care for it with maintenance and development. In fact, it was potentially justified and defensible in court for *land-squatters* to take control, in not ownership, by *squatting*. An individual needed only to move in, set-up quarters, work the land, and in time, without visitations or improvements or resistance by the actual owner(s), *squatters* could earn legal rights to land or parcels. Land is everything from their historically influenced breeding and teaching. *Land and freedom!*

Personally, with two, clearly-defensible positions, and I find that I am caught in the philosophic *middle* of the dilemma, I like to ask myself, "What would... Obama do?!" This would clearly define both sides of the proverbial fence. Any decision coming from the White House would automatically determine the obvious GOP position. The Grand Old Party would instantly take an exact opposite stance. There would be no "fence-sitting." A person would have to choose sides.

Big-business justifies rights of individual, property-owners and independent corporations (resort-ownership). They believe that business interests and expansion have sound, significant and better commonwealth interests of the entire community. They argue that the land's use is not presently justified because of tits vast loss of potential. Big-money would represent more opportunity and well-being for any displaced population. Allow big-business and government to assist the people with relocation. Present property-values and its interests and use would be magnified a thousand-fold.

History reflects several previous attempts to displace the people and get control of the land for big-business interests. In 1983, business won a powerful case when a wealthy, local land-owner claimed ownership and control with temporary, judicial-mandates. He moved swiftly with police and military backing to bull-doze and burn all the homes on the prescribed property in question. Land-dwellers who protested were arrested. In short order, the entire area was gleaned of inhabitants, and the land went into development. Presently, there are large, successful resorts on the land which serve thousands of tourists annually and employ hundreds of local workers for their enterprises.

Both sides seek government intervention. The People want protection and security from losing their heritage to rich and greedy, giant and powerful outside-influences. Business wants government mandates authorizing control and free-enterprise to flow-smoothly. It seems to be a feasible case of social Darwinism involving concepts of *natural selection* and *survival of the fittest.* Are these people *stronger and fitter* with government support on their side, or should an individual's interests fall to big-business's greater-good because he is *smaller and weaker*?

As a result of the 1983 case, *weak and unfit* losers became displaced inhabitants. Those properties were managed, developed and became sites to large corporate, resort development. However, still desiring to remain within their home bounds, many of the uprooted citizenry simply moved the short-distance across the river and took-up new residences. Today, it is this new region which has become the new, ***Mismaloyan*** *zone-of-conflict.* These days, heirs to the previous conflict from both sides are once again preparing for possible battle.

Once more, the landowner(s) claimants demand judicial support in their new quest to own and control the adjoining and potentially vast, development-area. The new property includes all land on the opposite-side of the community river and stretches from the other side of the main highway all the way down to the beach front. The owner-claimant states that the property is legally his to develop because he has properly purchased the land and pays all required taxes on it. He further states that the present inhabitants on the property are all illegal, land-squatters with no more ***Ejido*** protections.

The four-generational, throwback-families from the initial Ejido are again fighting this takeover. Some of these protesters were previous losers from the prior 1983 coup. Their argument is that ***Ejido*** rights have never been discarded. The people have lived on the land continuously and developed it ever since they received it. They further state that the supposed *owner-claimant* has never lived on the land, has never improved or maintained any of it and has made his illegal purchase-agreements for the property without proper sanctions.

Both sides are making serious claims advising warnings. The owner-claimant advises that police and military and government-action will arrive to assert his position and fulfill his takeover. The land-users warn that they will neither *leave without a fight*, nor go down *peacefully-in-the-night* this time. Threats and activity have occurred from both sides already in recent years over similar provocations. Predictions of violence and bloodshed have been issued by the people should any disturbances occur.

Matters seem to be heating-up. Everyone is looking to the Federal courts to see if any intervention may occur to resolve the situation peacefully. Some argue that the people could lose the fight because of big-money and big-business, but that they may be compensated for their losses. Others say that there is no amount of money which can compensate taking people's homes, their way-of-life and legacy from them.

We shall have to wait and see what happens. Stay tuned, Readers. Perhaps, there will be some current updates to offer before long. In the meantime, think about the issue yourself, and take a stand. Are you for big-business and growth and development and future prosperity for the whole region? Or, do you support inhabitants who claim to have family-history and past ***Ejido*** rights to the land.

Maybe it's similar to *eminent domain* where it's about civic-responsibility for the greater good. Is the *greater good* in this case validated by government stepping-in to remove inhabitants from an area which will then be developed into pristine, tourist-inviting mega resorts? Or, is the *greater good* leaving the inhabitants alone to continue living and working on the land which supports their quiet, humble and informal, rustic but quaint lifestyles in the face of surrounding modernization?

Should n*ew* win out over o*ld*? Does p*rogress* circumvent t*radition*? Should modernization succeed over antiquity? What is preferred for Mismaloya? How about 300, spectacular resort-habitations including suites and multifamily rooms, all with incredible vistas and impressive surroundings on dramatically beautiful property, a beach and bay *to take your breath away...* serving thousands of annual, vacation-visitors and time-share owners for decades to come?

Or, is ***Mismaloya*** better served by the status-qua? Should it continue with its humble areas of seclusion and dilapidated, private-abodes? What of the lives and businesses supporting three-hundred or so present inhabitants? These are people who have lived on this land for several generations, developing their own, quiet and private existences over many decades? Wow! It truly is a tough call.

Puerto Vallarta is growing. Hotels and resorts are expanding in size and number. The largest ones are presently in the process of developing Mexico's own version of *Disney World* to draw an even greater international, tourism-crowd. All along Route 200 from *Puerto Vallarta* to *Mismaloya* can be found many grand and picturesque resorts operating with several others presently under-construction. As those resorts expand and grow and prosper and continue promoting the region's beauty to the world's tourism industry, should Mismaloya remain behind and lose-out on inevitable, growth-potential? Is out-of-date really out-of-touch?

Or, is there a point in time when quiet, pristine and peaceful jungle deserves to be left alone to maintain its own, private tranquility? If growth and prosperity are inevitable, can they still be steered toward other locations leaving Mismaloya to continue drawing modest tourism yet maintaining its own, unique and personal identity? When there's no more jungle, will tourists still come for resorts?

EJIDO

***Ejido** promised land for us*
To pass down from each father.
With love, and work and in God's trust,
We worried not of others.

Yet, now we're told, "Times change so fast
That 'Deeds-of-Trust' are better,"
And though we're blessed with land possessed,
Control still needs a letter.

So, homes, our jobs and families
Are humbled upon alters.
We offer prayers for Mercy's grace,
"Return our peaceful squalor."

But, futures seldom seek their pasts;
Forces emerge to change them.
Though struggles seek to make things last,
Yesterday is condemned.

And steadily, encroachment flies
In face from cranes above.
Construction nullifies the lies,
And growth forsakes lands loved.

Passionate tranquility's loss,
Replaced by avarice's creed,
Brings unenlightened lives across
This land deemed for our seed.

Our lovely Mismaloya meant
To blend ancient with new
Will lose its face to bold intent-
A sacrificial view.

Yet, time will tell of modern haste
When all things come to pass,
"The future lays all trust to waste,
And nothing ever lasts."

"Mismaloya Blues"

Part 20: Essence of Nations: Hearts and Souls...

One of my favorite and laughable drinking-quips is the standardized but vacant toast, *Through the lips and over the gums, look out stomach, here it comes!* I suppose that toast will suffice for just about anything any of us plan to pour down our gullets, but it serves a warning to any amateur drinkers: *Beware and prepare!* However, one singular but *open-ended* toast I love to laugh over just before poisoning myself is the infamous warning: "Whiskey makes you frisky, Gin will make you sin, Vodka will rot ya, but ***Tequila*** means *ta kill ya*!" That toast always sounds a little foreboding, but *WOW*, it sure packs a punch-of-meaning when you follow it with a shot of your favorite brand of ***tequila.*** Actually, it doesn't even have to be your favorite; it can be whatever is on hand. Tequila is an amazing liquor and definitely worthy of its reckoning.

If there are things, or feelings or philosophies which may be deemed *"Souls" of nations*, then perhaps such examples worthy of reverence are some of our own familiar, natural or constitutional rights: *Democracy, freedom, liberty, land ownership, E Pluribus Unum, workers-unite, equality for all*, or *winner-take-all.* Choose for yourself or find and pick another.

In the good ol' USA, we are taught that above all else *freedom* exemplifies our nation's soul and its meaning and purpose. However, *majority-vote* determines appropriate *freedom* and *rules* over the masses. President Obama often speaks of a necessary *equal-playing-*

field for everyone to access *upward-mobility.* Freedom for all? Sounds fair.

"Upward-mobility" always sounds great in debate or on-paper until or unless you realize that you are at the bottom. Then, you might understand that you may have serious, uphill struggles ahead becoming included on that *equal-playing-field.* The positive point, however, may be the following: *In no other country on Earth in no other time in history has so much opportunity been available and possible for so many.* To me, with obvious pride and prejudices, but also with humbled experience, academic-studies, self-training, and travel, that unique *precept* stands significantly above all others to me. I believe it. I accept its basic premise as profound and resolute. It is a social commentary on the USA and its *free* opportunities for all. If you want it, go get it! Just earn it, or not...

As an alternate example, however, I offer England and its historically rich and diverse growth and development over virtual millenniums. Within Great Britain, on-the-other-hand, I fancy that the people's *soul* may be derived from historically famous, or infamous, antagonists. Some of those characters truly represent the meaning and purpose of British integrity and, therefore, perhaps its *soul.* From defiance of a King's rule as with King John and the Magna Carta in 1215, to Constitutional Monarchy excusing papal authority in 1558 with Elizabeth I, Great Britain has grown and developed as a nation, and an international power and force in human, social and governmental influence. The growth of democracy may be charted through its historical references. The Brits' almost rabid beliefs in *common good for the common man* are quintessential in their philosophy.

From hilarious, dry-humored Brits, I offer in tribute their annual celebration, primarily in Great Britain, which observes and commemorates *Guy Fawkes Night.* Its history begins with events of 5 November 1605, when Guy Fawkes and his celebrated *Gunpowder Plot* attempted to blow up the House of Lords! Initially, it was meant to focus dissatisfaction with Parliament's non-abeyance of Catholic and Papal support, but it eventually grew to represent an entire national unhappiness with anything Parliament screwed-up.

That, in itself, gave the *people* of England a never-ending supply of potential fodder for their disgust. Can you even begin to imagine a nationally-recognized, special-day set aside, in any nation, which honors "failure!" It was a *failed-attempt* at destroying the ruling, governing-body of that nation because many believed it to be an unworthy representative-body of officials who had *failed* to represent its constituents? *OMG!* I love it! It's a holiday jubilation for a collection of disgruntled attitudes and an annual celebration of impertinence!

But I digress... again. History hurts, but it usually says what you want to believe. Both England and the United States of America, I believe, were founded on principles and beliefs based upon the *common man and his common good.*

Mexico, on-the-other-hand, still a direct descendent of its likewise, influenced-parent, Spain, had similar, but significantly different, concepts. The difference appeared to be within the broader question, "Who made the rule?" Whoever controlled the *ink* determined the *stink*! To the *writer* goes the spoils!

Mexico was discovered, created, invented, or established as a country which would abide by whomever was *in charge.* Initially, due to Spanish conquest of the native Indian civilizations, Mexico's history reflects how it methodically bent toward whatever issue promised or suggested its ascent or climb to a self-serving higher-level. That desire to ascend or improve its position in world-markets allowed its philosophic attitude to encompass and accept its national-premise: *Who will pay the most?* That *barter* philosophy became the national-practice with nearly all available services or products. On the same level, and to an even more complex degree, government developed its own, similar precepts: *We'll give you what you want depending on what you'll pay.*

Gee whiz! Doesn't that have an *international, business-ring* to it? I think so. The only difference may be that in Mexico, there are seldom any price-tags attached to anything *for* sale. Everything is up-for barter: *This is how much I am asking, but what are you willing to pay?* This aspect promotes, if not encourages, attitudes of *getting, or taking*, what you can. Only prices of basic-commodities are permanently established and those things are usually strictly controlled by national or local governments. Everything else is up-for-grabs. With selling, "Get what you can; with buying, "Take what you can get." In both cases, accept outcomes.

That, in fact, may be Mexico's historically-based soul: *One gets what one can afford!* Therefore: *Take what you can get* more precisely means: *You get what you negotiate.* On the flip-side of this *getting what you negotiate* behavior is the attitude, therefore, of *accepting what you get.* The people seem content for the most part with *what they get.* Furthermore, they do not whine or complain over that which they do not have or cannot afford. They accept it.

For instance, if they can't afford a doctor's care or medicine, then they content themselves with their malady. For vast numbers of the population, they work hard at their daily endeavors yet earn relative pittance for their labors. They accept their place, however, and content themselves with having a beautiful environment within which to live and work and raise their families. It is natural to want more, but they accept their lot.

Nevertheless, if this aspect of *accepting whatever is negotiated* is the *soul* of Mexico's *essence*, then it is a national-prize always *up-for-grabs*. Whoever has the most money, or the most power, typically the same, wields the most influence on substantive matters. A *barter-economy* and *morditas* seem to go hand-in-hand. If you can't get *what-you-want* at the price *that-you-want*, then buy-them-off. A small, yet appropriate gesture of cash may transcend and correct a dilemma.

Everything is up for sale; everything is up for grabs! How much can you pay? Better yet, how much are you willing to pay? Regardless of the deal, a satisfied buyer usually only needs to travel a short distance away to another store, or shop or vendor and discover an even better deal. That, however, is the business you have chosen to *deal* in. It's a barter-economy.

In a fascinating reinforcement of this complex philosophy, however, is another unique fact. Prices to buy commodities or services in Mexico are still so low, regardless of demand or offer, that it's a *win-win* situation to be here in the first place. Imported items are exceptions, but other things like rents, food and beverages, utilities and bus transportation are very reasonable. To low-wage earners, prices are still difficult to handle, so they are extremely budget-minded. For us outsiders, however, with vacation funds to burn or steady sources of income, we maintain significant and distinct advantages.

With acceptable exceptions of special imports like wine, whiskey, name-brand food items, and such, everything else is mostly negotiable. Anything which has to be *imported* has reasonable tariffs attached to the price, so one can expect to pay more for it. Nevertheless, ask what something costs, and then offer something less. Negotiation will satisfy both parties with its closure. And everybody who discovers this fact wants to come here to take advantage of it. Of course, the major store outlets or chains have set prices on most things. It is typically street vendors and independent shop-keepers who can and will negotiate.

Alright! If I've suggested that Mexico's *soul* is *negotiable*, or up-for-grabs, then I failed! On the contrary, Mexico is a unique nation where by differing parties enter into *dialog* which is then fulfilled by mutually satisfactory conditions. *You get what you pay for.* Just like in the USA, tips are supposed to be dependent on service. It is not required to pay them, except in some exclusive establish-ments; however, supposedly, a patron rewards service they receive accordingly. Similarly, in Mexico, one need not conclude any transaction which he feels is not favorable to his needs or wants.

However, make no mistake, if every nation has a *soul,* then every nation also has a *heart* too. For the United States of America, many suggest that its "heart" lies squarely in the middle of *Wall Street,* New York City, NY. The difference between the USA and Mexico, perhaps, is that there is no *barter-economy* involved with the US dollar. You get something for whatever price is demanded.

However, everything is up for sale, and everything goes on-sale. Among the retail world, it is said, "If you pay full, retail-price for anything, then you are either a fool or impatient." Everything will eventually go on sale for significant savings. Coupons, and holiday special sales, and Black Fridays, and Cyber Mondays, and liquidation sales happen all the time. US Americans live for deals. We love 'em. That's another reason why Mexico's barter-system is so much fun and intriguing for its northern neighbors.

Oh, sure, in the USA, some things are negotiable, too, like home-buying or car purchases, for instance. Those commodities, however, are privately-owned and influenced by sales-parties like real-estate agents or auto-dealership, sales-department guidelines. Those external parties, but internal forces, determine built-in profit-margins for their own, personal benefit. Most other things, however, have set-prices, and buyers simply determine from reasonable research who sells a desired item at an acceptable price, and then they make a purchase, if desired.

Others argue that the USA's *heart* really can be found where Congress and its President work steadfastly in the people's interest in *Washington, D.C.*. Yeah, right! I am going to believe that when our President(s) and all our past (living), present and future congresspersons, both active and retired, pay for the same needs as the people of whom they serve. Give me a high-and-mighty break!

If you believe that, then have I got a *deal* for you! Remember that *Wall Street* place I mentioned earlier? Well, it just so happens that there's this *bridge* that goes to it, and I'll arrange a sale to you right away... for a small commission, of course! Oh, you don't buy that? OK, then how about a bridge-to-nowhere in Alaska? It's cheap; just send a small pittance, say ten-percent, and I'll arrange for Sarah Palin to make the deal. I believe she says, "You can see Russia on it, or it goes all the way to Russia, or something!" She needs the money too, so she can finance her GOP campaign to become President-elect in 2016.

Can you imagine? Only in American can buffoons regularly run for office and even get elected to high-office. They only need to have big, ...no, *enormous* mouths and even bigger egos. Plus, it helps to have extremely favorable margins of ignorant and empty masses who would dutifully and cheerfully follow the Pied-Piper straight into the river. Just play the right music for their ears. The point? If Washington, D.C. is the USA's *heart,* then we are all in trouble. It's almost as bad as saying, "The Dallas Cowboys are America's team!"

Oh, puke! That actually makes me sicker than American politics. And that nauseating comment came from a state which has sent more Presidents to Washington D.C. than any other. Three, in fact: Lyndon Johnson and G.H. and G.W. Bush. Furthermore, Dwight Eisenhower was born there, and he was a true American hero, but even he couldn't stand it there, so he got out quick and moved to Kansas as an infant.

Anyway, try kicking this thought-can down the road: Why do our elected representatives in Washington deserve free health-care for themselves for life after just one term in office? Why do they deserve full, retirement-benefits after serving just one term? Why can they receive multiple, full-retirement packages for every different elected position they held? Why are nationally elected-representatives and their children exempt from paying-back college student-loans? Why? Why? Why? There are many issues like these in American politics which approach and warn of pending catastrophe. It's wrong and borders on evil.

Even Thomas Jefferson, only our third, elected President warned the nation's people to beware of elected wolves in sheep's clothing. He held a serious distrust for career politicians. He believed, in fact, that every twenty years, or so, the nation's government should be purged of all its elected officials and start itself over again clean and fresh. Interesting prospect. Force Congress to operate with revolving doors: Send our Representatives and Senators packing after a couple of spins. Of course, give them a gold-plated watch and a "Certificate of Achievement" for their efforts, but get them revolved and *gone*!

Sadly, in our system, and probably all over the world, it's a game. Newly-elected officials are brought into private-offices of long-serving, powerful members of Congress. These green, idealistic Congressmen are advised how to play ball and told that, ultimately, they can eventually leave office smelling like winners. On-the-other-hand, if rookies argue or challenge rules, they are warned that they will lose out and their careers may end abruptly. Remember Wall Street's and Washington's rule: *Money talks, but bull-shit walks*!

Therefore, Thomas, I'm with you, in spirit anyway. I do not believe that our officials should continue to serve and award themselves with benefits unavailable to those constituents who elected them. So far, in my estimation with absolute certainty and undeniable disgust, I have determined that probably all our elected *representatives* are *self-serving* and reprehensible. I am a firm believer in term-limits. I think that our present, congressional determined terms should be lessened even more from their present status. Remember the famous quote of Sir John Dalberg-Acton: *Power tends to corrupt and absolute power corrupts absolutely!* He despised the immorality of powerful and influential people.

Am I ready to ex-communicate myself, however? Well, no, but I do gather a bit more insight, understanding and appreciation of the USA, *ex-patriot(ic)* attitude which persists here in Puerto Vallarta. Many live here because after lifetimes of working, paying taxes and contributing to the system back home, after retirement, they can't afford the USA. They cannot even afford a meager but reasonable life, let alone a comfortable one, where they came from. The option to remain home in the States and struggle with existence is unacceptable. That is why many visit here and then choose to remain.

Back at homes, the health care costs alone are prohibitive. Rents and insurances and daily living expenses are so high that many of these *ex-patriots* would practically live in squalor back home. Some argue that they would likely face homelessness as a circumstance.

Meager disability-incomes or social-security just don't go very far back home. Here, however, foreigners can find acceptable living conditions and wonderful weather and views for a fraction of costs back home. It's a no-brainer for those that discover Mexico's and Puerto Vallarta's cost-of-living truths.

To simplify things in my life, however, personally, I like to believe that the *heart* of America lies simply wherever my mother lives. Presently, that is just outside Yosemite National Park in Southern California. In the past, however, my mom carrying America's *heart,* faithfully ranged throughout and across the entire width and breadth of the United States. Born in the upper-Midwest of America, Mom traveled and lived from there to all points in all directions of the USA including Hawaii and Alaska. Sometimes, she traveled because of family, and other times she traveled because of desire, but she traveled, and grew and developed as a person, a mother and as a citizen.

What more may be expected of a nation's people? I believe that America's *heart* may be found in my mother. Nice place, great woman, terrific match! Mom represents the very best of the USA: Sacrifice-from-self, pride-in-country, and honor in relationships. She worked hard, very hard, all her life and raised her children with unconditional love, loyally following her husband everywhere he needed to go to supporting his family. Mom and Dad worked as mutually respectable team members. After their retirements, she cared for Dad before, during and after disease consumed him, eventually taking his life. Now, Mom lives very modestly in a retired-persons trailer-park. Even with foreboding eye-disease, she remains optimistic, active, supportive to all, and very loving.

Mom still travels with family members and friends, and she is always packed and ready for her next adventure. Mind you, for her eighty-seventh birthday, she chose to go sky-diving. No, you're right! She couldn't see what she was doing, but she felt the rush of air in her face. She said it was exhilarating! No doubt. I just watched her from the ground! She's a genuine national treasure deserving utmost support from her nation's government whom she gallantly served all her life.

On her modest pension and expensive, health-care plan, though, she never complains. She accepts her situation and makes the most of it. OMG! She would be ideal down here. Perfect, except for one condition, well, two: First, it's difficult for her to get around, so she requires a walker, and the streets, sidewalks and paths are treacherous down here; second, she is nearly blind from macular degeneration, so she would be unable to fully appreciate the incredible local beauty and vistas. But, she never complains, so she deserves front-row seat consideration. I know what! I'll make her an *honorary ex-patriot!*

The Toast of Jalisco!...

Can we not expect similar expectations, hopes and dreams from any nation's citizens? And what about the source and focus of this novel? What can we say about Mexico's unique and vibrant history? Certainly, it is rich and colorful. There have been long-standing power-struggles and political consequences, however, which have kept Mexico's enormous natural resources and agricultural potential on a proverbial back-burner. These issues along with its barter-economy have kept Mexico struggling as a third-world country unable to make-the-grade.

Similar to the USA is the ever-widening gap between *haves* and *have nots.* Unfortunately, in Mexico the *haves* are a significantly smaller portion of the whole population. They are a very elitist club, and it seems very difficult to gain admission or achieve membership. Mexico's population rises so quickly too, and its cities expand so rapidly that governmental conditions cannot maintain or keep up. As a result, Mexico always continues to struggle with its own identity. However, the key question still remains: Where does its *heart* lie?

A proud, leather-goods and footwear shop owner in ***Guadalajara*** boasted of ***Mexico's*** heritage and future potential. He loved his craft, and just as importantly, he was so proud of his ancestors and their skills. Like arts and fine wines and dining can be attributed to various nations, he believed the same could be true again for Mexico. He wrote of such on his store's web-page, and I paraphrase his message with the following:

> *"Just imagine **Mexico** getting its mojo back? Its future might become so much brighter if they stopped making crap like China and many other countries and instead worked to revive its own colonial heritage as purveyors of quality products (besides **tequila** and **mezcal**). I can imagine **Mexico** becoming a dominant player in the slow-wear clothing movement. It's very possible, and why not? **Mexico** has been producing quality leather-goods for over 400 years. **Mexico** has wonderfully skilled craftsmen too. The people who still use the old tools still remember how to do things the old way. Best of all, **Mexico** still has the heart!*
>
> -Gewebten Sandalen-
> Huaracheblog.com

The beautiful and intriguing truth is that Mexico has its own, unique past considering its historically referenced aspects. Its vivid history is filled with important characters who made valuable advances to its national persona and identity. Yet still, without a doubt, one singularly-special and totally unique product of Mexico carries more fame with it than all its other kin-contributors combined.

Mexico's contributions to world history, music and art, clothing, cuisine, and unique architecture and artisan-crafts are endless. Only a few of these include: but are hardly limited by the following: Aztec and Mayan civilizations with King Montezuma and Hernan Cortez, Emiliano Zepata and Poncho Villa, my wife and her ***Cuidad de Guzman*** upbringing, Herb Alpert and the Tijuana Brass, sombreros and ponchos, chili-peppers and hot tamales, mariachi music and salsa dance, leather and clay artisan products, drug cartels and illegal-immigration, and of course, the largest Spanish-speaking population in the world. The USA now is in second place, and that means that almost single-handed Mexico forced the USA to finally become bi-lingual! ***Bueno para nosotros*** (Good for them; better for us)!

However, this section has been talking about what makes countries tick? What winds their clocks? I suppose it's my nature to find as much of a country to poke fun at as I might in seeking their "essence," but I need to return to my second-love country: Mexico. What drives Mexico? It has all the third-world conflicts and issues, sure. It is a country definitely caught between a rock-and-a-hard-spot, so to speak.

On one hand are a nation's people proud of their heritage almost founded on festivities . The national government mandates specific days of celebration honoring, the government, national heroes, workers, independence and revolution, and of course, Christmas and New Years. Not statutory (federally mandated), but nevertheless festive occasions for parades and fireworks and parties to celebrate special events are civic-holidays commemorating battles, loyalty, heroes, victories, and adventurers, and more independence, and of course, Easter...

Steeped in heavy Catholicism, Mexico has a bountiful calendar of events to ignite the next group of celebrations simply referred to as traditional holidays to honor religious events and festivities and special events. The church designates many different, but important, honorarium such as the Epiphany, blessings, Carnival, Lent, various saints, dead or alive, and even a practical-jokes day (Day of the Holy Innocents) much like our April 1st. Also honored are special items like music festivals, benefits, races, and of course, fishing tournaments.

Wow! Okay. Fine. Mexicans celebrate a lot. Good for them. And, we know it is good for them. Mexicans are a fairly relaxed and jovial people. We talked about third-world aspects and their difficulties. We mentioned their pride and festive spirit, and that is to balance the other hand which is a nation reeking with leaders seeking their own well-being and not that of the people, ***la gente.***

Corruption and crime continues to keep this beautiful, resource rich country in the backwoods of national standings. It is based on the vastly wide variance between wealthy and poor. An elite few control most of the vast wealth with a very small middle-class and a huge, borderline poverty-stricken population. Yet, people carry on and seem happy and content with their situations. Perhaps, their festive-moods and many celebrations and festivities and festivals and parties and music help carry them through the years enjoying themselves.

All this bantering has led into my specific chit-chats about Mexico's national drink. Everyone knows ***cerveza.*** A beer and a pizza, I mean ***burrito***, go hand-in-hand, but everybody's got their own claim to their own, unique elements of style. Even in the good ol' USA, remember our own "America the Beautiful?" How about those *...amber waves of* grain, huh? Get it? Amber? Grain? Doesn't get much more obvious than that. There are lagers, ales, bitters, and stouts to please almost every taste. ***Mexico*** has plenty of their own well-known brands too. But if Mexicans love ***cerveza***, they live for ***tequila***!

What I'm talking about, however, is *national pride*. We have already been discussing tequila to some length. Now it is time to look at its characteristics and history to appreciate its meaning and value to Mexican heritage. Probably, two of those favorite holidays I enjoy mentioning occur on February 22, and on July 24. One honors ***margaritas*** and the other celebrates ***tequila.*** How about a country that designates not one, but two, days of national celebration for their pride: National ***Margarita*** Day and National ***Tequila*** Day! Sure, we have all heard of Oktoberfest. That is a festive period in Fall for various locations, places and people celebrating harvest time with excellent beers and camaraderie. It's lots of fun, to be sure. What I'm surprised and delighted to share is the occurrence and reverence of a national pride and love for their unique gift to the world, ***Tequila.***

Thank you, ***Mexico!...***

BOTTOMS-UP! I'LL DRINK TO THAT!...

If the river was whiskey,
And I was a duck,
I'd swim to the bottom
And drink myself up!

Anonymous

Ninety-nine bottles of beer on the wall,
Ninety-nine bottles of beer,
Take one down and pass it around,
Ninety-eight bottles of beer on the wall...

Ninety-eight bottles of beer on the wall...
(You get the picture)

Anonymous

And the beer I had for breakfast wasn't bad,
So, I had more for desert!

Kris Kristopherson

TEQUILA!

The Champs

I feel sorry for people who don't drink.
When they wake up in the morning,
That's as good as they're going to feel all day.

Frank Sinatra

All I ever did was supply a demand that was pretty popular.

Al Capone

Our love needs a transfusion, so let's shoot it full of wine-product

Tom Waits

Okay. That's enough! Need we go on? The previous quips were just a bunch of silly drinking jokes, or limericks or comments making fun or pleasure out of drinking. I imagine every nation on Earth (with exceptions of Muslim States-so they say, at least) has some comic-lines, lyrics or poems about drinking, warnings of its dangers or mishaps and silliness. Before we take a closer look at ***Mexico*** and ***t***equila in depth, however, let's look at some of the competition. Just to even-the-table, equal-the-odds or offer a fair, playing-ground, let's see what they've got. Bring 'em on! Set 'em up, Joe, and another for the road...

Alcohol, in some form or another, has been produced and consumed since the beginning-of-time. How about Adam and Eve, for instance, after a fallen apple accidentally fermented and they ate it and went on a wild, apple pickin' spree through the Garden?... Or, when His people were thirsty, Jesus even changed water into *wine*... Go figure! Which USA Amendment to its Constitution took yet another Amendment to cancel itself? Right, the one about Prohibition!

I guess nations and their people are just infatuated, if not intoxicated, with alcohol intake. First, we want to learn a little bit more about tequila. That is the actual purpose of this section, and we shall. First, however, what about some other forms of tranquilizers from alcoholic-intake?

Let's consider some of tequila's rivals: How about vodka for a starter? For over 900 years, from initially Russia and then beyond, alcoholic enthusiasts have been squashing and distilling acorns and such to create various stages of aromatic vodka to perfection. Now, the world is frustratingly plagued with drunken, alcoholic Russian demagogues who believe everyone should indulge themselves with their "water of life." Most of the rest of the world believe, however, that those Russians probably substitute vodka for their daily-requirement of water, anyway. It's difficult to communicate with drunks.

Today, vodka has spread its production and enthusiastic indulgences world-wide. The Smirnoff family has significant claim to its glory. Russia has one of the world's highest alcoholism rates in the world. That issue is demonstrated and emphasized no better than by recent, irrational actions of wanna-be, wishful-thinking-for-another-*cold-war"* leaders like the present ones. Likely, their personal-mottoes suggest as much: *Take another drink* (of vodka), *and be surprised! You'll recognize the world is RED through blood-shot eyes!"*

And what about famous grape-pressers of France, Italy and Napa Valley, Sonoma and Solano Counties of California? Those booze-producing ego-maniacs would sacrifice hearts of their offspring if they felt it would enhance the fertilizer fed to their precious vines. I attended a hometown, local wine-tasting fling-a-ding once, and I could almost swear I heard the Chief Vintner tell the following:

"I think of this Vintage as 'Heart-of-the-Child' to remind us of its naughtiness yet unique and spoiled fragrance and to honor its youthful benefactor and his effervescence. I named it after my dearly-departed, little grandchild, ('Uh, what was his name?... Oh, whatever!') Ahem! Anyway, it carries with it such a distinct aroma of giddiness yet abides with pleasing satisfactions of immaturity and vernal opulence. I take pleasure offering it now as: 'Wine for Whiners.'"

Good ol' vino has got to be one of the oldest, hangover or *spiritual-moment-producers* of all time. From original, Persian meads to the most recent world, wine-showing reviews, wine has progressed, improved, expanded, and continued its intoxicating grip on the world's drinking populations since times' immemorial. The only requirement for any desired drinkers was to decide which tastes they enjoyed the most and then partake in the flavors of their cosmic-consciousness:

> *"Wow, Man! Try this sweet stuff! It's called,* 'Nectar of the Gadzooks.' *OMG! It'll set you free! I'm not sure which drink sets you free, though, the second, or the twelfth-of-never, but you'll know when you get there,... or someone else will!"*
>
> *DTChapman*

> *His desire for this* (situation) *to be a joke was quickly replaced by a desire for whiskey.*
>
> *Ashley Straker, Infected Connection*

LA HISTORIA DE TEQUILA...

Alright. Enough chit-chat. We could spend all day "chatting" about various forms of booze and their dubious powers over human psychic, but enough. Let's get focused. Let's talk turkey! And I ain't talkin' 'bout *Wild Turkey*! Perhaps, there is one product which is truly the most significant and relevant source of Mexican influence throughout the whole world, if not the entire universe: *Tequila*!

Oh, sure, outside observers typically focus on those common themes of conversation and debate regarding Mexico: The terrible and horrible problems with drug cartels and US-Mexico immigration issues. However, what I wish to delve into is more genuine. I want to talk about ***tequila*** and its trans-formative nature on the Mexican psychic. No, I did not say, *drunken-nature*! That's one of the side-benefits, I suppose. I mean, *transforming-powers.*

I want to discuss how ***tequila*** *transformed* a nation's consciousness. How could a difficult but fascinating plant burgeon an entire economy? I would like to ook into the history, growth and development, production, and distribution of what may be considered the true *heart and soul,* the *Essence*, of ***Mexico.*** I feel it is relevant for this piece of writing for several reasons. One factor is partly because ***tequila*** originated right here in the ***estado de Jalisco,*** and that, of course, is where Puerto Vallarta and my lovely Mismaloya lie. Another reason is because of incredible industry and fiancial boon tequila production gave Mexico. A final element may be simply how its name, ***tequila,*** prompted another unique source for the world to share in the same festive nature as Mexicans are proud to exhibit.

One need not travel very far from Puerto Vallarta, on the way to ***Jalisco's*** capital of Guadalajara, to spot and recognized the renowned fields of the famous ***agave azul*** (blue agave) plant. Two points, initially, are worth mentioning: First, true ***tequila*** may originate only from blue agave plants. Second, the name ***Tequila*** has powerful patent and copy-right protections. We'll get into the history and explanation in a bit.

Referred to as: *The Essence of Mexico,* no other alcoholic liquid in the world is surrounded with as much history and colorful stories, legend, myth, and lore as ***tequila*** and its sister-beverage, ***mezcal. Tequila*** has the same world-wide name recognition and identity protections as does Champagne. You will never find another distilled, wine-product calling itself *Champagne* than that produced and approved by the regional board in Champagne, France. Its closest rivals, and offering similar if not distinctly closely resembling tastes, may refer to themselves as *Sparkling Wine*, but that is all. Champagne is to *champagne* just like Jalisco is to ***tequila.***

The same name recognition and protections hold true for ***tequila***. Since the mid-1900's, thanks to Mexican legislative, patent-protections, in the entire world, only ***Jalisco***, and a few adjoining, communal-areas, may call their distinctly distilled product, ***Tequila***. Even its distant ancestor, mezcal, comes from other states like ***Qaxaca*** and ***Guerrero***. Governmental protections insist that legally protected tequila processing must have a minimal, agave plant tequiliana Weber, variety azul (blue) of fifty-one percent (51%). The best tequilas all have a 100% blue-agave approval rating on their label to signify their purity. ***Tequila*** is special and unique unto itself, and one need not go to far to appreciate that fact.

Tequila production is a multibillion-dollar industry. It is extremely important to keep track of all tequila production and sales both here and abroad to assure government protections and controls. There are perhaps around 500 different names or brands of ***tequila***

produced, bottled and sold each year including the tequilas only sold or used in Mexico. In comparison, its sister, ***mezcal***, produces upwards of 100 brands. Certain ***tequila*** products are designated for sale to specific countries in the world. In fact, some special names were created to help sell products in certain areas.

Naturally, the finest produced tequila is only for sale and consumption here in ***Mexico***. There is no way to order shipments of what may be considered the finest ***tequila*** in ***Jalisco*** and have it sent to your foreign address. Government sanctions and personal, native-pride disallow the act. Also, it is understood, if not widely known, that the worst-produced ***tequilas*** are made, bottled, sold, and shipped to those countries with least known experiences with its tastes. Sorry, Russia, Europe and China, I was told by tour guides that you folks get the cheap stuff, but at a high price. Less-trained palates receive some of the worst varieties but still pay the same higher prices partially due to shipping costs.

Each product has slightly different adjustments to its nature from production processes. These elements include modifications such as harvesting times, sugar-breakdown processes, types of fermentation vats, number of distillations, length of distillations, aging periods, and even types of aging barrels. Any significant modification to any of those above-mentioned practices allows a producer to use a more unique or specific name for his brand ***tequila***. This is important when you discover and understand what gets shipped where.

When I began researching sources of background information on the history and importance of tequila to Mexicana heritage, I found a fun and interesting web-site from an online Cabo San Lucas Magazine which featured a good article by one of its writers, Ryan Thomas. In the piece, Ryan explained clearly what I desired regarding tequila's history, definition and meaning. The following writings explain concisely much of what I wanted to offer my readers:

> *As North America's first distilled drink, and its (first) commercially produced alcohol, the history of tequila is long and*

rich. Its roots reach back into pre-Hispanic times when natives fermented sap from local maguey plants into a drink called pulque. The history of tequila's development from traditional beverage to the modern spirit parallels the often turbulent, chaotic growth of Mexico herself and is equally obscure to outsiders.

Mezcal wine, tequila's grandparent, was first produced only a few decades after the Conquest that brought the Spaniards to the New World in 1521. It swas variously called mezcal brandy, agave wine, mezcal tequila and finally simply "tequila"-appropriately named after Tequila, a small town in a valley in Jalisco state, Mexico.

The word tequila is itself a mystery. It is said to be an ancient term. The Nahuati were the original people who lived in the area. The word means "the place of harvesting plants."

Incidentally, by the 1940s, it had been determined that the agave pulque used to make the very best tequilas came only from the agave tequiliana Weber, blue variety. Furthermore, growers, producers and thus the government learned that the "blue agave" plant only grew in ***Jalisco*** and a few other small, adjoining areas. Therefore, in 1944 the Mexican government proclaimed protective laws were enacted proclaiming to the world that "only varieties from the blue agave plant grown, processed and produced in the ***Estado de Jalisco*** could legally call themselves ***Tequila***.

By the way, I want to mention that Ryan Thomas writes for the colorful and informative, online-publication, *LosCabosGuide.com* and its owner, Joseph A. Tyson of Tyson Promotions. Obviously, they team up to provide useful and interesting information about ***Los Cabos***. Specifically focusing on guides for visitors to the popular, vacation spot, the online magazine also develops topics of high interest for all readers wishing to learn more about Mexico in general, and in our case, ***tequila***.

Now let's get back to our guest writer, Ryan Thomas, who continues with his informative outline on the history and development of ***tequila***. He continues:

> *Distillation of pulque, tequila's distant ancestor, into something stronger may have originated with the Conquistadors as early as the 1520's. After the Conquest, the area around today's Jalisco State was originally called New Galicia by the Spanish conquerors. The community we now know as Tequila officially became a village in 1656. In the 1700's, mezcal wines became an important product for export because the town of Tequila lay on the route to the newly opened Pacific port of San Blas.*
>
> *The first licensed manufacturer was a gentleman by the familiar name of Jose' Antonio Cuervo. Sr. Cuervo received the rights to cultivate a parcel of land from the King of Spain in 1758, and the rest is history. However, tequila did not achieve its prominence until after 1821 when Mexico attained independence, and Spanish products were more difficult to obtain.*

Of course, like most others in the USA, I cut-my-(tequila) teeth with Jose Cuervo brands, and somehow managed to live through it. Everybody has their own favorite brands, though, and Mexicans are passionate about their choices. I had to laugh at some "drinkers" I spoke with regarding different tequila flavors, tastes and brands. They reminded me of some beer-brewer discussions I'd had previously. *Big was bad! Small, elitist-breweries were better!* By connection, ***Cuervo's Tequilas*** were bad because he sold so much; small processing plants, on the other hand, focused more on flavor... Yeah, right! I challenge any of them to a blind-fold test. After two shots, it's all great! Don't get me wrong. The really good, aged and mellowed stuff is very smooth to the palate, whereas the younger, clear tequilas can burn!

Today, Jose Cuervo's fields of blue agave plants are enormous. By the mid-1900s, Cuervo's agave fields had more than 3,000,000 plants. By 1880, the company was selling over 10,000 barrels of ***tequila*** each year in ***Guadalajara*** alone! No question, Jose Cuervo is the largest manufacturer of tequila in all of ***Jalisco, Mexico***. Their international export business is staggering. And still, there are many other distilleries which do great business with world-markets as well as sales at home. There are some, such as the extremely popular ***Tres Mujeres*** brand which only distill, bottle and sell in ***Mexico*** alone. It is held in high-esteem among ***tequila*** purists.

During this period, however, events arrived which would catapult ***tequila*** into becoming a major source of national pride. Two significant developments helped to foster tremendous support for Mexico's homegrown product. One was Mexico's own, short-lived, mini-revolution against the French in 1862 when ***Cinco de Mayo*** gained notoriety. The French were temporarily defeated, and the date stuck later on as an important and major commemorator of Mexican will and courage against great odds. Later, after the French were permanently disposed, the Mexican people needed to replace unpopular and unavailable French products with items from home. Tequila sales were perfect. Plus, it doubled as a celebration agent!

Another important factor was its northern, friendly-neighbor. That's right, us! The USA. Remember prohibition? Tell children that they can't have something, and oh, they cry and want it even more. Adults are even worse. American history is bred, born, and bled on the notion: If you can't have it, take it! When our government banned all *sassy sauce* from production, sales and use in 1919 until 1933, anyone who wanted to drink liguor simply went to whatever sources supplied them.

The black-market was rampant, and *Mexico* was delighted to support our national, bad-habits through US-Mexican elaborate, smuggling-operations. Now, we should be able to appreciate why there is so much successful, yet illegal, smuggling of products and people across our border. There is significant, welcomed and celebrated history behind it. It still seems apparent today: When people want something, they will find a way to get it.

Less than a decade later, ***tequila*** grew even more popular within the USA because of WWII. When European spirits were hugely limited because of the war effort, ***tequila*** was our potent, friendly ally to the south. ***Tequila*** sales sky-rocketed. Today, there is an enormous, world-wide sales effort supporting ***tequila*** enthusiasts. Whether you're a purist who takes his shots straight, or an ***hombre machista*** (macho man) even without salt and lime, or a lover of ***margaritas***, ***tequila*** sunsets, or a hundred other popular drinks partaking of ***Mexico's*** own treasure, once experienced, no one ever forgets the unique taste, charm and potential impact from its pleasures.

TEQUILA MEANS 'TA KILL YA!'...

I suppose now is a reasonable time to interpose one of my own, personal and anecdotal experiences involving the consumption of ***tequila***. Granted, on the particular occasion I shall now describe, I might have indulged myself with any other alcoholic beverage to serve my needs, but I didn't. I chose ***tequila*** because of its very unique, welcoming and captive nature. Being here in ***Puerto Vallarta, Jalisco*** and visiting a new friend, ***tequila*** seemed the obvious choice to bring along for a visit.

Additionally, I selected a fine brand of *tequila*, a **reposado** (at least a year of aging) of 100% blue agave. It seems further fitting to tell this story because the *incident* I shall share happened just recently here in ***Mismaloya-Boca de Tomatlan*** and occurred during the actual writing of this section on ***tequila***. It's like *destiny* or something; however, it's not pretty. I'm not necessarily proud of what happened, and it's not for squeamish-of-heart. Nevertheless, it's all true and presented to you now in all its gory and troublesome details...

Once upon a time, in a land far, far away... No, I only wish this story was a fairy-tale, but it's too basic, crude and real to be fantasy. There's no mystique or charm about it, just cold, cruel facts. I drank more than I should have on a particular occasion, and as a result, I probably slipped, fell and nearly broke my neck. Okay, that's the core of what happened. Here's the bloody, colorful facts...

About two-weeks ago, Angelina and I decided to take a four-hour, trail-hike through the jungle to beautiful ***Playa las Animas.*** The trek passed through the dusty village of ***Boca de Tomatlan*** and then followed over a concrete footbridge crossing the ***Rio Horcones.*** Once across, we turned right, toward the ocean, and followed the delightfully crude and haphazardly worn but well-used path past many private ***casas*** and rental units along the often steep cliff-side. Eventually, our trail twisted and turned and weaved itself through jungle and lovely, pristine beaches along the way to our ultimate and delightful destination.

The hike was a little tiring but a thoroughly enjoyable exercise-outing. Our visit at ***las Animas*** was well worth our tour effort. We had an inexpensive meal, and afterward, just sat back, relaxed in our lounge chairs and enjoyed the day. When evening arrived and we had soaked up enough sun and surf and filled our tummies ***con la comida mexicana***, we flagged down a water-taxi and got a desired and deserved boat ride back to ***Boca de Tomatlan.*** Once there, we caught a local bus and rode the shorter distance returning to our home, ***Casa Quantica.***

That was the set-up. Here comes the background... Recalling our journey that day, however, sometimes the path we followed going to ***Playa las Animas*** was rugged, and other times it was fairly smooth. As the trail climbed up and down the cliff-side of the ***Rio Horcones*** which flowed through ***Boca de Tomatlan*** to the ***Bahia de Banderas***, we passed so many dwellings and private residences of all shapes and sizes and qualities. Some homes were beautiful, ***mexicana*** designs and secluded up the hill from the cliff-side trail for privacy. Others were stoical fortresses tucked away into the jungle's forest.

Still other dwellings were simple, crude, sloppily-fashioned abodes suggesting amateurish, unskilled construction. These ***casas*** showed no signs of basic amenities including electricity and running water. This was authentic, remote-living along a jungle trail, I rationalized.

As we freely but carefully edged our hike forward, though, I would casually and amiably greet passersby. We even stopped to talk to a few, local residents for short times regarding their potential rental-properties. Soon, though, the more populated and crowded area seemed to thin out as we ventured deeper along the ***Playa las Animas*** trail. Ultimately, we came upon one particularly crude building with a somewhat grungy-looking character leaning against his outside wall above us. He was obviously relaxing and enjoying the early afternoon while inspecting any trail-hikers passing by.

I greeted him amiably as he acknowledged our passing. His was a tough and weathered, rough-cut, unshaven, and fairly worn fellow. He looked like a genuine survivor, mountain-man. The building that he appeared to be living in coincidentally seemed to be an equally rough-shod and worn-down structure. His apparent home was old and weathered and made of concrete blocks, bricks and cinder-block slapped together with some mortar. The place looked like it had been shoved and mismatched together in haste to accommodate its meager trappings.

I stopped to visit with him for a minute, though, and casually but quickly questioned him regarding his circumstances. I surmised that he was another rough-cut American, ex-patriot who had just recently moved to that area but had, in fact, been living in Puerto Vallarta for twenty-nine years already. He seemed very congenial, and ours was a brief but friendly conversation. I was prompted to depart, though, by my waiting and anxious, if not impatient and annoyed, wife to keep moving because we had a long hike ahead of us. Curiosity gained the upper-hand of my attention, though, so I suggested that sometime soon, I might drop by again for a longer visit. He pleasantly welcomed a return visit. We bid goodbye, unknowingly setting a date for doom.

About a week later came an opportunity to follow-up on that visitation promise. I had been in town doing a little research on the ***Mismaloya*** property-topic I was studying. While meandering down the city's pebble-stoned streets, I passed a somewhat scroungy-looking character whose visage gave me a momentary flash of familiarity. Since there was no immediate connection, though, I let the spotty recognition go. Maybe I knew him, but I had already seen or met quite a few *wasted-looking* characters during my travels, so probably not.

Later, during the bus trip home, I had stopped-off in ***Mismaloya*** to visit a new contact and continue my research project. Once my interview was completed, I signaled another bus to pick me up to finish my evening's trek home. Climbing aboard, I settled down to relax and consider new and valuable information gathered from the day's interviews. In fact, I had gained a whole new perspective on the disastrous, ***Mismaloya*** property squabble. Suddenly, my concentration instantly dissolved by a surprised greeting from the character I'd seen in town. His excited call from back of the bus erupted, "Hey, Buddy! Aren't you the one who walked past my place last week?"

I paused for a moment, then turned to see who was talking. Of course, immediately, I identified the scruffy, unshaven face. It was the same *guy* I'd seen in town too. Aha! I *had* actually recognized someone I knew wandering down the same streets in town that morning. This day, however, and this time, he was wearing a baseball cap. That hat must have been what had thrown me earlier. I laughed, though, and responded with a grin and a resounding cue, "***Si, que soy yo!*** (That's me!) Hey, Guy, ***es usted*! *Que pasa***?" (...it's you! What's up?)

I had remembered his name too. It was *Guy*, and I had told him when we introduced ourselves that it would be easy to remember his name because that was my father's name. What I hadn't told him was that even more than that, he reminded me of my loving, kid-brother, Kerry, who passed away several years ago. No matter, I figured that on some future visit we'd share more personal info. There were so many curious, if not intriguing, people whom I'd met during my travels in Puerto Vallarta. Perhaps, this *Guy* would turn out to be another. It would be worth the visit, I thought.

In fact, I did actually think about interviewing him. What is it that takes people (like him) to places they end up? Whatever brought a character like *Guy* to this beautiful part of the world? How long had he been here? How did he manage to stay and survive? What was his status or relationship with his native country, our USA? What were his future plans? I suppose, however, that I wanted to learn his life-story as much for my own curiosity as I did for any potential inclusion in my book. Perhaps, I was questioning and seeking answers to my own queries and aspirations. What could bring someone down here and then keep them? I was truly interested in anyone's response whether despondent or defensive.

Anyway, before my own bus-stop approached, I arranged another visit at his home. We agreed that I'd come by in a day or so. Guy assured me that he'd be there for a few more days. The bus came to my stop, and as we parted, we agreed our visit should occur fairly soon before he left again. He had a part-time job in the mountain jungles somewhere. I chuckled to myself regarding the day's coincidences of seeing him in town then curiously again on the irregular, bus-ride home. I supposed it was fortunate, if not comical, circumstances too that after a week's activities and the day's events, he had remembered me.

Now fcome the bloody facts... Two days later, an opportunity presented itself. Angelina needed to go into town early for some personal business, so I had the afternoon all to myself. I had told her that when she returned, if I were not yet home, I would probably be visiting the "guy" over in ***Boca*** across the river. She understood and agreed, I believed, and she was off on errands. It was late morning. I decided to make the excursion to find my new acquaintance's place.

It was nearly noon by the time I had collected my gear and wits. I had been writing that morning but reached an appropriate stage to resist continuing. The mid-day sun was out. It had developed into a spectacular day for a walk and, in this circumstance, a visit. However,

I acknowledged to myself that I had unwittingly and foolishly not eaten anything for breakfast, or lunch for that matter; I'd had a roll and coffee was all. I decided that, regardless, I had no hunger cravings. If desired, I could eat in the local town of ***Boca de Tomatlan.***

Besides, I can easily play down hunger or nutritional needs when displaced with enthusiasm or intentional focus. If I am doing something important, I can forget about eating. My past teaching career, sole-proprietorship businesses, writing endeavors, and any activities could usually negate or block out thoughts of hunger. I am always anxious to get going or keep going. I'll eat later.

Anyway, I locked up our apartment and tossed the house keys into our secret, storage-spot for Angelina to find upon her return, if needed. I'd like to say I *bounded* up the stairs to the roadside above, but I seldom *bound* anywhere these days. Nevertheless, I was delighted to be *bound* for somewhere. Feeling particularly energetic that day, I chose to make it a full-outing and at least hike part of the distance to ***Boca de Tomatlan***. I turned right and headed up the road toward the little, fishing village.

It's a fairly narrow highway and can be really treacherous for oncoming and rear-coming traffic. I needed to stay clear of cars as much as possible. Drivers are speed demons on that route, especially taxis and bus drivers. Most could-not-care-less about a whimsical pedestrian dawdling up the roadside. Around here, it's an absolutely accepted rule: *Pedestrians do **not** have the right-of-way*. Furthermore, *offensive-driving* techniques are most decidedly practiced. That exercise was evident to me everywhere, and most drivers were typically very *offensive* to me.

Anyway, I was hiking, and along the way, I spotted an interesting stick, picked it up and considered that it would make a fabulous, hiking-staff. So, stick in hand, I continued meandering along the roadside, whistling away to a *traveler's* tune and whittling away at my new prize to make it more presentable and useful. It never takes much to please me. I'm pretty much a *happy-go-lucky* fellow and fairly easily amused. To wit, I'm easily entertained. Give me a knife and a stick to whittle on, and I am comfortably amused for minutes at a time.

After a fairly short distance, though, I decided a bus-ride would help immensely. My feet, legs and especially knees usually always bother me somewhat; rheumatoid arthritis slows my gait a bit. Sometimes, I am limited by terrain or distances I can travel depending on occasions or my mood. Today seemed like a good day, but I did not want to push my luck. It was still a significant and slightly difficult and awkward hike to the jungle trail leading to my friend's place. I wanted to enjoy my day, not exhaust myself.

Plus, I had a return hike home, and if by chance, Guy were not even there, I'd have to turn right around and go home. Yes, a bus-ride was a good idea. Besides, it is very inexpensive, about fifty-cents a ride. The bonus for me also was that here they had no problems with some character climbing aboard their buses with a big stick in his hands. It seldom seemed like drivers or other passengers even gave it a thought. That was probably because all kinds of folks came aboard buses with all kinds of stuff: Fishing poles, buckets, laundry, groceries, scuba equipment, guitars, machetes, and even some weirdos with long sticks in their hands. Everything was fine so far. I was in cool company. Life was good.

So, a bus and friendly driver picked me up, and off we went for the final distance to the community of ***Boca de Tomatlan***. Herein lay my second mistake-of-judgment. Remember that I had skipped breakfast and lunch? Now came the moment in which I made a near-fatal decision on that ominous day. I decided to drop by a local market and buy my host a house-warming gift. A bottle of wine, perhaps? Naahh! Wine was for sissies. What we needed to kick off Guy's new house celebration was something appropriate, yet special: ***Tequila***! Nobody knows how to throw a party better than ***Jose Cuervo***.

I greeted a young, store-clerk, quickly made my selection and purchase and stuffed the ***tequila*** bottle inside my backpack. As mentioned earlier, it was a nice choice. I was sure we'd both enjoy it. At least, I would. Out the door and I was off again for the route through town. I crossed the narrow highway, went South up the country road a bit and then turned down the steep hill toward the village and river via a broken and dilapidated stairwell. Passing by several abodes, I reached a worn down, cobblestone street which seemed to have laid there for ages. I turned and followed away from the village, then turned right again and took another beaten stairway all the way to the ***Rio Horcones*** edge. There I followed a dirt road upstream alongside the river to a footbridge which crossed over to the other side, my required route.

These types of bare, nearly one-way, foot bridges are scattered throughout the municipalities of ***Puerto Vallarta***. They are used to access both sides of the many surrounding rivers in the area. Some of them are very shaky, and people must use serious precautions when crossing. Others, such as the one I was presently crossing were made of solid concrete and were relatively stable. In fact, I had already used this one several times previously including one time to rescue a frightened, abandoned dog stuck on a large rock in the middle of the quick moving and rapidly rising current. I was very comfortable with that bridge. So was the rescued pup, too, once he was set free and raced home across it.

Finally, I was on the river-edge path winding along the *Potpourri-Trail* to my final destination. I call it the "potpourri" because it is scantily and crudely constructed of wild and crazy assortments of passage materials which kept any traveler focused, amused, fascinated, and moving forward. Some parts were simple and basic, dirt-paths. Others were slabs of concrete poured as accesses to the river or abodes up the cliff's side. Then there were dirt, rock and concrete steps built up and down the cliff-sides to continue progress. Also, there were large deck walks made from poured concrete and others of wooden pilings and boards.

Still, further along the *Be Careful Trail* came huge, barren tree-trunks growing alongside the river which required stepping over, bending under and navigating around. Then came climbs over boulders which had been chipped, broken and carved into usable steps. Of course, several sections of the *Piece-meal Path* were deliberately constructed of large, relatively flat rocks used as stepping stones. Occasionally, the path worked itself right through somebody's front yard and then just as haphazardly passed beyond and through weird, over-growths disappearing into jungle foliage only to reappear again clearly in daylight after a brief lapse. Hikers just had to keep their wits about them and take certain parts of the trail with serious precautions. Nevertheless, it was authentic, and that made it interesting and almost romantic.

I could only vaguely remember where I had initially met Guy at his jungle abode that earlier visit. Therefore, I asked people I came across, ***"Disculpa, por favor, pero ?sabe usted donde Sr. Guy vive cerca de aqui?"*** *(*Excuse me, please, but do you know where Mr. Guy lives near here?)

Everyone politely and considerately pondered the question intently, but then each respectively responded, ***"Lo siento, yo no lo conozco."*** (Sorry, I don't know him.)

At first, of course, I figured it was my poor Spanish or bad accent. Alright, it was probably both, but still I did understand them, and I recognized their simple lack of knowing *Guy.* Okay, *unknown* is still better than *nothing*. If there is *no such thing*, then we are working on a scheme, or plan or thesis based on zilch, zero, nada. It's just ignorance and foolhardy and a wasteful time of energy.

However, if the matter simply requires more information, more insight and knowledge, then we can just keep working, struggling and researching toward an ultimate solution. I simply had to keep going and keep asking, ***"Donde esta mi amigo, Guy? Donde estas?"*** (Where is my friend, Guy? Where are you?) He'd turn up, or I'd finally recognize his place, and he'd be there or not! I'd soon see.

Lo and behold! I came across a young man moving swiftly up the trail past me, and I pursued his *knowledge.* ***"Perdone, pero ?sabes Guy? El veve cerca de aqui."***

I lucked out! Not only did he understand me, but he knew Guy, and he spoke English! *Da, da, da, da, da, da, da, da, da, da, da, daaaa!* Success! I mentally hummed the fight song of the UC Berkeley Bears! I did it! Persistence pays off. Just keep trying. Don't stop. Don't quit. The answer will get closer. Success is just ahead, just around the next bend. Keep going...

The young man even gave me explicit directions: "Yeah, I know Guy. He lives in the small house just past the beach, picnic-tables and the big, orange place with the orange bench on the trail. It's the next place after that." You can't get directions much clearer than that. This young fellow was specific, knew exactly who I was looking for and told me in excellent English. I was almost there.

A minute later, and I spotted the beach tables, then the orange house with its bench and suddenly, I was standing in front of Guy's ***casa. "Donde estas, mis amigo, Guy?"***

Immediately, a yell came out from inside the abode, "Hey! Yeah, Dan, you made it! Great! C'mon up."

I found the crude, uneven steps up to his abode about eight feet above the trail, and I climbed up his entrance way. A quick review and I noted the pretty much crude, ramshackle and rough-shod conditions. Let's see.

Right away, Guy met me at his doorway and extended his hand for a shake and a welcome, "Glad you made it! Let me show you the place. It's a little rough right now because I just moved in, but I'm fixing it up as I go along." Okay. That was positive, but I did realize that the place appeared to need a lot of *fixing-up*.

Guy took my backpack, hat and staff and set them aside and offered the quick tour of the grounds. He definitely was one of those dwellers who required very little subsistence. His one room, cinder-block residence was absent of all the typically needed or desired amenities. No running water, electricity or gas lines were evident. His bathroom facilities appeared to be the nearby river and the outside jungle. Those aspects combined with the rather challenging and awkward walk hiking to his place made me fully aware of his somewhat reclusive nature and hermit-like existence. Certainly, I was curious and planned to find out more.

A quick tour and question-answer period followed, and many curiosities were resolved. The place was crude and rough right then, but guy had plans for it. Eventually, he would clean-out sewer lines and bring water to a flushing toilet he would install in the back. In the meantime, welcome to the great outdoors! Although, there were no plans for electricity, lamps and candles would suffice. He would do very little cooking. His own, personal diet would consist of whatever he could get in trade for shrimp that he caught in the river with his many traps. He also earned cash occasionally as a gardener and landscaper. However, it was the plans for his inside apartment for which he was most proud.

I sat down at his small, camper table to ask more questions and hear his stories. Also, this began the third and next-to-last mistake of my adventure that ominous day. I opened the bottle of ***tequila***, and announced, "A toast to you, Guy, and your new home! May you thrive here in peace, joy and tranquility." We touched glasses, "***Salud***!" and the session was on.

Guy proceeded to give me the high-lighted version of his life's history. Similar to a few others I had already interviewed, Guy was extremely well-traveled. During his youthful and fearless years, he had been a fairly high-powered executive for a Canadian shipping company. His work took him throughout the world establishing contacts and business for his firm. In fact, that is what ultimately brought him to Puerto Vallarta in the first place. ***"Salud,*** Guy!"

Once here, the most internationally common saga of all-time occurred: Guy met a young, beautiful and vivacious Mexican girl; they both fell desperately in love; he left his steady, foreign employment to remain here with his woman; she immediately got pregnant; they quickly married (she was Catholic, no kidding); they had a healthy and handsome son; soon, she became disenchanted with his now weak, employment opportunities; and finally, they divorced. Herein, however, lies the distinguishing part to Guy's character. He chose to remain here in Puerto Vallarta's vicinity to be close to his child and help rear him. What could I say, "The honorable thing to do, Guy! I toast you. Drink up!"

Having been divorced, myself, years earlier from the mother of my four children and having chosen to remain near by to support them, I related to Guy's circumstance. Obviously, it had been quite a bit easier for me because my employment had been in the same community as my children. However, I sensed from Guy his mutual temptation to run away at that time and start over again in some distant place. In a way, we bonded perhaps because both of us had honorably chosen fatherhood. Additionally, I found kindness, responsibility, creativity, self-sufficiency, and a still smoldering desire to excel. He was a naturally decent man. We continued to talk and to drink.

Eventually, it was necessary to relive myself. I'd already had the outdoor tour, so I knew where to go for the *natural* toilet. I laughingly and jokingly advised him of the imminent flood and to thus prepare for damages. I clearly recall working my way out his front door, carefully maneuvering up and over the awkward steps and dirt, concrete path to the bathroom grounds. Business complete, I edged my way back over the path, down the step and back into his castle. A couple more jokes ensued, a couple more shots were poured and polished-off and our stories continued.

Naturally, I had filled him in on my own situation and had already cleared his story with permission for possible inclusion in my book. Most people are relatively comfortable with any potential claim-to-fame. Almost everyone wants their story to be shared especially if it is relatively colorful even to them. He respected my promises and conditions. I would speak openly about him, but appropriately, or not at all. Both of us felt fairly comfortable sharing his successes and mishaps.

It appeared obvious, also, that Guy had slipped and traveled a long way down-hill from the peak he once strode upon proudly. However, he didn't sound depressed and seemed to accept his position in life, his slide, so to speak. He even spoke cheerily with bravado, if not humor, of his situation and shared very matter-of-fact manners about his life. As he talked, I took notes and we both took turns filling each other's shot glasses, "Wow! Interesting. You did that? *Cheers*!"

The visit was really getting interesting and particularly humorous when an occasion for a chess match developed. I had noticed his board and curios pieces, and he had proudly and appreciably explained their native, Mexican Indian heritage to me. Moments later, a game was on with all the noise and hoopla and wildly excitable exclamations which seldom accompany or typically resemble any reasonable, thoughtful and/or sober contest. "Wow, man! You killed my pawn! You got me! Look the f---out! Nice move, though. Here, Let's drink to that!"

Guy continued his personal log of experiences since remaining in Puerto Vallarta for the past twenty-nine years. I was interested and remained an avid listener. He had moved around over the years from one task to another, dabbling in rentals, sales and then care-taking for some rather exclusive establishments. All the while, he had developed a love of orchids, and through his knowledge, demeanor and effort became a reasonably well-known local specialist, if not expert, in the field.

Guy was proud enough to show me his published article under his pseudonym, *The Orchid Guy.* It was a long article in a local newspaper which served local, ex-Patriots and English speakers by offering interesting tidbits and useful information. Guy's column involved origins and history of orchids including their enormous varieties and accessibility to potential, local growers or garden variety enthusiasts. He sounded extremely knowledgeable, and as he spoke I continued sipping on my tequila in genuine interest.

Throughout, I also attempted weary concentration on our chess match while valiantly focusing on absorbing Guy's incredible details of orchids. Listening, questioning, taking notes, learning, focusing on the game all became somewhat blurry to me. I was awash in an information flood. And so, in time once more, another urge emerged to relieve myself. I needed to rise and go out back...

Obviously, I had made it outdoors. Because I had not covered myself in urine suggested that I even managed the "relieving-myself" gig. However, the actual very next moment I recall was when Guy, with his shoulder under my arm, was helping me back inside his apartment to sit back down.

His voice sounded anguished, and he was emphatically pleading with me, "No, Dan, we've really got to get you to the hospital. You need stitches bad, Dan. Your eye is cut! Oh, wow, Man! It looks really bad!"

Of course, in my typical, heroic manner, I just mumbled, "Oh, I'm fine, Guy. I'll be okay. Just let me sit down and rest here for a minute."

Guy began sounding more anxious and urgent, "No, man, you've got to go now. I'll help you back to the bus stop."

By now, I was not arguing or even pleading. I felt too dazed and confused to do either; however, I was aware of a "forfeited" chess game if I could not continue. I remember chidingly mentioning it to Guy, "Gee, just when I was starting to win, and now you want me to leave." I laughed at my own dull humor but gingerly rose to find the door with Guy's assistance.

With no mirror to review my condition, and actually feeling little pain, I agreed to leave right away with one stipulation. Once he helped me stagger out his doorway and down his awkward and difficult steps to the rock and dirt trail below, I laughingly demanded, "Okay, Guy, if it's that bad, then you've got to take my picture for us to remember the occasion."

I stopped and wobbled for a moment, fumbled a camera from my pocket, shakily turned it on, extended my arm in Guy's direction to accept the thing. Then, in that evening's early twilight with exaggerated and dramatic form, I leaned against the eight-foot concrete, retainer wall beneath Guy's patio and grinned. Striking a deliberately carefree pose for the moment's memorabilia, I finally inquired with utmost curiosity, "By the way, Guy, what happened?"

He just shook his own shocked head and solemnly replied, "Man, you fell! You fell off the wall you're leaning against and landed on these rocks right here. I thought you were dead, Man! C'mon! It's getting late. We gotta get going!"...

The rest of the story is fairly a blur for my memory. I remember casually asking Guy a few times to wait while I sat down and rested to catch my breath. Even still, I was feeling very little pain or discomfort, just dazed and groggy. Afterthoughts advised me with complete cognizance that Guy had heroically placed his arm under mine and assisted maneuvering me toward the bus-stop nearly a mile away and an hour's walk.

I have no doubts he struggled quite a bit that evening against my weight and imbalance while lifting, straining and helping me along that difficult path. We trudged on, though, up the cliff-side trail, then across the narrow, foot bridge, down the town's dirt, riverside road, and then up the concrete, cobblestone drive to the hill's top where a bus still waited its departure. What I really recall was actually how swiftly we arrived at the bus stop. Like I mentioned, I was feeling no pain and probably enjoying myself for the most part.

At this point, Guy needed to return to his own, unprotected home,. After helping me aboard, he bid me goodbye asking for a return visit. I gripped the bus door bars and hoisted myself up and into the coach. When I had finally fumbled out eight pesos for the ride's fare from my pocket and handed the change to the driver, I became aware of his alarmed face. What could I say? I needed his assistance to deliver me to the hospital in town, but I didn't want to stress him.

So, I half-jokingly mused, "***Lo siento, pero me cai luchando con Jose Cuervo!***" [I'm sorry, but I fell down fighting with Jose Cuervo (***tequila***)!] I received a nod of acknowledgment yet still a stern look and shaking head as he shoved the gear shift into place, and we roared off for town about thirty-five minutes away.

I sat in the front seat behind the driver and angled myself toward the exit doors for a quick getaway once we arrived in town. I was regularly aware of the surprised looks on new passengers' faces as they entered the bus and glanced at me while handing their fares to the driver. Obviously, I must not have looked too pleasing, but all I could think about in response was the joke, "Oh, yeah? Well, you ought to see me from this side!"

Similarly, to the long hike to the bus stop, the bus ride to town seemed to pass swiftly, and before long, we were near the arrival point. The bus still had two blocks left to its cycle, but the Medisi Hospital was conveniently across the highway from our route. The driver pulled the coach to a stop, opened the doors and this time with an understanding and kind look upon his face, pointed at the hospital, and coaxed, "***Ahi esta. Tienes que ir alli.***"

I carefully exited the bus and slowly made my way across a parking lot to a highway crossing leading to the hospital's entrance. I remember chuckling to myself thinking, "Wouldn't this be a mess if I got hit by a truck trying to cross this highway getting to Emergency?" Fortunately, I was somber and sober enough to consider the possibility even with humor, so I steadily eased my weaving body across the thoroughfare and up the entrance steps to the hospital.

Once the automatic doors opened, I felt a sense of relief. I knew I was in good hands now. I had visited this same Emergency Center a few times earlier in my previous visits. My first visit had been for horrendous, flue-like symptoms. I guessed that American, flu-shot vaccinations did not work effectively against Mexican viruses. This was the real jungle down here, after all, not the concrete kind like back home. Another visit had been an ear infection. Go figure. I came to swim, but got swimmer's ear. My kind of luck. Then another visit had been a chronic, ongoing and nagging cough. I wasn't the only one, though. Around ***Mismaloya***, people referred to it as: *The 100 Day Cough!*

Fortunately, I have Kaiser Insurance. My emergency, care-costs while away from any nearby Kaiser Center in the USA are always respectfully, speedily and cheerfully reimbursed by the corporate claim's department. I am fortunate for that. And yet, medical attention and care down here is relatively inexpensive compared to back home in the States. In Puerto Vallarta, I can almost afford to fall down and break my crown, and then *get put back together.* Regardless, I guess I'm grateful that I didn't end-up falling-down like Jack or ol' Humpty Dumpty!

I love history. Some of the funniest historical events written about, if not best stories, come from origins of nursery rhymes. Take a look, for instance...

I suppose that my circumstance could have ended up a nursery rhyme too, or at least a local joke among these parts. Fortunately, as with the meaning of Jack's character's, my debacle didn't end up resulting with the government lowering the quantity in a serving of beer (tequila) in local saloons for the same price. Furthermore, I fell off a wall, but unlike King Richard III of England who was defeated in battle at Bosworth Field in 1485, (doctors and nurses) did put me together again. Or, if you like, I was a huge canon (*Humpty Dumpty*) which tumbled defending a walled community (the church of St Mary-at-the-wall) when the wall supporting it collapsed from Parliamentary gunfire in 1648.

Of course, neither rhymes vividly exemplify my own pathetic circumstance. True, it was tequila involved, not beer, and when I broke my proverbial *crown*, that bottle of "Ta-kill-ya" became the most expensive drink I ever bought. And even like that moron, *Jack,* I did *climb up a hill* to fetch a (drink). But there was no Jill tumbling after, and the closest thing to her was Guy scrambling to pick me up.

Therefore, I tend to lean toward (no pun intended) the Humpty riddle. True, I did get put back together and was victorious in that aspect. Additionally, I was raised from the (near) dead, and I have lived to once more *fire again* (pun intended)! But, more specifically, and important, was the date for Humpty: 1648. Think about it! I was born 300 years later ...exactly to the year in 1948! I mean, there's some kind of eerie coincidence there that is truly remarkable and significant. Unfortunately, I have no idea what, how or why, but I'm jazzed!

There's a connection for me in history. I've got to start telling this story and really glamourize it for effect. I've got a new nickname, *Humpty*. Or, better yet, *Unhumpty* because, historically, I *did* get put back together again. Of course, maybe there's a combination of the two rhymes because Richard III is referenced *historically* to having been a *hunchback,* and I did hurt my back too. Well, it was actually my shoulder that I, apparently, partially landed on. If a big ol' bump decides to grow there, then there you go! History is in the making! I'm going to be *infamous*! Babies will cry in their cribs when mamas whine legends of my exploits to them. Then moms will cease, and babies will be alright again...

Anyway, back to the hospital. Once I entered, the front room staff all gasped in unison and rushed into action. They actually remembered me. This place already had a computerized chart on me in their files. No, I didn't share my nursery-rhyme theories with the staff. I was actually relatively happy. I was *feeling no pain* kind of like the broken car that works fine when you go to the mechanic. It's just that the body got destroyed is all!

I heard later, though, that an inconsiderate, disloyal, and likely AA-member nurse informed my wife on the phone that I had been incoherently mumbling a bunch of gibberish, *and* she smelled alcohol on my breath! How dare they do that to me? And, I was so sweet and helpful and considerate as they carried me into the Emergency Procedures Room and wiped up the blood covering my entire body. I even remember offering to pay for their additional laundry bill. I told them *red* was my favorite color like my Grand Cherokee Jeep Laredo. I even think I began quietly sobbing a moment or two because I missed my car so much.

And so, ten stitches later, four underneath the tear on the skull, and six to patch my eyebrow together, and I was good to go. Well, not exactly. An IV was stuck in my arm, some X-Rays were done to check severity of the concussion I had received, and I was left in the hospital room to sleep off my situation. Angelina showed up thanks to our benevolent landlords' transporting her to the hospital, and she advised me as to how *embarrassed* she was. Hey! I'm the one who was *embarrassed,* for cryin' out loud! ***Me cai y me rompi la corona!*** (I fell down and broke my crown!) And I love this crown so much... I miss it!

I was proud of her, though. I remember her telling me the next day while I was slurping away on some delicious jello that she had dutifully defended my honor (and hers) when she exclaimed to everyone, "Daniel drinking? Why, I'm as shocked as you all are!" I mean, I don't think I drink a lot, but sometimes, maybe it's more than it should have been. This was, perhaps, such a case.

So, there were many lessons to be learned from that disaster. If you ever plan on indulging in *liquid fire,* do so on a full stomach. Sipping tequila is usually preferred, but remember that one shot of tequila, or any liquor, is equivalent to one beer or one decent glass of wine. It's all similar alcoholic-intake. Six shots of tequila or anything is typically about the same as a half-gallon of beer or two and one/fourth quarts of wine. So, know your limits. Like Clint Eastwood said as Dirty Harry in *Magnum Force,* "A man's got to know his limitations!" And that goes for all you women, also. A woman's got to know her man's limitations too!

I'm happy to say that this episode had a *happy ending.* I'm not making up any excuses, but I have some really good ones already on hand. I explained to my loving and supportive wife that, true, I had been drinking. Yes, it had been the equivalent to over half a gallon of ***cerveza*** (six or more shots of tequila), but our drinking session had been spread out over several minutes, I mean hours.

And, furthermore, at the time of the incident, I was gravely involved in a challenging chess match and was maybe on the verge of winning or gaining the upper-hand. Of course, that could be a complete miss-truth. I'll never know. Guy may have had me check-mated in two more moves. But, I don't think so because he had been drinking too. Get it? Hah! I think I had gotten him on the ropes when I conveniently took a wrong turn. *Forfeit, my eye!* Oh, the anguish!

However, additionally and foolishly, I had skipped meals beforehand, and I should have fixed breakfast that morning... for both of us, but I hadn't. Shame. Furthermore, I slipped, tripped, staggered, and fell off a dangerous staging. My head got split open on a big, flat rock below, and I was knocked unconscious from a concussion. Of course, I stammered and drooled and behaved incoherently. I was a bloody mess, but I had had my wits about me enough to request Guy take a photo of my pathetic, yet grinning posture.

To my new friend's credit, I visited Guy once more as requested, and I was astonished to see what he had accomplished since I had fallen off his deck. Not only was a reasonably safe bathroom zone prepared, the inside of his concrete cabin had received a complete makeover. It was comfortable, interesting and an authentic, rustic-motif but of a Mexicali-hippie nature. Brick cleaning, white-washed and decorated walls, mortar-filled crack repairs, wall-hangings, furniture, decorations, and genuine cleanliness greeted any welcomed and impressed visitor.

I was delighted at his handiwork, craftsmanship, creativity, and ingenuity. Plus, outdoors I immediately had noticed the *piece de resistance*: Guy had built a strong and sturdy, bamboo-railing where I had fallen to protect future dive-bombers from going over-the edge, so to speak. He had even named it for my sake. He calls it the *Dan-rail. What a guy!* I like this *Guy!*

It's been nearly a month since my accident. I've had serious time to reflect on the incident and my mishap. Once more, for some inconceivable reason, I was spared from some unthinkably, horrific ending. I have often considered reports of others more unfortunate than I. Many committed lesser grievances and perished for their actions. I would be less than veracious were I not to admit or consider for myself an arguably charmed existence.

This calamity was really only the next one in a fairly long list of mortal situations I have found myself surviving,. Once again, I am so immensely grateful for this episode's final circumstances. And my Angelina is still with me here to the end. She becomes frustrated, even maddened, at my continual barrage of foolish antics. I charge forward, often without looking, and I fall. Yet, my *Angel* shows up to pick me up. I've got a keeper. I've got to keep her. I'll love her until it's time for a better place for me to go.

I have often considered that perhaps there is still some mysterious task, or challenge, which lies ahead yet waiting for my fulfillment. I haven't completed it so far, therefore, I have subsequently been granted survival from termination and allowed continuation with this life-form. I still have not yet earned a ticket, deserved an exodus, been cleared for passage, or deemed ready and prepared to leave this life. There is still something I need to manage or finish. Perhaps, that task is fulfilled or accomplished and ends with the completion of this novel.

Once this book hits the shelves, so to speak, the world will discover it and me. It will read and rediscover me again. Possibly then, my work here shall be done. I shall finally and rightly and justifiably join the cosmos. Maybe with this book finally atoning for all my past grievances, I will be able to relax and go on to the next phase of my existence...

Then again, I'm still having too much fun. If that's the case, and this book is the barometer of my demise, then I shall just keep on writing. This will be the longest book ever written... What is written so far is just an *Introduction*. I'm going to continue with a veritable set of encyclopedias.

Get ready for letter ***A*** in my next volume: *The Traveler Series: Seeking Aardvarks!...* Let's go to Africa together! I want to write about an African Safari experience... from the animals' points of view. I'll start with aardvarks and continue through to zebras! Yeah, that's it! What's it like for *the king of beasts* to wile his time away in the jungle and have to stand there to have his picture taken?

I'll offer a personal interview...

This *Traveler* isn't done *traveling* yet. I've still got dozens of *travels* yet to experience, write about and share with my readers, and miles to go before I weep...

To be continued...

‘TIL THE VERY END

Before dimmed lights wound meager views
Of spoilt visages come askew,
Doleful refrains sadly take cue
From wanton pleasures lost in lieu.

Hence, with emotions’ silent play,
And nights consuming lustful days,
Let mental morals fade away
Ingesting love without delay.

False-teeth laid cleansing in a glass,
While bleeding gums’ trauma does pass,
Yield depictions construed so crass
That wanton needs become harassed.

As chronic struggling fails to talk
From choking phlegm and mucus blocks,
Anxious, yet denied, speech takes stock
Of lost time’s tally on the clock.

And macular degeneration,
Spent vision's interpretations,
Imagines love's invitation
With creative innovations.

Alas, days' gliding-walks are past;
Arthritic cripples cannot last.
Gnarled fingers protruding from casts
Seek supportive hands holding fast.

And canes or walkers serving weak
Hardly justify pores that leak.
Their convoluted odors seek
A private place and space to reek.

'Tis true, aged-skin sags wearily
O'er bones incised so hauntingly.
Yet, jaundiced tones warn acutely:
"*Time's essence* always is the key."

Thus, on oath's trust, unless I mend, This
promissory note does send:
"While brain and digits join with pen,
I'll love you 'til the very end!"

"Mismaloya Blues"

Part 21:
Hasta el Proximo Ano!...

Oh, gee whiz! "Hasta el proximo ano," is just about all I can muster up without *tearing-up.* "See you next year," keeps reminding me that this journey has nearly run its course. As initially planned, once the book-writing phase began, I understood that at some point my writing task would be completed. I mean, even Leo finally had to accept his situation and say, "Okay, Mona, that's enough! Thanks. Smile, you can go home now."

I've still got several other things to do besides finishing the book. There are at least two special places that I want to dive and see their sights. One place I have already gone to before while on a boat excursion with about fifty other snorkelers, and it was very distracting. It was to Los Arcos, an area of several, locally well-known, enormous rocks jutting out in the Bay a short distance from the shoreline near Mismaloya. At the time, I had wanted to burst away from the frolicking crowd and really see something, but I didn't want to get so far away that I'd not hear the return-call and take a chance of *missing the boat.* But the rocks have got really fun, big caves in them, so it should be interesting.

Another place I want to dive is right inside the cove of Mismaloya. It is the place notable from a scene in *Night of the Iguanas.* I've walked to the setting, but the water there looks very inviting. If I ever see the movie again, at least I can holler, *"Right there! That's where I went swimming!... No! Elizabeth Taylor wasn't there. She wasn't even in the damned movie! But I did give Arnold my autograph! He was just next door!"* … NOT!

I guess I'm nearly ready to go home too. What's left for my book is just a little touch-up, here-and-there, and I've got to find a frame... But, I still need to sit back, take the manuscript in hand and peruse it carefully for omissions, errors,editorial review, and organizational aspects. Hopefully, then I shall recognize any aspects still requiring updates and fulfillment. Therefore, now seems to be a reasonable time to review the individual stories and bring them to acceptable conclusions or, if possible, closure with the most current tidings. So, what boxes are still left open?

Best Wishes, Mismaloya...

Among topics we have shared which may deserve final acknowledgment might be updates regarding the ***Mismaloya*** community and its future. Where might ***Mismaloya*** be going from here and now? Over the years, crises have developed before, and violence has occurred to end disputes. No one wants unfortunate circumstances to blight the area and affect business or personal lives. People live here. It's supposed to be the land of *tranquility.* Que pasa?

It has been a difficult case for local magistrates to consider because so much ill-use and improprieties and corruption have occurred in the past and still exist today. In an election year, to boot, violence or blood-shed would serve no one's cause. ***Mismaloya*** has a fruitful image for tourism, and property and business owners can ill-afford to see a visitor scale drop-off due to unglamorous headlines. It remains a tenuous and difficult situation.

I had opportunities to speak with and interview many sources from both sides of the issues. There are those who feel pressured and forced to grab their families and belongings and leave their homes and potential livelihoods. They worry about the local school and the education their children receive there. They worry about where and what they may have as any option to go. They harbor negative sentiment because of unscrupulous demands from rich and powerful landowners and developers. They believe that their fathers were cheated, and now they want retribution.

Other villagers, recently antagonistic toward the protestors, support the area in question being redeveloped and sanitized with an eye toward expansion and a beautifying future. These villagers, who live on the opposite and previously-developed side of ***Rio Mismaloya*** which separates the entire community, resent the other side 's squabbling and squatting townsfolk who are profiting without payment. There have been obvious tones of jealousy, envy and frustration. It sounds strange because of all the prior, enchanting verbiage of *tranquil* lives.

Anyway, a mutually satisfactory and resolving communication is being developed. It is still necessary to bring these adversaries back together again as a complete family moving forward in a *tranquil* community. ***Mismaloya*** deserves a positive focus toward a pleasing future for all. Anger seems to be abiding, and the people and community appear to be more relaxed and settled. Protest signs are still up, but many have come down, and it appears like a consensus is in the making. I believe that the entire Mismaloya community will resolve its differences and continue its extremely relevant partnership with a growing and modernizing ***Puerto Vallarta.*** We'll see.

Something's Fishy!...

Another aspect deserving attention could be the latest developments with my step-son, Adam, and his incredible, Sailfish catch. It was so large, we should have expected that it might not end up so inexpensive. Furthermore, naturally, because of so many personal and somewhat similar dealings regarding money and services in Mexico in our relatively modest experience, Angelina and I should have anticipated potential discrepancies regarding final, fulfillment of any contractual agreements. Once money is forked over in a transaction, the person handing over the funds is pretty much committed. That aspect definitely provides the receiver with significant power and position.

Mexico has an unfortunate reputation of service-providers adding *small-print* to contracts *after-the-fact*! "We don' need no *stinkin'* contracts! Just pay me more!" seems to be an all-too-often abridgment and consequence of doing any business here. There's still a little time left before our verbally agreed-upon delivery of the fish to its new home with its catcher and owner, Adam, in Sacramento, CA. Unfortunately, I believe a new equation has been developed for their delivery formula. The new date of delivery is directly proportional to full payment of the new and *unapproved*, final pay-off figure.

As we review our final, fishy-story notes before they're just in "water-under-the-bridge," we need to reexamine our initial, *stinkin'* contract... Let's look at the initial cost of their brochure-advertised, and Captain Freddie provided *contractual agreement.* Keep in mind that all numbers and credit-card information and signatures were exchanged immediately during the incredible excitement and frenzy of Adam's capturing that *lord of the sea*. Sealing a deal for stuffing that magnificent fish in all its glory so that it could be shipped to Adam's home and proudly hung on his mantel was not cheap, in the first place, but it was very reasonable, it seemed, to similar services done in the States.

The *deal* was for hiring a local taxidermist with whom they were in cahoots, I mean did business with. Originally, the taxidermist fee was $1,150.

That's USD (United States Dollars) not MXN (Mexican Pesos). After a required sixty-percent down-payment of $725, immediately due upon acceptance, there was a final balance due to be paid to the taxidermist before shipment of $425. Not included, however, was an understood and agreed-upon, necessary transportation fee of sixty-five dollars ($65) also to be paid to the taxidermist to cover shipping costs. This is the point where we should have smelled something *fishy*.

Considering standard costs of typical, regular shipping for basic items to and from Mexico, $65 seemed like a price that was *too good to be true*. You know what they say about that!... Anyway, the technical part of the taxidermist's job was nearly over. They wanted the balance due and payment to arrange shipping. They needed those funds before their next moves. *Furthermore,* now came the spoiler:

They discovered that the Sailfish was much larger than they had initially been told and had calculated.

Apparently, the length given to them was ninety-five inches (7'11"); the actual length turned out to be (8'1"). However, *Fishy* turned out to be 100 lbs, not 120 lbs, as expected. He was taller (longer) and skinnier than we had been informed on the boat. In any rate, therefore, additional labor and materials had been required. That meant more money to cover expenses. Additionally, the size of the package, and therefore, the delivery, would require extensively higher costs due to initial underestimations.

Surprise! We were informed that as soon as payment was received to cover balance-due, including all additional-costs, shipment of the merchandise would be activated. However, the new costs would require an *additional $800. OMG! What?* We agreed to fiberglass-coating, not platinum! And we did not request *overnight-delivery*! *What*? Regular shipping, is all? One month still? Are you sure it's not going by *Pony Express*?

Curiously, the supposed, initial 60% down-payment now reconfigured to exactly 40%. Curiously? How about *coincidentally*! Nevertheless, it was a large down-payment, and it was obviously non-refundable, especially in Mexico. Ouch! I find myself arguing for calmness and not anger.

The taxidermist is in control of the situation, and we are foreigners dealing with standard, local business practices. Adam just needs to *suck-it-up*, accept it, deal with it, handle it, and *pay for it!* Besides, with that spectacular, sea-monster eventually hanging on his wall somewhere, and all payment costs behind him, Adam is going to have two great, fish stories to tell: The first one will be of *him* "catching" his *fish-of-a-lifetime;* and the second story will be about *him* "getting caught" *like a fish* by Mexico's somewhat unscrupulous, business and fiscal practices.

It's the kind of stuff when legends are made... I'll see about that!

There's No Place Like Home...

And now, after having experience my latest four months to date in this paradise, I have recognized a terrible error in my book as of late. I am absolutely remiss. I have provided no recent advisory reports for potential travelers to this area regarding weather conditions. I am just now realizing that I have barely mentioned the absolutely pristine weather experienced since arriving at the beginning of January this year. I suppose my negligence has been due to the weather being so remarkably nice that I have simply taken it for granted, "Oh, look! I think I see a cloud in the sky way over there! Oh, no, never mind. It's just an airplane. Pass me the suntan lotion, please... and another ***cerveza***"

I am now into May, and it has been some of the finest weather of an entire year. Oh, sure, November and December were spectacular months when we lived here a couple years ago. It is also true that January through April so far match them for comfort and pleasure. I should also mention pleasure derived from these high-season months because we have enjoyed them virtually without any critter invasions and insect trauma. It has been rare, indeed, to spot tan occasional mosquito or solitary gecko buzzing or creeping around de ***nos casa*** (our house).

I have already mentioned that I am expecting heat, lots of sun, for May. That is what all my friends and contacts tell me. Yeah, but how about my trip home at the end of this month? Is it going to *rain on my parade*? Are the rains going to pour by then? Are the rivers going to gush? Is the ocean going to rise? Am I going to half to swim to the airport to catch my flight home?

And wait a minute! Just where is *home*! Remember yesterday when Angelina and I stood at the airport waiting for her plane? We both pretended to put on our red sneakers, stand up and tap our toes together three times repeating, "There's no place like home!... There's no place like home!... There's no place like home!" Instantly, in a flash, Angelina was gone! Yeah, true. While she laughingly waved her arms passing X-rays, she had slipped through the baggage-check gate and had vanished. Instantly, she had disappeared from my sight...

Me, on-the-other-hand? Why, I was just standing there all by myself. Maybe it's because my shoes were actually just Jelly Belly, flip-flops, but there were some red jelly bean designs on them, and I did whisper the right words... Or, maybe this is the place *there's no other place like*! Maybe this is the place I love... *Home*? If this is home, then, does that mean that going back to California will actually be like my *vacation time*? That is really not a bad way to look at things. "Home" is *here*, and "vacation" is t*here*... I might *actually* make *there* (my old home) a really fun and entertaining experience.

After all, I'll be on *vacation* when I go there! I like the idea! When I am with my wife at our place in Suisun City, California, I shall behave as though I am n *vacation*! Everything I do will be like an entertainment activity: "Let's see! What's on our activity schedule for this (whatever) day? What? "Mow the loan?" Wow! What great exercise! I'll become a natural-health machine!... "Take out the garbage?" Whoa! What an adventure I might have! Can I accomplish the task without falling down or spilling any? Every step will be a challenge which I must conquer!... "Water the plants?" OMG! Our gardens will become veritable jungles! I'm going to grow the greenest roses ever!...

"Get off your lazy, pathetic a-s and stop watching so much sports!" Oh, well, okay, some places and things are the same everywhere.

Television, however, will now transport me hypnotically to anywhere else I wish to go. That is, of course, just in case I get bored while I'm on vacation! "Hey, *Nati*onal Geographic! What country are you takin' me today?" Or, my major love, "Hey, Baseball Game! What city are we playin' in today?" When I shall be on *vacation*, TV will be my prime source of entertainment! Today I feel like playin' golf! Okay, what channel is PGA on? Don't know. I ain't got the *remotest* idea! Get it? Oh, wow! Now, that's funny! See? *Vacation* is *fun*!

I must admit, though, that ***Puerto Vallarta*** has reasonably taken over a special part of my heart... and my life. Anymore, it is difficult imagining *not returning* here again for another determined period. Having spent almost eleven different months here so far out of a year's twelve, I can honestly confess and admit to preferences and priorities. Having experienced the varying conditions available throughout those varying months of a year, I have undeniably selected my favorite times to visit. Furthermore, I have determined my much less favored months and already mentally arranged *not to be on vacation* during those periods.

I suppose, though, that someday I shall return here for the month of June just to complete my annual calendar of months visited; however, June is still low-priority because of what I have already heard and read and *Googled*. May is already initiating its heat wave, but that, in itself, is fine with me. I have a fan! June brings with it heavy rains and bugs. Thanks, but no thanks! I am already familiar with July's heat and humidity and rain and bugs. And I am fully aware that August brings with it even more still, and that September is probably the crisis month and *full of it*: heat, rain, humidity, and biting insects and critters!

Puerto Vallarta has reasonably taken over a special part of my heart... and my life. Anymore, it is difficult to imagine not returning here again for another undetermined period. Well, actually, having spent approaching eleven different months out of a year's twelve, I can honestly confess and admit to preferences and priorities. Having experienced the varying conditions available throughout the months of a year, I have undeniably selected my favorite times to visit and my much less appreciated times to stay away.

In the meantime, below represents a simple and practical chart for casually gauging your visits to this area. Start by ignoring my reports. Keep an open-mind. Remember: *One person's garbage is another person's treasure*! What I don't like, you might love! What gels my psyche, might make you... *scream*! Some worship the *sun*. Others rant and rave and chant to *rain dance* lyrics. Some are allergic to anything non-human. Others are wanna-be Entomologists. How do I know what you might enjoy? All I can show you is a very general and personal chart highlighting typical weather patterns for ***Puerto Vallarta's*** region:

MISMALOYA'S WEATHER REPORT:

Bien! Buenos Dias, Vallartans!
Today's weather report
Is brought to you by:
'Heaven or Hell.'
You decide
Which one
Now!

November – April	= Mild, Sunny and Dry!	= Heavenly!
May	= Warm!	= Nice...
June	= Hot and Rainy!	= Uncomfortable.
July	= Hot, Rainy and Humid!	= Miserable...
August-October	= Hot, Rainy, Humid, and Insects!	= Hell!

The seasons come varied in range
Forcing inhabitants to change
From soaking-up a winter's sun
To drowning in Hell-fire's fun!

Insects, rain and hot, wet air
Engulf your flesh in bleak despair
While critters crawling on the floors
Find open-spaces under doors.

The days are spent helter-skelter
In pouring rains seeking shelter.
One storm causes awkward faux pas;
Then two more seek menage a trois.

Tropical, torrential down-pours
Force humankind to hide indoors
As creatures of the air and earth
Forage from ravenous rebirth.

Hell converges in Summers' months
And torments 'til the Falls announce
Departure of torture's ill-vents
With Glory's weather heaven-sent.

"Mismaloya Blues"

Part 22:

Adios, mis amigos mexicanos ...

Finally, I need to express my thoughts regarding some of the wonderful and amazing people with whom I have shared time and experiences. Granted, some have naturally been more meaningful than others; however, I learned from them all. I have met and visited with such a varied crowd of unique individuals. Some locals know this region because it is in their blood. I have shared some of their stories and insight because they promote the heart and soul of Mexico. They talk about ***Vallarta*** and its *tranquility* not as a methodology or exercise but rather as a way-of-life.

Others migrated here because they had heard and learned of ***Puerto Vallarta's*** own special charm from their own native States, regions or homes within ***Mexico***. Perhaps, similarly to Angelina and me, they initially arrived here on vacation or visits. As a result, they too recognized ***Vallarta's*** charm and value as a permanent residence. They, of course, were significant with expanding the well-doing and nurturing of ***Mexican*** culture with ***Vallarta's*** growth. Through their use both personal and business interests, they encouraged others to come and play, visit and stay.

I have met yet others who came here to stay or have been returning regularly for years and years during the same general periods. They are like *snowbirds.* They usually arrive during close proximity and depart in similar time frames. They all come and go for an assortment of reasons or explanations. ***Vallarta*** is a second home.

Long-term, ex-patriots I have met are a unique breed who accidentally, or otherwise, found this beautiful spot on Earth and claimed it as their own. I appreciate them opening their personal lives' storybooks for me.

To be honest and fair, though, and to make things a little nastier, I'll even include some of the lousy experiences and characters. I mean, these trips haven't all been roses and daffodils *all the time.* There have been a few dandelions in the mix, a few weeds, and some were were real stinkers. After all, that's life, right?... *Sometimes, roads less traveled are that way because they are more hazardous...*

We've all had the experience of meeting someone, becoming good acquaintances, even friends, only to have that person do something pretty rotten to us. Something that would likely never earn your trust again. The worst cases are those that continue through a deceiving relationship with handshakes and back-slapping greetings. Once they are *found-out,* they slip out the side-door when they see you coming. If there is finances involved, and there usually is where friendship's deception takes place, you can kiss the money goodbye.

Our feelings are hurt. Some people even get extremely perturbed or angry over the situation. Typically, the anger or frustration may be directly-proportional to the amount of funds or value it has to the victim. We all consider, ponder and attempt to rationally explain why someone we thought was our friend would do something harmful or deceiving to us. We can likely categorize that negative behavior and identify it as one or more of the following factors:

1. Your own *naivete* or ignorance by failing to use proper judgment;
2. You're a sap, a softie, an *easy-touch,* and they *saw-you-coming* a mile away*;*
3. You are generous, and you let others take advantage of that quality;
4. You are *A-have,* they are a *Have-Not*, and they want what you have;

5. You have morals, ethics, responsibility, and character, and they have no scruples;
6. Some people believe when money is involved, there are no *friendships*;
7. You enjoy hanging-out with a seedy crowd.

Please note that over half of the *factors* are your fault. You cannot be responsible for the behavior and actions of others, but you can control your own. Therefore, when something unfortunate happens, and there is little legal recourse, use better judgment the next time. Also, there is something else you must do:

Get over it! You won't do business with them again. You will probably never see them again. Let it go! Forget them, and forgive their sad, miserable lives. Afterward, they are still the ones hurting, but you have a story to remember.

?HABLAS ESPANOL O CHINO?...

"T*e veré de nuevo pronto*." ("I shall see you again soon,") is a phrase I am beginning to use more frequently these days. Anytime I make contact with an acquaintance or friend I have made over the past nearly two years of visiting here, I use the phrase just in case I miss seeing them again before I must leave.

Mis amigos americanos just stare at me thinking, "Okay. Nice. Now speak English!"

Mis amigos mexicanos just look at me appreciably, but quizzically, thinking, "Okay. Nice try. Now speak English!"

I am certain that I used the correct words: I G*oogled* the words beforehand. It must be my *pronunciation*. Oh, what the heck! *I don' need no stinkin'* ***pronunciacion!*** I've got sign-language!

Whether I speak in English or Spanish, I use my hands and arms fluently. As I carefully mouth out each syllable, while speaking, I exaggerate my meanings with shaking and twisting hands and by aimlessly flopping my arms about for special effects. And that's just for my *English*! My *Spanish* is pretty visual too. But at least I'm attempting to communicate. Sometimes, though, I think that others just subconsciously tune out my voice pretending that we are in some sort of game of charades...

It's like when I greet my friends in town, and I practice, "***Hola, amigos!***

Que pasa? Como estan ustedes? Ustedes quieren ir al cine? ?Has visto la vuelta al mundo en ochenta dias?" (Hey, Buds! Sup? How you all doing?

Wanna go to the movies? Have you seen *Around the World in Eighty-Days?*)

At first, they just blankly stare at each other for a moment, then they all enthusiastically jump right into the conversational game, "Oh, okay... Circle?... World?... Infinity?... Eight?... Zero?... Stupid?... Everything?... Dazed?...

Days? *Around the world in eighty...?* Have we been ***Around the World in Eighty-Days?***"

"Yeah. Right. Close enough. That's what I asked. So, do you want to go to see a movie, or not? It's got English subtitles, by-the-way!"

Oh, it's frustrating sometimes, but I don't care. At least, I'm trying. It's my hand-gyrations, though, not my Spanish, that gets it for them. Hey! Wow! I just thought of something. Maybe I should learn Italian. I'm perfect for it!

And no, naturally, my friends don't want to go see a movie. *Subtitles*? Am I kidding? That means they can't *flat-line* their brains during the show. They'll be forced to provide multitasking efforts by viewing *and* reading simultaneously.

"No?"I shrug in obvious disappointment, "Oh, well, and in case you were all wondering, it's not the recent version with Jackie Chan. It's the original with ***Cantinflas*** and David Niven!"

Again, they all stare at me blankly, and in unison quiz, "Who?"

I suppose I should have used my hands to explain, but I let it go and just laughed, "C'mon, you guys need some brain food. Where's a taco-stand?"

I'm teasing, of course. I could never learn Italian... That's another 100,000 vocabulary-word language to memorize, and my arms will get way too tired! Besides, my Mexican friends, with the exception of my wife, tolerate my ***espanol***-language inadequacies. Sometimes, some of them even offer helpful corrections or lessons when I am incoherent or request help. They are always good-natured.

The fact remains, too, that most of tmy Mexican friends are quite adequately bi-lingual. Many of them are comfortably fluent with English-language skills. When you travel a lot to foreign destinations, you meet many people who are multilingual. Perhaps, the explanation is because *Travelers* learn to communicate with people and places they visit, like me with my *sign-language.* It goes with me everywhere. It's universal.

The EU and US...

European citizens, however, are nearly all fluent in several languages. It's because of three, basic but important reasons: The first reason is because their borders are next-door to other foreign-language, speaking cultures. It behooves them to learn their neighbor's tongue. Some European countries are virtually surrounded by other-language speaking nations and cultures. It is useful and valuable to be able to relate to them in their own, native tongues...

"***He, Jean-Pierre, votre chien merde sur ma pelouse a nouveau aujourd'hui*** (Hey, John, <Petie-boy>, your <stinkin', rotten, no-good-for-nothin'> poodle just <shit> all over my lawn again!), came a borderline, smiling, yet stern and nasty, but neighborly criticism.

The suave and debonaire,yet frowning, reply came, "Ach ja, Oskar, und es war fur ihn gesund, aber Ihre Kinder warfen Steine auf meinen Armen, wehrlosen Welpen, kleine 'Chevalier.'" (Oh, yes,Oscar <Mein Fuhrer>, and it was <such a delightfully satisfying> a healthy poopoo for him<and me>, but your <miserably brutal and fiendishly sadistic> children threw rocks at my poor, defenseless puppy, little "Chevalier!)

And with a menacing gleam in his neighborly, squinting-eyes, and a wildly gesturing threat to his tone, came his eastern, unfriendly warning: ***"Ach ja, et la prochaine fois, ils utiliseront des balles!"*** ("Oh, yeah, <weakling-boy>, and the next time <you can bet your

French Champagne> they <my protective and obedient children> will use bullets!"

See? It's meaningful to understand and communicate with our other-language, speaking neighbors. How else can we recognize what attitudes are most deeply in each others' psyches? We need to appreciate our individual feelings and share our emotions. I think that the United States and Mexico have already learned this truth. Just look at how well our countries communicate on either side of our borders.

Have you ever noticed how many Mexicans in USA border-communities already speak English? Why, is that, you may earnestly inquire? Do Mexicans learn to speak English because they cherish cohesive-bonding between neighboring allies and wish supportive communication with their Northern neighbors? Well, no! There's actually a much more pragmatic explanation.

It's heavily dependent upon our own, American health-crisis. Our laws regarding medical-care, medicine costs and enormous insurance premiums are so astronomically unfair, biased and limiting. That frustrating and fiscally corrupt issue causes shadowy crowds of Americans to regularly sneak across the border in order to quickly buy cheap and unlimited *pharmaceuticals* inside Mexico. Mexicans learn English so that they can avoid being cheated by these angry, desperate, skin-flint, and conniving addicts.

English-language skills also aid Mexicans in developing and defending their own business acumen against their own, collapsing-economy and devaluing peso. Speaking fluent English aids their entrepreneurial-spirit with a more powerful and efficient tool and effective means in order to sell Americans their craved medicines: Drugs and tequila. It makes good business sense.

On-the-other-hand, have you observed the huge groupings on the American sides of the border who are highly competent and fluent with Spanish-speaking abilities? Why, too, does that humanistic-quality and coincidence exist, you may ponder? Is it also because ***norteamericanos*** crave friendship and brotherhood and camaraderie with their friendly neighbors to the south? Well, no, as a matter-of-fact, it's not. There's actually a much more ideological explanation.

It is heavily dependent upon our own American immigration-crisis. Those *huge numbers of inhabitants* on the US side of the border are mostly recent, illegal-immigrants who have been aggrandized by the American press and now reap presidential reprieve from our wannabe *Universal President.* Those *illegals* (Mexicans) *only* speak Spanish. I wish to emphasize that they *can* speak *English,* but they will *only* speak *Spanish*!

That way, in case of a highly-unlikely chance that any of them are actually caught, and then detained and asked *who they are*, they can cheerfully claim, "***No se porque yo no hablo Ingles, pero Obama me quiere. ?Donde esta WalMart? Tengo algo que vender a Sam.***" (I don't know because I don't speak English, but Obama wants me. Where is Walmart? I have something to sell to Sam!"

After all, ol' Walton wasn't named *Sam* by coincidence either. Don't you get it? Haven't you ever heard of *Uncle Sam?*

Secondly, nearly all European nations' educational-systems require English as a mandatory, second-language course. Why? With so much transient and migratory movement among EU (European Union) people seeking work and opportunities in neighboring countries, the schools are filled with many different, native-tongues requiring education. Because these countries are always bickering over which one is at the top of the food-chain, and occasionally fight over the concept, they needed an objective, outside language by which they might all learn and thus, become educated and communicative.

Furthermore, the United Kingdom refused to join the fiscally fragile, EU monetary-system. They've always had a *sink or swim* dynamic to their *essence.* Also, pride, I think. The UKs (United Kingdomers, pronounced *Ukes... No, not Uckies, Youks or Yewks!*) are just as bad as us *Yanks*, maybe even worse. They're an island people with easily distinguishable borders, yet they've managed to spread their influence and language all over the world. When they speak, can we understand them, though? *Fuhgeddaboudit*!

Even George Bernard Shaw, the great, Irish playwright jeeringly quipped, *"England and America are two countries separated by the same language!"* Have you ever listened to them when they talk? What bloody-well kind of accent is that, anyway? And, to be sure, they can barely understand each other. Put an Englishman, Welshman, Scotsman, and a Northern Irishman all together in the same room, and what do you get? Absolutely utter chaos! I'm talking about their *Parliament*, of course! And forget about the Irish language. Nobody understands them at all, including themselves! Or worse, who cares?

When visiting Great Britain, however, speak English or remain idle, ignored and ignorant! After all, it is the King's language, er, *Queen's*! That fact, along with the UK's sharing a common bond with each other's wonderfully melodic and frantically popular music and Hollywood-franchised, American film-industry together with BBC productions, made English a no-brainer choice for international, communication-appeal.

Everybody loves *The Beatles* and *Elvis*. Sometimes, EUers lip-sync if they choose. Sometimes that's better than sub-titles, but straight-up *English* gets it done the best. And the world adores *Arnold Schwarzenegger* and *James Bond*! *Britain's Got Talent* and *American Idol* are models to all the rest of the EU for which to aspire. In comparison, their leading talents are merely monkeys bouncing on pogo-sticks!

Third, many of the EU's favorite television programs and theater movies are offered in English, or they have English subtitles. As a second language, English is everywhere, and it's very popular. EUs love Hollywood and Bruce Lee movies with English subtitles. From an early age, impressionable children are continuously entertained and sabotaged by American and English shows, programs and movies. These *diversion* vehicles are actually subtle and deliberate academic and psychological instruments providing EU viewers with dynamic but fake action accompanied with English subtitles.

They are also relevant, instructional tools using this methodology to impress our friends and subjugate our enemies with our capabilities: *"Wow! You mean Americans can already go to Mars? And Brits have a submarine that can go 20,000 leagues under the sea? Whoa! They're bad! We'd better make sure we're on their side and can communicate with them. Let's all learn English!"*

BIENVENIDO. MI CASA ES TU CASA.

English:	Welcome. My home is your home.
Welsh:	Croesawu. Fy nghartref yn eich cartref.
Scots Gaelic:	(No human translation can be found!)
Irish Gaelic:	Failte. Diya brung any gren beers wiya?
German:	Herzlich willkommen. Mein Haus ist dein Zuhause.
Swedish:	Valkommen. Mitt hem ar ditt hem.
Dutch:	Welkom. Mijn woning is uw huis.
Finnish:	Tervetuloa. Kotini on kotisi.
French:	Bienvenue. Ma maison est votre maison.
Spanish:	Bienvenido. Mi casa es su casa.
Portuguese:	Bem-vindo. Minha casa e sua casa.
Italian:	Bienvenuti. Miacasa e la tua casa.
Polish:	Zapraszamy. Moj dom jest Twoim domem.
Czech:	Vitej. Muj dum je tvuj dum.
Lithuanian:	Sweikas atvykes. Mano namuose yra jusu.
Russian:	Ao6po nokkanoBaTb. Mon AoM-Baw AoM. (???)

Swahili: Karibu. Wageni mwakaribidhwa!
Hawaiian: Ahola! E komo mai.
Latin: Domun (My home). Cor meum tuum est (My heart is yours).
Kurdish: Bi xer hati...

{Greek/Hebrew/
Persian/Hindi/ – !@#$%^&*/*-()_+{}+|:"<>? (Go figure!)
Chinese/Korean/
Mongolian: Xanx!

There are patterns to languages;
Groups seem to correlate.
Yet, any phrase said with a smile,
Is welcomed in this State.

!Viva Mexico!

“Mismaloya Blues”

Part 23:
In America, Bilingual Means ‘Two-faced’...

It's simple fact: English is the third most commonly spoken language in the world. In fact, it is just behind Spanish which is way behind Mandarin Chinese, the top spoken language by a far stretch. Notice I said, "spoken." No body can *read* that gibberish. And *up-and-down*? You can't ever keep your place in line!

Therefore, although China is rapidly becoming a dominating, world economic-leader, the rest of the world is not going to submit to learning Chinese *scribble* just in order to communicate with them. There are over 20,000 characters in the Chinese vocabulary. Although only around 8,000 are necessary to be fluent, they still use about 370,000 words to express themselves. *Fuhgeddaboudit!*

English, on the other hand, demands less than half that number to be truly fluent and demands a mere 171,000-word vocabulary. Spanish comes in well back in the pack of "word" requirement levels matching French or Italian with a mere 100,000-word dictionary. *Words? Words? We don' need no stinkin' words!* No wonder they call the Latin languages (Italian, French and Spanish) the *Romantic Languages*! They run out of words to say really fast, so they have to use their hands! They are lovers, not talkers.

It sort of makes sense too, though. Fewer words means *easier to learn.* Oh, I guess so. I'm learning Spanish words okay. I already know a whole bunch. It's just the proper order to put them in which confuses hell out of me!

And I still get amused at that European-based joke about language-learners. It goes something like this: Early one morning, a couple of neighboring-nation Europeans are sitting in a bar (naturally) and discussing the day's worldly events. their chit-chat. Suddenly and curiously, the first one asks the other, "Hey, I was wondering, Jean-Pierre. What do you call someone who speaks *four* languages?"

The other responds quickly, "*Quad-lingual*, or *multilingual.*"

The first one nods, "*Ja!*" in appreciation and understanding and then asks, "What if they speak *three* languages?"

With slightly conceited annoyance, the other rapidly quips, "*Trilinque, naturellement!*"

The first one nods hastily again and happily exclaims "Oh, Ja, Oskar, I get it! And if they speak *two* languages, that means that they are *Bi-lingual,* right?"

The other nods his head, "O*ui,*" in appreciation and support. However, the first one still looks confused, so he asks a final question, "Well, then what do you call someone who *only* speaks *one* language?"

With a smug sneer on his face, the other retorts, "Hah, *American*!"

How About a Universal Language?...

Yeah, now that's a funny joke! Even *French Canadians* get a kick out of that one! But, here's a fine and fancy little fact for everyone to comment upon. Gallup polls suggest that, in fact, around one in four Americans can carry on a conversation in a second-language. Sure, three-fourths of us are *monolingual,* but unlike those Europeans, we are that way regarding spouses and lovers too. *We only talk to one of them at a time!* But, I'm changing my evil ways. I'm going to speak Spanish to *all* my women... and use my hands a lot too!

I think that the reason for that other one-fourth of *Mr. Smarty-pants, show-offs* and *bi* or *multilingual* Americans is probably because of the terrific immigration opportunities that the USA offers. Anybody can sneak into this country. All you do is tell the guys at the border that you have something to sell in the States from China. "Step right on over! Go talk to Sam! He'll buy anything!"

Have you been to WalMarts lately? Trying to find something in those stores which *isn't* "Made-in-China" is like some kind of cru-el-hoax, scavenger-hunt game. Impossible! You lose! And Sam & Company had it all figured out a long time ago. They own many factories in China where they make and build the stuff themselves using cheap, Chinese labor. When they proudly exclaim to the world that they are employment leaders in China because they offered their workers a thirty-three and a third percent (33 1/3%) wage increase, what they didn't explain is that just took their workers' wages from fifteen cents (15) to twenty cents (20)!

But they are clever... and smart and sneaky too. As the Chinese economy grows, so grows Walmart. They just keep building more factories to make more stuff to sell in Sam's Clubs and WalMarts all over the world. Steadily, they will progress building and buying up all the other Chinese factories until one day, they will have the monopoly. When China eventually controls and rules the world, everyone will hear about it over loudspeakers...

> *"Attention, WalMart Shoppers! Congratulations! Today only there is an 'International Special' going on right now on Aisle Number Four. That is where you must buy a bargain-priced volume of the world's new and required, single-language study to be memorized over the coming weekend. Your new, compulsory, spoken-language was developed by our benevolent dictator, Premier Sam. It's called* 'Walmartian,' *and all non-compliant learners will be forced to stand forever in non-serviced register lines!"*

Oh, whatever. I'm into languages. This Spanish-learning has been more fun than I thought. And I feel like I'm doing my part to leave the world a little better off than when it found me. Communication is the key. We've all just got to keep talking to each other. Regardless the language. Even if we get loud sometimes, we're still negotiating, still conversing. We just need to nicely ask each other to calm down and share the conversation; it's always a two-way street. And we must always remember to keep our hands to ourselves unless we're holding each others.

And I'll speak *Walmartian,* if they want me too, as long as they keep those 'blue light specials" going on. I love a good WalMart sale!

Mass Attack: Spanishitis...

But, I mean, there's lots of languages spoken in the USA. Just travel to any major city in the States. Every corner has its own national language identity. Take a trip to my own stateside, home-zone in the California Bay Area. In my *City by the Bay*, San Francisco, there are so many unique, sub-districts which voice their own language: Chinatown, Japan town, Russia town, Little Mexico, and many other vicinities which favor, flavor and flaunt their own native tongues like Vietnamese or Philippine Tagalog. And, of course on March 17th, everyone speaks Irish, only nobody can understand anybody! Now, that's a weird language! It's so confusing... so green!

But, the point is that America *is* becoming multilingual,. At minimal, at least, the general, American population is steadily becoming *bi-lingual.* So many families of one native tongue teach that language to their children while those same kids learn English in school. And the massive, Mexican immigration is effectively raising the language bar for all Americans. We can't stop 'em. We can't beat 'em. So, let's join 'em!

Hilary could really do her 2016 Presidential Election hopes serious justice if she'd just start guaranteeing: "I'll put a tamale in every pot!" I think Bill promised something similar, however, and he probably was busy fulfilling his promise until he got caught. He did get elected, though!

But, trying to get our government to openly support bilingualism is a very tenuous situation. Our government has hysterically, I mean hi*storically,* believed that American citizens are too lazy, indignant, volatile, or stupid to quickly adapt to another language such as Spanish. So, instead, our leaders cleverly plot, they think, with business dynamos (like Walmart) to use store advertising and government services to subtly educate everyone in Spanish fluency.

They are doing this right now by providing sales-offers and/or directions in both English and Spanish languages together. Just go anywhere in town and note the ads and directional instructions posted everywhere! Federal, State, County, and Local governments provide nearly all their rules and regulations on both English and Spanish forms or signs:. Just look: Enter-***Intro***; Exit-***Salida***; Open-***Abrir***; Closed-***Cerrada***; Upstairs-***Arriba***; Down-***Abajo***; Sale!-***Venta***!; No more-***No mas***; Pay your taxes!-***Paque sus impuestos! Hablamos espanol!***

Also, have you checked out your cable companies' programming lately? Half of all our TV program-channels are in Spanish-language. The next-step will be requiring all English-language programs to provide Spanish sub-titles. I know what our leaders are thinking. They are in cahoots with Carlos Slim, the richest man in the world and Mexico's communications-maggot, er, *magnate*! Every time someone says something on a phone in Mexico, Carlos makes a peso. Our leaders drool over his power and crave learning his concept of snatching similar profits for themselves, "***Ustedes estupidos americanos!*** You don' need no stinkin' English!"

Wow! What about when I start going back to church? I just finished translating all the Latin into English so I could understand priests during mass. That's why I left the church's confines in the first place. I never knew what they were saying, and I was an Alter Boy! Recently, I just finished studying and struggling and learning all the necessary Latin for Sundays' masses. Now, I can finally hold my head up proudly when I return for services.

And what did I hear that they want to do? Now they want to worship in Spanish? Oh, wait! That's impossible! Latin won't translate into Spanish. There's not enough Spanish words to do it. They'll have to use some form of *Latish,* instead, I suppose. The local, deviants like to poke fun and joke around saying, "It's really a form of *Spatin*'," but I don't abide with that. Humor. I'm just trying to return to the church. I'm not going to do anything to reap the wrath of you-know-who,... His Wholeness, Pope Frankie. No, thank you, Hallelujah, Amen.

Back to the *conspiracy-theory,* though... Every time you buy something in the States which requires completing a *Registration* Document or *Operations* Manual, the forms come in English language and Spanish too. For our really ambitious language-learners, though, many *Installation* pamphlets also come in German, French, Swahili, and Irish. No one understands Irish directions, though, especially themselves. But, our leaders put *Irish* directions in those pamphlets to humor them in case an Irishman's fixing something on Saint Patrick's Day. None of them ever do, though. They're too busy getting drunk on green beer!

Nevertheless. we truly are *a land for all people,* even including the Irish! It's not *free,* though. Our taxes will have to pay for it, but we're always searching and complaining for more freedom. It's our adventuresome spirit! We don't always know where we're headed, but we keep on looking. Becoming bi-lingual is all part of of the *master-plan.* But, who's the master? *Carlos Slim*? It's working, too. Our government anticipates and tells us that by 2,500 AD, the USA will be, officially, bi-lingual... in Spanish and Chinese!

It's similar to our earlier *metric-system* discussion. Americans, our benevolent governments' leaders believe, are too indignant, spoiled, volatile, or stupid to learn a much simpler method of measurement. Stupidity has been ingrained and devolved within our educational system for so long that even our foolish and lazy politicians are afraid to tip-over the scales of ignorance. They are so afraid of attempting to change something dramatically for the better good cannot be done during one term of office, so they balk. And yet, think of the obvious for goodness sake: *10 x 10 x 10* would sure make a lot more sense than this: *12 inches equals 1 foot; 3 feet equals 1 yard; and 1,760 yards equals 1 mile.* Weird!

But our government promises that in the United States of Chinese America, we shall all convert to a new measurement system, too, *before 2,500 AD.* By then, we are advised, citizens will be using a not-so-new, but very controlled economic scheme: One chicken egg equals twelve sheets of toilet paper; one cigarette will get us extra daylight-time in the exercise yard. Good behavior will earn any of us extra-opportunities to study our *WalMartian Bibles.* It's going to be revolutionary! ***Y hablamos espanol con Kung Fu!***

“Mismaloya Blues”

Part 24:
We’ve Got ‘Manifesto’, and You Don’t!...

Until then, we Americans just keep trekkin' along. When it comes to home, today we are a fairly liberal and welcoming nation. It wasn't always that way. Oh, sure, we went through our awkward teen years while growing-up. We caused others a lot of pain every so often when got a little big for our britches.

At one point, we even warned all of Europe to stay out of our half of the globe. The *Monroe Doctrine* of 1823 was fairly explicit: *"Any attempts by European nations to colonize land or interfere with states in North or South America would be viewed as acts of aggression, requiring U.S. Intervention."*

Wow! Now that's stingy. And I can hear Chinese and Russians giggling in the background, though. Have you been to San Francisco or New York City? Chinatown and Queen's Forest Hills District are packed with, you guessed it, Chinese and Russians! Apparently, they both felt obligated from Monroe and had green lights to *colonize* wherever they were smuggled or could lie to get into. And, boy, they spread out too.! Today, you can have your pants cleaned in laundromats in almost any city in the Western hemisphere, and then you can have those same, shiny-new britches pick-pocketed as soon as you wear them! Good thinking! Thanks, James!

Of course, a few years later around the mid-1840's, we felt obligated to tighten our belts a little. We felt like we needed more room to grow and define our borders a little better. We wanted to sew-up our own continent as a sure thing for U.S. Expansion. Therefore, our leaders cleverly devised a phrase which invoked divine sanction for territorial expansion for ourselves. *Manifest Destiny* basically suggested that God gave the USA *Supreme authority* to follow Horace Mann's advice and*:* "Go West, Young Men!"

And we did, *from sea to shining sea!* Naturally, our moves upset a lot of Mexicans and Indians, but what could they say? *God was on our side!* Actually, it was pretty much just an attitude justifying the previous war against Mexico.

Remember the Alamo? Well, not that battle. Mexico kicked our *butts* good there, but about ten years later, in 1846 Mexico declared war against us for our outright A*nnexation and Statehood of Texas.* We defeated them in an expensive and high-casualty war. As a result, Mexico's Supreme General Dictator, Santa Ana, officially signed-over the Texas Territory in a deal to save his own hide and career.

Texas had immediately became a State following its Mexico-unapproved annexation in 1845. Of course, the subsequent war and our victory also freed up territories west ward including New Mexico and California. We were still moving, growing and expanding. Finding gold in *them thar' hills* of California in 1849 pretty much sewed up the Westward Movement too. Statehood in 1850 for California made the words "...from sea to shining sea" in the song *America the Beautiful,* patriotic braggadocio of direct fact, not just inspirational words.

Other lands became territories and all fell like dominoes to our *divine destiny* theory for Statehood. Each one progressively *organized* itself, applied for Statehood and was greedily welcomed into the inner-circle. Mexico could only wearily and begrudgingly stand by watching helplessly as all the lands which they had previously usurped from local Indians for over two-hundred years fell to the Americans. After all, it was their *destiny.*

The Indians, who were simply trying to exist quietly and privately, for the most part, in spite of our Westward Movement, were nomadic peoples . Most slept in teepees and followed buffalo migrations. Plus, they used their hands to communicate. (I'm not sure, but I believe that they must have spoken Italian.) Anyway, their smoke signals and buffalo tracks let others far away know when they were leaving. So, as soon as they moved on, our ancestors moved in. And there you have it again... A national trend had begun.

The earliest records of the *Jeffersonian Movements* were started. No, not *Thomas*; granted, he was originally responsible for sending Lewis and Clarke off to explore our, or rather the Indians', countryside from coast-to-coast. They then brought back to Washington D.C. America's future dreams, hopes and aspirations for expansion and upward-mobility. However, I'm talking about the *other* Jeffersons. We were "moving on up, to the (*West)-side!"* Our plans, though, were to take the *whole,* darn pie!

Yes, we keep moving. Sometimes, I think we really don't understand where we're going. It's like we just keep heading where Captain James T. Kirk of the Starship USS Enterprise always said, *"Out there!"* Going West obviously meant going into the Pacific Ocean, too, because Hawaii became our 50th State in 1959. Oh, and we didn't stop there. We have *protectorate* (protected) islands scattered all over the Pacific Ocean.

There is even a small, political contingent in the Philippines which lobbies, promotes and campaigns for official USA Statehood. But, realistically, they're too far away and can't afford to keep sending Representatives to Congress. Their ex-Presidents Ferdinand and Imelda Marcos saw to that.. Ferdinand stripped the treasury and then split; Imelda spent what was left on shoes! But, yeah, can you believe that? A nation where a husband and then *wife* became *President.* No way! ***Increible!*** Besides, Manny "PacMan" Pacquiao, the boxing legend, has other, ulterior motives for the Philippines... once he is elected *God.*

Our more recent ancestral fathers (and mothers) even had ambitions of going South. Now, there was a convenient location for a perfect holiday vacation State: Cuba! Oh, sure, Hawaii is cute and entertaining with all its sweet, provocative hula dancers and such, but Cuba was going to be *nasty fun*! There were power-brokers and politically ambitious demagogues who drooled over making that *Cuba* a virtual, fantasy playground. It was going to make Sin City, (Las Vegas) seem like a nursery school for priests' and nuns' illegitimate babies.

A land-of-milk-and-honey, you inquire? Hardly! Our leaders saw it more like a showcase *State* for limitless booze, and totally legal drugs, and prostitution, and gambling, and street-racing, and chicken and dog fights, and bull-fights! Oh, well, no, that's too bloody. But, oh, wait! That's right1 We already have that other stuff right now in Nevada and New Jersey. My bad. I forgot. It's been twelve years now since I last went there and lost all my money...

Unlike Vegas and Atlantic City, however, was an important difference: It was true, *what happens in Vegas stays in Vegas,* but *what happens in Cuba stays in the whole entire State of Cuba!* All visitors would be in a legalized *State of Sin!* How would you like to be one of its Congressmen? You'd be everybody's best friend! Cuba would have no actual Governor there, *only* a "Vice"-Governor!

Anyway, it's a moot point. Unfortunately, in the late 1950's until today, Fidel has been selfish and greedy and won't play ball with us. Why should he be Vice-Governor he is already King! And they even offered him his own MLB team too: *Havana Commies*. But he doesn't watch sports; he just chews on cigars. Now, great baseball players from Cuba have got to swim ninety-miles, first, before they can get drafted. Castro defied our *destiny!* So much for that. Thanks, Fidel!

But we keep searching. It's adventurous, and we keep looking for something. We've just got to see what's around the next bend. Who knows? There might be a new oil-field or gold deposits we can pilfer. I've been told that even our Space-Age focus was instigated by some warped, half-Irish Communist-scientists who wanted the moon for themselves. They believed (still do) that it is made of *green cheese.* They wanted ***queso verde*** as *snacks* to go with their ***cerveza verde*** *on St. Paddie's Day celebrations!*

Why do we explore? We do it because it's fun! We enjoy exploring our horizons for curiosity's sake, for knowledge and for adventure. Why do we expand? For fun-and-profit! And it's in our *Manifesto.* No! No! I mean, it's in our *Divinely Manifested Destiny.* The *Manifesto* is the Chinese Communists' trip. It's cool, though, because they are all atheists anyway and don't buy-into our crap! Besides, with Sam's help, today we're moving into China, and that's the *East Side*!... We are *movin' on up!* There's a big job ahead of us... We've got to get 1,500,000,000 Chinese to learn English. But, Hollywood is helping with its *laundromat*-image of Chinese immigrants and with guys like Charlie Chan, Jackie Chan and Bruce Lee. First, it's *hello* sub-titles, then it's all out, "Ni hao, Joe!"

# QUIENES SON?	# WHO ARE THEY?
Viven entre tantas razas	They live among many races
Mas no saben de que raza son.	But do not know what breed they are.
Senalan a unos, senalan a otros	They point to some, then point to others,
Y encuentran que Norteamericanos son.	And find that they are all Americans.
Adventuros son hombres y mujeres	Adventurers are men and women
Explorando siempre estan	Always exploring
Aqui y alla, ababjo y arriba	Here and there and up and down
Porque aventureros son.	Because adventurers are explorers.
No tienen raices	They have no roots
Porque de todos lados son	Because all sides
Y atraidos hacia lo desconecido	Are attracted to the unknown.
Buscan y buscan, pero	They search and search, but
?Quienes son?	Who are they?

Norteamericanos son	Americans are
Nacieron libres o buscuson libertad	Born free and seek freedom
En tierras de libertad,	In all lands of liberty.
Buscan todo,	They are always looking
Porque aventureros son.	Because adventurers do.

Para Daniel y Angelina de Sergio y Deyanira
-2015-

Who Are We?... How About Bermuda Grass?...

On the previous page, was the poem, *Who Are They?.* It was written, and given to my wife, Angelina, and me as a very personal gift, by our very kind and benevolent landlord living above us here in Mismaloya-Boca. I believe readers can appreciate the tribute Sr. Sergio seems to offer to our *American spirit.* Of course, I had to read his original, Spanish version and then translate it into reasonable English for better understanding. In discussing its meaning with Sergio regarding his poem, he emphasized how he has observed behavior of US citizens and some Canadians who venture to this area for respite or new lives.

Sergio has previously told me that he is always amazed and impressed with we ***norteamericanos*** and our desire to explore and seek new adventures. He has also confided in me his rationale for our aggressive-explorer attitudes and behavior. He says that he believes that our nation is still so young, and because of that we have no roots to identify ourselves. In the same manner, because we are so new and virile everybody who comes to America becomes part of the adventure. Eventually, there are no distinctions to anyone's membership.

As Sergio believes: *We look around to see (who is what), and all we see is other Americans.* It was both touching and humbling; he made me proud to be an American, and I considered his own, Mexican heritage in terms of his words.

I appreciated Sergio's comments. Just as importantly, I was gratified by his respect. Our conversations always leave me asking more questions of myself, and life's meaning, and our existence. He makes me consider concepts which I had not previously thought about. Sergio's admiration for our *freedom-loving, adventurous spirit* is also apparent when I share with him details of our most recent adventures down here.

Sergio, and his charming wife, Deyanira, are typically surprised, occasionally alarmed but then usually delighted from tales of our various activities: Long hikes through jungles, open-ocean swims to island retreats, horseback rides everywhere we can, our deep-sea fishing expedition, snorkeling and diving exploits for sea shells, car rentals and bus transportation to distant, historical, entertainment-sights, visits to and participation in all the *by-boat-only* access sites, and even our seeking out all the various, festival-activities and then joining in the mix with such bravado.

Occasionally, Sergio dutifully offers subtle advice and warnings for some of our antics, but he enjoys hearing stories of our escapades. He flippantly teases, "There seems to be nothing stopping you Americans. You just go everywhere you want!" Then he adds, "Because you don't stay put, however, you never establish any roots." He even uses *Christopher Columbus* as a comparison for Americans' spirit, "Just like (him) you are all adventurers and explorers of the unknown." He guesses maybe it's in our DNA. He may be right. I am a *boomer-baby,* after all!

I laugh and offer-up in humorous exchange:

Perhaps, we Americans are more like the very invasive, Bermuda grass: It too puts down shallow-roots from its joints

> *as it spreads. With dashing, self-survival instincts, it ventures out anywhere possible. Additionally, it seems to enjoy exposing itself in every nook and cranny. Furthermore, it is difficult to eradicate. Plus, another mollifying feature is that once Bermuda grass is damaged, it is capable of rapid, self-repair making it extremely resilient. A potentially final tribute is that when it is nurtured and allowed freedom to grow, it really is quite charming and pleasant to look at!*

Both of us being readers of history, I feel compelled to remind him, also, that they (Mexicans) are attributed to Chris's explorations. Americans and Mexicans both have similar ancestral ties and *roots'* time-lines. We each have direct ties to Spanish (and later English for *norteamericanos*) explorations.

I mean, for Heaven's sake, it was the Spanish Explorer and Conquistador, Juan Ponce de Leon, who first set foot into what would later become Florida looking for the *Fountain of Youth*. Americans have been looking for it ever since. I mean, Disney found it in the swamps there later, and they've been making people feel young for decades! Maybe de Leon brought in the first Bermuda grass or crabgrass too! If it's anyone's fault or responsibility, he should be to blame, or get credit, for Americans' exploratory or *exploitative* nature. Thanks, *Ponce*!

Even Dr. Oz gets adventurous every day on TV when he explores all sorts of new, tricky and sneaky routes to get richer. He is constantly getting (mostly) women all riled-up in delirious-frenzy when he excitedly and daily exclaims that *he has found it* (over and over again)! Each week, it's a new *fountain-of-youth, weight-loss-product* or *emotional-stability-pill* that he has discovered. Then he proceeds to sell his *miracle* (crap) on TV and the internet for handsome profits.

I mean, didn't anybody get it at all when Oprah first introduced him? *Dr. Oz*? C'mon! *The Wizard of Oz? Oz the Magnificent?* Give me a break! That *Wizard of Oz* shyster was also a likeable guy in person, but on stage he was a vicious and cruel hoaxer for power and wealth. He wanted control of all Emerald City. Oprah is probably turning over in her grave right now because of *Dr. Oz*! *Huh? Oh!* She's not *gone* yet? Sorry. *Wow! My bad!* Come to think of it, maybe she *owns* his show. She *owns* everything else! Get it? "OWNs" *Oprah Winfrey Network*! There's nothing like shoving it down our throats!

Anyway, I'm sorry. I'm probably just a little jealous and miffed with her rejection of my first book on her *Oprah* TV show as a Reader's Club Selection. In fact, as an added insult, she never even mentioned it or returned my review-copy to me for consideration, or even pay for it. Ten bucks down the drain! My book is probably lying there on her nightstand right now. She reads from it each evening *for free* to put her into thoughtful, pleasant or humorous slumber...

She's probably not even aware that my book of poetry which, by the way, is cleverly named *The Book of Daniel: Lasting Impressions. Of Life, Love and Laughter and* is available... "... *right now at your local bookstores, or at Amazon.com or www.AmericanShoppingMall.com in paperback or Kindle, e-book purchases. Buy it now!" Ooops!* Sorry... That was really cheap advertising... In fact, it was *free*! But, I tried to tell Oprah that each poem would make her feel younger at heart, and she'd probably lose weight just from laughing so hard! *Plus,* I told her I'd autograph a copy for her... for a small fee! Thanks, Oprah!

Getting back to the *Oz* fiasco, though, I hope that his term-in-office at Emerald City (Oprahland) has term-limits. As for me, I've had enough of his claims of youthfulness-agents and weight-loss drugs. After the first, half-dozen, or so, products that I purchased from *Oz Productions,* I simply refused to follow his *yellow-brick road* anymore!

And, now I'm still just as wrinkled, fat and depressed as ever, no thanks to *him*. Plus, I'm even more *broke* than I ever used to be... *thanks* to him*!*

"I want to go home! There's no place like home... There's no place like home... I want to stay home... I want to stay in ***Puerto Vallarta***!" Thanks, Dr. Oz!

Mexico's history is directly connected to Spain's globalization practices. The *Black Ship* and the *Spanish Armada* were pretty intimidating vehicles on the world's ocean-markets scene. ***Mexico's*** history is also filled with a glorious, expeditionary past. Hernan Cortes (de Monroy y Pizarro) was the supreme, Spanish Conquistador and Explorer who conquered a whole empire and gave their vast lands over to Spain for control. In a previous section of this book, we shared details about Cortes's own influence on local ***Puerto Vallarta*** history. After all, he was inadvertently responsible for naming our local bay, *la Bahia de Banderas*.

Hernan was only nineteen years old when he first set sail a mere dozen years after Christopher's first voyage in 1492. During his prime, this adventurous soul defeated a magnificent civilization, the Aztec Empire, in 1521,and brought its wealth to his motherland, Spain. In the process, of course, just like us with the Indians, he pissed-off a lot of Aztecs. And you know what we all deservedly earned from that huge miscarriage-of-justice: *Montezuma's Revenge*. Think about that the next time you run to the bathroom! Thanks, Hernan.

But Sergio's comment about America's connection to Columbus through mutual spirits of adventure and exploratory drives caused my reflection. Christopher was indeed an ambitious fellow who spurned commonly taught theories of the day and marched to the beat of his own mind. He believed that the world was round, and he could sail West around it to find a shortcut to the Emerald City (the East Indies). And he dreamed of fame and wealth and power. Chris just had to *sell* his *miracle concept* to the right audience. He needed Dr. Oz!

Chris believed in himself, too. He had spirit and heart! It was that, or he had an unhealthy OCD craving for silk and black pepper. After all, Chris's mom cooked and cleaned, and his father made fancy clothes. Chris probably had a few fetishes. Furthermore, Columbus was an Italian. That means he was Catholic too, and it was natural for him to speak at least three languages: Latin, Italian and Sign-language, naturally... All Italians know Sign! They can't help it. They wave their arms and shake their hands when they speak all the time! It's in their DNA.

But, Italians don't like boats, and they can't swim, so Chris had to leave home in order to seek adventure, become sea-worthy and prove his theories... At age fourteen Chris began his sea travels. After years of sea-travel experience, Chris finally met his map-maker brother, Bartolomeo, in Lisbon, and the two of them began pressing the Portuguese and Spanish Kings for ships and money to sail off on Chris's proposed shortcut to the Far East.

Columbus was getting anxious. He continued getting his petitions for support turned down by the narrow-minded royalty, disbelievers. And he was tired of people laughing at him, "Hey, Chris, when you fall off the edge, remember: You can't swim!" And "Hey, Genius, if God had wanted Earth to be round, then he wouldn't have made the sun revolve around us!" And their favorites, "Hey, Hero, don't forget to take extra-rations along to feed the Sea Serpents. They love Italian food!" And the real ball-buster, "Hey, Moron, don't get seasick!"

Chris was no quitter. He persisted with his insistence on bringing back wealth and prosperity to the king which backed him. Eventually, the Moors were forced out of Spain, and Chris finally got a chance through the help of King Ferdinand and Isabella of Spain. He had to promise to bring back to His & Her Majesties of Spain all the wealth and riches that he found, and he had to promise to spread Christianity for the Pope's approval. Chris was a real gamer. He felt sure that he would get rich and famous and powerful all at the same time. I think he was looking for the Emerald City, or something.

The rest is history. Of course, Columbus never actually found the East Indies. Ultimately, he believed that he had simply found some islands or landings off the Japans. And unfortunately, after four expeditions, Chris never did bring back any reasonable gold or riches to Spain. Furthermore, the forts and men he left behind to colonize the (Caribbean) Islands and South American mainland and Central America were all burned down, deserted and his men were killed by the natives. But Chris made that incredible trip four... get that? Four times! And for nothing... he died, sick, broke and disenchanted that he had never actually proven his fervent belief in a short-cut to the East Indies. What a colossal failure, huh?

Columbus and his men, apparently, were *takers* and not *givers,* though. They kept asking, "Where's the gold? Anybody seen anything really, really shiny laying around? What are these rags you're wearing? Don't any of you have any fancy, silk clothes? Don't you ever get dress-up? Oh, you *are* dressed-up! Sorry. And what about your spices? Not these scorching ***jalapenos***; they're killin' us! We want *black pepper and tea* for civilized folks back home!

"Oh, alright then," Chris persisted, "Here, hold still! Let this Priest bless you! He can save your mortal soul and give you everlasting life. Just offer him ***un poco de algo par mojar su pico*** (a little something to wet his beak), a ***mordita,*** if you will,... for his plate… to show your appreciation..."

Well, it seems that the natives already had religion; they prayed to some rocks, I think. And they didn't *appreciate* the Spaniards at all. To make matters worse, those frustrated seamen-turned-merchants became very discouraged. Apparently, Chris's Homeboys were not too kind to the Indians. Even Chris was put on trial, himself, for abuse to the Indians and even to some Spaniards.

However, Columbus had little to offer the Indians for their needs. Frankly, the Indians had nothing much except coconuts to offer in return. Both sides became upset, and the Natives became *very restless.* It was probably the origins of a *Mexican stand-off!* But, brutally, the natives ended Chris's adventures. They destroyed the Spanish claims to anything. Nothing was left behind except misery and disappointment.

Little did the natives realize, however, that by burning down the forts and killing everyone, they had merely opened a door to a future, Spanish invasion.

Inadvertently, they had left an impact on imperialistic forces in Europe, especially Spain. Chris's misfortunes had actually set the stage for a non-sympathetic, revengeful and future Spaniard, El Conquistador Hernan Cortez, to enter the area. He would conquer, kill or enslave everyone and seize all for Spain. Thanks, Chris!

Anyway, that was all a long-winded approach to analyzing Sr. Sergio's comments on "who we are." I think we need to have an understanding of where we came from first. *Deep down*, I believe, we *all* are *adventurers.* We all explore; it's just in different ways and to different degrees.

Some of us explore the wild, blue-yonder. Others have got to see what's down some road, or river or over a mountain or a sea. Still, others like to check out the new, local Walmart over and over again while another chooses exploring local, beachfronts for eye-candy. The gifted love to explore their own personal, artistic talents or those of someone else. And, there are those who enjoy seeking power, wealth and influence. Of course, thinkers are always searching for knowledge and depths of the human mind. Certainly, humanists seek peace and goodwill and communion with God or nature or whatever excites them.

An adventurous spirit is in all of us, I believe. It just comes in different forms. It's in *all* our hearts, blood and DNA. But an interesting, intelligent, knowledgeable, skilled, talented, and extremely kind individual helped me to consider such things. I appreciated his influence on my reflections.

Gracias, mi amigo, Sergio.

"Mismaloya Blues"

Part 25:

Te Vere de Nuevo Pronto...

Oh, yes, *'I'll see them all again soon,' and* I shall remember them. I actually made a list of all the different friends and acquaintances whom I have made down here over the past twenty-months. It's odd to me realizing that our several visits and time down here to date have been encompassed, so far, within a mere twenty-months. It seems like I've been here longer. I feel comfortable, and I tend to lose track of time. I sort of fit in with the landscape. Soon, I may sense an *odd-eeling* upon awakening each morning and not having coffee with an ocean-view.

Unfortunately, I know better. Reality check: We're still newcomers who must earn and make their way down here each return-trip. The advantage Angelina and I have, which is distinct over many other renters, is that we always have a promised vacation home in which to return whenever we choose. We simply need to advise our hosts of when we wish to be accommodated.

El senor y la senora Salazars han hecho sentir bienvenidos (Mr./Mrs. Salazar have made us welcome). They have made us fully aware and gratified that ***su casa es nuestra*** casa (their house is our house). At all times in the future, we simply need to be appropriately courteous and responsible advising them as to any potential, future visits. Our (their rental) home here will be ready and available for us. We have first-call for use. First dibs! Anybody would be fortunate to have similar arrangements with a vacation-rental and its residence-owners.

Mismaloya is a very comfortable area in which to live. True, we do have an on-going time, distance and inconvenience factor with a bus-ride into town. Each time we want or need something unavailable at a local market which, by the way, still means a brief, bus-ride, we must factor in the thirty-minute jaunt to town. However, although we lessen our "wants and needs" trips to multitasking ventures, the longer bus ride is still pleasant enough and interesting.

Plus, with our wonderful location, spectacular views, quality living-conditions and amenities, multiple-services, and most importantly, friendships and camaraderie, we just cannot beat the deal. It's an inexpensive pleasure to return here. It could be like an annual, Christmas-gift to ourselves, and indirectly to the Salazars too, for us to drop-by each year for a few month's visit.

If I have any concerns, they are the possibilities or probabilities that others else may request to rent the condo for potentially six-months or more, from November through April or May. After all, those are the highly-desirable months, the beautiful period, the high-rent season. We could not fairly deny the Salazars several months' potential rent simply to accommodate our getaway wishes. That may yet develop into an unresolved issue.

Nevertheless, ***Tanto*** (both) ***el senor Sergio y su esposa, la senora Deyanira Salazar,*** have helped to make our visits here so much fun and relaxing and interesting. They are true friends on an international scale. I believe the feelings are mutual; there is trust and support between us. We consider needs of each other. Remember the anecdote about the Salazars inviting us to their home and then providing a special and personal Thanksgiving celebration for us while we were here and away from our own children and families in California?

How about my earlier "tequila-episode" segment? Remember the account mentioning the Salazars' role? When I had called Angelina to tell her of my mishap, I was a bit banged-up (and intoxicated). I knew, however, that she needed to know where I was and that I was okay. At first, she wasn't sure where to go or what to do. There were no more buses that late at night and no way to call for a taxi. Justifiably, however, and correctly, she went upstairs to our landlords, Sergio and Deya Salazar, also our friends.

Their almost spontaneous-reaction bringing Angelina to a local emergency hospital was both impressive and heart-warming. After all, it was in the dead-of-night. Yet, they reacted to Angelina's worry with immediate service and swift assistance. Deya called the hospital to confirm reports and location; Sergio rushed to his car making it ready and available for Angelina's transport. After telephone confirmation and vaguely offered information, Sergio and his accompanying son, who had been visiting, rushed Angelina to the hospital to be with me. Once there, furthermore, the two of them waited in the lobby until Angelina felt comfortable leaving me overnight. Sergio then returned Angelina back to our ***casa***. What can I say? "Righteous people." Thank you, Sergio and Deya.

I mean, bottom-line, we are simply renters who lease their property for specific periods each year; it's a financial arrangement. However, they go far beyond the call and requirements of landlords. We share time, energy, talents, interests, food, activities, and recreation together. That's what I call a *mutually-satisfying, working-relationship.* For that, and so much more, we are extremely grateful.

In our many visits and activities together, Angelina and I have learned much from Sergio and Deya. We have also learned a lot *about* each of them. Both are intriguing and interesting people dedicated to self-improvement aspects of minds, bodies and spirits. As a modest and humble tribute to them, I would now enjoy briefly sharing some of their key points of knowledge, interests, goals and activities, and future endeavors. They are both very busy individuals and very talented. The following mildly and generally describes their lives :

Ladies first...

La senora Deyanira Salazar

Our, friend, Deya, is a very kind, warm and charming woman near our own ages and very youthful. She and Sergio have been married many years with children and grandchildren who live quite some distance away in ***Mexico.*** When her husband, Sergio, retired and moved here to follow his dreams to be an artist and to build them a new house, Deya had remained at their home near family until things were adjusted here. A few years ago, she rejoined Sergio in their new, exquisite ***casa*** which he designed and built himself (including our rental unit). She has remained here with him ever since keeping active with her new, varied, unique, and multiplicity of activities.

Years back, Deya was university educated. In fact, she graduated from law school. However, after her exams and real-life, street-wise introduction into Mexico's legal-system, Deya became irreconcilably disenchanted. She made a huge, personal decision to forsake her legal, educational-training and leave the field of practicing law completely behind. Deya simply felt mentally, physically and emotionally not up to the daily, soulless grind of wheeling-and-dealing within Mexico's pathetic, criminal and corrupted business and legal schemes requiring both allegiance and obedience.

Instead, Deya turned her attention and legal background to working with Federal Programs serving her hometown's local people with Federally-mandated, health-care. She rose high up the medical-services echelon administrating medical care and services to the general and indigent populations. It was a lengthy and rewarding career, and Deya remained there for upwards of thirty-years until she retired in 2009. Following retirement, Deya rejoined Sergio for their new, retirement-life together here in Mismaloya.

Additionally, throughout her years with family and while pursuing her many other passions and interests away from career, Deya also developed world-class level, culinary-skills. Having sat at her dining table several times and enjoyed numerous delivered snacks and meals, I can offer personal testimonial to her wonderful cooking talents. Naturally, Mexican cuisine is her specialty, and I can joyously attest to the fact that her chile rellenos are simply *out-of-this-world* delicious! And, I rather pride myself as a somewhat *expert* and knowledgeable gourmet with chile relleno tasting!

Furthermore, Deya has studied beyond typical, cooking ingredients and also focuses on whole-health elements of herbs and spices and vitamins and minerals found naturally in garden variety vegetables and fruits. She creates specialties with her naturally-sweetened, exotic-fruit and vegetable shakes. Her cooking is good to eat and good for you! Lucky Sergio!

Sin embargo, la cocina no es suficiente para satisfacer la energia y la curiosidad de Deya (However, the kitchen is not enough to satisfy Deya's energy and curiosity). Her active mind is always searching, seeking knowledge and training and development with her many varied methods and multiple disciplines. In the brief time that we have known each other, I can personally bear witness to Deya having studied, fulfilled requirements and graduated from at least three, technical-training institutes.

When we first met, Deya was finishing an advanced, computer-skills, training-program. Angelina was invited and went to her graduation ceremonies.

Following that feat, during our next visit, Deya had begun a six-month minimum, formal, massage-therapy training-program for personal, massage-therapy licensing. I personally know that she fulfilled that goal because I was asked, volunteered and was selected as one of her final-exam volunteer patients. Deya got an A+. She was excellent. However, did she stop there? Hardly.

Being a licensed masseuse still did not completely float-her-boat, so-to-speak, so Deya continued her technical-training and education focusing on a sister-field of facial massage therapies and facial treatments. She has since completed that program too. Presently, I am aware that now, when Deya chooses, she can virtually channel all her skills and talents at once. An imaginative description somewhat representing what Deya's business acumen and planned, professional strategies might encompass are addressed in the following description:

> *First, through use of her computer-generated program for business development, sales-coordination and client management, Deya greets potential patients at her home/office and wonderful, rooftop-balcony, therapy-room with its spacious, magnificent-viewing and mentally, physically and emotionally therapeutic environment...*
>
> *Once patients arrive, Deya relaxes with each one, individually, and personally designs and creates thorough computer-analyzed assessments of potential, client-patients' needs including beneficial, facial-makeovers. After agreement, she then proceeds to fulfill and complete an agreed-upon therapy providing partial or full-body massages with specifically designed focuses.*
>
> *Finally, with part of her 'Whole-treatment Plan,' Deya provides facial massages and/or facial-makeovers including 'masks' using complementary, unique-oils, ingredients and her own, personalized and specialized hands-on-approach treatments.*

Okay, so far. This may describe Deya's potential, practical endeavors including her other dreams and future plans; however, I am still not so sure. You see, her mind is always working and thinking and developing. Each day, Deya is always creating something delicious in the kitchen unless she and Sergio are out on-the-town sampling other chef's delights. Yet, besides the cooking, Deya is offering massages and facials, and keeping all her records on a computer program.

Deya is completely and fully immersed in her *whole-health* strategy paradigm and belief-structure. Not only is she a believer, student and practitioner of holistic-medicine, Deya is an ardent reader and researcher of various, supportive themes and topics. She is always seeking new, and potentially constructive advice, instructions and teachings from fellow, holistic-servants. As her cooking skills improve, so do her human-art skills improve too.

Because of her humanistic-qualities and an eager, inquisitive and sharing mind, Deya recommended a book of health-secrets to me knowing of my own, personal health-issues. Previously, Deya has spoken to me, and demonstrated with her cooking knowledge, the benefits of herbal therapies. She has also suggested several other methodologies and techniques including diet, massage-manipulation and specific, natural-ingredients to aid with my particular ailments. I have always appreciated Deya's knowledge, sharing-care and interest in my well-being as well as for others. She is very sensitive and generous with her learning and knowledge.

Just as Deya cares to share, I recognize her spirit and humanistic qualities which seem so typical of the kind people living throughout Puerto Vallarta. Both she and her eloquent, educated, bi-lingual and philosophical husband share a bond with me in our searches for human truth regarding our minds, bodies and our spirits. Above all else, though, I appreciate Deya's caring generosity and her sharing heart. Oh, yes, and I really enjoy her great cooking! Thank you, Deya.

Sr. Sergio Jose Gomez-Salazar

Where shall I begin with a man such as this? Sergio's curiosity, his inventive and constructive past, his artistic and creative talents, and his philosophical mind have all led him down his own, *long and winding road* of personal search and self-discovery. He is a man of many talents and has pursued many endeavors. We have regularly had brief chats, and I am always impressed, if not bewildered, by what analysis or assessments he offers regarding his own social, political, moral, or existential views.

Sr. Sergio has continuously astounded me since our initial meeting twenty-months ago. In that time, I have learned to both admire and recognize in his character a modern example of the *Renaissance Man*. In my estimation, he can be reasonably compared to a modern *Leonardo da Vinci*. As a young child his interests focused and developed as a builder and artist (painter). Later, he honed those skills with education and became a professional architect and community developer-builder all-the-while pursuing his interests in art and philosophy.

Throughout his life, Sergio continued to study, develop and progress with his art talents. He became a sculptor too which seemed a pleasing and smooth transition from builder to artist. With his architectural, career-growth, Sergio increased his professional-skills with real-estate developing and banking-management. Toward the end of his jammed, crammed and rushed working schedule and career, he even built, opened and operated (including Chief Cook and Bottle-washer) his own restaurant. It failed miserably, as Sergio attests, but (at least) it was an exhausting, painful and terribly-expensive experience.

All the while, he studied, researched and learned from all the relevant thinkers, both past and present, of their ideas, concepts drawings, and writings regarding religion, philosophy and astrophysics, his favorite. Today, Sergio is completely immersed in his latest phase: Philosopher/author. He has become both a questioning and resolving philosopher. As a writer, he is recording all his thoughts for young intellectuals and any questioners. I need to add that recently he dabbled at my professed art, poetry, and I offered a selection of his earlier in this writing. It was very thought-provoking and enjoyable. I appreciated it very much.

In his present work, Sergio is recording all his beliefs regarding the history, meaning, purpose, and future of mankind. Finally, it is evident that Sergio loves his gardens and can be seen regularly nurturing and watering them. Like I said, a regular *da Vinci*. The only thing missing? I told him that I'd loan him one of my harmonicas to develop his musicianship skills. Then, he and *Leonardo* would practically be twins!

In his heart, I believe that Sergio seems himself first and foremost as an artist and then philosopher. Although he made a highly successful and rewarding career as a builder and developer with his laudable, architectural-skills, knowledge and business acumen, Sergio always found outlets to paint. He began his portraits and images at a young age, and his focus has continued to the present.

Following Sergio's formal education in ***Monterrey, Nuevo Leon, MX***, he became the consummate professional. As an educated-man and trained, master-architect, Sergio began the major focus of his architectural career: He became an organizer, real-estate developer and builder of entire, large communities in ***Saltillo***, a city in his home-state of ***Coahuila de Zaragoza***.

In order to fulfill this community-development dream, Sergio had to see and steer through his original, building-dream plans with their many, unique-concepts, its total, required fiscal-management, its design, development, implementation, construction, adjustments and modifications, and ultimate sales and financing stages from start to finish. He was a sort of Frank Lloyd Wright, Guy F. Atkinson and J.P. Morgan all-in-one. Impressive. Oh, yeah, by-the-way, did I say that he paints like *Leo*?

However, Sergio and I share a common-bond with similar health issues. After years of intensive concentration on his career and its demands, stress attacked his body without mercy. Although he had already recognized that enough was enough, and it was time to leave the high-pressures of his work, the stress lay inside waiting to strike. At forty-five years of age, Sergio retired and moved to this wonderful, relaxing and tranquil area of ***Mismaloya-Boca***.

Once here, he began to paint in a frenzy and felt like he was finally filled with peace, or so he thought. Stress will do that nasty trick of turning-up when least suspected. Deya came to visit him and discovered him seemingly wasting-away at fifty-pounds too light for his height. He looked sickly, but he could not explain it. Then he began losing his breath and appetite completely. Quickly, Deya put him on a rigid diet of proper, health-foods, proteins and liquids. Under her care and Sergio's continued painting and soul-searching, steadily he recovered.

After retiring and swearing not to design or build anymore, Sergio took time away from his first love, painting, to build one more thing. In the early 2000's, Sergio began construction of his and Deya's dream home here in ***Mismaloya-Boca***. It took him several years of difficult effort with designs, development and construction because the home was literally built into a solid-rock, cliff-side. The finished product became a premier home all along the cliff highway.

Sergio is a master-designer, and he utilized constructional-attributes learned from architectural geniuses like Frank L. Wright. His design integrated balance with aspects like wind-direction, morning and setting sunlight, expansive ocean-views and open-air areas. Brilliant whites countered sunlight and heat and other natural colors, and plant-life blended with his running pool of water. Everything melds and flows together and is beautifully incorporated within his aesthetic personal, artistic touches. Even his *cosmic* sculptures are evident to all passersby.

The rental unit which I presently live in was deliberately built as the fourth level below his top, veranda floor. My rental nearly matches his above-levels for expansive, ocean-views. His, of course, have greater distance viewing, which is to be expected from their respective heights. But my very comfortable, large one-bedroom/one-bath condo has full-kitchen offerings and a comfortable, dining-table area immediately beside a small but relaxing living-room area. The two-level stairwell is steep but manageable, and the garden-like walkway to the front door leaves me relaxed and joyful both coming and going. I truly enjoy it here.

Today, Sergio busies himself with thinking and writing. His plans are to complete his volume on modern philosophy where he shall answer all the critical questions in the world and make his book readily available to eager minds everywhere. The book will analyze the growth and development, the evolution, of modern man. Sergio plans to use many of his paintings at appropriate stages in the volume to illustrate what he feels his writings may fall short in expressing. Also, the paintings chronicle an entire life (his) of personal maturation and evolution. I firmly believe that Sergio may be creating his masterpiece, if not the world's.

I enjoy teasing Sergio about his volume's philosophic content. When I asked him once about various concepts he was analyzing and postulating for his book, Sergio told me that he was examining: ***The*** *'essence of nothingness.' What is 'nothing?'* He instructed me that *we first had to comprehend the meaning of 'nothing', in order to understand... 'everything else!'*

During yet a later visit, Sergio informed that his topic at that time was analyzing: ***The** concept and meaning of 'truth.' What is 'truth?' How do we know when something is 'true,' or what is not 'truthful?'*

Whooossshhhh! Okay, Sergio, sorry. Those went over my head like comets. You actually lost me both times at... 'The'... Then, straight-faced, each time I just responded, *"Well, I don't know. What? Why don't you just Google it!"*

Later on, during yet another visit, I fibbed to Sergio that many of my friends had inquired regarding the subject-matter of his future book. That earned his curious attention, and he sought my response to them. Straight-faced but chuckling, I chided, *Sergio, when my friends ask, I just tell them, 'Oh, he's writing about 'nothing,' but he wants to know the 'truth' about it!'*

Fortunately, Sergio has a *sense-of-humor*. I think he understands by now that for one to associate with me for very long, one needs to have it! He laughed, though, and told me that would tell all his friends what I said. I hope *they* all have senses-of-humor. Sergio is fairly respected amongst his peers down here, and they may *not* joke-around! My lovely wife is Me***xicana***, and she definitely doesn't appreciate my humor! But wives seldom do. Or, she ignores me. That's their job!

One of Sergio's future goals is to return to painting again. Once an artist, always an artist, I hear! He has been side-lined for years due to his writing, but you can feel his love and devotion of art when he shows his previous works and talks about that part of his life. Sergio focuses on a variety of themes, but many of his portraiture's subjects are truly impressive and moving. He is a tremendous talent.

Not wishes for his artwork to become mere wall decorations for another's home, Sergio dreams of one day donating all his paintings for display to a significant museum somewhere for the world to see and appreciate. This will follow his authorship publication because many of his artworks will be featured in his volume. He also wishes for his book to be eventually accepted as preferred reading material for university, undergraduate and philosophy programs. Go, Sergio! And, Thank you, Sergio!

Additionally, both he and Deya dream and make plans to travel. They have both mentioned desires to travel while they are still able. Sergio is an excellent and avid table-tennis player and practices regularly, twice a week for many hours.

Deya busies herself with studies and projects, but they both look forward to breaking-away from their routines to see the world. They have even opted to sell-out their wonderful home here in ***Mismaloya*** to finance a future lifetime of travel elsewhere in the world. They have visited several places overseas, but they both wish for more.

If and when Sergio and Deya Salazar leave Puerto Vallarta, I shall miss our local camaraderie and friendship. Of course, I'll have to find a new, lovely home somewhere in ***Mismaloya-Boca***, but I could do so, reluctantly, if necessary. I shall miss our wonderful visits and ventures together too. But who knows? It may just turn out to be the next step in an evolving relationship of world-class, travel-buddies. One fact is always a certainty: They will always be welcome at our home in California. ***Nuestra Casa es Su Casa*** (Our home is their home).

"Mismaloya Blues"

Part 26:
Seek, and Ye Shall Find Something, Anyway!...

Reading is an important and favorite pastime for me. Here, in ***Mismaloya-Boca***, during my visits, reading is both critical and essential. I must read a great deal to complete areas of my own writing. I daily read from the Internet to keep abreast of the affecting world and local news. I read each night as a final sedative to relaxing for sleep. If that book is gripping, I have to be careful because I might likely be awake until the wee hours of the morn. But reading is important to me, and it is a great source of pleasure and relaxation and thought.

Although I am most fond of Historical-Drama, both fiction and non-fiction, I also enjoy occasional Fantasy/Sci-Fi too. Suspense, mystery and modern drama will captivate my interests also consuming much of my relaxation-ime down here. Besides as a sleep-aid, a good book while stretched out on my couch, a deck chair or on a blanket sprawled-out on a beach somewhere taking in the sun or simply nature's ambiance does my heart wonders.

Another appreciated source of reading material for me are the multitudes of self-help and life-organizing material. I am a firm believer in each of us taking charge of our own lives and determining what it is that will fulfill us. We all deserve happiness, and most of us need direction or focus by which to find it. That is why I have such deep respect for truly great books of historical, and physical, and mental, and spiritual value. So many people find peace from their messages.

Once again, I reiterate that I respect others' interpretations of great works and great-writings. However, I prefer my own studies and analysis. I don't want another's strict opinion for my own. Certainly, I shall fashion my own beliefs from others' ideas, of course. None of us need to *reinvent the wheel.* That is what study of literature, history, philosophy, science, mathematics, art and nature does for us.

We are all *fashioners* because we utilize everything in our lives to *fashion* our own philosophies. We are all unique products of our own, personal experiences, learning, imaginations, and thought.

None of us experience anything exactly the same way as another. We all have our own, completely unique-styles and fashion by which we relish our vision, taste, touch, smell, sound, or imagination of something. Therefore, we all should clearly recognize, accept and appreciate a very simple truth: We may *honestly* say, *No one else in the Universe is like (me). (I) am unique in all the world.*

Deya has suggested numerous avenues for me to seek better health and harmony for my body and mind. Often during our discussions, Sergio speaks of mankind's need and search for understanding and peace and tranquility. So many people down here seem focused on finding and relishing personal nirvana as a priority for one's life. I am sure that faith and church help many, but people discuss *tranquility* as a way-of-life, it seems. Besides healthy cuisine, an almost religious devotion to self-help and massage-therapy, Deya constantly seeks to improve herself and offer advice to others. She has suggested certain authors for me to read of their wisdom too, and even recently, she recommended a particular book on self-help for my review. Truly, Deya is a giver. I like that about her.

I believe that we are all *originally* born (not in *sin*, for *God's* sake, but rather) into a *Universal Spirit.* Regardless of what priests, pastors, preachers, and wannabes like to expound upon emphasizing their own knowledge-base, self-worth, qualifications, benefit, power, control, and judgment, they just pass on the same, worn-out, precisely unchanged definitions handed-down from times immemorial.

Others have their own prophets or concepts or sources which show them ta way to a spirituality. Still, others have none. Jesus shows a way, *His* way, to recognize and accept that *spirituality.* We don't need to be *born again* or *saved.* Jesus is there inside us all-the-time anyway, regardless. None of us can stop *His* presence; none can dispose of it either. We can only accept, or not. Acceptance offers peace-of-mind; non-acceptance or denial offers... nothing. We may choose to have something, to be something, or we may choose to be nothing with nothing.

Because we are all of *God's* Spirit, we are G*odly.* We can simply accept our mutually connected existence and be comforted, or not. It's a personal choice. God and Jesus are there within us because *we are of them.* If you follow my reasoning, then it should also follow that all others (holy people, believers, non-believers, agnostics, atheists, and otherwise alike) are there too. We are *all* part of this *universal existence.* We're together in *universal energy,* a *spiritual cosmos,* if you will... Cosmic-consciousness.

My *faith* is very personal. It's mine. It is not for anyone else. I *believe*, and that works wonders for me. I need no one else telling me how to think or what to say or pray. Because of my *belief,* however, I am encouraged to maintain an open-mind about everything else. Because of Deya's *sharing-spirit*, therefore, I shall continue my reading of her recommendation for curiosity and pleasure.

However, although I have healthy respect for medical people, I am not so naive that I do not recognize common attempts at legalized extortion and selling-out on one's principles. Remember my ranting about Dr. Oz? Even so, if I am willing to accept professed blessings and personal satisfactions of Bible readers, then I shall remain open to others who exalt their varieties of holistic-medicine. Unless deliberately initiated as a scam, most sources are well-meaning.

In fact, I believe that there are some *scams* developed which ultimately and naively probably served some others with well-being. *Belief* is incredibly powerful and significant. So be it. To each their own. Who am I to judge? I *believe* in my own faith: With *acceptance* of God, we each have the right to believe whatever we wish. We just do not hurt anyone (with exceptions, of course). Thank God, the Occidental countries are free and open for personal thought, questioning and debate. Still, healthy skepticism, I think, helps nurture meaningful philosophy. *We ask questions, we challenge and in the process, we seek and discover our own truths...*

Faith in A Mustard Seed...

To me, *faith* is *belief* in a *Cosmic-consciousness*. Ultimately, the *faithful* shall all fulfill rightful and designed merging with *God* in this abstract, *Universal Energy*. Non-accepting, disbelieving or disputants will also merge but will likely be unaware of their status. For them, I suppose, *ignorance will be bliss*; but, they would miss out on the *big-picture:* Membership, participation and awareness within *Universal-consciousness*. We *faithful-believers*, on-the-other-hand, shall fulfill cosmic destinies because we already recognize that in our present, *states-of-being,* we are already a part of God in our magnificent Universe.

Skeptics, Doubting-Thomas's, or others who refuse to accept such seemingly far-fetched *faith* and amusingly laugh at such an absurd or preposterous idea, may immediately challenge this belief with appropriate questions: What about infants, or babies and unaware children or adolescents who die during youth? What about anyone without any formal, scientific, social or religious training? What about developmentally-disabled persons? Mentally-ill?...

How can these people speak, or question or even *pray* for themselves? Who will speak-up for those suffering from brain-trauma, nerve damage or the chronically-deprived people pained from minimal vitamin, mineral and protein deficiencies? These people can't speak let alone think for themselves about *faithful* issues of *cosmic-con-*

sciousness and such. Who *speaks* for them? What happens when *their* time is up, and they are greeted by the *thresh hold*?

Like the parable says: *Oh, ye, of little faith... Go stuff your faith in a mustard seed and see what happens!* Or, something like that... Can you understand or accept, however, that since everyone is involved in this *Cosmic, Universal-Consciousness,* all those special people and unique cases *are already included!* They are examples of automatic-inclusion. Regardless, everyone is involved, perhaps with exceptions of refuters. They know no better. But, blessed-children and others are already destined for merging and blending within our universally cosmic, energy, our fabric-of-consciousness.

The *Bible* and other works such as *Al Qur'an, Zen teachings, Confucius's lessons,* or even the *Kama Sutra* for those who seek Paradise through extreme, physical-activity, are all equally supreme sources for understanding. Each offers solutions and answers and means to appreciate, channel and eventually find their readers and studiers forms of *Nirvana* and tickets to the *Promised Land* or *Cosmic-Consciousness.* Still, others may read works from previous and present great minds, including agnostics and atheists, and then develop their own approaches. Even those who believe in *nothing* believe in something, even if it is *nothing.*

But, let's not get too silly or metaphysical here. Our appreciation and understanding of this relatively basic concept need not be so complicated. ***Es increible y magnifico***, but it's still just nuts and bolts! No sense trying to *reinvent the wheel.* Remember: "KISS it!" *Keep it simple, Stupid!* The meaning and purpose of our *lives* and *afterlives* are not difficult to grasp:

> *We are born into an expanding Universe; we are all given an unique opportunity to experience and share life in varying, but still meaningful, degrees; then, we merge into Universal Energy.*

Einstein knew what I mean, and he would still agree: *E=mc^2*. Cool! Pretty simple. I know that there are many others who have likely already considered this *Belief.* After all, it is obviously nothing new under-the sun! Besides, most thoughts we have, at least considering spiritual, faithful and afterlife-matters, someone else already considered them and wrote a book about them too. Read their ideas and learn. Then, make up your own mind. That is another great aspect of our *state-of-being's* mental freedom... *free will!* Choose.

None of us accept the same facts, let alone life-philosophies, with the same understandings or appreciations. Similar yes, exact same, hardly... We all devise our own *truths* based upon our own degrees of experience, learning, and contemplation. No two of us are alike. That point exemplifies my own, *faith-based,* belief-structure. It's all good. Just like the *here-and-now* on Earth, we shall all be together *there-and-then* in our futures, in joined, after-life consciousnesses, (*or not!*). No sense fighting it; it will happen regardless of opposition. Perhaps, it's simply whether-or-not the *opposition* shall be *aware* to enjoy anything!

The *Good Book(s)* mentioned above, and many others are all filled with stories, biographies, lessons, or teachings from people who had (have) already discovered *truth* on their own and on their own levels. Each found a *healing nature,* or a source, or path, or ways-and-means by which to develop or connect to a relationship with God, or *Universal Energy.* The book I am presently reading, *The Healing Code,* offers yet another methodology or process in which to discover that connection. Supposedly, when one uses the *Code* instructions, one is able to find their body's source of healing by *connecting to God* and then using that *spiritual energy* to heal any maladies from which one may suffer.

Regarding *spirituality,* however, we can go there anytime and find it for ourselves... NOW! God, in a Universal sense, is still a Personal God. He is "It" and is there in-the-open waiting for our calling. We need only ask... That's it! Remember the wonderful Jack Palance character, Curly, from the *City Slickers* movie? In one scene

Curly instructs Mitch, the Billy Crystal character, about *finding-the-meaning-of-life* and issues. He did so by holding up one, extended finger and announcing, "…Find the *one thing* that is most important in life."

Huh? That's it? Yeah! How about that? It's *that* simple… *Believe.* God wants us to resolve torments in our lives through discovery and reckoning with ourselves and acknowledging that we are all truly part of a Cosmic Energy. When we learn and know what is most important to us, *the one thing*, in our lives, we shall then completely understand God's presence in our lives. We shall appreciate our existences within God's Universal truth, awareness, consciousness, and energy.

For me, what worked, *the one thing,* was a true *gratitude-for-life.* It immediately gave me an understanding and acceptance of purpose and meaning with my existence. After acknowledging Jesus Christ as my Personal Savior, and on a larger scale, my own ownership and membership within a grandiose scheme of Eternal Energy, I was able to determine other *related-aspects* which were also significantly important in my life…

These *aspects* are ever-changing, too. They are ever-growing in number, in dimension and are continuously modified as my life and existence also change. Births of my children, career-changes, residential moves, divorce, education, re-marriage, new ambitions and dreams, and travel all affect my consciousness and relevant aspects of my life. Everything is interconnected and interrelated. It is like *Cosmic-consciousness,* but it is for this life. I finally understand and appreciate how all things in our lives are related to each other and influenced by each other. And, I realize that *all things*, all those combined '*its' in the Universe,* actually began with births! *Births of* ***babies*** *to births of* ***stars****!*

Birth is a beginning, a natural and continuing *state-of-being* for life. That's right! We are in a *state-of-being* for our entire lives! Cool, huh? Fundamentalists may argue that *conception* is the beginning, but I'm not going to labor that point. I'm not going to get pigeon-holed into a futile debate over abortion-issues. I could never tell another person what to do with her body. Advise, yes, but never demand. Furthermore, like my *belief-system* explains, all life, regardless of its stage, is part of the fabric of universal-energy. Nothing is ever lost or wasted.

At the other end of our *state-of-being,* comes death. Death is also as natural to life as birth. But unlike birth in-the-beginning, death is not the end. It is merely a threshold, a step-over, from a *state-of-being* to merging naturally into the cosmic form of energy and *state-of-Universal consciousness.* Extending our lives, our *states-of-being,* through appropriate channels surely may extend our presence. Proper diet, exercise, health and attitudinal-care, security, and of course, avenues of modern, medical science, *all* assist with extending our lives, our *states-of-being.* They do not, however, keep us from avoiding eventual thresh holds we are all meant to cross-over and new, cosmic-existences for which we were created.

But we need not die so soon. We can develop healthier, happier lives. We can extend them through simple, basic-recognition, understanding and acceptance of our eventual place in the C*osmos* and through our relationship with *God* and *Universal-consciousness.* Our searches for identity can be over! We can learn who we are and understand, appreciate and enjoy our present place under the sun.

Then, we could all appreciate where we are bound and from what we originated. Genetics and DNA are all great! They are instrumental role-players in designing significance with the miracle of life and its energy. But that is just the point; they are role-players in an eternal, ongoing-how... The Big show! The everlasting, never-ending story of ageless, universal existence and its Cosmic-consciousness of Energy.

Even atheists may live longer because, whether they accept my paradigm, or not, they too believe in *God.* They simply have not recognized *Its* face or refuse to identify *It* as the source of their eventual but denied supernatural, cosmic, state-of-consciousness. Presumably, they accept a Universe which they can believe in because of its real, proven, physical, and natural-state. They understand "it" as a growing, expanding and developing Cosmos. What they don't *get* is that *conceptual-grasp* ***is*** already a form of *acceptance* of *Cosmic-consciousness,* in itself.

If they can recognize their own existence, their part, or place or membership in our universe, regardless how small or insignificant they may feel it is, then they can accept a place or value in all of a universality of all things. Then, they may understand that all things, including themselves, have an alliance, a place and part in our *Cosmos.* Perhaps, they believe it is only "Earth to earth and ashes to ashes."

Once they *understand* even this "earth or ash" connection, or alliance, they may accept that their body's energy is in an entire relationship with the *Cosmos*, which again, I repeat, is *God.* Again, if they can't, or won't, or don't, or refuse to follow this train-of-thought, so to speak, then so be it. They may not be along for the ride or even aware of it. And *Traveling* is so much fun! What an experience! *That relationship* just may end-up being the best *trip* of all!

When ultimately, these naysayers die, however, nothing will change the fact of their passing-over a thresh hold at the time of their death, anyway. They simply may be unaware of the whole process. They will, nevertheless, still become part of the Universal-fabric; they may just be oblivious and *unconscious* of it, like colorless and empty moth-holes. Like we all say, ignorance is bliss. In their case, however, it may simply be: *ignorance is oblivious*!

Furthermore, this *understanding and acceptance* of Cosmic-consciousness also brings along with it *social consciousness.* Just because someone can say, "I've got it! By Jove, I've got it!" doesn't mean that someone *gets it!* Assuming that we all automatically have *merging-beings* into *eternal-awareness* does not give any of us freedom to do as we fantasize. There are no issued, *007 License-to-Kill,* or permissions (or not) to maim, harm or bring discomfort to any other human being, or other living things, for that matter.

Of course, there are exceptions for governmental obligations, social requirements, self-defense, or food-chain issues. But, we are created for this Earth and any other future, life-holds to experience life to our fullest and to whatever degree we can or may without bringing deliberate harm or consequence to any other living-forms. Those that do, don't *get it*, and they *won't get it!* True, *Cosmic-consciousness* is not for them.

In a way, we are all dying. From our births, or conceptions if you must, we are all on a straight or raggedy path toward death. Some of us, by accident or circumstance, rush toward death or are handed it prematurely; others stretch out their road making it *longer and more winding* with many ups-and-downs. For me, a wonderful explanation is like *The Beatles* lyrics in their song, *The Long and Winding Road.* As the song so eloquently, beautifully and brilliantly notes:

The long and winding road
That leads to your door
Will never disappear
I've seen that road before
It always leads me here
Leads me to your door

And, we are all on our way to that inevitable destination, that special door-way to the-other-side. Eventually, we shall all cross-over, aware of the fact, or not, and then we may all *see the way*... Accept it... Just, *Let It Be!*

Explained in that sense, you may then understand this: *I am dying now and have been for sixty-seven years, so far.* I am incredibly fortunate that so many previous mishaps haven't sent me through the doorway already. You see, that's another advantage to "*understanding and acceptance*" of cosmic-consciousness: *I'm going to 'get it' anyway, so I may as well enjoy the ride getting there!* I want it, but I don't need it right now. *Understanding* and *acceptance* of my awareness is enough at the moment. I can wait some more until I *get it.* I've still got some more mishaps to survive first.

In the meantime, just as Loyd writes in his book about a '*Code*' to good health, *dying* people, like myself, can search for alternatives or additives to modern, medical-science to treat our maladies. I have High Blood Pressure (HBP), Rheumatoid-Arthritis (R-A, although presently in remission) and congestive heart-failure (CHF). Most medical professionals agree that HBP is caused by inordinate, chronic stress. R-A, on the other hand, is unknown for what triggers the condition, but it is explained as the body's immune-system attacking itself. And CHF? Who knows where that came from? My mom? Well, that's just great! I allow everything on the outside to attack me making me sick, and then I attack myself from the inside.

That's one hell (no pun intended) of a partnership or alliance! I can imagine filthy, *Disease-Forces* rubbing their clammy, sickening hands together gleefully while vomiting and spewing-out their slimy and nasty aggressions:

> *First, we'll* stress *him with* ***pressure*** *from the outside until he breaks; then, we'll* ***inflame*** *and* ***tear-him-down*** *from inside!*

OMG! That sounds like our Washington, D.C. Pentagon Generals talking...

> *First, we drop bombs and missiles all over their (God-forsaken) country until they're immobilized. Then, when the country is pained and starving and anguished, we let its own people revolt, overrun and destroy their government from the inside! Yeah! Sounds like a plan! Bruuuahahahaha!*

But I'm always ready for those menacing threats with my own calm recant, "Oh, yeah?" I meditatively counter while simultaneously massaging my sore, aching-knees and flexing my tingling and numbing feet, "I can take it because *I have understanding and acceptance!... And you don't! Na na na na naa naaa!*"

In Search of Self...

Regarding my own, personalized, reality, health-check reviews, though, I have been forced to recognize and understand also that my HBP has been directly-related to Stress-Disorder. For much of my adult life, and likely since infancy, I have been victimized by stress. Even my parents and Mom's sisters and brothers told me continuously how I cried all the time during babyhood. As an adult, I have since advised them all to its explanation, "It was the pressure,... the pressure! It took childhood before I could develop skills to simply *grin and bear it!*"

Later, it was always my need to achieve and to experience new sights and people. School was difficult, and to excel I had to stay in top-form and work very hard all the time. Other, typical pressures perhaps affected me more than they did my classmates. I had dreams, and I needed to achieve them. I wanted acceptance and appreciation. I needed that too.

Plus, I was cognizant of the fact that intelligence varied among creatures. Furthermore, I begrudgingly understood and accepted the premise that I was not the "sharpest light-bulb in the six-pack!" So, I assessed, *If I couldn't be more intelligent, then I needed to become smarter, or more knowledgeable.* I'd have to work harder than others more intelligent because I 'needed' to do so. *Stress!*

I mean, in Algebra I through College Calculus, I was constantly stunned, yet impressed and stupefied, by others' *brightness*, and by how quickly those *others* could grasp relatively serious theorems. We would still be in a classroom with the teacher scrawling laborious equations on the chalkboard. I'd just stare at his proofs and ponder deeply to myself, "Huh?" Then, I'd catch the two-hour bus ride home, or hitchhike and spend that evening trying to make sense of what Evan, Tom, Buck, Susan and Jack all understood already upon leaving class each day. Awful stress!

College was a long struggle dealing with new, untapped emotions and new forms of stress. As a liberal-arts major focusing on Education, I was all caught up in the 1960's movements. Whatever government activity was going on, I opposed it. Down with the Vietnam War! Up with Peace! Down with bias, prejudice and discrimination! Up with Civil Rights. Help Chavez and this struggling, migrant, Mexican-workers! Up with farm-labor wages and rights! Down with Gallo Wine!

If there was a protest going on anywhere, I tried to be there, so I could also run from the police! They were exciting times. And the girls liked *runners,* too, I mean *us-protesters*! All we guys may have been yelling, "Down with the government!" But, in our pants, I mean *minds*, though, we were hoping we'd get to go *down with the girls*! Those were emotional times, and they were *mental.* It was fun; but it was stressful!

Everything else caused anxiety for my well-being too. Our government's greedy, power-mongering, influence-peddling, anti-communist, fear and anxiety-driven, big-business, and war-machine-sponsored Vietnam War pressured me until I was finally forced to submit and join the Marine Corps Reserves in 1970. Those six years were simply more stress. Only this time it was dressed-up, covered-up and disguised in a uniform. The war continued with daily drudgery's reminders of disappointment and frustration on everyone's psychic. The continually sad news of casualties was disheartening and *stressful* throughout my entire enlistment. I was discharged in 1976 one year after the war ended.

In the meantime, and following, daily-life and its routines brought along with it all the other stuff dedicated to raising anyone's blood-pressure: Continuing university studies, marriage, divorce, career demands, career changes, marriage, having children, health-issues, career changes with new demands, business-opportunities, divorce, and the 10:00 news. It all took its toll on me. Although I sensed health issues coming as a result of stress overflow, I ignored their heated and tingling sensations over my face and just carried on.

Career stress had a lot to do with my health factors too. A thirty-year, teaching-career predominantly with a daily-grind in community-based, high-risk youth, secondary, education-programs definitely used stressful-anxieties to punish any remaining well-being I may have had. Each day at my school and in my classrooms were unique, often violent and always difficult endeavors dealing with angry, disturbed, dysfunctional, anti-authority, and often gang-member student populations. I loved teaching; I cared so much for those kids, and I wanted such success and happiness for my students. Yet, every day was a struggling challenge to reach them and teach them.

My stress was anything but dormant too. It wasn't just there in-hiding. I had feelings of anxiety from everything, and I didn't just *feel* high-blood pressure. Sometimes, my blood would just *boil*! Stress was fixating throughout my body searching and seeking outlets. It wanted to manifest itself in some violent, angry fashion. I think that stress in our lives and diseases in our bodies give us warning signs. We need to be willing to recognize them early and correctly act to ward them off. My stress was obvious and unapologetic. It was trying to punish me with blatant symptoms causing irreparable harm to my body. I was probably just an *accident-waiting-to-happen...*

Then, a mental-sign occurred. I remember the day. It was that fateful afternoon on October 17, 1989. I was at my Bay Area home standing near our dining-area's open rear-door, looking out at the yard and trying to make a phone call. The World-Series was on TV in the background. Suddenly, trees in our yard began swaying, and I started wavering and buckling as well. Of course, after a brief-period,

I deduced that it was a pretty rough earthquake. It was, in fact, that terrible Loma Prieta earthquake which brought such unfortunate destruction to so many Californians in the Bay Area.

Let me explain, however, the *mental-sign* which occurred and my point: When the earthquake hit, and I was weaving all around the room with a phone in my hand and swaying with the walls, my first reaction was, "OMG! I'm having a *stroke* or a *stress attack!* My students' (ill-behavior) has finally gotten to me. I'm going down!"

Shortly thereafter, I understood the reality of the moment and raced to the TV set for updates. I was still unaware of the horror in the cities and extent of the catastrophic damage, yet, I clearly remember chuckling to myself and mentally apologizing to my students: "Sorry class!" It was an immediate, spontaneous, unwarranted, and ill-based accusation. It wasn't a *stress-attack*, after all!

It was, however, a ready, clear and focused *mental-sign* of recognition, though. I thought to myself *that reaction* might very well be the *real-thing* next time. If I thought that my ill-behavior was caused by stress, then stress was probably hanging around. I checked into a doctor's office right away for a diagnosis, and I've been under treatment ever since. Thank you, Students!

Then, years later while in my fifties, I began noticing that progressively all my body-joints intermittently began painful and agonizing aching and swelling.

There seemed no rhyme or reason to it. One time, it would be an ankle; the next time, it could be a shoulder; after that, it might be a thumb-joint. I never knew where the pain would locate and bring-me-down. It was very frustrating, and each incident hurt like hell for a long, painful time.

Initially, it was like some creepy monster crawling underneath my skin moving about from one joint to another. At each stopover during its course of ill-intent, it would make that joint throb with pain. I actually became shockingly aware of how a single, attacked-joint had a polarizing alliance with entire body-parts and/or limbs. If my baby-finger knuckle shut-down with agonizing pain, I would lose use of the entire hand. I didn't even want rustling wind to disturb me.

If I moved it, or a breeze whispered by, the whole hand would ache with excruciating pain, and I'd holler, "Ooooohhhh! Ouch! Don't touch! Leave it alone. Give me some Ibuprofen quick!" If an elbow went inactive from throbbing discomfort, my entire arm was useless. Effectively, I could use no part of that limb because any movement made the elbow's focal point hurt that much more.

Our body truly is an incredible, interdependent, moving, and working machine. Like a regularly smooth-running, efficient engine, one tiny and damaged ball-bearing can eventually bring the whole mechanism to a crushing halt. It will take time, but something will break. However, unlike an engine where we often need only replace a damaged or broken part, the human-body is only masked with medications or treatments or therapies. Are there any cures?

Similarly, we rely on every part of our body to work in unison with its co-partners. If something is broken or out-of-whack, it affects the entire rest of the body. If it is gone, then that's a different story because we make up for absences or weaknesses. But as long as a part (of our body) is supposed to be doing a job, and it doesn't, then there will be painful costs until it is repaired or administered.

Yet, I know and fully recognize and understand, however, that HBP is a *silent-killer.* And who knows how long I may continue with my present, treatment-program warding-off those agonizing symptoms of R-A. For both, however, a strict-regimen of specific medications, supplements and bi-monthly, Humira-injections are holding a huge predominance of pain and discomfort at bay. I am aware too of the dangers. It's sort of an emotional and medical-choice roller-coaster ride which carries my options: No drugs, and I die in painful agony; medications, and my life is extended with both quantity and quality. It's a no-brainer! But, I want both without drugs. How, then, can I make that happen?

Left untreated, symptoms from stress are very real and painful. They affect everything good or bad in my life. Happy thoughts are diminished, and sad, negative thoughts are polarized. I feel HBP's wave of heat and anxiety flowing through my veins and focusing on my facial skin and head. It's not pleasant, and I know that without medication, symptoms can bring about strokes or *premature doorways!* "Just a minute," I cry, "I'm not ready to go yet! Quick! Where's those pills, anyway?"

Finally, diagnosis and medicine helped a great deal treating symptoms with both maladies. Regarding HBP, I also need to learn new ways to relax. That never comes easily even after trying all those fancy, mental-operatives: T-M, Yoga, EST, Scientology, and nearly all the other newer, upstart self-awareness methodologies. Of course, I was too cool for Christ back then. I needed to nearly die in order to discover that He had been inside me all my life, already.

Even then, acknowledging an awareness of Jesus' spirit within me became a lifetime struggle dealing with this newly found meaning and purpose. I continued my rebelliousness toward organized religions, and I just simply sat back quietly with my own, smug, personal *acceptance* and *state of grace.* It has taken all these years *and recent months* for me to appreciate my present *state-of-being* and grasp my understanding and acknowledgment of *Universal-consciousness.* I've been aware of it for many years, and I took pride and pleasure in my own circumstance and relationship with God and Jesus. I just never did savvy the bigger-picture.

It's like I said before about being a little *slow-to-catch-on.* Maybe everybody else in class got '*It*' already, and I should have studied harder, but I didn't. I knew enough to satisfy myself and maybe even enough to fill me with a false sense of security. I could even snicker and mock others who said that *they had already gotten 'It.'* I *really* didn't have a clue as to what *really* mattered.

I understand a meaningful and positive-relationship that I have with God. I know Jesus personally and appreciate ultimate, *Cosmic-consciousness.* Yet, I still suffer from my maladies and emotional-disharmony. I feel relatively secure with my *afterlife,* and I am even mentally and emotionally prepared to leave this life, when circumstances warrant such. Granted, however, I shall never encourage death's premature arrival except by occasional, stupid and thoughtless behavior.

But, my life is still not right. Something is missing... It's like some of my old-trainers used to teach: (I'm) not *focused...* (I'm) not *centered... (*I've) lost the *one thing... (I've) lost that loving feeling...* No, Sorry! I just remembered the *Righteous Brothers.* But, Jesus is in my *Soul.* Eventually, I'll see God and become part of the G*reat-Magnificence.* Still, I am not *right* with God. What can I do?

I am still seeking truth and more understanding. Never in my life before have I taken focused time to truly contemplate my life and meaning and that of the Universe. It is truly a blessing and a privilege to do so. I do not enjoy sitting in compartmentalized zones being dictated to or having *meaning* explained to me. I must discover answers on my own and determine my own truths. I believe self-discovery is God's universal-design as with plans set forth by Moses, Jesus, Muhammad, Buddha, Confucius, Laozi (Taoism), and rightfully, a score of other great minds, religious and otherwise.

Each of those great thinkers help us by paving a way for our understanding and enlightenment. By reading, reflecting and pensive contemplation, we can determine our own meaning and significance. Of course, short-cuts are simply allowing words of someone else to spoon-feed us and be our spotlights getting us through the darkness of ignorance. It's okay. It's easier, but it's lazier, and all the preachers are happy to deliver their interpretations. Plus, you need not become confused or bewildered with so many other options and explanations and beliefs.

Just allow someone else to choose one for you, put your blinders on, and proudly wear your badge of loyalty. What was that saying about... *bliss*?

In the end, though, we all shall figure out what ideas or which concepts or teachings make us feel most comfortable. Personally, I asked Jesus to help me, and He did. However, I enjoy, appreciate and value much of the teachings and instructions from other great minds. They all have something significant to offer. There is common sense, peace-of-mind, tranquility, and truth, both personal and worldly, in the words, writings and instructions from other great-thinkers who took precious, thoughtful and selfless time assessing their lives and *states-of-being*. These people dedicated their lives to studying, reflecting, considering, developing, and offering means by which we others might more easily find our own ways.

They all have something to say. And most agree: *There is more to life than just 'life.'* What we think, and what we do in our lives and with our lives and our minds, is extremely important. We all need to come-to-grips with our *states-of-being*. I'm sure of it, but it is fascinating learning what others believe too.

It has not been until I began reading, thinking and writing while living down here in my beloved ***Mismaloya*** during these visits to ***Puerto Vallarta*** that I began the wonderful process of "coming-to-grips" with my own life. I have needed the peacefulness, serenity, calmness, and opportunity for addressing my own, personal issues and trying to finally get *on the right track*. Opportunities to sit and think, while reflecting and writing about impressions of what I have experienced, have been doing wonders for my soul and, hopefully, my health.

I understand that my *Salvation* is the *One-thing...* I love my wife and children and family with all my *heart*, but I love God and our Universe and Jesus' *Saving Grace* with all my *soul*. This life shall pass... I want to be ready, prepared and willing for the next phase, the *truest existence.* I understand my eventual and ultimate merging with *Cosmic-consciousness.* But, I want to know my way with God *now.* I want to know *joy* in *this* life. I *need* to know what I must do.

My answer is clear. I need to do that which *pleases me. Curly* had it right all along: Find the *One Thing...* above all else. It *pleases me* to be a good human-being, *at 'One' with Jesus* and *happy...* I want *joy* in a good *state-of-being.* I'll never be a Moses or an Einstein. Everything I might think of has already been thought. But, I can be my very own, *'happier' better-person.* I simply need to try (all the time) to be *'better'* than I was and *'happier'* about it.

How can I be *better* than I was and also find true *happiness?* If my S*alvation* is secured with the *One* (most pleasing) *thing,* then what is it that will fulfill my other desires of being *'better and happier about it?' I know!* I've got it! *I shall continue to write and share my experiences because I am:* ***The Traveler.***

Peace and meditation have a way of opening-eyes. I offer my brief analogy of the "advancement of civilization" which may clearly explain my epiphany:

When there was finally enough bread on the table and others tilling the fields for more, there was time for thoughtful persons to contemplate their lives.-DT Chapman: 2015-

VALLARTA, MI AMOR Y MI PRECIOSO MISMALOYA

Adventure brought me to your shore
From dreams which opened vision's door
Seeking imagination's quest
Before interminable rest
Delivers mortal spirit's core
Unto eternal peace possessed.

Discovering tranquility
Sustains peaceful communities
With unexpected pleasures caught
In nets of simplicities sought
And offers opportunities
To seek significance untaught.

When hopes surpass expectations,
Reassessing situations
Fulfills primitive wanderlust
Acknowledging that living trusts
In rewarding brief durations
Before our spirits readjust.

Thus, cosmic-consciousness is force
Designating natural course
Leading us through subconscious dreams
Advancing earthly human schemes
Which may challenge with vague remorse
Or accept God's blessed self-esteem.

Regardless, Vallarta, my love,
Appreciated notes above
Exclaim how precious time was lent
Examining how lives are meant,
And faithful beliefs I approve
Protect my soul's abandonment.

EPILOGUE

Homeward Bound...

I think that I am ready to go home. Better than that, I am *preparing* to return. I am preparing in body, mind and spirit. I still have a long way to go in fixing my body and mind issues, but I'm working on them. I have a new focus and new direction. Home. Perhaps, I shall treat *home* as though it were vacation-time. That would be different and maybe fun. Angelina and I shall be together again, and that is always better than being apart. I suppose there is truth to the old adage: *Absence makes the heart grow fonder.* I know that I have missed her since she needed to return home. I have missed her because I am quite *fond* of my *Angel*ina.

I recognize the difficulty that she endures being away from our home and children while being with me here in ***Mismaloya-Boca***. Don't get me wrong, Angelina *endures* quite well down here during her visits. She has always kept fairly busy with art-classes, or visits, or walks or Googling. Three-month sojourns away from our kids and Grandchildren, though, is too long for her. And, to give credit-where-credit-is-due, Angelina actually tied her previous record of ninety-two straight days away from home. I can imagine better schedules and arrangements in the future to accommodate her travel wants, though. But, she is my *travel-buddy, and* we shall see a lot more of the world together.

I am going back to our *other* home with a new spirituality too. I am the same person, but I do not feel the same. God, Jesus and *awareness* are on my mind and *soul-searching* is relieved, for the time being anyway. I am working on mending personal relationships which means a great deal to me. Finally, my body is in repair, but there are obvious health matters which I must consider and at least attempt to deal with more satisfactorily: I need to continue avoiding unhealthy diets and feed myself with proper nutrition; I need to really work on my cardioid-vascular regimen and keep my body-joints limber and exercised;. Mentally and emotionally I need to concentrate on *living-in the moments* and appreciating my present mind-conditions while focusing on *being-better.*

There it is in another *mustard seed: The Three Health's: Diet, exercise and living.* Big surprise, huh? Body, mind and spirit again. Oh, don't laugh. I know that I'll probably screw-up again, sometime. No matter what, it seems to come up. It must be in my DNA. Thanks, Ancestors!

And, if-and-when-I-do slide, occasionally and probably right afterward, I will deliberately step-back for a moment just to see where I've been and maybe reconsider where I'm going. Fresh perspectives will help maintain my focus too. I'll get to stop, look and recognize what I'm doing while I'm doing it. Then, I'll even have an opportunity to reevaluate where I'm really going with it after all.

And as I mentioned earlier, it's a changing world with new demands and so many new and different responsibilities. I need to be prepared for adapting and modifying to new circumstances. It's all good. It's a big, growing and evolving planet. I just do not need to change my own, core-beliefs, my *state-of-being.* That goes with me to everywhere that I shall travel.

And I shall make plans to go everywhere. Well, I'll go wherever I am reasonably able. Angelina will be with me too as well as she is able and willing. I've already plotted out our Fall exercises. For her next birthday in September, we are cruising up to *Alaska*! It's a bucket-list thing.

I have a goal to travel through all fifty-states eventually, and I've already visited the most difficult one... Texas! Just kidding! NOT! I actually mean Hawaii, though. I took Angelina there for our Honeymoon almost thirteen years ago. She loved it, well, most of it. Initially, we went to Molokai, but after we almost contracted leprosy-of-boredom, we chose to visit Maui the next day. But, if she's willing, we'll see all the rest of the USA together too. As I mentioned, we'll be adding Alaska to our repertoire soon.

The cruise to Alaska is special for two reasons: First, is that we shall be sailing out of San Francisco. The flight to Seattle, WA or Vancouver, BC is nice, and we've already been there and done that. This time it's another *bucket-list* item again because we shall be sailing directly underneath our incredible *Golden Gate Bridge*. It's one thing to see its majesty from the *City by the Bay* or the *East Bay*, but it's an entirely different angle to see it from below, I imagine!

We may even get a fish-eye view of the next plunge when someone takes a suicidal dive because of a non-reconciled and anguished *state-of-being*. It's too bad that the jumper hadn't read this book first to help resolve matters A sense of humor can do wonders to rejuvenate our senses. But then, there's always the possibility that it was an accident. It wasn't a *jumper,* after all, but rather a *faller* who had slipped while trying to throw this book off the ledge. None-the-wiser.

Sounds logical, right? Something's missing, though... Oh, I know: A good joke. Sorry. It was an insensitive attempt at humor and an obvious *back-slide* from my *better 'state-of-being.'* Sorry... I just hope to *You-Know-Who* that a *diver, jumper, faller, or slipper-er* doesn't *splat!* on our ship. That would be annoying and a regrettably hideous incident. In fact, it would probably delay our cruise while some really unfortunate employee had to clean the Poop-Deck. Or, would it be: C*lean the deck-poop?* Go figure.

Anyway, the Golden Gate Bridge view ought to be magnificent! And remember? I'm allowed a *back-slide* once in a while. I'm not *perfect,* you know, just blessed!

Second, of course, is visiting Alaska, itself,now that Sarah Palin has fortunately removed herself from any spot-lights. Or, Republicans *turned-them-off* once they finally were, themselves. Of course, it was due to chronic, Palinesque embarrassments, but as is typical of the GOP, they just traded-in her antics for those of other fools. However, now I can begin imagining a rebirth, a new intelligence arising once more from that "Final Frontier State." For so long now, actually since Palin became Alaska's Governor, as a matter-of-fact, that poor state as been stagnant or in a nose-dive of decline, like a bridge-to-nowhere.

I am once again excited about going there, though. It's been a long time since I dreamed of venturing to Alaska. Probably, it fell off my *bucket-list* when Timothy Treadwell, famous for wildlife-advocacy and living-with grizzly bears, and his girlfriend were eaten by a brown bear while living in the wilds of Alaska in 2003. Apparently, *grizzlies* liked him, but (he) was a delicacy to the *browns.*

Anyway, we'll be on a ship, so no worries! Any bears we might see should be from the "Viewing-Decks" only... It would be refreshing to actually see one in the wild for once as opposed to staring at those sad, horrific creatures suffering confinement in those absolutely miserable, tortuous imprisoned conditions in ***Mismaloya's*** lesser-known, lowest-quality ***Zoologico de Vallarta.***

Although a few visitors had provided pleasant enough reviews online, I simply sensed that those responders had not *gotten-out-much* before at least with zoo visitations. ***Vallarta's*** zoo made me slightly more pleased with our own, USA animal-rights advocate activists demanding reasonably decent prisons, I mean *zoos,* for our animal captives. Regardless of where, however, "Three-squares-a-day, a roof-over-their-heads and a ten-foot, barricaded-wall separating them from civilization.".. seems like a fairly secure, sheltered-life. When they're really old and immobilized, it's probably not such a bad gig at all. All they need do is sleep, eat and ignore the constant flow of unimpressed, truly-sheltered and gawking, civilized-sorts from the ruling species.

I'll have to remember on cruise-stopovers for scheduled port visits, however, not to *gawk* too long at grizzlies-in-the-wild, or even at any of those parading down *Main Street.* They've got *no barricades,* and they've probably *got a place to sleep,* so they may just be looking for one of their *squares.* I may *seem square,* but I don't want to be one of *their "squares.'*

And finally, I can begin retelling the "Alaskan Dream Tale" to others:

Visit in ***Summer****; stay through* ***Fall****; survive* ***Winter***; and if you are still *alive in* ***Spring, you'll never want to leave!*** We'll see about that. That's a tough pill to swallow. If rain, heat, humidity, and bugs are bad, how bad are freezes and bears?

Ah, but the time has finally come to make that adventurous leap going "North to Alaska!" It works out just fine too because it's in the near-*future*. Get it? *North to the Future!* Clever, huh? It's great too because Alaska's sure been goin' s*outh* for awhile! And besides, the best part is that I might even get a chance to see Russia from my ship-cabin's porthole! Do ya think? Thanks, Sarah!

How about it, though? We can go North to Alaska for Summer months, and then head South to ***Mismaloya*** for Winter-Spring. I like it! Oh, alright, though. My conscience is nagging again... To be fair and *a better-person,* I'd be less than honest if I didn't admit to a hidden-agenda plan of mine regarding *Alaska.*

That little cruise might just be testing-the-waters, so to speak, for a future, potential and short-term adventure up there. Now, that's an idea which is beginning to swell in my brain, and it sounds, "Swell!" Here's a crude outline starting to formulate in my devious, but *sportsmanlike* and delightful mind:

> *We come home to Suisun City, California for our vacation from* ***Mismaloya, PV*** *in late* ***Spring*** *in order to beat-the-heat, mow the lawns, water the weeds, hug the Grandchildren,*

> *and check our mail. Then, we depart for Alaska during spectacular-viewing **Summer**-months. Next, we return home to **Suisun City** for **Fall** to beat the freeze, mow the lawns, water the weeds, hug the Grandchildren, check our mail again, and stuff our faces during family-gatherings. Then, in mid-**Winter,** we head back to our second-home here in lovely **Mismaloya** where we shall begin the entire process over again...*

Oh, I'm getting excited now! And if Alaska doesn't work out (too many Republicans, or something!), we can always find somewhere else. We still have places to go, people to see, and things to do: The Amazon river to feed Piranhas on a tropical boat-ride; the Marrakesh Express or Trans-Siberian Railway to observe Westerner kidnappings and prisons inside frozen-wastelands, respectively, of course; or, the Holy Land to leaves our flesh and DNA on the Western Wall.

Anyway, we've got to go somewhere, but where do I begin? Oh, yeah! I've got it! *I'll start a brand-new game of 'Marital Bliss!'* "Angelina! Wanna play?" !!

I'm really looking forward to Alaska, though, or whatever happens. It's all fine with me. I mean, I can't expect every journey to go calmly and smoothly without any hitches. They're not always entertaining. A couple of previous jaunts were sort of busts. They had their moments, though, and they brought new sights, sounds and people. I was happy. Occasionally, it may be who you are traveling with that makes the vacation a little less inspiring. It's to be expected. I mean, even Angelina... thinks I'm a drag, sometimes! Can you believe that?

I even have our next vacation planned *after* Alaska. It will be with one of my favorite travel-buddies, Mom. She just loves cruises, and those are really excellent and inexpensive ways for folks to travel and vacation. With her poor vision and ambulatory-limitations, cruises make sense for ease of travel.

So, Mom's next holiday escape will be cruising in November through the Caribbean again. This time, my sister, Barbara, put the plan into action and included Angelina and me There are actually a couple of stop-overs where Mom and Barbara have never been before, which surprises me. Those places will all be new for Angelina and me, though. We'll all have a good time. Mom is such a pleasant and easy-going traveler that she will make the trip pleasing for everyone.

What needs to be accomplished for all these getaways, though, are just basic saving and planning strategies. Sure, they're not free, but with advanced searching, we can get really good deals online. Plus, a travel-club which I joined a few years ago offers some excellent and competitive bargains. As I've mentioned before, Angelina is a *Google-maniac*, and she thrives on finding the best deals anywhere with flights and hotels. I handle any cruises from my club venues and certain attractions and rental cars, but we make a good, travel-plan team.

Hello, Honduras, Belize and ***Cozumel*, *Mexico*** in the Fall, and who knows? Any one of those port-stops could be the next scheduled, short-term vacation for Angelina and me. I know that I'm always looking, and thinking, and dreaming, and sometimes planning. Angelina and I might just step-off another gang-plank and instantly, *fall-in-love* again with a brand new Walmart or, better yet, a new city! It will be incredibly difficult to win me away from ***Vallarta*** and ***Mismaloya-Boca***, though. I'm surely leaving a piece-of-my heart here when I leave soon.

And leave soon, I must. I'm already organizing my final days: Let's see: There's three days left to lay on the beach and soak up the sun; there's three other days to find some more snorkeling spots; there's four days at the end to show-off the area to my next-door neighbor friends from back-home who will be visiting; there's time needed to finish saying good-byes; and I have to pack and clean-up this condominium to my wife's standards... Uh, oh... *Houston! We've got a problem*! If I start cleaning right now and work until I need to race to the airport to catch my plane, that's still not enough time to get this place up-to-par for that woman. Oh, Angelina, you set the bar so high!

Knowing my gal, Angelina will call to check on me the day of my return. She knows the last thing I pack is my Wi-Fi phone. Hopefully, she'll call just to wish me a happy flight like I would do for her; however, I know better. So, when she calls inquiring about the cleanliness of our rented-condominium, I'll be alright.

Naturally, it's like life-and-death for Angelina. Her entire life's-reputation is on-the-line with my cleaning-habits, of course. I'll be ready for her, though, and of course, I'll be prepared. Of course, I'll answer, "Of course!" when responding to her endless *Mexican Inquisition* queries:

Did you change the bedding, fold the blankets and sort and separate the dirty-laundry for them?---"Of course! Huh? Wait! It's *their* laundry?"

Did you clean the toilet, shower and bathroom sink? Did you use bleach?---"Duh, yeah! Of course! The whole bottle! In fact, I got nauseous!"

Did you wipe-off the water-stains and polish the chrome?---"Of course! But, *h*ey! It's not a car, you know! It's a shower!"

Did you clean-off all your junk from the cabinets, dressers, table, and roller-tray?---"Jeesh! 'Course! Wait a minute! It's not junk! I'm bringin' it home!"

Did you clean the refrigerator completely, plus the freezer and wipe them both down too?---"Of course! I even defrosted the frost-free freezer!"

Did you thoroughly sweep and mop including under the bed and under the table?---"Of course, I did! Plus, I even picked-up the couch to sweep and mop under it. I think of that stuff, you know!"---*Oh, c'mon!*

Did you wipe down the kitchen-sink, counter-tops and clean the dish tray?

---"One better! I threw the *dish tray* out! It was disgusting!"---*OMG!*

Did you dust?---"Huh?"---*I knew it! You never do!*

Did you empty the garbage?---"Oh, shoot! Ooops!"---*Oh, Daniel!*

Observaciones Finales...

I've taken a couple, short walks through town recently to once more remind myself of its pleasantries, absorb the surroundings, greet the folks, and enjoy all its ambiance. It has become familiar to me, and as much as I shall recall its pleasing offerings, I shall miss its tranquil nature. I suppose that having to leave just when the climate is spectacular seems a conflict-of interests with memory too.

It's been warm during May, so far, but not hostile and uncomfortable at all. Clear, ***azul*** skies complement calm, clean and bright blue, ocean-waters gently lapping against pristine, sandy beaches with inviting, almost tepid, surf. Restaurants provide neatly arranged, large, bamboo ***palapas*** or umbrellas with cushioned, lounge-chairs. It all offers relaxing mood developers but protection from the bright but dangerous ultra-violets.

It is unusually quiet these days. Far fewer, if any, cruise-stopovers from passenger-liners are arriving now. The weather is becoming intolerable for tourism some say. With coming rains, and really intense heat, and humidity, and insects, the community knows to customarily slip back into low-gear until Fall. For me, personally, I could still enjoy it. When it rains, it's refreshing but I'd simply find shelter. When it's hot, I'd jump in the ocean or a swimming-pool or turn on all the fans or AC, if I'm fortunate enough to be near it. Ditto for humidity. When the insects come... in swarms... hungry and thirsty... seeking human flesh for their tiny-bug fiestas... then...

I'd just... cover-up! Hide! Fight back! Aaaaarrrgh! Oh, well, like I said,... "It's time to go!"

From my comfortable, double-duty, dining-table turned office-desk, I sit to eat, write, think and sometimes just stare while absorbing the incredible beauty and magnificent expanse of the deep blue, smoothly calm Bay of Banderas. My table views, or nearby lounging couch or deck chairs all allow me relaxation and vantage points to keep track of the still plentiful two-way, ocean parades. Small, fishing-boats, larger, tourist-attraction catamarans, passenger boats, private yachts, and water-taxis for isolated, school-children still continue their daily voyages.

Brilliant weather or the less comfortable summer months make little difference to the populations here. They adjust their lifestyles and move on. Sort of like I shall. There is obviously much less work now because of the drop-off in tourism, so workers seek other employment elsewhere. Likely, many shall move inland to the big cities or North, even to the USA, for field-work or anything else.

There is already a steep decline in traffic and congestion going into ***PV*** or locally here near ***Mismaloya***. Fewer people or cars are needed to manage the vastly lessened tourist-crowds. City-shops are noticeably closing down for either longer hours or seasonally. On the beaches, steady streams of independent, souvenir-vendors flock toward the few remaining, unsuspecting, stray-tourists to offer their special sales of knickknacks. The mostly empty restaurants and food or beverage shops greedily welcome sparse visitations.

Construction continues to be in full-swing. The huge, resort-builders and real-estate developers are steadily working toward their future goals. By the coming Fall, or least this time next year, a virtual transformation may likely have occurred down here. There will probably be several new and a couple huge tourist hotel/resort openings. The big-money folks can see a prosperous future with their plans for growth and development even during these marginal times.

I still suspect something complicated but grandiose will evolve within my lovely ***Mismaloya*** area. Unfortunately, its huge but crude, haphazard and minimally-utilized potential is taunting the powers-that-be with realizations of lost, possible revenue. Temporarily, the surface stress and anxiety has been waylaid, delayed or covered-up with coping measures, promises and exercises not likely meant to be maintained or kept.

I mentioned earlier that this is an election year. Politics are the same everywhere. A crisis situation anywhere is unwelcome in any constituency, so common, election-year propaganda persists: *Promise the unhappy or unruly roses; get their votes; then give them lilies.* Whomever remains or comes to power will likely already understand the potential of an expanding and prosperous ***Mismaloya.*** They will naturally expect ***mordidas*** *for their support to* influence change coming to the area. Politics in bed with big-business and corruption? Oh, wow! Like that's not internationally rampant. Unfortunately, it is still a sad commentary which most of the people living here all recognize, agree and attest: M***exico*** thrives on it.

In more recent developments, some parts of Puerto Vallarta have literally blown-up in proportion too. Apparently, and also due to possible government and election overtures, notorious cartels have flexed their muscle locally to show their strength with drug-trafficking. Horrific violence occurred several weeks ago with ambush-attacks against local police resulting in many deaths and casualties. In the city, outbreaks of drug-gang-related violence occurred with organized proficiency. Banks, ATM's, gas stations, and some other establishments were bombed and/or set on fire in demonstrations of power and authority by drug cartels. Even a military helicopter was shot down close by.

Narco-blockades were even established in several points by a powerful, J***alisco*** cartel intent on controlling areas and fighting-back against government attacks on their leadership and control. Many vacationers and tourists were effectively caught-in-the-middle of bloody, war-zone shoot-outs between the heavily-armed cartels and government military-operations. It was a brief, reminiscent period, reflective of similar actions three-years ago over also in ***Guadalajara, Jalisco*** over related issues. Cartels fight for supremacy, the government reacts and innocent bystanders and citizenry plead for safety and a stoppage to all the corruption and crime on both sides.

In ***Guadalahara,*** the Capitol City of ***Jalisco,*** an ultimatum warning was recently announced by the criminal cartel to the government: The army (will) withdraw its military forces completely by the end of May 2015, or according to a written-form of cartel propaganda, the ***narcomanta,*** "We will kill every soldier we see in the street." Nationals and tourists alike have been advised and warned to stay away.

This is all, of course, extremely sad and disheartening news for ***Puerto Vallarta*** people in general. These types of headlines will work inversely and negatively keeping tourism stagnant if not declining. I even heard that major, tourist cruise-lines were eliminating visits to ***Puerto Vallarta***. That, in itself, in not unusual, however, due to typical, seasonal-changes. If their actions were to persist into next Fall, the consequences could be startling, if not devastating. It will be very interesting to see what may happen in the future to curtail, alleviate or eliminate these potentially destructive forces of noticeable drug-cartel presence in the ***Puerto Vallarta*** community.

Many of the ***Vallartans*** I have recently spoken with accept the violence as typical and unavoidable. In their evaluations, they observe corrupt and criminal government-actions continuously throughout their daily-lives. To see violence within their communities from private, citizen-forces fighting back or seeking to *get-their-fair-share* is not any historically new development. However, many realize the potential harm that violence would do to their businesses, or work or incomes, so they do not relish open, flagrant or even indirect attacks on potential tourism. After all, it is well-established that tourism is the blood of ***Puerto Vallarta***. Danger or harm to the economy's stream of visitors would be both a painful and agitating disease. Thanks, Cartels.

As we shared during earlier historical references to ***Puerto Vallarta's*** spectacular growth over a relatively short period of time, it makes sense that there would be *growing pains*. ***PV*** has enjoyed an illustrious, though recent, extremely high-status among *safest tourist-sites in Mexico.* For those reasons, visitors flocked here, cruised here or drove here in staggering and impressive annually-increasing numbers. Some growth-stints are likely to be minimally awkward in their beginnings during initial stages. Let's face it too, ***Puerto Vallarta*** is still a relatively young city with enormous recent years' growth.

Let's face it, no doubt even ***tequila*** sales have sky-rocketed. I know, for a fact, I have done my share with improving the market's sales-dynamic over the past two years. ***Tequila*** is available everywhere practically. And now, the drug-market seeks to get in on the action. Where there are crowds, there are likely *users. Subtly advertise, seek, approach, and sell the contraband to whomever will buy* is a cartel's norm. Until recently, little police or military intervention has occurred. Of course, cartels would just as soon have neon-sign billboards promoting their products, but as long as business increases, they are happy.

What cartels obviously cannot appreciate, or care about, is that their presence has many negative consequences. Opposing gangs will commit to warfare in order to establish dominance. Drug-dealers always demand some form of hierarchical, pecking-order or territorial, control-zones. Drug-dealers cannot think for themselves; they are clearly in need of instruction and orders to do their business using accepted, appropriate and well-established behavior and rules. On-the-other-hand, drug-users cannot think for themselves either. Otherwise, they wouldn't be seeking drugs and using narcotics and marijuana to soothe, escape, expand, or open-their-minds in the first place.

Wherever there are drugs for sale, there is always trouble. When there is trouble, there is always violence, and violence will always meet-the-press. Unfortunate news will fuel an already growing apathy for future, potential tourism to any infected-area. When potential vacationers seeking *La-La-Land,* resort-sites for their personal, special, exotic, annual getaways, they will use news and research provided through computer-accessed web-sites. These potential visitors will seek information from what everyone else may suggest.

Borrowing a mild modification of the *USS Enterprise's* proud mission: *To boldly go where (everyone) has gone before,...* the internet will not lie to them. In an instant, an early-morning, violent, gang-related scuffle on a ***PV*** street somewhere will be announced and available for worldly-review on some informational blog or twitter account by that same afternoon. Their response will likely be something of this sort: *Why would I want to go there? I've got all that violence right here in my own back-yard! What is out there that is 'beautiful, fun, inexpensive, and drug-free?'*

Well, we all know the answer to that is probably, "Nowhere!" But, if drugs and violence are in the news, then that makes it too current for thoughtful travelers. Look at Acapulco and Mazatlan as examples. Both been hit mercilessly by tourism declines, yet both were previously highlight cruise and stopover spots for tourists. Then drugs and its ensuing violence attacked their shores and communities. Now, they both suffer from verdicts which testify: *And the crowds stayed away in droves!*

News spreads fast too. In fact, initially, I heard some mixed-reports about the recent drug-cartel, police and military activities, and Iwas terribly alarmed. Then, shortly afterward, I began hearing less except occasional opinions when I specifically or deliberately sought them. But the internet was full of reports. If I needed or wanted to know something, I just asked Angelina to Google it for me, or I did it myself. The internet coverage was current, clear and very explicit.

That is one thing I really appreciate about Western nations' journalism: *It may not be pretty, but if it's news, it will be printed.* Mexico is no exception to that special, journalistic heroism, and it has a long, colorful history of letting the press or various other publication-avenues voice its people's outrage or joy. Of course, there are many wealthy politicians, corporate world executives and criminals also who get to exercise their own "freedom of speech!" Some even belong to all three groups. Some even own the airwaves!

Readily on-hand opinions of circumstances were willingly offered too during conversations. Yet, the varying perspectives all had one main theme: How did current situations directly affect them individually? If ***Vallartans*** live out-of-town, then they care little about city-violence as long as it does not affect their travel-plans or lifestyles. If they live in-town, then they are either apathetically unconcerned or frustrated if violence occurs which might affect their sales-traffic. Some down-play the violence as a mere passing storm unlikely to return. They seek peace-of-mind, tranquility and status-quo.

Local nationals and natives see the violence and drug culture as inevitable. Its face is the direct result of corrupt and profiteering governments whose officials first take money from cartels and then turn their backs on them to suit any political purposes. Many Mexicans also curse American drug-dependence and its decadent cravings from Mexican providers. They emphasize that if US Americans did not want drugs, then it would never have become an issue.

Finally, then, are the outsiders: Snow-birds and long-term visitors and ex-patriots. Ignorance is bliss is their seeming motto. Drugs and its usage is nothing new. If they do not like to associate with its culture, then they remain aloof within their protected circles. If they are users, then their access just improved. But, it all remains private, personal and within non-advertised, non-committed, alliance-connections. It's there if you want it or ignore it, but "Shhhhhh!"

Anyway, I had to discover many of my facts on the Internet, myself. It was the Internet that provided me with current updates on local incidents. What I now know is also available for any and all readers simply by Googling or using any favorite search-engine to inquire upon. Press a couple of buttons and instantly we are made aware of words, thoughts, behaviors, or actions all around the world. No! The universe even!

That's what I was describing earlier with my *Cosmic-consciousness* vociferates. Nowadays, we are all an inter-connected, inter-related, inter-dependent, and international species, anymore. Everything is becoming known to everyone. Life is a constant struggle made up of personal choices. We each decide what we are going to do. We each have to make our own choices and determine our own directions. All of us focus on what we choose, what we really want for our own minds, bodies and souls. We choose, and we live with it, or not.

This violence is a new growth phase in ***PV*** obviously, and its issues may very well become more extreme before they subside into acceptance, oblivion or vague, territorial-aspects. Nevertheless, I hate to see any harm come to this incredibly entertaining city that I love. I have to face the truth, though. In my own hometown, or my other *cities by the bay*, San Francisco or Oakland, I could probably ask any taxi-driver or pedestrian on any street-corner where to go to buy whatever I requested. That's an unfortunate aspect of modern, (civilized?) city-life. Of course, if one travels to the countryside, one may then get to experience the natural growing and producing zones. Go figure.

I can only wish this beautiful part of the world a serenity to its resolve. It is too magnificent a place to be sheltered, denied, or made fearsome to outsiders. There must be some form of peaceful resilience for the community. There is still a long ways to go for ***Puerto Vallarta*** to find some meaningful and substantial arrangement between the drug-culture, the government and those caught in the middle. *Tranquility* is still the mantra here. I can only hope and trust that it will remain to be maintained and savored. May God Bless ***Puerto Vallarta.***

Acknowledgments

Cheers! To the Home Crowd!...

Everything any of us ever accomplishes in our lives was a co-effort with support and gratification and assistance from another or others helping us succeed. We have all heard the long, almost endless list of names offered in gratuity by Hollywood's stars when accepting an award for whatever. And each recipient was correct to do so. There were likely many others left unnamed who also aided in earning that special recognition for that celebrity.

We are all similar. Any successes or accomplishments we have achieved in our varied lives are the result of many influences on our lives from practically birth. These include our own unique experiences, learning, training, study, in-sight, and awareness from other people's personal reflections. We arrive at specific stages in our lives through access to other people's influences.

This book is no exception. Throughout its pages, I have attempted to discuss, if not exaggerate for sake of humor, on a variety of influences from other people and activities which helped open-my-eyes for observational learning and experiential reasoning. Many, I chose to identify in person, by name, because they were particularly important for the essence of this book.

Obviously, I cannot name everyone for spacial factors, but I figure that even people like my third-grade teacher, Mrs. Tresler, already know and understand. They all have my gratitude and sincere thanks. Everyone and everything else from my entire life which helped influenced, teach, educate, instruct and support me deserve my special thanks and appreciation. I accept the bad with the good too. We learn and are influenced by everything, aren't we? That's life.

Others whom are clearly focused upon in this book, however, deserve mentioning. Again, I may inadvertently exclude some, and for that I am sorry. There have been so many conversations, connections, acquaintances and impressions that I simply cannot address them all. But, I still appreciate their time.

Some others, I shall deliberately exclude because having earned a reference in earlier passages, once was enough. Still, some others will be included and thanked once more because of their special and more significant influences.

Reflecting over the past five-visits and twenty-months of living down here in my lovely ***Mismaloya-Boca*** truly gives pause for thought. Where shall I ever begin? Oh, okay, I know... At the beginning...

How did I ever end of here? First of all, thanks again go to Mom, Dad, my aunt Jean, and Phyllis for encouraging my "Traveler" spirit. Mom, we've still got some more miles to go before we sleep. My beautiful wife, Angelina, I appreciate for putting up with my travels and especially for joining me on many. Also, I adore her willingness to join me for our experiences in ***Puerto Vallarta*** and our time together there. I also apologize, but offer her due credit, for her acceptance of the unreasonable time I spent writing this book while obviously ignoring her needs. I love you, respect you, appreciate you, and thank you.

Next, would come appreciation for and thanks to our combined children who accepted and supported our lengthy stays away from physical family-contact. I particularly want to thank my daughter, Deborah, who initially house-sat for us while we enjoyed our first three-month sojourn down here. Her on-going phone contact was truly desired and appreciated. My son, Michael, I thank for his phone updates, efforts with our home's care and very worthy assistance and resolve dealing with an emotional issue involving our pet dog, Smiley.

Cynthia, Terasa, Michael, and Adam also served as drop-offs or pick-ups for our going and returning transportation. I thank them all so much for their time and trouble and caring. To Cynthia and Adam, Angelina's children, but my kids too, I thank for their fun and entertaining visits with us while down here. To all our other children and grandchildren, including Alonzo, Jessica, Terasa, and other family members, I thank for their phone and email contacts and family updates especially during lonelier times.

Certainly, thanks go to Angelina's sister, Teresa, and Angelina's friends, Yadi and her mom, who visited and made our own stay more pleasing to share our joy.

Also, regarding other friends from home, I also wish to express my thanks and appreciation for our next-door-neighbors, Vic and Anna Cuellar, who came to visit ***Puerto Vallarta*** at the end of my recent, five-month stay. They watched over our residence back home in our absence, collected some mail, visited by phone, and were generally what good-neighbors exemplify. Plus, we had a really pleasing time enjoying the merits of ***Puerto Vallarta*** together.

Additionally, certainly worthy of appreciation were the many phone calls from other family and friends who kept us connected during regular, phone-contact. Repeat thanks go to Mom, sisters

Barbara and Kelly and our children Terasa, Deborah, Michael, Alonzo, Cynthia, Adam and many others who reached out or received our calls.

Special thanks also go to my "Limey-Rusky" friends from Doncaster, England, Ian and Natasha Galloway, who stayed regularly in-touch with me through use of SKYPE. Ian never failed to keep me informed and laughing, over his demented views on world-politics and future excursions. I always enjoyed our banter and always make plans to visit with them both again soon.

Another SKYPER friend was Roger who called many times to chat and keep me up-to-date on my mother's well-being. Also, a special back-home friend and fellow-Traveler, Marty gets appreciation for regularly returning calls because he would never answer when I called!

Naturally too, I must express love and appreciation for all the voices, comments and conversation from our grandchildren which always brought smiles and laughter to our days. Thanks go to Angelica, Cecelia, Alexis, Eric, Isabel, Francesca, Xoshi, Alyssa, Elias, and Hunter for making us smile. To any and all others, mistakenly or absent-mindlessly excluded, I truly wish to thank them too.

Salud! To Local Favorites...

Now, I need move on to inclusion and appreciation of so many friends and acquaintances made while visiting our beautiful ***Puerto Vallarta*** and while living in our happy and comfortable ***Casa Quantica #D*** in my lovely ***Mismaloya-Boca***.

Some of these relationships were far more important, valuable and gratifying than others, but that is to be expected. A few of these friends were even previously involved in sketches, reflections or anecdotes within this book's content already.

Some will be mentioned again; others, perhaps not. Some no longer reside in the area as they were only temporary visitors, somewhat like Angelina and myself, and have subsequently returned to their homes at their vacations' closings. Others continue living here because they have additional-time on their leases, they are native-born, and this is their home, or they have made Puerto Vallarta their new, *ex-Patriotic* home. Regardless, they all left impressions on me, and I wish to thank most of them by name, if possible:

My closest ***amigo*** in all of ***PV*** and ***Mismaloya*** has been my next-door-neighbor, Charlie McDaniels. Next to our host/friends, Sergio and Deya, Charlie has had the most impact and influence from any friendships. In all honesty, perhaps Charlie has been even more so because there were seldom any restrictions on visits or discussions limited by language-barriers. Charlie is one of the more than fifty-thousand, ***Puerto Vallarta,*** local, ex-Patriots living here. I met him while talking over issues with local inhabitants, and he became my friend.

Of course, one cannot honestly or fairly talk about Charlie, or include him in any discussions, without talking about his wife, or soul mate, or mistress, or girlfriend, or daughter, or *best-friend* in his world. Naturally, I am referring to ***Sombra,*** Charlie's pet, *Havanese* dog. A who, or what? Yeah, I thought so too. Charlie says they are the national pooch of Cuba. Okay, similar to a cross between a *Mini-poodle* and a *Jack Russel Terrier,* I think, but Charlie insists, however, that ***Sombra*** is from a 100% purebred-species,. I simply claim ignorance but refuse to confirm it through Google because I just trust his word. ***Sombra*** is Spanish for shade, by the way, but she is absolutely Charlie's constant ray of sunshine.

'Theirs' is one of those relationships which is envied by even the most, happily-married couples. It is a pleasure to watch them together, and it needs to be, or otherwise, one would soon have their full! Anyway, I need to thank Charlie (and ***Sombra***) for their many enjoyable visits and generous company. We have shared many fine meals together, some serious discussions and plenty of visits.

Charlie is a good friend, too. He lives in a very comfortable studio apartment next door. Several years ago, Charlie made the fantastic jump from Colorado to ***Mismaloya*** as a potential ex-patriot. He has transformed his life within his inexpensive, cliff-side residence, comfortable lifestyle and what he loves to refer to as his: *Million-dollar view!* You could check him out at his online-moniker, but it's private!... *Thanks, HRH Charlie &* ***Sombra.***

I think I may have even shared stories with Charlie of my own, first childhood-pet, *Dollie*, my pet frog. Or, I don't know, maybe I didn't; it was pretty personal-stuff. For instance, I think... my next pet, *Tiger the Cat*, ate him, or her, or it, or whatever; I mean, I could never tell the difference! I didn't look really-hard to figure it out, either. I just assumed that it was one of those: *Who cares?* or, *What-does-it-matter?* issues. These days, I just blame my poetic laziness back then on my previous, "non-awareness nature" regarding *cosmic-consciousness...*

A really nice couple we met near the very beginning during our first stay in 2013 were Nelson and Jan Kelm. Nelson and I began a Spanish class together, and Jan was attending a similar but alternate-day class. We all became friends outside of school and have remained so. Several months before Angelina and I made our venture, Nelson and Jan had already made a complete break from their families and home in Colorado. They up and moved to ***Puerto Vallarta*** cold-turkey. They have made the most out of their visit so far and are considering leasing again once their present lease is up in 2016. they have expressed a strong desire to remain and continue enjoying the tranquil nature. We'll see. They are *Travelers* now.

Both extended several kindnesses toward us. We, in turn, enjoyed our visits nd multiple times on the beach and in the surf. I enjoyed visiting them in action and respect their activities which fill up their days. Each volunteered with a local, theater-group preparing a theater and stage for performances. Of the two, Jan is the more adventurous hiker, climber, explorer, and swimmer type. Nelson is a retired scientist, quite pragmatic in nature and spends lots of time exploring the internet, learning from You-tube and making things for their home or activities. We had several fun times together. Thanks, Nelson and Jan. *Happy travels.*

I made another set of friends from another classmate too. Per Warolin joked and laughed and studied very hard through the class with me. On occasions, I enjoyed dinner and entertaining chatter with him and his charming wife and daughter, Sophia and Isabella. Per and I even ventured through the ten-run, crazy zip-line adventure through one of the jungle areas. He was a great sport, and it was a fun male-bonding experience. Except instead of just a few words, as I recall there was a lot of screaming!

They are an adventurous couple from Sweden who had taken their nation's generous, child-birth leave and had come to Puerto Vallarta for one year to study Spanish. I understand that their family is growing, and they are always planning new getaways. Great people! Thanks, Per, Sophia and Isabella. *Congratulations!*

By mentioning the Spanish class, then I must credit our ***maestra,*** Lizbeth, an instructor for the University of Guadalajara Extension Program for language-classes. She was an excellent teacher and obviously a patient person. Per's and my classroom-antics would probably have forced many teachers to resign. I understand that Lizbeth had future changes ahead of her and that she had a passion for Salsa dancing. Hopefully, she is fulfilling her dreams. Muchas gracias, senorita profesora Lizbeth, mi amiga!

Another notable acquaintance was Luis, the U of G Language Program's Administrator. He was very supportive and responsible for placing me in the Early-Beginner Class due to my entrance-exam scores for Spanish fluency.

After class, I'd visit Angelina during her art-class with her *art-throb* instructor, Sr. Manuel. Mostly, though, I'd often sit at a nearby cafe drinking cerveza, snacking on ***nachos grandes y practicar mi espanol*** with two pleasant waiters and helpful ***amigos.*** Thanks, ***amigos***, *Miguel y Miguel.*

Friends or acquaintances from the communities of ***Puerto Vallarta*** and ***Mismaloya*** included several people who took time to share their thoughts or attitudes regarding various issues I researched. I owe thanks to Sr. Enrique of the Central Tourist-Bureau for his informative guidance regarding issues of the town.

A couple of activity-vendors/time-share agents, Saloman and Jose, spent too much time trying to fleece us regarding activities and car rentals. We mistook them both as friends and trusted them until the end when we realized they were dishonest and conniving. Oh, well, it was really their losses, and both were finally forced to leave town under duress from threats. I heard that they had skipped-town and moved-on to Mazatlan. New territory.

A more recent activity-vendor and friend of ours was Sr. Ricardo Petrocena. He was always pleasant and obliging for our visits to town. Regularly, we'd stop for a chat, and I'd question him for updates or attitudes regarding local issues and news of the day's *happenings*. He is a relaxed, tranquil man with big dreams encouraging his business's expansion. I appreciated his honesty and kindnesses.

From the community of ***Mismaloya*** are two local, native-born brothers, Jose and Pedro Lopez. Both have lived there and watched growth and development and ups and downs for their entire lives.

Each was extremely kind and generous extending time to me for interviews regarding perspectives on ***Mismaloya's*** issues. Pedro and Jose were certainly intuitive, knowledgeable, and historically accurate.

Additionally, being lifetime-locals, both were quite refreshingly opinionated. Pedro was extremely frank and sincere about the problems that he sees in his own community, and Puerto Vallarta, Jalisco, and Mexico too. The levels of crime and corruption within governmental-political, corporate-big business, military-police and cartels-gangs were obviously very distressing to him.

Both being active and historically aware of ***Mismaloya's*** best and worst aspects made them both sensitive. I was grateful for their opinions and candid honesty. I could sense their love and appreciation for country, community and lifestyles.

Visiting even deeper into the town of ***Mismaloya*** is a young man, Hector, who works as a tour-guide for ***Mister Tequila Tasting Gallery/Mismaloya***. From Hector, I received a personal, one-on-one guided-tour of their facility and an enthusiastic history of the production of ***tequila***. He was very knowledgeable and informative about the ***tequila*** industry, the travel-industry (his personal, career choice) and local issues in ***Mismaloya***. I wish him well in his endeavors.

Of course, I wish to thank some other neighbors who were gracious to me and allowed me into their home and lives. All locals, or from ***Guadalajara***, Beto and his fiancée, Rachel, were very kind to me as were their roommates, Pablo and Luis. Beto is a local SCUBA diving-instructor and Activities-Agent for ***Vallarta*** *Adventures* in ***Mismaloya***. Beto has loaned me snorkeling gear and invited me to share events at his home. Rachel is a recent Post-Graduate who focuses on her career of Holistic-lifestyles. Her parents are forty-year residents of the distant, isolated and beautiful, protected, Indian-land and ***playa***-community of ***Yelapa*** with access by boats only. Nice neighbors.

In the same complex are other friends with whom I enjoyed company. Christina and her husband, Raphael are two kind persons. Christina is a young, local artist by dream and spare-time and a past, cruise-line employee who keeps industriously busy working for the many contacts she makes through her artwork. Wonderfully fluent in at least three languages, Christina is a long-term, ex-Patriot from Hungary. Raphael is originally from Mexico City and works for a major, international cruise-line. Thanks for your friendship.

Thanks, and appreciations go to other inhabitants of the various bungalows which fill the rental complex next door. Emma and Jose, landlords themselves, have extended kindnesses. They are both Mexican Nationals who have lived here locally much of their lives. They are *Travelers* too. One of their renters are Kathy, an ex-Patriot herself, and her husband Mic who invite me and everyone else to her organized activities. Very spirited and kind annual returnees.

Another renter and neighbor is Sandy, an ex-IRS agent. Down here, Sandy busies herself with a career as a fellow-author who has written many works on tax issues and short-novelettes. Presently, she is excited, busy and engrossed in a children's literature focus. You can find her on Amazon, I enjoy telling her, "You go, girl! Write on!" Best wishes, Sandy.

Another nearby neighbor is Dave. He plays this own favorite music and enjoys plunkin' on guitars and tweetin' on harmonicas. We obviously share similar musical tastes. I enjoyed sharing his hospitality. Thank you guys.

Also, I wish to pass thanks on to others who invited me into their homes for camaraderie. There were Reggie and Max from Toronto, Ontario, Canada. These buddies have been coming down here to their Mexican, cliff-side ***casas*** for thirty or more years. Larry and Joanne are from Arkansas and have been returning to their ***casa*** in the same fashion. They all come for the beautiful, winter weather, and that makes them all true-blue, snowbird owners. They all typically arrive around the same time each year in November and depart around the same time in late April. All of them are very industrious, kind and generous.

Additionally, I appreciated visits with a couple of young, industrious and intellectual travelers, Nathan and Brian, who are down here for their first stint as long-term lease vacationers from Seattle, WA These guys are planning to move into a downtown area called Gringo Gulch for their next lease. They probably prefer to be nearer to city-action. It's too quiet around here for a couple of party guys! Ah, to be so young and exploring the world and doing so with a "travel-buddy." It's the best of all worlds. Have great travels. It should be fun.

Finally, in closing, I shall thank my friends and next-door-neighbors from back home, Victor and Anna Cuellar, who traveled here during their own vacation to spend time with me visiting my lovely ***Mismaloya*** and ***Puerto Vallarta***. Victor obviously loves the sights, sounds and action of the area, and Anna loves the mellow, tranquil nature and the sun and surf. Great combination and good friends. Thanks for the Lobster-fest! And, thank you for sharing your time.

To everyone, I enjoyed your company, kindnesses and sharing. I look forward to future visits. Who knows? Perhaps, we'll visit again next year!

Thanx2all.

QUOTES FOR THE TRAVELER

And whether or not it is clear to you,
no doubt the universe is unfolding as it should.
Therefore be at peace with God,
whatever you conceive Him to be.

Max Erhmann (From: *Desiderata*

I am not in this world to live up to your expectations, nor are you in it to live up to mine.

Bruce Lee

The best things in life are unexpected –
because there were no expectations.

Eli Khamarov

Dreams should exceed expectations.

DT Chapman

Adventure encourages imagination
creating dreams which promote adventure.

DT Chapman

About the Author

Dan Chapman has always been a poet at heart. Although meaningful since his youth, Dan actually began the established poetry phase of his life during his academic-career. Initially, he used personal poetry in his classrooms attempting to better reach his students. Later, promoting his unique style for post-graduate studies, Dan used poetry to enhance his assignments, projects and dissertation.

Dan's prose career came along comfortably with his first effort in *The Traveler Series.* His first book introduced and connected ideas, attitudes and humor from Dan's past life and experiences. Surreptitiously entitled *The Book of Daniel: Lasting Impressions of Life, Love and Laughter*, Dan explored human nature as he saw *fit* regarding issues of people's lives, hearts and conditions. His poetry was a study of and testimonial to people: Life with its curious aspects, strengths and frailties; the human-heart minding both requited and denied love; and of course, Dan's signature humor as relating to aspects of both.

Dan enjoys pursuing his own, personal and unique style-of-writing with *The Traveler Series.* Utilizing a prose of story-telling combined with poetry and Spanish-language studies, Dan attempts to blend multiplicity-of-style while describing his experiences searching the globe for *truth.* He follows his heart and mind through distant, adventures observing, learning, recording, and teaching about impressions of people, places and things while soul-searching with humor.

In Dan's next book, *The Traveler Series: Where to Go?*, he plans reviewing the *Snowbirds* enigma: *Travelers Annually Heading North for Summer and South for Winter.* "They are a uniquely colorful group worthy of renown and migratory story-telling and deservedly needy of descriptive, comic-relief poetry," says he.

When I am not traveling or living-abroad with my 'travel-buddy' wife, Angelina," Dan likes to quip, "I reside in Suisun City, California with her and my faithful, fun-loving, loyal, selfless, considerate, and dependable, etc. computer.

About the Book

Messages *from Vallarta* sets the background and stage for Dan Chapman's entire *The Traveler Series.* The book introduces its readers to Dan's progressively developed love of travel and its meaning and benefits to him. In the issue, Dan further explores how he emotionally manages travels' often confounding and conflicting experiences. He then takes his readers along his own visionary walk and profound, personal-growth through an exotic and distant vacation-site. Dan explores his own, personal-growth experiences and reflections while living within ***Mismaloya's*** profound, spiritual-nature. Further, Dan's often poetically recorded journey also describes ***Puerto Vallarta's*** unique and colorful characteristics, characters and lifestyles which left many, mixed-impressions upon him.

In the book, Chapman offers us a *different set of eyes* to view and consider circumstances and consequences of travel to this incredible and beautiful destination he describes as his own "lovely ***Mismaloya***" within the bounds of ***Puerto Vallarta, Jalisco, MX.***

You will visualize with him a bountiful and precious, yet fragile, vacation destination in ***Mismaloya-Boca, Puerto Vallarta***. At the same time, you will experience and appreciate his growth, progression and development through various stages of conflict, challenge, questioning, and search for ultimate awareness, truth and understanding.

Welcome to Dan Chapman's: *Messages from Vallarta: The Traveler Series.*

Welcome to his world and His universe...

The End

CPSIA information can be obtained
at www.ICGtesting.com
Printed in the USA
LVHW102051161222
735389LV00001B/6

9 781950 101009